Spanish in Review

SECOND EDITION

Spanish in Review

John B. Dalbor

H. Tracy Sturcken

Pennsylvania State University

JOHN WILEY & SONS, INC.

New York   Chichester

Brisbane   Toronto   Singapore

ACQUISITIONS EDITOR	Mary Jane Peluso
PRODUCTION MANAGER	Katharine Rubin
DESIGNER	Dawn L. Stanley
PRODUCTION SUPERVISOR	Nancy Prinz
MANUFACTURING MANAGER	Lorraine Fumoso
COPY EDITORS	Richard Blander & David Thorstad
PHOTO RESEARCHER	Jennifer Atkins
PHOTO RESEARCH MANAGER	Stella Kupferberg
ILLUSTRATION	Ishaya Monokoff
COVER COMPUTER ART	Marjory Dressler

Library of Congress Cataloging in Publication Data:

Dalbor, John B.
    Spanish in review / John B. Dalbor, H. Tracy Sturcken. –2nd ed.
        p.   cm.
    Includes index.
    ISBN 0-471-60093-8 (pbk.)
        1. Spanish language–Grammar–1950-   I. Sturcken, H. Tracy.
    II. Title.
    PC4112.D254   1992
    468.2'421–dc20   91-34200
                                                      CIP

Printed in the United States of America

10 9 8 7 6 5 4 3 2 1

Recognizing the importance of preserving what has been written, it is a policy of John Wiley & Sons, Inc. to have books of enduring value published in the United States printed on acid-free paper, and we exert our best efforts to that end.

Preface

The second edition of *Spanish in Review* presents a review of basic Spanish grammar and a variety of materials and activities for different learning modes and situations. The organization and content of the text have been substantially revised, and a number of new features have been added.

PASOS PRELIMINARES. The textbook begins with two optional **pasos preliminares** that introduce succinctly some basic elements of Spanish grammar, many of which are taken up later in greater detail. The instructor should feel free to use or omit these **pasos**.

GRAMMAR UNITS. The grammar is presented in 48 units rather than chapters for maximum flexibility in syllabus planning. We felt that smaller segments of material are easier to arrange in a syllabus than are traditional chapters, which inevitably turn out to be uneven in length and degree of difficulty. These units offer simple and clear explanations accompanied by charts, tables, abundant examples, and a variety of exercises—both traditional and communicative—designed to help the students acquire a basic competence in the language.

ILLUSTRATIVE MATERIALS. Journalistic realia are incorporated at regular intervals and strategic points to help illustrate points of Spanish grammar and vocabulary and aspects of Hispanic life and culture.

LECTURAS. Eight journalistic pieces of varied content offer the opportunity at given intervals to help the student improve reading skills and also to enhance awareness of various aspects of Hispanic life.

DIVERSIÓN Y PRÁCTICA. To provide a change of pace, these brief interludes present game-like activities dealing with a variety of cultural, geographical, and everyday topics.

VAMOS A ESCRIBIR. Writing skills are practiced in these review exercises, which gradually increase in difficulty as they cover grammar recently presented in class.

WORKBOOK. This accompanying manual with tear-out pages provides exercises for extra writing practice. These exercises follow the material presented in the main text but are different. The Workbook also includes audio drills available on accompanying cassette tapes. The Workbook has its own vocabularies.

AUDIO TAPES. These cassette tapes are designed to improve the students' aural comprehension and their ability to produce correct spoken responses. They contain oral exercises that are different from the text exercises.

COURSE OUTLINES. Following are sample outlines that divide the basic grammar content of the text into suitable assignments. Not included here are the **Diversiones** and the **Lecturas**, which provide additional/optional materials that can be used to satisfy the design and needs of specific review courses. One is for a 15-week semester (assuming three class meetings per week) and the other for two 10-week quarters (also three meetings per week).

SEMESTER

Week	Material
1	**Pasos preliminares I, II**
2	Units 1, 2, 3, 4
3	Units 5, 6, **Vamos a escribir...** **(1)**, units 7, 8
4	Units 9, 10, 11, 12, 13
5	Units 14, 15, 16
6	Unit 17, **Vamos...** **(2)**, units 18, 19, 20, 21
7	Unit 22, **Vamos...** **(3)**, units 23, 24
8	Units 25, 26, 27
9	Unit 28, **Vamos...** **(4)**, unit 29
10	Units 30, 31
11	Units 32, 33
12	Units 34, 35, 36, **Vamos...** **(5)**
13	Units 37, 38, 39, 40, 41
14	Units 42, 43, 44, 45
15	Units 46, 47, 48; REVIEW

FIRST QUARTER	SECOND QUARTER
Week	**Week**
1 **Paso I, Paso II** (half)	1 Units 27, 28
2 **Paso II** (half) unit 1	2 **Vamos . . . (4)**, units 29, 30
3 Units 2, 3, 4	3 Units 31, 32 (half)
4 Units 5, 6, **Vamos . . . (1)**, unit 7	4 Units 32 (half), 33
5 Units 8, 9, 10, 11, 12	5 Units 34, 35
6 Units 13, 14, 15	6 Units 36, **Vamos . . . (5)**, unit 37
7 Units 16, 17	7 Units 38, 39, 40, 41
8 **Vamos . . . (2)**, units 18, 19, 20, 21, 22	8 Units 42, 43
9 **Vamos . . . (3)**, units 23, 24	9 Units 44, 45, 46
10 Units 25, 26	10 Units 47, 48; REVIEW

JOHN B. DALBOR
H. TRACY STURCKEN

Acknowledgements

The authors and publisher wish to thank the following reviewers who provided valuable guidance during the revision stages of the text. The appearance of their names does not necessarily constitute their endorsement of the text or its methodology. Hilde Cramsie, Mt. San Antonio College; James F. Horton, University of Arkansas; Zulma Iguina, Cornell University; Theodore W. Jensen, Eastern Montana College; Philip W. Klein, University of Iowa; Beverly Leetch, Towson State University; Carol Maier, Bradley University; Leo Ortiz-Minique, Clark University; Irma Perlman, University of Wisconsin–Milwaukee; Miguel Tirado, Los Angeles City College. The authors also wish to thank Juan Liébana, Hobart & William Smith Colleges, and Jorge H. Cubillos, Pennsylvania State University, for their assistance as linguistic consultants.

Contents

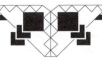

Spanish in Review

Paso preliminar 1

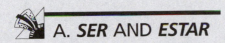

A. *SER* AND *ESTAR*

PRESENT TENSE

	ser to be	**estar** to be
yo	soy	estoy
tú	eres	estás
él/ella/usted	es	está
nosotros/nosotras	somos	estamos
vosotros/vosotras	sois	estáis
ellos/ellas/ustedes	son	están

1. Ser and **estar** are two Spanish equivalents of the English verb *to be*. They are never interchangeable.

2. Estar indicates location: **No está aquí** *He is not here.*

aquí here	**ahí** there	**allí** there
aquí mismo right here		

—¿**Dónde está usted?**	"Where are you?"
—**Estoy en el aeropuerto.**	"I am in the airport."
—¿**Dónde están ustedes?**	"Where are you?"
—**Estamos en la estación.**	"We are in the station."

3. Estar is used with adjectives to describe conditions.

Estamos muy ocupados.	We are very busy.
Mi amigo está enfermo.	My friend is sick.

4. Estar also expresses condition with adverbs of manner.

—¿**Cómo está la comida?**	"How is the food?"
—**No está mal.**	"It's not bad."

1

| bien | well | mal | bad | mejor | better | peor | worse |

—¿Cómo está su padre?   "How is your father?"
—Está mejor.   "He is better."

—Hoy estamos bien.   "Today we're fine."
—Pero mi hermanita está peor.   "But my little sister is worse."

5. **Ser** links any combination of nouns and pronouns.

—¿Quién eres?   "Who are you?"
—Yo soy Gerardo.   "I'm Gerardo."

—¿Quiénes son ustedes?   "Who are you?"
—Somos los amigos de Mariluz.   "We are Mariluz's friends."

6. **Ser** is used with adjectives that describe basic and inherent characteristics.

Son venezolanos.   They are Venezuelan.
Ella es alta.   She is tall.
Es inteligente y amable. She is intelligent and friendly.

7. **Ser** expresses when and where events take place.

Nuestro examen es el viernes.   Our exam is on Friday.
La reunión va a ser en un aula.   The meeting is going to be in a
                                         classroom.

Diga en español (*Say in Spanish*).

1. We are here.
2. You are there.
3. She is right here.
4. Where is the book?
5. The exam is Friday.
6. Who are you?
7. I am busy.
8. The meeting is in the library.
9. How is the food?
10. It's not bad.
11. Today it's worse.
12. Today it's better.

B. SUBJECT PRONOUNS

yo	I		nosotros/as	we
tú	you (*familiar*)		vosotros/as	you (*familiar*)
usted (**Ud., Vd.**)	you (*polite*)		ustedes (**Uds., Vds.**)	you (*polite, familiar*)
él	he		ellos	they
ella	she		ellas	they

1. Since Spanish verbs indicate by their form the person and number of the
subject, subject pronouns are used only for emphasis, clarity, and contrast.

Ella no sabe que él sabe   She doesn't know that he knows
la verdad.   the truth.

2. Spanish has two ways to say *you*. **Tú** is used with family, friends, and class-mates, i.e., usually a "first-name" relationship. **Usted** is used in more formal relationships. Its plural **ustedes** is used over most of the Spanish-speaking world also as the plural of **tú**. In Spain, however, the plural of **tú** is **vosotros/as.**

3. Several subject pronouns have masculine and feminine forms: **nosotros/nosotras, ellos/ellas.** The masculine plural is used for mixed groups.

4. Spanish ordinarily has no equivalent of English *it* when it is the subject: **Es mi libro** *It is my book.*

C. DEFINITE AND INDEFINITE ARTICLES

DEFINITE ARTICLES	INDEFINITE ARTICLES
masculine / feminine	**masculine / feminine**
el hombre / la mujer the man / the woman	**un hombre / una mujer** a man / a woman
los hombres / las mujeres the men / the women	**unos hombres / unas mujeres** some men / some women

1. Spanish nouns are either masculine or feminine. Nouns that refer to males and most nouns ending in **-o** are masculine. Nouns that refer to females and most nouns ending in **-a** are feminine.

2. Spanish nouns that end in a vowel add **-s** for the plural. Those ending in a consonant add **-es.**

3. Spanish adjectives agree in gender and number with the noun they modify.

un hombre bajo	a short man
una mujer baja	a short woman
los hombres altos	the tall men
las mujeres altas	the tall women

4. Spanish has two contracted forms of the definite article.

de + el = del	**Son los juguetes del niño.**	They're the child's toys.
a + el = al	**Vamos al mercado.**	Let's go to the market.

5. Spanish expresses possession with the preposition **de.**

—**¿De quién es el bolígrafo?**	"Whose pen is it?"
—**Es de Mario.**	"It's Mario's."

¿Cómo se dice en español...? (*How do you say... in Spanish?*)

1. It's Teresa's book.
2. The men are here.
3. The children's toys.
4. She knows that he doesn't know the truth.
5. Whose book is it?
6. It's Blanca's.

D. THE USEFUL VERB *TENER*

tener to have
tengo tienes tiene tenemos tenéis tienen

tener cuidado   to be careful
tener miedo   to be afraid
tener razón   to be right
no tener razón   to be wrong
tener suerte   to be lucky

Diga en inglés.

1. Paco no tiene cuidado.
2. Tienen mucha suerte.
3. Tengo razón.
4. Tú no tienes suerte.
5. La niña tiene miedo.
6. Él no tiene razón.

tener que (+ *infinitive*)   to have to (+ *verb*)

Diga en español.

1. We have to be here.
2. You have to read more (**leer más**).
3. They have to eat less (**comer menos**).
4. She has to study (**estudiar**) more.

tener hambre   to be hungry
tener sed   to be thirsty
tener sueño   to be sleepy
tener frío   to be cold
tener calor   to be hot

Diga en inglés.

1. Tienen mucha hambre.
2. Yo tengo sed.
3. ¿Tienes frío?
4. ¿Tiene Ud. calor?
5. No tengo sueño.

tener éxito   to be successful
tener prisa   to be in a hurry
tener ganas de (+ *infinitive*)   to feel like (+ -ing)
tener . . . años   to be . . . years old

Diga en español.

1. We are in a hurry.
2. She is three years old.
3. I feel like going out (**salir**).
4. They are successful.
5. I am not in a hurry.

E. EXPRESIONES ÚTILES (*USEFUL EXPRESSIONS*)

SALUDOS Y CORTESÍAS

—Hola, Felipe. ¿Qué tal?	"Hi, Felipe. How's it going?"
—No estoy seguro. Tengo tres exámenes hoy.	"I'm not sure. I have three exams today."
—Veo que tienes prisa. Aquí tienes una carta de tu novia.	"I see that you're in a hurry. Here's a letter from your girlfriend."
—¡No me digas! Pues adiós.	"You're kidding! Well, bye."
—Hasta luego.	"See you later."

—Buenos días, señorita Cruz.	"Good morning, Miss Cruz."
—Muy buenos, señor Amado. ¿Cómo está?	"Morning, Mr. Amado. How are you?"
—Bien, gracias.	"Fine, thanks."
—¿Y la señora?	"And Mrs. Amado?"
—Ella está bien.	"She's fine."

LOS DÍAS DE LA SEMANA

lunes	Monday
martes	Tuesday
miércoles	Wednesday
jueves	Thursday
viernes	Friday
sábado	Saturday
domingo	Sunday

The masculine definite article (**el/los**) expresses *on*.

Voy a estar aquí el martes.	I'm going to be here on Tuesday.
Siempre salimos los viernes.	We always go out on Fridays.
Hoy es lunes.	Today is Monday.

LOS MESES Y LAS ESTACIONES DEL AÑO

se(p)tiembre		marzo	
octubre	} el otoño	abril	} la primavera
noviembre		mayo	
diciembre		junio	
enero	} el invierno	julio	} el verano
febrero		agosto	

¿Cuál es la fecha de hoy?   What is today's date?

Hoy es el cuatro de julio.   Today is the Fourth of July.

Mañana es el primero de abril.   Tomorrow is the first of April.

LOS COLORES

amarillo/a yellow		**morado/a** purple	
anaranjado/a orange		**negro/a** black	
azul blue		**rojo/a** red	
blanco/a white		**rosado/a** pink	
gris gray		**verde** green	
marrón/castaño/(color) café brown			
azul oscuro dark blue		**verde claro** light green	

Al español, por favor.

1. What is today's date?
2. Today is the first of October.
3. Tomorrow is November the fourth.
4. I'm here on Mondays.
5. Good morning, Miss Flores. How are you?
6. Fine, thanks.
7. Today is Thursday.
8. We have class on Wednesdays.
9. The blue books are here.
10. Whose is the gray sweater (**suéter**)?

F. INTERROGATIVES

¿Cómo? How?	**¿Quién(es)?** Who?
¿Cuándo? When?	**¿De quién(es)?** Whose?
¿A qué hora? At what time?	**¿Dónde?** Where?
¿Qué? What?	**¿Adónde?** Where?
¿Cuál(es)? What? Which one(s)?	**¿De dónde?** From where?
¿Por qué? Why?	**¿Cuánto/a?** How much?
	¿Cuántos/as? How many?

1. Interrogative words have a written accent on the stressed vowel.

2. **¿Qué?** asks for an explanation or definition. **¿Cuál?** means *What?* in the sense of *Which one?*

—**¿Qué tiene Ud. ahí?**	"What do you have there?"
—**Tengo mi horario de clases.**	"I have my class schedule."
—**¿Cuál es tu teléfono?**	"What's your phone number?"
—**Es el 321-4567.**	"It's 321-4567."

Diga en español.

1. What is this (**esto**)?
2. Why are we going (**vamos**) tomorrow?
3. Why don't we go out (**salimos**) today?
4. What's your phone number?

5. Which one is your son (**tu hijo**)?
6. At what time are we going?
7. Where is he from?
8. How many tickets (**boletos**) does he have?

G. MÁS PALABRAS ÚTILES

esta noche tonight	
siempre always	
también also	
temprano early	
tarde late	
más tarde later	

cerca de close to	
lejos de far from	
delante de in front of	
detrás de in back of	
a la derecha to the right	
a la izquierda to the left	

casi almost	
una vez once	
dos veces twice	
sólo only	

pues... well...	
por eso therefore	
luego then	
cómo no of course	
a lo mejor maybe	

nunca never: **No estoy aquí nunca a esas horas/Nunca estoy aquí a esas horas.** I'm never here at that time.
nada nothing: **No tenemos nada/Nada tenemos.** We have nothing.

y and (**e** before **i-** and **hi-**): **padres e hijos** fathers and sons
pero but **porque** because

> **hay**   there is, there are: **Ahora hay once alumnos en mi clase.**
> There are now eleven students in my class.
>
> **había**   there was, there were: **Ayer había doce.**   There were
> twelve yesterday.

Al español, por favor.

1. There are only six students in this class.
2. Yesterday there were seven.
3. We are never here early.
4. On Mondays?
5. We are sleepy.
6. Of course.

Diga en español.

1. Julio and I eat (**comemos**) early.
2. We eat late also.
3. We are always hungry.
4. We eat a lot of burritos.
5. Close to downtown (**el centro**) there is a pizzeria (**pizzería**).
6. But it is far from the dormitory (**residencia**).

Cerca del centro hay un sitio
bueno y barato para comer
algo, pero está lejos de aquí.

Paso preliminar II

A. DEMONSTRATIVES AND POSSESSIVES

DEMONSTRATIVES	POSSESSIVES
este/a/os/as — this, these ese/a/os/as ⎫ aquel/aquella/ ⎬ that, those aquellos/aquellas ⎭	mi/mis — my tu/tus — your (*familiar*) su/sus — your (*polite*), his, her, its, their nuestro/a/os/as — our

1. The demonstrative forms above agree in number and gender with the noun they modify: **Estos libros son del profesor** *These books are the professor's.*

They take a written accent when they are used in place of nouns: **Éstos son de la profesora** *These are the professor's.* **Aquéllos son de ella también** *Those are hers also.*

2. The possessive forms above agree with the thing(s) possessed, not with the possessor: **sus lápices** *her pencils,* **nuestro auto** *our car.*

Exprese en español.

1. This book is Anita's.
2. I have my books.
3. Anita also has Federico's books.
4. That's her book.
5. These are our books here.
6. Those burritos are Julio's.

B. *IR* TO GO / *QUERER* TO WANT / *DEBER* MUST, SHOULD / *PODER* TO BE ABLE, CAN—present tense

ir to go
voy vas va vamos vais van

Vamos pronto. We are going soon. / Let's go soon.

Voy ahora. I'm going now.

Ir + a + *infinitive* is used for actions to be done in the near future.

Van a venir esta noche. They're going to come tonight.

querer to want
quiero
quieres
quiere
queremos
queréis
quieren

¿Cuándo quieres comer?   When do you want to eat?

Quieren ir ahora.   They want to go now.

Ella quiere salir, yo no.   She wants to go out, I don't.

deber (+ *inf.*) must, should
debo
debes
debe
debemos
debéis
deben

Debe leer más.   You must read more.

Julio debe comer menos.   Julio should eat less.

Deben llegar a tiempo.   They ought to arrive on time.

poder to be able, can
puedo
puedes
puede
podemos
podéis
pueden

No podemos ir ahora.   We can't go now.

Ud. puede ayudar.   You can help.

Uds. pueden ayudarme.   You can help me.

¿Cómo se dice en español?

1. She wants to go out tonight.
2. But we want to leave early.
3. Let's go now.
4. We must arrive on time.

5. We can't arrive late.
6. Don't you want to help?
7. Your mother can come too.
8. I'm going home. Goodbye.

C. *GUSTAR*   TO BE PLEASING (TO SOMEONE)

Gustar is generally used in the the third person (**gusta/gustan**) with an indirect-object pronoun: **me** *(to) me*, **nos** *(to) us*, **te** *(to) you*, **le/les** *(to) you, him, her, them*. The usual word order is object pronoun + verb + subject.

Les gusta la novela.

They like the novel ("To them is pleasing the novel").

¿No le gusta ir al cine?

Doesn't he like to go to the movies?

Me gustan las enchiladas picantes.

I like spicy-hot enchiladas.

Diga en español.

1. I like to eat.
2. We like the book.
3. She likes to go to the beach (**playa**).
4. They like the novel.
5. Does he like this music (**música**)?
6. Do you like (**las**) enchiladas?

D. USES OF THE VERB *HACER*

hacer to do; to make
hago
haces
hace
hacemos
hacéis
hacen

¿Qué hacen ahora? What are they doing now?

Ahora mismo no hacen nada. Right now they are not doing anything.

Van a hacer el trabajo más tarde. They are going to do the job later.

Los tejanos hacen burritos, los mexicanos, no. Texans make burritos, Mexicans don't.

WEATHER CONDITIONS

¿Qué tiempo hace?	How is the weather?
Hace mal tiempo.	The weather is bad.
Hace buen tiempo.	The weather is nice.
Hace fresco.	It's cool.
frío.	cold.
calor.	hot.
viento.	windy.
sol.	sunny.
Hace mucho frío.	It's very cold.
Hace poco sol.	It's not very sunny.

TIME EXPRESSIONS

¿Cuánto tiempo hace que Uds. tienen el piso?	How long have you had the apartment?
Hace ocho meses que estamos aquí.	We have been here for eight months.

The construction **hace . . . que** indicates the time period something has been going on. Both verbs are in the present tense.

¿Cómo se dice?

1. It's very hot.
2. It's not very sunny.
3. What are you doing?
4. I'm not doing anything now.
5. How do they make (**las**) tortillas?
6. What's the weather like?
7. It's bad. It's not good.
8. It's very windy.

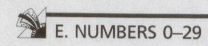

E. NUMBERS 0–29

0	cero	10	diez	20	veinte
1	uno/a, un	11	once	21	veintiuno(-ún)/una
2	dos	12	doce	22	veintidós
3	tres	13	trece	23	veintitrés
4	cuatro	14	catorce	24	veinticuatro
5	cinco	15	quince	25	veinticinco
6	seis	16	dieciséis	26	veintiséis
7	siete	17	diecisiete	27	veintisiete
8	ocho	18	dieciocho	28	veintiocho
9	nueve	19	diecinueve	29	veintinueve

1. Uno and numbers ending in **uno** (**veintiuno**) shorten to **un** or **-ún** before masculine nouns (**un hombre, veintiún hombres**) and become **una** or **-una** before feminine nouns (**una mujer, veintiuna mujeres**).

2. Numbers from 16 through 29 are written as one word: **dieciocho, veintisiete, veintinueve.**

Exprese en español.

6 + 6 = ?
Seis y seis son doce.

1. 3 + 11 = ?
2. 7 + 12 = ?
3. 10 + 10 = ?
4. 9 + 9 = ?
5. He is fifteen years old.
6. She has twenty-two pesos.
7. There are twenty-one burritos.
8. With thirteen (**Con el trece**) I am lucky.

F. MORE NUMBERS

30	treinta	31	treinta y uno (un)/una		
40	cuarenta	42	cuarenta y dos		
50	cincuenta	53	cincuenta y tres		
60	sesenta	200	doscientos	600	seiscientos
70	setenta	300	trescientos	700	setecientos
80	ochenta	400	cuatrocientos	800	ochocientos
90	noventa	500	quinientos	900	novecientos
100	cien, ciento				

250 **doscientos cincuenta**	643 **seiscientos cuarenta y tres**

1.000 **mil**	2.000 **dos mil**	1.000.000 **un millón**	2.000.000 **dos millones**

1. Compound numbers from 31 to 99 are written as separate words with **y**: **treinta y una mujeres, sesenta y tres estudiantes.**

2. *One hundred* is **cien. Ciento** is used when a smaller number follows: **ciento nueve** (109), **ciento ochenta y seis** (186).

3. Multiples of 100 have a feminine form in **-as**: **quinientas mujeres**.

4. In numerals Spanish uses a period where English uses a comma: **60.761** (60,761).

5. Mil is used to express the years in dates: 1920 **mil novecientos veinte**.

6. Millón takes **de** before its modified noun: **un millón de dólares, dos millones de pesetas.**

Practique estos números.

100 hombres	200 niñas	1.000 mujeres
35 clases	350 pesos	4.000 cartas
92 libros	500 pesetas	el año 1930
63 dólares	930 personas	el año 1850

G. ORDINAL NUMBERS

primero	first	**quinto**	fifth	**noveno**	ninth
segundo	second	**sexto**	sixth	**décimo**	tenth
tercero	third	**séptimo**	seventh		
cuarto	fourth	**octavo**	eighth		

1. Ordinal numbers agree in gender and number with the modified noun and precede it: **la tercera lección, la Quinta Avenida.**

2. Primer and **tercer** are forms used before masculine singular nouns: **el tercer mes del año.**

3. Spanish has ordinal numbers higher than *tenth* but cardinal numbers regularly replace them and follow the noun: **la lección trece, el siglo veinte.**

Continúe según (*according to*) el modelo.

1. Enero es el primer mes del año. Febrero es...
2. El lunes es el primer día de la semana. El martes es...

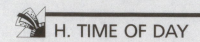

H. TIME OF DAY

> **¿Qué hora es?** What time is it?
>
> **Es la una.** It's one o'clock.
>
> **Son las dos y cuarto (quince).** It's (a) quarter past two.
>
> **Son las tres y media (treinta).** It's three thirty.
>
> **Son las cuatro y cuarenta y cinco.** It's 4:45.
>
> **Son las cinco menos diez.** ⎫
> **Faltan diez para las cinco.** ⎬ It's ten to five.
>
> **Son las seis menos quince.** ⎫
> **Faltan quince para las seis.** ⎬ It's (a) quarter to six.
>
> **Son las siete en punto.** It's seven o'clock sharp.
>
> **a las cinco de la mañana (tarde)** at five in the morning (afternoon)
>
> **a las ocho de la noche** at eight in the evening (at night)
>
> ---
>
> **al mediodía** at noon   **a (la) medianoche** at midnight

1. The feminine article **la/las** is used in clock time because it agrees with the implied **hora/horas.**

2. Minutes after the hour are expressed with **y: la una y veinticinco** (1:25).

3. Minutes before the hour are expressed either with **menos** (**Es la una menos cinco**) or with **faltar...para...** (**Faltan cinco para la una**) (12:55). A more formal way is to add the minutes as in English: **Son las cuatro y cuarenta y cinco** (4:45).

4. The word **minutos** is usually omitted when telling time.

5. ¿Qué horas son? *What time is it?* is often used in some areas of American Spanish.

¿Qué hora es?

5:00	11:00	9:30	7:55
8:00	5:15	10:10	6 A.M.
1:00	6:20	4:45	7 P.M.

WRITTEN ACCENT MARKS

The written form of a Spanish word indicates the vowel that receives voice stress (loudness or emphasis).

1. An **í** or a **ú** with a written accent next to another vowel in the word shows that it is pronounced as a separate syllable. Compare the following pairs of words.

   vía/viaje   leí/ley   gradúa/graduado   baúl/aula

2. Stress normally falls on the next-to-the-last syllable if the word ends in a vowel, **n** or **s**.

> **novela   burrito   hacen   joven   menos   meses**

3. Stress normally falls on the last syllable if the word ends in any other consonant (but **n** or **s**).

> **español   tener   usted   veloz   reloj   anorak**

4. If a word is an exception to rules 2 and 3 above, stress is indicated by a written accent.

> **está   millón   inglés   fácil   dólar   López   teléfono**

5. Interrogative and exclamatory words take a written accent on the stressed vowel, even in statements.

> —**¿Quién es?**   Who is it?
> —**No sé quién es.**   I don't know who it is.
> **¿Cuántos hay?**   How many are there?
> **¡Cuánto me alegro!**   How happy I am!
> **¡Qué hombre!**   What a man!

6. A written accent is also used to distinguish between two words identical in spelling but different in meaning.

> **si** if   **sí** yes   **solo** alone   **sólo** only
> **el** the   **él** he   **esta** this   **ésta** this one

Regular and stem-changing verbs in the present indicative

A. REGULAR VERBS

	hablar	**comer**	**vivir**
yo	hablo	como	vivo
tú	hablas	comes	vives
él, ella, usted	habla	come	vive
nosotros, nosotras	hablamos	comemos	vivimos
vosotros, vosotras	habláis	coméis	vivís
ellos, ellas, ustedes	hablan	comen	viven

Regular verbs in the present indicative replace the infinitive ending (**-ar**, **-er**, **-ir**) with person-number endings. The voice stress is on the stem except in the first- and second-person plural. Below are some regular verbs.

-ar	
acabar to finish, end	**estudiar** to study
apagar to turn off	**explicar** to explain
bailar to dance	**llegar** to arrive
bajar to take down, go down	**mandar** to send, order
cantar to sing	**mirar** to look at, watch
cenar to have dinner, supper	**pasar** to pass, spend (*time*)
desayunar to have breakfast	**preparar** to prepare
enseñar to teach, show	**tocar** to touch, play (*an instrument*)
entrar to go, come in	**tomar** to take, eat, drink
escuchar to listen (to)	**trabajar** to work
esperar to wait (for)	**viajar** to travel

-er	
aprender to learn	**deber** to owe; must
beber to drink	**leer** to read
comprender to understand	**responder** to answer
correr to run	**romper** to break, tear
creer to believe, think	**vender** to sell

-ir	
abrir to open	**discutir** to discuss, argue
admitir to admit	**escribir** to write
asistir to attend	**recibir** to receive
cubrir to cover	**subir** to take up, go up, get on (*a vehicle*)
decidir to decide	

1.1 Påra cada infinitivo dé (give) la forma indicada del presente de indicativo.

1. yo—bailar/ explicar/ deber/ abrir/ asistir
2. nosotros—cenar/ vivir/ leer/ pasar/ vender
3. ellas—correr/ subir/ enseñar/ romper/ estudiar
4. usted—cubrir/ trabajar/ recibir/ creer/ beber

1.2 Complete con el presente de indicativo. Los verbos se encuentran ahí arriba. Tras esto léalo todo en voz alta.

USTED NECESITA SABER IDIOMAS

Apréndalos con facilidad y rapidez en un centro especializado

el despertador alarm clock	**oigan** listen (*command*)
a lo español Spanish-style	**ida y vuelta** round-trip
un cacho a piece, slice	**el billete** ticket (*Spain; in Spanish America it is* **el boleto**)
a todo gas at top speed	
a veces sometimes	**en todo caso** in any case
parecido/a similar	**los gastos** expenses
a tiempo on time	**atónito/a** dumbfounded

A las seis el despertador _____ (breaks) el silencio. Frank me pregunta si _____ (we'll attend) a clase hoy. Le digo que sí. _____ (We have breakfast) a lo español, café con leche y un cacho de pan muy duro.

_____ (I turn off) la luz y a las seis y veinte _____ (we get on) al autobús. _____ (We spend) media hora en el camino. _____ (We live) lejos de la universidad y _____ (arrive) cansados. La verdad es que

A las seis y veinte subimos al autobús. Pasamos media hora en el camino. Vivimos lejos de la universidad y llegamos cansados. La verdad es que trabajamos casi toda la noche...

_____ y _____ todas las noches.
    we work   *study*

_____ otro café en la Unión mientras Frank me
   I have (tomar)

_____ afuera. Mi amigo me _____ la lección para hoy
   waits for   *explains*

y _____ listos para el sacrificio.
    we go in

· · ·

La profesora _____ tan lejos como nosotros. Ella
                doesn't live

_____ sin problemas y _____ a clase temprano.
  has breakfast   *arrives*

_____ que es una buena profesora que _____
  We believe   *understands*

nuestros problemas. Pero _____ español a todo gas, y a veces nos
                           she speaks

_____ a la pizarra.
  sends

Otras veces _____ la guitarra y _____ cantar.
            she plays   *we must*

_____ muy bien y _____
  We don't sing   *we don't understand*

ni una sola palabra. Claro, ella _____ muy bien los verbos y
                         explains

nosotros _____ atentos cada palabra. Ella _____ en
               listen   *reads*

español y nosotros _____ algo parecido.
                   write

· · ·

Hoy ella _____ la puerta y _____ a la clase. Primero
           opens   *comes into*

dice: «Ustedes nunca _____ a tiempo. Y _____ las
               arrive   *you don't prepare*

lecciones. Tú, Tom, ¿por qué _____ la lección?» Tom
                      don't you finish

_____ y _____ el eterno problema del
　　　doesn't answer　　　　*we discuss*
tiempo.

　　Pero pronto ella dice: «Oigan todos. Una gran sorpresa. Mañana la

clase entera _____ conmigo a Navarra, allí donde _____
　　　　　　　　travels　　　　　　　　　　　　　　　　*run*
los toros. Allá en la oficina _____ billetes de ida y vuelta. En todo
　　　　　　　　　　　　　they sell
caso, yo _____ los gastos.» La _____ atónitos. ¡Qué
　　　　　cover　　　　　　　　　　　*we look at*
profesora ésta! Una santa para nuestros días.

1.3 Reconstrucción

1. ¿A qué hora oyen (*do they hear*) el despertador? (**A las seis**...)
2. ¿Qué quiere saber Frank? (**si van**...)
3. ¿Con qué desayunan? (**con café con**...)
4. A las seis y veinte, ¿qué hacen (*do they do*)? (**suben**...)
5. ¿Dónde viven?
6. ¿Qué hacen todas las noches?
7. ¿Vive lejos la profesora?
8. ¿Cómo cantan los estudiantes?
9. ¿Qué explica muy bien la profesora?
10. ¿Cuál es el eterno problema de los estudiantes?

B. STEM-CHANGING VERBS

Some verbs of all three endings change the stem vowel in the present indicative when it is stressed: **e→ie** and **o→ue**. The change occurs in all forms except the first- and second-person plural.

e→ie		
cerrar (ie) to close	**perder (ie)** to lose	**sentir (ie)** to feel, regret
cierro	pierdo	siento
cierras	pierdes	sientes
cierra	pierde	siente
cerramos	perdemos	sentimos
cerráis	perdéis	sentís
cierran	pierden	sienten

comenzar to begin	**defender** to defend	**mentir** to lie
empezar to begin	**encender** to turn on; to set on fire	**preferir** to prefer
negar to deny	**entender** to understand	
pensar to think	**querer** to want; to love	

o→ue		
contar (ue) to tell, count	**poder (ue)** to be able, can	**dormir (ue)** to sleep
cuento	puedo	duermo
cuentas	puedes	duermes
cuenta	puede	duerme
contamos	podemos	dormimos
contáis	podéis	dormís
cuentan	pueden	duermen

almorzar to have lunch	**devolver** to return (*something*)	**morir** to die
colgar to hang (up)	**llover** to rain	
costar to cost	**morder** to bite	
encontrar to find, meet	**mover** to move (*something*)	
mostrar to show	**volver** to return, go, come back	
probar to prove; to test, try out		
recordar to remember		
soñar to dream		

Adquirir (i→ie) and **jugar** (u→ue) follow the same pattern.

adquirir to acquire	**jugar** to play
adquiero	juego
adquieres	juegas
adquiere	juega
adquirimos	jugamos
adquirís	jugáis
adquieren	juegan

Oler *to smell* is written **hue-** instead of **ue-**: **huelo, hueles, huele, olemos, oléis, huelen.**

Some verbs in **-ir** change **e→i** in the same places that the **e→ie** and the **o→ue** changes happen.

pedir to ask for	**competir** to compete	**perseguir** to pursue, harass
pido	**conseguir** to get, achieve	**repetir** to repeat
pides	**despedir** to see off, dismiss	**seguir** to follow, continue
pide	**elegir** to choose, elect	**servir** to serve
pedimos	**impedir** to prevent	**vestir** to dress, wear
pedís		
piden		

1.4 Complete con el presente de indicativo. Los verbos son los mismos que ve Ud. arriba. ¡Ojo! En muchos casos hay que cambiar la vocal radical (*stem vowel*).

la siestecita short nap	el ambiente atmosphere, environment
la librería bookstore	la venta sale
la película film, movie	podrido/a rotten
envidioso/a envious	el chiringuito open-air restaurant on beach (*Spain*)
parar to stop	
además furthermore	el boquerón anchovy
lo difícil que es how difficult it is	el porrón wine pitcher with side spout

Guillermo Cornejo _____ cuentos de detectives. Hoy miércoles
                writes
_____ sus costumbres de toda la vida. Cornejo _____ a
  he follows   *arrives*
su estudio a las ocho. _____ la chaqueta y _____ una
              He hangs up   *sleeps*
siestecita.

_____ nunca la luz y el estudio _____
  He doesn't turn on   *acquires*

la atmósfera que desea. Cornejo siempre _____ de negro. Así
wears
_____ el efecto deseado. _____ con adquirir una gran
he achieves   *He dreams*
fortuna.

• • •

A su amiga Adriana le dice: «Tú no me _____ ,
understand
muchacha. _____ que gano un montón de dinero. Si
I don't deny
tú me _____, _____ más que yo. Las librerías
dismiss   *you lose*
_____ todos los ejemplares de mis novelas. Y ahora
sell
_____ a hablar de películas. Pero mis enemigos, los en-
they begin
vidiosos, me _____ sin parar. Además _____
harass   *they lie*
mucho. _____ en lo difícil que es escribir una novela
They don't think
policíaca.»

• • •

En las novelas de Cornejo hay mucho ambiente. _____
It rains
mucho. Y hay nubes oscuras que _____ lentamente por el cielo.
pass
Cornejo _____ sus personajes con cuidado. Su último «best-seller»
chooses
ahora _____ todos los récords de venta.
breaks

Los dos se encuentran en
un chiringuito en la Costa
Blanca, donde almuerzan
con boquerones fritos y un
porrón de vino blanco.

El título de este fenómeno: *Algo* _____ *a podrido en*
smells
Calahorra. En la novela los dos protagonistas _____ mano
compete
a mano en un duelo a muerte. Pero no _____ nadie. Los dos se
dies
_____ en un chiringuito en la Costa Blanca.
meet
_____ con boquerones fritos y un porrón de
They have lunch
vino blanco. Todo esto _____ lo que _____ el autor:
prevents   wants
un final trágico.

•   •   •

En una cafetería Guillermo _____ ahora a comprender
begins
su situación. _____ una carta de Adriana pero no la _____ .
He receives   opens
Primero _____ : «Si ella _____ conmigo . . . »
he thinks   is playing
_____ un vaso de leche fría. Guillermo _____
He asks for   doesn't take
bebidas alcohólicas. La carta _____ : «Lo _____
begins   I regret
mucho . . . » Esto no _____ a rosas, _____ Cornejo. La
smell   believes
muchacha lo _____ .
dismisses
«¡Leche!» _____ Guillermo, y se _____ los labios.
repeats   bites
Afuera _____ a llover.
it starts

1.5 Reconstrucción

1. ¿Qué escribe Guillermo Cornejo?
2. ¿Cómo se llama su amiga?
3. ¿Qué gana Cornejo con su trabajo?
4. ¿Vende muchos libros?
5. ¿En dónde llueve mucho?
6. En su «best-seller», ¿quién muere?
7. ¿Qué pide Guillermo en la cafetería?
8. ¿Qué bebidas no prueba nunca?

AQUÍ HUELE
A MUERTO...
(¡PUES YO NO HE SIDO!)
Una película de ALVARO SAENZ DE HEREDIA

Diversión y práctica 1

Más expresiones útiles

¿Quiere (puede) Ud. repetirlo, por favor?	Would (could) you please repeat it?
Un poco más despacio, por favor.	A little slower, please
¡Claro! **¡Claro que sí!**	Sure!, Of course!

¿Se puede?	May I come in?
¡Pasa! **¡Pase Ud.!** **¡Adelante!**	Come in!

Te quisiera presentar a mi amiga Loli.	I'd like to introduce you to my friend Loli.
Encantado/a.	Pleased to meet you.
Mucho gusto.	Glad to meet you.
Igualmente.	The same here.

Perdón.	Pardon me. Excuse me. (*to attract someone's attention or apologize*)
Con permiso.	Pardon me. Excuse me. (*when passing through a crowd or asking someone's permission to do something*)

Hasta luego.	See you later.
¡Nos vemos!	⎰ Be seeing you! ⎱ See you soon!
Adiós.	Goodbye. (*also used for "hello" when people pass each other and do not intend to stop to chat or when they have recently spoken to each other somewhere else and happen to see each other shortly after*)

Suena el teléfono.	The telephone is ringing.
¡Dígame! **¡Aló!**	Hello!
¿Julia? (Te) habla Juan.	Julia? This is Juan.
¿De parte de quién, por favor?	Who (may I say) is calling, please?

¿Qué dices en las siguientes situaciones?

1. Hablas español con alguien y no entiendes lo que dice por la rapidez con que salen las palabras.
2. Yo te ofrezco un puesto en mi compañía que paga un sueldo increíblemente alto. ¿Cómo me respondes si te pregunto si vas a aceptarlo?
3. Tienes cita con tu consejera para discutir tus notas del semestre pasado, que son bastante bajas. Llegas a la puerta de su oficina. ¿Qué dices antes de entrar?
4. ¿Y qué responde la consejera?
5. Quieres presentar un nuevo amigo a tu compañero de la residencia universitaria. ¿Cómo lo haces?
6. ¿Qué responde tu compañero de cuarto?
7. Y luego, ¿qué dice el nuevo amigo?
8. Quieres buscar tu asiento en el estadio pero tienes que pasar por entre un gran número de gente que ya está viendo el partido. ¿Qué les dices?
9. Te tropiezas con (*bump into*) un desconocido en la calle. ¿Qué le dices?
10. Vas a ver a tu compañera más tarde en el comedor de la residencia, pero ahora tú la dejas en la biblioteca porque tienes que ir a clase. ¿Cómo te despides de ella?
11. Tú ves a unos amigos que caminan por la calle. No puedes parar y charlar porque tienes prisa. ¿Qué les dices?
12. Quieres saber el nombre del desconocido que llama por teléfono y que quiere hablar con tus padres. ¿Qué le preguntas?
13. Suena el teléfono y tú contestas. ¿Qué dices?
14. Una amiga que se llama Cristina te llama por teléfono. Cuando tú le dices —¡Aló!, ¿cómo responde ella?

Unit 2

Gender and plural of nouns

A. GENDER OF NOUNS

The following types of nouns are usually masculine in Spanish:

1. Those ending in **-o**: **el aparato, el paso, el río**
    Common exceptions: **la foto** *photo*   **la moto** *motorbike*
    la mano *hand*   **la radio** *radio* (although some speakers prefer **el radio**)

2. Geographical names: **el Guadalquivir, el Caribe, el Everest, el Sahara**

3. Days of the week: **el lunes, el martes** . . .

4. Modified months of the year: **el lluvioso abril** *rainy April*

5. Cardinal points (on the map): **el norte, el este, el sur, el oeste**

6. Cardinal numbers: **el tres, el siete, el trece**

The following nouns are usually feminine:

1. Those ending in **-a: la cita, la corbata, la mesa, la cama**. Common exceptions include many words of Greek origin usually ending in **-ma** or **-ta** that simply must be memorized.

el clima climate	**el crucigrama** crossword puzzle
el día day	**el sistema** system
el drama drama	**el telegrama** telegram
el fantasma ghost	**el tema** theme
el idioma language	**el cometa** comet
el panorama view	**el planeta** planet
el poema poem	**el poeta** poet
el problema problem	
el programa program	

The only two common exceptions ending in **-pa** are **el mapa** *map* and **el Papa** *the Pope*.

2. Nouns ending in **-dad**, **-tad**, **-ión**, and **-sis**.

la ciudad	city	**la lección**	lesson
la libertad	liberty	**la pasión**	passion
la conexión	connection	**la crisis**	crisis

Two common exceptions:

    el análisis analysis   **el énfasis** emphasis

3. Letters of the alphabet.

la a	a	**la hache**	h	**la ere**	r
la be	b	**la ele**	l	**la ese**	s

Some Spanish nouns referring to human beings have only one form for both the male and female. Many of these nouns end in **-ista.** The modifier indicates the gender (and thus the sex of the person).

el artista / la artista	artist	**el / la estudiante**	student
el / la astronauta	astronaut	**el / la intérprete**	interpreter
el / la atleta	athlete	**el / la modelo**	model
el / la ciclista	cyclist	**el / la periodista**	journalist
el / la egoísta	egotist	**el / la testigo**	witness
el / la guía	guide	**el / la turista**	tourist

Other nouns for professions and occupations have different male/female forms.

el abogado / la abogada	lawyer
el doctor / la doctora	doctor
el ingeniero / la ingeniera	engineer
el jefe / la jefa	boss
el secretario / la secretaria	secretary
el traductor / la traductora	translator

Some nouns have completely different meanings depending on gender.

el capital capital (*money*)	**la capital** capital (*city*)
el cometa comet	**la cometa** kite
el cura priest	**la cura** cure
el frente front, battlefront	**la frente** forehead
el orden order (*arrangement*)	**la orden** order (*command; religious organization*)
el Papa Pope	**la papa** potato (*Spanish America*)

2.1 Escriba en español.

1. Elisa is the boss of the team (**equipo**).
2. The athletes (*male*) are all cyclists.
3. They are also guides for the tourists.
4. The team has three interpreters (*female*) and two lawyers (*female*).
5. Elisa has one secretary (*male*).
6. The athletes (*female*) are also students; they are going to be engineers.
7. The French fries are for the Pope?

Oye Listen	**estar contigo** to be with you (on your side)
algo sordo somewhat deaf	**no faltaba más** how absurd, this is ridiculous, the "last straw"
ver la tele (visión) to watch television	**el proceso** trial
¿Eso qué tiene que ver? What does that have to do with anything?	**las lentejas** lentils
	¿están ya? Are they (ready) now?

2.2 Lea en español.

La difícil comunicación

PURI: Oye, hombre. Mira. Aquí hay un telegrama de María.

PEPE (*algo sordo*): Ningún programa para mí. No voy a ver la tele esta noche.

PURI (*gritando*): ¿Eso qué tiene que ver? ¡María va a ser testigo!

PEPE: ¿Que si estoy contigo? Sí, mujer. Qué pregunta. No faltaba más.

PURI (*más fuerte*): ¡¡La llaman para el proceso del jueves!!

PEPE (*paciente*): Sí, mujer, también los jueves estoy contigo. Las lentejas, ¿están ya? Tengo hambre.

B. PLURAL OF NOUNS

1. Spanish nouns ending in a vowel add **-s** in the plural: **hija** / **hijas**.
2. Nouns ending in a consonant or in **-ey** add **-es**: **flor** / **flores**, **rey** / **reyes**.
3. The plural of nouns ending in **-z** is spelled **-ces**: **luz** / **luces**, **voz** / **voces**. There is no change in sound.
4. Nouns ending in an unstressed vowel and **-s** are invariable.

el análisis / los análisis	el lunes / los lunes
la crisis / las crisis	el tocadiscos / los tocadiscos
el cumpleaños / los cumpleaños	el paraguas / los paraguas

Family names are also invariable: **los López** *the López's*, **los Santana** *the Santanas*, **las Ochoa** *the Ochoa women (girls, daughters, sisters)*.

los agentes	police	**los domingueros**	picnickers
arrojado	thrown	**la ira**	wrath
la canasta	basket	**patrullando**	on patrol
cotidiano/a	daily, everyday	**la persecución**	pursuit
deportivo/a	sports (*adj*)	**el poder**	power
los dibujos	cartoons	**se basaron**	were based
doblada al catalán	dubbed into Catalan	**se cruzan con**	run across
(*a Romance language spoken in northeastern Spain*)		**los tebeos**	comics (*Spain*)

2.3 Preguntas y comentarios

1. Determine the gender of these nouns used below: **serie, planeta, cantidad, programa, guardián, parque, vigilante, televisión, emisión, habitante.**
2. Infinitives used as nouns are masculine: **el poder** / **los poderes**.
3. Is **cumpleaños** below singular or plural?
4. Some nouns like **la víctima, el ángel, la persona** are invariable in gender and refer to individuals of either sex.

18.30
DOCUMENTAL

Aniversario. En 1938, en la publicación *Detective Comics*, apareció la primera aventura de un superhombre llegado de otro planeta con poderes fuera de lo común. En él se basaron programas de radio, series de televisión, películas y gran cantidad de tebeos. ¡Feliz 50ª cumpleaños, Superman!

4.25
SERIE

Miami. Mientras se hallan patrullando, Crockett y Tubbs, la pareja protagonista de *Corrupción en Miami*, se cruzan con un automóvil deportivo blanco que avanza a gran velocidad; los agentes, en su persecución, observan cómo al doblar la calle un cuerpo es arrojado fuera del vehículo. La víctima es una mujer muy joven y resulta ser una prostituta conocida por el nombre de Florence Italy.

18.45
DIBUJOS

Oso Yogui. TV-3 ha iniciado la emisión de la serie de dibujos animados protagonizada por el oso Yogui, pacífico habitante del parque de Yellowstone cuya vida cotidiana está llena de involuntarios desastres que provocan las iras del fiel guardián de la zona. Serie ya conocida, que ahora se emite doblada al catalán. Las víctimas propiciatorias de Yogui son los domingueros con sus apetitosas canastas y el ya citado vigilante.

Unit 3

Subject pronouns

A. USAGE

Subject pronouns in Spanish are usually omitted since the verb ending and context often make clear who the subject is. They are used, nevertheless, in the following cases:

1. For emphasis and contrast: **Tú no lo sabes, pero yo sí.**
2. To avoid ambiguity: **Él sabe que ella no viene.**
3. For politeness with **usted** and **ustedes**: **¿Conocen Uds. a mi amigo?**
4. After **ser** as the equivalent of *it* in *It's me*, *It's her*, etc.

    —**¿Es ése nuestro mesero?**   —**¿Eres tú, José María?**
    —**Sí, es él.**   —**Sí, soy yo.**

5. Spanish has no equivalent of *it* and *they* as inanimate subjects of the verb.

    ¿Esas cajas rojas? Son papeleras.   Those red boxes? They're trash
                                              baskets.

6. To answer **quién** or **quiénes.**

    —**¿Quién habla portugués aquí?**
    —**Yo hablo portugués.**

B. *TÚ* VS. *USTED*

In most Hispanic countries **tú** is used with family, friends, children, and fellow students of the same age. It is thus used to address anyone with whom the speaker might be on a first-name or friendly basis. **Usted** is used everywhere else. It may indicate respect, courtesy, and social distance. **Tú** and **usted** may both occur in the same conversation: an adult addresses an adolescent with **tú,** and the youth answers with **usted.** Conversations among children and teenagers use only **tú.***

*In Argentina the use of **vos** for familiar address (called **voseo**) is virtually universal, although the use of **tú** (called **tuteo**) is taught in schools. In several other parts of South and Central America **vos** is used for extreme familiarity, along with **tú** and **usted**, which are used in the customary way. Present-tense forms with **vos** are **hablás** (for **-ar** verbs), **tenés** (**-er**), and **decís** (**-ir**).

The plural of **tú** in Spanish America is **ustedes** (with third-person plural verb forms). In Spain it is **vosotros** (with second-person plural verb forms).

> **¿Qué hacen, niños?** (*Spanish America*)
> **¿Qué hacéis, niños?** (*Spain*)

C. *NOSOTROS* AND *VOSOTROS*

Nosotros and **vosotros** have feminine forms: **nosotras** and **vosotras.** The masculine may indicate males only or mixed company.

nosotros los canadienses	we Canadian men/ we Canadians (*male and female*)
vosotras las canadienses **ustedes las canadienses**	you Canadians (*female*)

Lea el diálogo de abajo y note el uso de pronombres como sujeto del verbo. (Note also the form of address the speakers use with each other.)

la madrugada dawn	**No es para tanto.** There's no reason to get upset, It's no big deal.
¿Cómo «soy yo»? What do you mean "it's me"?	
dime (tú) tell me	**se lo explico** I'll explain it to you
cálmese calm down	**de veras** truly, really

Encuentro nocturno

Es de noche en Villalba del Monte. Silencio total. Luna llena. Todo tranquilo. A la madrugada se oye *tun-tun-tun* a la puerta.

MANUELA (*dentro*): ¿Ángel? ¿Eres tú?
VOZ INCIERTA (*fuera*): No, señora, soy yo.
MANUELA: ¿Cómo «soy yo»? ¿Tú qué quieres?
VOZ: ¿No me recuerda usted, señora? Soy yo, Andrés. Estuve aquí anoche, con Ángel. ¿No recuerda?
MANUELA: ¿Andrés?
VOZ: El mismo y en persona. A sus órdenes, señora.
MANUELA: Pues dime, Andrés, ¿qué le ha pasado a Ángel?
ANDRÉS: Es que fuimos Ángel y yo allá a Nájera a las fiestas . . .
MANUELA: ¿Vosotros a Nájera? Ay, Dios.
ANDRÉS: Sí, señora, cálmese usted. No es para tanto. Es que Ángel y ella . . .
MANUELA: ¿Ella? ¿Quién es ella?
ANDRÉS: Por favor, señora, aquí fuera me vienen a saludar todos los perros del pueblo. Usted me deja entrar, por favor, y se lo explico. No es nada, de veras . . .

Unit 4

Ser and *estar* with adjectives

A. *SER* + ADJECTIVE

Both **ser** and **estar** are used with adjectives. **Ser** is used to express characteristic qualities of the subject, i.e., what kind of a person or thing you are talking about.

—**¿Cómo es el jefe?**	"What's the boss like?"
—**Es alto, guapo e inteligente.**	"He's tall, handsome, and intelligent."
—**Y su esposa, ¿cómo es?**	"And what's his wife like?"
—**Ella es seria, pero amable y cariñosa.**	"She's serious, but nice and affectionate."

If a noun modifies the subject, it is preceded by **de**.

La blusa es de seda.	The blouse is silk.
La cartera es de cuero.	The wallet is leather.

B. *ESTAR* + ADJECTIVE

Estar is used when the adjective modifying the subject describes a condition or state.

El té está caliente.	The tea is hot.
La plancha está encendida.	The iron is (turned) on.
Tiene fiebre, está enferma.	She has a fever; she's sick.
La pera está podrida.	The pear is rotten.
La ventana está sucia.	The window is dirty.
El aparato está descompuesto.	The set is broken.
El piso está limpio.	The floor is clean.
Todos están muertos.	They are all dead.

Estar is often the equivalent of the English verbs *look, taste, act, seem, feel*.

Para los años que tiene, Antonio está muy joven.	For his age Antonio seems (looks, acts) pretty young.

¡Qué elegante estás hoy!	How elegant you are (look) today!
¡El viento está tan frío!	The wind is (feels) so cold!
La gasolina está muy cara.	Gas is very expensive (now).
El postre está muy rico.	The dessert is (tastes) very good.

C. CHANGE OF MEANING WITH ADJECTIVES

The meaning of many common adjectives changes depending on whether **ser** or **estar** is used.

Bárbara es lista.	Bárbara is smart (clever).
Están listos.	They are ready.
Eduardo es vivo.	Eduardo is lively (quick-witted).
Todos están vivos.	They are all alive.
Las uvas son verdes.	The grapes are green (*in color*).
Las uvas están verdes.	The grapes are green (*unripe*).
Simón es rico.	Simón is rich.
El postre está muy rico.	The dessert is (tastes) very good.
¿Cómo es?	What's she like?
¿Cómo está?	How is she (feeling)?

4.1 Escriba en español.

1. What is the professor like?
2. She is friendly.
3. Her husband is intelligent and serious.
4. Mario is the best.
5. He is Italian.
6. His mother is Spanish.
7. The food (**comida**) that she prepares is delicious.
8. It's not spicy (**picante**).
9. But today the coffee is cold.
10. The road is frozen (**helado**).
11. The car is broken.
12. The air is (feels) chilly (**fresco**).

4.2 Haga Ud. oraciones con un sustantivo (*noun*) del primer grupo + **ser** / **estar** + una frase del segundo grupo. Frases razonables, por favor.

esa habitación	ancho/ estrecho
mis camisas	caro/ barato
su esposo	fuerte/ débil
Magdalena	limpio/ sucio
la avenida	abierto/ cerrado
Joaquín	oscuro/ iluminado
la oficina	contento/ triste
mis amigos	alto/ bajo
esta sala	satisfecho/ enojado

Unit 5

Irregular verbs in the present indicative

A. VERBS WITH *G*

The verbs below have a **g** in the first-person singular. **Traer** also has an **i: traigo.**

salir to go out, leave	**poner** to put, place	Verbs like **poner**
salgo	pongo	**componer** to compose
sales	pones	**disponer** to dispose
sale	pone	**oponer** to oppose
salimos	ponemos	**proponer** to propose
salís	ponéis	**suponer** to suppose
salen	ponen	

valer to cost, be worth	**traer** to bring	Verbs like **traer**
valgo	traigo	**atraer** to attract
vales	traes	**caer** to fall
vale	trae	**distraer** to distract
valemos	traemos	
valéis	traéis	
valen	traen	

The following verbs with a first-person **g** also have a stem change. **Decir** is like **pedir (e→i). Venir** and **tener** are like **querer (e→ie)**, except for **vengo** and **tengo.**

decir to say, tell	**venir** to come	**tener** to have, possess	Verbs like **tener**
digo	vengo	tengo	**contener** to contain
dices	vienes	tienes	**detener** to detain
dice	viene	tiene	**entretener** to amuse, entertain
decimos	venimos	tenemos	**obtener** to obtain
decís	venís	tenéis	
dicen	vienen	tienen	

B. VERBS WITH *ZCO*

Some verbs ending in **-cer** and **-cir** have **-zco** in the first-person singular.

conocer to know, be acquainted with	Verbs like **conocer**
conozco	**agradecer** to thank
conoces	**aparecer** to appear
conoce	**merecer** to deserve
conocemos	**obedecer** to obey
conocéis	**ofrecer** to offer
conocen	**parecer** to seem
	permanecer to remain
	pertenecer to belong
	reconocer to recognize

traducir to translate	Verbs like **traducir**
traduzco	**conducir** to drive; to lead
traduces	**introducir** to introduce
traduce	**producir** to produce
traducimos	
traducís	
traducen	

C. VERBS WITH *Y*

Almost all verbs ending in **-uir** have **y** in the singular and in the third-person plural.

concluir to conclude	Verbs like **concluir**
concluyo	**construir** to build
concluyes	**contribuir** to contribute
concluye	**destruir** to destroy
concluimos	**distribuir** to distribute
concluís	**huir** to flee
concluyen	**incluir** to include

D. VERBS WITH Í OR Ú

In some verbs ending in **-iar** and in all verbs ending in **-uar** the stress is on the **i** or the **u** in four forms and is so indicated with a written accent. **Reunir** is similar.

enviar to send	continuar to continue	reunir to gather
envío	continúo	reúno
envías	continúas	reúnes
envía	continúa	reúne
enviamos	continuamos	reunimos
enviáis	continuáis	reunís
envían	continúan	reúnen

However, **cambiar, estudiar, pronunciar,** and many other **-iar** verbs are completely regular and have no stress change. They must be learned individually.

E. OTHER IRREGULAR VERBS

Other verbs irregular in the present indicative are below. **Reír** follows the pattern of **pedir,** and it takes written accents like the verbs in section D above.

dar to give	haber to have	saber to know	ver to see
doy	he	sé	veo
das	has	sabes	ves
da	ha	sabe	ve
damos	hemos	sabemos	vemos
dais	habéis	sabéis	veis
dan	han	saben	ven

oír to hear	reír to laugh	Another verb like **reír**
oigo	río	**sonreír** to smile
oyes	ríes	
oye	ríe	
oímos	reímos	
oís	reís	
oyen	ríen	

5.1 Para cada infinitivo dé la forma indicada del presente de indicativo.

1. yo—traer/ venir/ conocer/ dar/ oír
2. ellas—contribuir/ enviar/ oír/ decir/ ver
3. tú—haber/ reunir/ traducir/ huir/ venir
4. nosotros—dar/ enviar/ conocer/ decir/ reír
5. él—valer/ continuar/ decir/ caer/ merecer

5.2 Haga las combinaciones más convenientes (*most suitable*).

No dice nunca	su ayuda
No obedecen	lo que digo
Cae ahora	en nosotros
No siempre oyen	las leyes
No vale ni	la mitad (*half*) de lo que cuesta
Ya no (*no longer*) confían	a las cuatro de la madrugada
Salimos	una lluvia fuerte
Agradezco mucho	la verdad

5.3 Traduzca ambas cartas. Escriba la traducción.

Querida Irene,

Supongo que no vienes a verme el sábado. ¿Qué hago yo para merecer esto? Tienes que decirme la pura verdad. Confío en ti. ¿Por qué huyes de mí? Sé que continúas amando a Eugenio. ¿Es que no valgo nada a tus ojos? Te agradezco una respuesta clara y que no deje lugar a dudas.

Gregorio

Dear Gregorio,

You want to know the truth. You deserve the truth. The truth is that I am not going to see you Saturday. I have to study. What more can I say? Who is Eugenio?

Irene

Diversión y Práctica 2

Números, letras y el clima

A. VAMOS A HACER UN POCO DE MATEMÁTICAS.

1. *Números pares* (empezando con cualquier número elegido). Por ejemplo:
   Treinta y dos — treinta y cuatro — treinta y seis ...
   Ochenta y seis — ochenta y ocho — noventa...

2. *Números impares.* Por ejemplo:
   Diecisiete — diecinueve — veintiuno...

3. *Adición.* Por ejemplo: Cuatro y cuatro son ocho.
   Once y trece...
   Treinta y tres y quince...
   Cincuenta y siete y doce...

4. *Sustracción.* Por ejemplo: Cuatro menos dos son dos.
   Dieciocho menos tres ...
   Cuarenta y cuatro menos veinticinco...
   Setenta y seis menos veinticinco...

5. *Multiplicación.* Por ejemplo: Cuatro por cuatro son dieciséis.
   Cinco por cinco...
   Siete por seis ...
   Ocho por nueve...

6. *División.* Por ejemplo: Treinta dividido por seis son cinco.
   Cuarenta dividido por cuatro...
   Setenta dividido por dos ...

B. LAS LETRAS DEL ALFABETO Y SUS NOMBRES

a	a	**j**	jota	**r**	ere
b	be	**k**	ka	**rr**	erre
c	ce	**ll**	ele	**s**	ese
ch	che	**l**	elle	**t**	te
d	de	**m**	eme	**u**	u
e	e	**n**	ene	**v**	ve
f	efe	**ñ**	eñe	**w**	doble ve
g	ge	**o**	o	**x**	equis
h	hache	**p**	pe	**y**	i griega
i	i	**q**	cu	**z**	zeta

Notas

1. **Ch**, **ll** y **rr** representan letras sencillas (*single letters*) y un solo sonido cada una.

2. **B** y **v** representan un solo sonido (como la *b* de inglés) tras **m** y **n** (**hombre, invitar**) y al principio de un grupo de palabras (tras una pausa) (**Bien, Vamos**). Estas dos letras representan también un solo sonido (es decir, una **b** muy suave sin contacto completo de los labios) en otras posiciones, sobre todo entre vocales (**está bien, no vamos, lobo, tuvo**). Para distinguir entre estas dos letras, muchos dicen **la be alta** o **be grande** o **«be de burro»** y **la ve corta** o **ve chica** o **«ve de vaca»**.

¿Cómo se escriben estas palabras y estos nombres? Deletréamelos (*Spell them for me*), por favor.

honor	breve	comenzar	David
Gerardo	kilómetro*	Joaquín	calle
maravilla	niño	wáter	chiflado
suyo	perro	explicar	zapato

C. EL CLIMA—¿QUÉ TIEMPO HACE?

Llueve. It rains.		**Está lloviendo.** It's raining.	
Nieva. It snows.		**Está nevando.** It's snowing.	
Está nublado. It's cloudy.		**Está lloviznando.** It's drizzling.	

(*Paso preliminar II—parte D* tiene otras expresiones climatológicas.)

¿Qué tiempo hace generalmente en los lugares indicados abajo según las fechas indicadas? No olvides que las estaciones del hemisferio sur ocurren al revés de las del norte del ecuador. Por ejemplo, cuando hace calor en Toronto, hace bastante frío en Santiago de Chile.

1. El veinte de junio en Houston.→Hace…o…
2. El tres de enero en Buenos Aires.→
3. El veinticinco de diciembre en Minneapolis.→
4. El quince de febrero en Rio de Janeiro.→
5. El cuatro de julio en Montevideo.→
6. El primero de agosto en Cleveland.→
7. El dieciocho de julio en Asunción.→
8. El diez de febrero en Kennebunkport.→

*Di «o con acento» para **ó**.

Unit 6

Spelling-changing verbs in the present indicative

The spellings **gi** / **ge** / **ja** / **jo** / **ju** represent in Spanish one consonant sound at the beginning of each of these syllables. In some areas it is like the *h* of English. In other areas it is a sound we do not have in English—the consonant in German *Ach!*, Scottish *loch*, or Yiddish *chutzpah*. Verbs in **-ger** and **-gir** change the **g** to **j** before the **o** of the first-person singular. This keeps the spelling consistent with the sound.

dirigir to direct	Verbs like **dirigir**
dirijo	**coger** to pick up, grab
diriges	**corregir** (**i**) to correct
dirige	**escoger** to choose
dirigimos	**elegir** (**i**) to choose, elect
dirigís	**fingir** to pretend
dirigen	**proteger** to protect

The Spanish spellings **gui** / **gue** / **ga** / **go** / **gu** represent one consonant sound at the beginning of each of these syllables, like the *g* in English *gone*. Verbs in **-guir** change **gu** to **g** before **o** in order to follow the rules of Spanish spelling, showing that there is no "u" sound in these verbs anywhere.

distinguir to distinguish	Verbs like **distinguir**
distingo	**seguir** (**i**) to follow, continue
distingues	**conseguir** (**i**) to get, achieve
distingue	
distinguimos	
distinguís	
distinguen	

The Spanish spellings **ci / ce / za / zo / zu** represent one consonant sound at the beginning of each of these syllables. In American Spanish it is like the *s* in English *see*. In Castilian Spanish (the standard usage of Spain) it is like the *th* in English *think*. The first-person singular of **vencer** *to defeat* and **convencer** *to convince* is written **-zo**: **venzo, convenzo**.

Para cada infinitivo escriba la primera persona del presente de indicativo.

conseguir / dirigir / convencer / coger / seguir / fingir / corregir / vencer / elegir

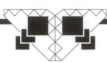

Vamos a escribir ... 1

Presente de indicativo

Completar la narración que sigue, utilizando el presente de indicativo y algunas frases con un infinitivo. Después, leerla en voz alta y sin parar. Si hace falta (*If it's needed*) consultar el vocabulario (más los verbos alfabetizados) que se halla al final.

VIAJE A ESTOCOLMO

A las cinco de la mañana _____ para el aeropuerto. Mi compañía
I leave
_____ ayuda técnica que _____ en países
offers *it distributes*
del mundo entero. Yo _____ el material informativo. Voy a
translate
_____ un viaje bastante largo y _____ a toda veloci-
make *I drive*
dad. _____ una llovizna, pero no molesta. Los otros conduc-
Is falling
tores no me _____ de mi propósito de _____ lo más
distract *arrive*
pronto posible. _____ siempre _____ temprano al
It pleases me *to arrive*
aeropuerto.

Además, _____ un boleto superganga. Si _____ el
I bring *I don't make*
viaje, _____ el dinero. _____ conduciendo a ciento
I lose *I continue*
treinta kilómetros por hora. A las cinco y media _____ en el
I am
aeropuerto.

La línea aérea que _____ es SAS. Le _____ el boleto a la
I look for *I give*
agente del mostrador y le _____ mi pasaporte. Ella _____
I show *laughs*
un poco al ver la foto. Qué amable señorita. Otro empleado de la línea
me _____ facturando las maletas, y me _____ los
continues *he gives*
talones.

—¿_____ equipaje de mano?—me _____ la
Do you have *asks*
señorita.

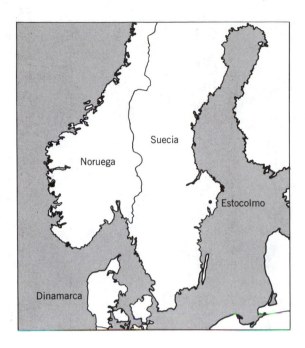

—Sólo este maletín que _____ mis papeles—
                                contains

_____ .
I answer

   —Bien, señor—me _____ . —Usted _____ en la fila
                        she says   _are_

veintitrés, en el pasillo. El vuelo _____ completo. Puerta
                                          isn't

dieciséis. Buen viaje.

   A una amiga le _____ una tarjeta postal. _____ un
                      I send   _I have_

café cortado y un bollo en el bar del aeropuerto, donde los precios

_____ de escándalo. Ahora me _____ una buena idea
      are   _it seems_

_____ los aseos, y_____ , «¿Dónde _____
  to look for   _I ask_   _are_

los servicios?» Alguien me _____ , «Allí al fondo, a mano
                                 answers

izquierda».

                    •   •   •

   Algo más tarde _____ solo y _____ a dos hombres
                        _I am_   _I see_

enormes que _____ a parar junto a mí. No los _____ .
                  come   _I know_

¿ _____ terroristas? En estos días uno _____ y
   Are they   _doesn't know_

_____ . Uno de ellos _____ :
        I am afraid   _begins_

—¿Adónde _____ , señor? Le _____
              are you going   _we want to propose_

_____ a usted un pequeño negocio.

Oigo palpitar mi corazón y comienzo a sudar. Por el momento no recuerdo adónde voy. Ah, a Estocolmo...

_____ palpitar mi corazón violentamente y _____ a
 I hear   *I begin*
sudar. Por el momento _____ adónde _____ .
                           I don't remember   *I'm going*
—A Estocolmo— _____ por fin. —Y con su permiso me
                   I answer
_____ ahora subir al avión.
 I propose
—¿Usted _____ a Suiza?— _____ el que
             are going   *asks*
_____ el más imbécil de los dos.
 seems
—No, _____ Suecia, idiota— _____ su compañero.
       it's   *explains*
—¿Y _____ escala en París?
     don't you make
—Afortunadamente no, señor. Ahora, si Uds. me
_____ ...
 permit
—Usted nos _____ un gran favor— _____
               can do   *says*
el más listo de los dos, y _____ :
                             he explains
—Aquí _____ un libro que _____ hoy a
         I bring   *has to arrive*
Estocolmo. _____ mucho. _____ el
             It is worth   *We want to send*
libro con usted, en su misma persona. _____ en usted,
                                         We trust
y se lo _____ .
         we thank
Me _____ en la mano un libro que curiosamente
     he puts
_____ muy pesado. Entre las páginas _____ un billete
 is   *there is*
de cien dólares. _____ esto, _____ .
                   I don't deserve   *I think*

_____ el libro. _____ una novela de Guillermo Cornejo.
(I look at) _(It is)_
_____ el título: _Al asesino le_ _____ _los boquerones_
(I recognize) _(are pleasing)_
fritos. Me _____ los dos y yo _____ nerviosamente.
(smile) _(laugh)_
Precisamente en ese momento _____ a un guardia del aero-
(I see)
puerto que nos _____ sospechoso.
(looks at)

—¿ _____ algún problema?— _____ .
(Is there) _(he asks)_
—Ninguno— _____ .— _____ todas las
(I answer) _(I obey)_
leyes de este país, y además la verdad es que _____ a esta
(I don't belong)
pequeña reunión que _____ aquí—. Y en el acto le _____ al
(you see) _(I give)_
guardia el billete de cien.

—Aquí _____ lo que _____ yo a la
(you have) _(contribute)_
agencia de beneficios para empleados—. Me _____ con estupor
(he looks at)
y yo _____ hacia mi puerta, que es la dieciséis.
(flee)

Una vez a bordo nos _____ bebidas frías. Pero de pronto
(they serve)
me _____ una duda. Aún _____ conmigo la novela que
(distracts) _(I bring)_
pesa como diez. Por lo visto _____ más que palabras. ¿Qué
(it contains)
_____ ahora?
(shall I do)

---

bastante largo rather long	**(el café) cortado** coffee "cut" with a little milk
la llovizna drizzle	**el bollo** roll
lo más pronto posible as soon as possible	**los aseos** toilets, restrooms
superganga supersaver (_fare_)	**los servicios (públicos)** toilets
el mostrador counter	**el fondo** back, rear
facturar to check	**un negocio** a business deal
la maleta suitcase	**sudar** to sweat
el talón stub	**Suiza** Switzerland
el equipaje de mano hand luggage	**Suecia** Sweden
el maletín briefcase	**la escala** stop (_on a flight_)
la fila row	**pesado/a** heavy
el pasillo aisle	**en el acto** at once, right away
el vuelo flight	**el estupor** amazement
completo full, booked	**de pronto** suddenly
la puerta gate	**pesar** to weigh
la tarjeta postal postcard	**por lo visto** clearly

agradecer	distraer	merecer	poner	sonreír
buscar	distribuir	mirar	preguntar	tener
caer	empezar	mostrar	proponer	tomar
comenzar	enviar	obedecer	querer	traducir
conducir	estar	ofrecer	reconocer	traer
confiar	explicar	oír	recordar	valer
contener	gustar	parecer	reír	venir
contestar	haber	pensar	responder	ver
continuar	hacer	perder	saber	viajar
contribuir	huir	permitir	salir	
dar	ir	pertenecer	ser	
decir	llegar	poder	servir	

Ahora reconstruya la historia.

1. ¿A qué hora sale el viajero?
2. ¿Adónde va en su coche?
3. ¿Cómo conduce?
4. ¿Cuándo prefiere llegar al aeropuerto?
5. Si no hace el viaje, ¿qué pierde?
6. ¿Adónde va el viajero?
7. ¿A quiénes ve el viajero?
8. ¿Por qué le palpita el corazón?
9. ¿Dónde está Estocolmo?
10. ¿Qué cosa trae a bordo el viajero?

LECTURA I

Read straight through the passage first. Then complete the verb-form exercise before re-reading the article. Questions for comprehension follow.

«¿Qué pasa?»

En las calles neoyorquinas está de moda[1] entre anglos[2] saludar diciendo: «¿Qué pasa?». Pero «¿Qué pasa?» curiosamente es también el nombre de una publicación en inglés que pronto parece que va a publicar textos en español. Esto es sólo una indicación más del vertiginoso° ascenso del periodismo en español en Estados Unidos. — *dizzy*

¿Dónde se encuentran[3] los clientes para tanta prensa° en castellano[4]? Hay cada vez más° periódicos hispanos que prueban su fortuna en el mercado°. ¿Con qué público cuentan los periódicos? Claro, un público que se siente como en casa cuando sigue los acontecimientos° del día en español. Un público que pide cada vez más ejemplares. Un público que vuelve una y otra vez° a la página de deportes° y noticias° en español. — *press* · **cada**... *more and more* · *marketplace* · *events* · *again and again* · *sports / news*

Los Estados Unidos hoy es el quinto país del mundo en número de hispanoparlantes°. La mitad de éstos se hallan en Tejas y California. La cuarta parte vive en Nueva York, La Florida y el Suroeste. La ciudad de Nueva York sigue como la gran metrópoli de habla española. Pero en Miami es donde *The Miami Herald*, con la publicación de *El Nuevo Herald*, prevalece últimamente en el campo del periodismo. — *Spanish speakers*

El Nuevo Herald es una edición totalmente independiente, de más de 30 páginas a todo color. Se vende con su hermano mayor° por el mismo precio. Llega a diario a los 94.000 ejemplares. Y no en vano—la población hispana aquí, preferentemente de Cuba, representa ya el 43% de los dos millones de habitantes del Gran Miami. — *bigger (older)*

Casi todos los 30 redactores° de *El Nuevo Herald* son bilingües. Fácilmente saltan del español al inglés. Su director repite que es un diario en español que publica las noticias que le interesan al lector hispano de Miami. Utiliza también las técnicas de los periódicos norteamericanos. Esas «técnicas», con sus ruidosos titulares° de primera página («PRESO EX BANQUERO POR LAVADO DE DINERO»*) son las que más chocan° a un lector español recién llegado. — *editors* · *headlines* · *shock*

La principal competencia (en Miami) es *El Diario–Las Américas*, el periódico exclusivamente en español de mayor tirada° en Estados Unidos. El incansable° Horacio Aguirre lleva varios lustros° fustigando° diariamente desde este periódico al régimen castrista. El diario sigue siendo de lectura obligada para la gran mayoría conservadora emigrada de Cuba. — *press run* · *untiring* · *five-year periods / lashing out at*

*"FORMER BANKER ARRESTED FOR LAUNDERING CASH"

DIARIO LAS AMERICAS

Membro de la Sociedad
Interamericana de Prensa

Fundado el 4 de
Julio de 1953

NUMERO 36

AÑO XXXVIII

Por la Libertad, la Cultura y la Solidaridad Hemisférica.

MIAMI, FLA...MIERCOLES 15 DE AGOSTO DE 1990

EDICION DE 24 PAGINAS – 2 SECCIONES

25 CENTAVOS EN MIAMI

Al Cerrar la Edición

Nueve piden asilo en Cuba

ABRE EL REFRIGERADOR Y HALLA UN CADAVER

LA NACION

AÑO IV No. 187 — VIERNES 10 DE AGOSTO DE 1990   NEW YORK — NEW JERSEY

EL PERIODICO DIARIO DE LOS HISPANOS

35¢

EL VOCERO DE PUERTO RICO

COPYRIGHT CARIBBEAN INTERNATIONAL NEWS CORP. 1990

VOL. 8 NUM. 5927 SAN JUAN, P.R.
JUEVES 9 DE AGOSTO DE 1990

40¢

El precio de EL VOCERO fuera de NY, Boston, Hartford, Filadelfia, Norte de NJ y C

Emboscada en plena vía pública

MAFIOSOS

NOTICIAS del MUNDO

NUEVA YORK 35¢

Fuera del área metropolitana de
Nueva York y Nueva Jersey 40¢

VIERNES 10 DE AGOSTO DE 1990

el Nuevo Herald

30 PAGINAS

MIAMI, FLA., MIERCOLES 14 DE FEBRERO DE 1990

CIAS
IERRE

tos y Heridos

TAXISTAS EX

Siguen los Asaltos y lo:
Piden les Permitan Po

ATACADA SEDE COMUNISTA

Sucedió en Dushanbe, a
1,600 millas de Moscú

KGB revela mate

Siguen los sacrificios humanos en México

ASESINATOS ATRIBUIDOS AL DEMONIO

DESFILE
DOMINICANO,
UN EVENTO
QUE DIVIDE A
LA COMUNIDAD

IMPACTO

Latin News

AÑO XXI, Nº 788

(New Jersey & Sorrounding Areas   50¢)

AGOSTO 8-14, 1990

40¢

LOS ANGELES TIMES

Los Angeles Times

Nuestro Tiempo

A Monthly Bilingual Section / Una Sección Mensual Bilingüe

THURSDAY, DECEMBER 14, 1989

METS GANAN A FILADELFIA 8-4 P. 44

CAMPEON DE LOS HISPANOS

el diario / la prensa

DOMINICANA
Resistencia laboral a
las alzas de Balaguer
P. 13

35¢

NUEVA YORK, JUEVES 9 DE AGOSTO DE 1990

Edición Metropolitana

'No pasarán'

Médico afirma que peligra
carrera de Maradona
Página 69

SUPER BOWL XXIII
la fiesta es en Miami
Páginas 71-72

Higuera no empezará
temporada por operacion
Página 58

CAMPEON DE LOS HISPANOS

el diario / la prensa

VOL. XXXV 12655

UN PERIODICO
GANNETT

¿PROBLEMAS?
LLAME A NUESTRA
LINEA CALIENTE
(212) 807-4700

Edición Metropolitana Aérea $1.25

NUEVA YORK, DOMINGO 22 DE ENERO DE 1989

$1.00

SE BUSCA
ASESINO PELIGROSO

LA VOZ
HISPANA
NEW YORK'S LARGEST SPANISH WEEKLY NEWSPAPER

El retorr
de ur
gran
Hé

AÑO 14 — No. 642 • 9 DE AGOSTO AL 15 DE 1990

el expreso
La Nueva Fuerza Del Periodismo Hispano

New York, Junio 1990-Edición de Prueba

Policias Asaltan Residentes NY

EL EXPRESO, tendrá diariamente
un resumen de noticias colom-
bianas, las informaciones serán
suministradas desde aquella nación
por el bloque de prensa de la empresa COLMUNDO que dirige el
periodista Carlos Alvarez.

NOTICIAS

**SUPLEMENTO
DE REPUBLICA
DOMINICANA**

60¢

EL ESPECIAL™
EL SEMANARIO HISPANO DE MAYOR CIRCULACION EN LOS ESTADOS UNIDOS

Muchos diarios y semanarios en español sueñan con competir en un mercado potencial de cerca de dos millones de habitantes, pero el caso más singular es el de *El Diario–La Prensa*, el decano de la prensa hispana fundado en 1913.

Nueva York, sin embargo, es el mejor campo de pruebas°. *proving ground*
Muchos diarios y semanarios° en español sueñan con competir *weeklies*
en un mercado potencial de cerca de dos millones de habitantes.
El caso más singular es sin duda el de *El Diario–La Prensa*, el
decano° de la prensa hispana fundado en 1913. Persigue su for- *dean*
tuna ahora dentro de la cadena° de periódicos más poderosa de *chain*
Estados Unidos, la Gannett Company, propietaria del *USA Today*.
En competición con *The Daily News* y *The New York Post*, El Diario
compite con grandes titulares rojos con textos como «BALEAN EM-
PRESARIO EN OFICINA»*. Las noticias de los barrios hispanos,
el deporte o los acontecimientos lejanos de Hispanoamérica son
los contenidos de este diario, popular entre la población puertorriqueña.

El ascenso del español llega también a las ondas°. En tan *airwaves*
sólo° 10 años el número de estaciones de radio que emite en *only*
español se ha doblado a 211. Los 16 canales de televisión se han
convertido en 22, mientras la cadena de televisión de España aquí
en EE.UU. cuenta con casi 300 afiliadas. Las grandes compañías
de la comunicación no quieren perder en la carrera° desesperada *race*
por controlar las redes° de distribución de programas para la co- *networks*
munidad hispana.

Notas

1. **Estar de (última) moda** to be *fashionable* is one of several idiomatic expressions with **estar**: **estar de acuerdo** to *agree*, **estar de vacaciones (viaje)** to *be on vacation (a trip)*, **estar de buen (mal) humor** to *be in a good (bad) mood*.
2. The word **anglos** is generally applied to all non-Hispanics.
3. **Encontrarse, hallarse,** and **quedar** are other Spanish equivalents of **estar**: **¿Dónde están (se encuentran, se hallan, quedan)?** *Where are they?*
4. With many Spanish speakers **castellano** and **español** are synonymous terms.

"MANAGER GUNNED DOWN IN OFFICE"

Prácticas

Los siguientes verbos aparecen aquí en el orden de su uso en el texto. Complete la frase en tercera persona, singular o plural, sin referirse, claro, al texto de arriba.

1. ¿Dónde se (encontrar) los clientes?
2. Estos periódicos (probar) su fortuna en el mercado.
3. ¿Con qué público (contar) los periódicos?
4. Es un público que se (sentir) como en casa cuando (seguir) las noticias en español.
5. Un público que (pedir) cada vez más ejemplares.
6. Son clientes que (volver) a la página de deportes en español.

7. Los directores (repetir) que van a publicar las noticias que le interesan al lector hispano.
8. Muchos diarios (soñar) con competir en este mercado.
9. *El Diario–La Prensa* (perseguir) su fortuna dentro de la cadena Gannet.
10. *El Diario* (competir) con grandes titulares rojos.
11. Las grandes compañías no (querer) perder en esta carrera económica.

Comprensión

1. ¿Qué dicen los neoyorquinos si no dicen «*Hi*»?
2. ¿Qué país es el quinto del mundo en número de hispanoparlantes?
3. ¿Qué es un bilingüe?

4. ¿Cuál es el periódico exclusivamente en español de mayor tirada en Estados Unidos?
5. ¿Por qué se llama *El Diario–La Prensa* el decano de la prensa hispana?

Unit 7

━━

Direct-object pronouns

me	me	**nos**	us
te	you (= **tú**)	**os**	you (= **vosotros/as**)
lo	you (= **usted**) him it (*masc.*)	**los**	you (= **ustedes**) them (*masc., masc. + fem.*)
la	you (= **usted**) her it (*fem.*)	**las**	you (= **ustedes**) them (*fem.*)

Direct-object pronouns agree in gender and number with the nouns to which they refer. They are placed before a conjugated verb form and after the negative **no**.

¿El pasaporte? No lo necesito para este viaje.	The passport? I don't need it for this trip.

In verb + infinitive constructions they may either precede or follow.

¿La leche y el azúcar? Ella los va a comprar. (Ella va a comprarlos.)	The milk and sugar? She's going to buy them.

The pronouns referring to **usted**, **ustedes** are **lo**, **la**, **los**, **las**.

Pablo lo ayuda (a Ud., señor).	Pablo will help you (sir).
Yo las oigo (a Uds., señoras).	I hear you (ladies).

In Spanish America the plural of familiar **te** is **los**, **las**, corresponding to **ustedes**. In Spain, **os** is the plural familiar form corresponding to **vosotros/as**.

Le and **les** (rather than **lo** and **los**) are used in Spain for males.

Le respeto (a Ud., señor).	I respect you (sir).
Les respeto (a Uds., señores).	I respect you (gentlemen).

Direct-object pronouns are used when a noun object precedes the verb.

Este libro no lo necesito.	I don't need this book ("This book I don't need").

CALLE GUARDIA, 9 - Teléfono 32 38 15

VALDEPEÑAS

Mesa núm. _____

D. _____

CONCEPTOS	PESETAS
1 Ensalada	100
1 Solomillo	900
1 pan	25
vino	100
1 flan	150
1 cafe	50
1 coñac	75
	1400

¿Conoces el Mesón de la Virreyna? Con su cocina casera, se come bien y barato, y se bebe mejor. Tú puedes ser feliz con su arroz a la marinera, que es gala de la casa. Y cocidos todavía se comen, con toda solemnidad y en días fijos.

Menú

Sopas / Entremeses
(appetizers)

Sopa de pescado

Gazpacho andaluz (*cold vegetable soup*)

Caldo gallego (*broth w/ greens*)

Jamón serrano con melón
(*cured ham, honeydew melon*)

Angulas en cazuela
(*baby eels in hot garlic sauce*)

Gambas (camarones) al ajillo
(*garlic shrimp*)

Almejas a la marinera
(*clams, wine, tomato, onion*)

Carnes / Aves

Pollo asado (*roast chicken*)

Cochinillo asado con romero
(*roast suckling pig, rosemary*)

Parrillada criolla (*Argentine mixed grill*)

Bistec de ternera (*veal steak*)

Solomillo a la bordelesa
(*filet mignon Bordelaise*)

Chuletas de cerdo (*pork chops*)

Postres

Helados variados
–fresa, vainilla, piña

Flan de naranja (*orange caramel custard*)

Tarta borracha (*whiskey cake*)

Brazo de gitano (*sponge cake, rum cream*)

Quesos manchegos (*La Mancha cheeses*)

Ensaladas

Ensalada mixta (*w/ tuna, egg, olives*)

Lechuga y tomate a la vinagreta

Legumbres

Menestra de verduras (*stir-fried vegetables*)

Lentejas con chorizo
(*lentils, chorizo sausage*)

Pimientos rellenos (*stuffed peppers*)

Alcachofas salteadas con jamón
(*artichokes, ham*)

Arroces

Paella valenciana (*rice, seafood*)

Pescados / Mariscos

Bacalao a la vizcaína (*cod, Basque-style*)

Langostinos a la plancha (*grilled crawfish*)

Zarzuela de mariscos (*shellfish stew*)

Merluza a la sidra (*cider-steamed hake*)

Besugo al horno (*red snapper w/ potatoes*)

Bebidas

Vino–tinto, blanco, rosado

Cerveza–marcas importadas

Sangría

Refrescos (Gaseosas, *Spain***)** (*soft drinks*)

Agua mineral

NOTA: EL BAR DE TAPAS ABRE A LAS 12 H.

Boquerones en vinagre
(*marinated anchovies*)

Tortilla española (*potato omelet*)

Pescaditos rebozados (*tiny fried fish*)

Calamares a la romana (*squid deep-fried*)

Gran surtido de especialidades de la casa

7.1 Traduzca usando pronombres del complemento directo (*direct object*), según el modelo.

/a usted, **Adela Gómez**/ I see you. → **La veo.** I listen to you. → **La escucho.** But I still (**aún**) do not know you. → **Pero aún no la conozco.**

1. /a usted, **Rafael Alonso**/ I hear you. Then I help you. But I do not understand you.
2. /a ustedes, **Jaime y Nilda**/ I look for you. I find you. But I do not need you.
3. /a ti, **Tere (Teresa)**/ I don't know if I really know you. But I love (**quiero**) you.

7.2 Convierta los complementos directos (*direct objects*) en pronombres. En algunas frases no hay complemento directo.

de lujo first-class	**la carne** meat; beef
el mesero (camarero) waiter	**a la parrilla** grilled
la minuta menu	**un poco roja** medium rare
el pescado fish	**la cuenta** bill
a la romana deep-fried	

1. Julia llama a su hermana Marisela.
2. Mañana celebran el cumpleaños de una amiga.
3. ¿Conoces *El Bodegón*? Es un restaurante de lujo.
4. Decimos al mesero que preferimos la mesa ahí, en el patio.
5. El mesero trae la minuta.
6. Y pregunta:—¿Qué les apetece?*
7. Yo recomiendo el pescado, a la romana.
8. ¿Cómo quieren la carne?
9. —A la parrilla. Un poco roja.
10. El mesero sirve la comida y dice:—Buen provecho.*
11. —Aquí tienen la cuenta.
12. —No pago estos precios.

---

*¿Qué les apetece? and **Buen provecho / Que aproveche(n)** are expressions often heard in restaurants. The first is often said by the waiter, and it means "What would you like to have?" The second is also said by the waiter after serving the main course or by someone who sees friends dining. It expresses the hope that your well-being improves after eating your meal. With friends the implication is also that the speaker will not be joining his friends at the meal.

Personal *a*

1. The personal **a** is used in Spanish before direct-object nouns that identify specific people.

Conocemos a Luis y a todos los invitados.	We know Luis and all the guests.
La policía va a detener a los terroristas.	The police are going to arrest the terrorists.
¡Llama al médico!	Call the doctor!
No veo a la enfermera.	I don't see the nurse.

2. If a class of people is referred to, and not particular individuals, the personal **a** is not used.

Necesitamos enfermeras y médicos.	We need nurses and doctors.
Buscan una secretaria trilingüe.	They are looking for a trilingual secretary.

3. Personal **a** is not used with **tener** when **tener** means *to have*: **Tienen tres hijos.** It is used before interrogatives and relatives (**quien, cual, cuantos**) and the indefinite pronouns **alguno, alguien, nadie, ninguno**, and **cualquiera**, whenever these words are direct objects and refer to persons.

—**¿A quién conoces aquí?**	"Who do you know here?"
—**No conozco a nadie.**	"I don't know anybody."
—**¿Conocen a alguien?**	"Do you know anyone?"
—**No conocemos a ninguno aquí.**	"We don't know anyone (a single person) here."

Restaurant

Especialidades:

• **Cazuela de Mariscos**
• **Crema de Cangrejo** •
Lunes
• **Sancocho de Pescado**

Lleve su familia, a su esposa o a su novia a pasar un rato ameno en un ambiente familiar.

Haga frases con las palabras indicadas.

1. la enferma / no conocer / esos médicos
2. nosotros / no esperar / nadie
3. ¿quién / llamar / tú? / ¿José María?
4. ella / escuchar / el profesor Pérez
5. yo / tener / amigos / en Santander
6. la compañía / buscar / más obreros
7. ellos / querer / consultar / el jefe
8. ¿cuál / de los chicos / preferir / tú / para el equipo?

Indirect-object pronouns

me	(to, for) me	**nos**	(to, for) us
te	you (= **tú**)	**os**	you (= **vosotros/as**)
le	⎧ you (= **usted**) ⎨ him ⎩ her it	**les**	⎧ you (= **ustedes**) ⎩ them
(**le** → **se**)		(**les** → **se**)	

1. Indirect-object pronouns indicate *to who(m)* and *for who(m)* something is given or done. English often omits the word *to*. The Spanish pronouns are placed before a conjugated verb form and after the negative **no**. In verb + infinitive constructions they may either precede or follow.

Nos mandan los boletos.	They send us the tickets. (They send the tickets to us.)
No les doy nada.	I don't give them anything. (I don't give anything to them.)

2. English often uses a possessive form to indicate the person who experiences or is affected by an event, but Spanish always uses an indirect-object pronoun in such cases. The direct object is often a personal belonging, a part of the body, or clothing.

They cut our hair.	**Nos cortan el pelo.**
He wastes all my money.	**Me gasta todo el dinero.**
I take their temperature.	**Les tomo la temperatura.**
The nurse takes off his shirt.	**La enfermera le quita la camisa.**

3. English often expresses the indirect-object noun or pronoun with a prepositional phrase, but Spanish always uses an indirect-object pronoun in such constructions, even when a prepositional phrase is present.

I give the money to Ana.	**Le doy el dinero a Ana.**
She sends the check to them.	**Les envía el cheque a ellos.**

4. Indirect-object pronouns precede direct-object pronouns.

Me lo mandan a fines de mes.	They send it to me at the end of the month.
Nos las entrega ahora.	She hands them in to us now.

5. The indirect-object pronouns **le** and **les** become **se** when used with a third-person direct-object pronoun (**lo**, **la**, **los**, **las**).

Se lo doy.	I give it to him (to her, to you, to them).
Se las entregamos.	We hand them in to him (to her, to you, to them).

6. The meaning of **se** is clarified when necessary with a prepositional phrase. These phrases can also be contrastive and emphatic.

Se lo doy (a él, a ella, a Ud., a ellos).	I give it to him (to her, to you, to them).
Se las entrego a él, no a Ud.	I hand them in to *him*, not to *you*.

9.1 Reemplace la frase preposicional al final por un pronombre de complemento indirecto (*indirect object*) y combine las palabras para formar una oración completa. Por ejemplo:

la mujer / dar / los boletos / a Javier → **La mujer le da los boletos.**

1. Raquel / no entregar / el dinero / a nosotros

2. yo / mandar / los regalos / a Consuelo

3. el gobierno / no ofrecer / ayuda / a los obreros

4. el profesor / no explicar bien / el problema / a Gloria

5. el entrenador / no decir / nada / a los jugadores

6. la vieja / contar / una historia / a las niñas

9.2 Traduzca utilizando pronombres de complemento indirecto donde sea necesario.

1. Rodolfo has to go to the hospital.

2. He is very sick.

3. I know Rodolfo.

4. He doesn't like hospitals.

5. They take away (**quitar**) his clothes.

6. The nurse takes his temperature.

7. Someone cuts his hair.

8. Another person shaves (**afeitar**) his head.

9. Finally Rodolfo is better.

10. They give him back (**devolver**) his clothes.

9.3 Traduzca convirtiendo los complementos (*objects*) directos e indirectos en pronombres. Por ejemplo:

I give the money (= *it*) to the cashier (**cajero**) (= *to him*). → **Se lo doy.** (i.e., *I give it to him.*)

1. He gives the money to me.

2. We give books to the libraries.

3. They give the house to their children.

4. You give the tables to the carpenter.

Unit 10

Preterit past

A. REGULAR VERBS IN THE PRETERIT

Spanish has two simple past tenses, the preterit and the imperfect. The preterit of regular verbs is formed by adding person-number endings to the infinitive stem.

entrar	aprender	recibir
entr é	aprend í	recib í
entr aste	aprend iste	recib iste
entr ó	aprend ió	recib ió
entr amos	aprend imos	recib imos
entr asteis	aprend isteis	recib isteis
entr aron	aprend ieron	recib ieron

Verbs in **-er** and **-ir** have the same endings. Verbs in **-ar** and **-ir** have the same forms in the first-person plural for both the present and the preterit. Context determines whether **entramos** means *we go in* or *we went in*.

Stem-changing verbs in **-ar** and **-er** show no stem change in the preterit. Stem-changing verbs in **-ir** do have changes, which will be taken up in Unit 12.

The preterit reports actions or states as finished in the past.

Le compré un estéreo.   I bought her a stereo.

¿Le mandaste otro cheque?   Did you send him another check?

B. SPELLING-CHANGES IN THE PRETERIT

The rules of Spanish spelling require a spelling change in the first-person singular of many **-ar** verbs since the consonant in question precedes **é**.

In all **-car** verbs (**buscar**) c → qu: **busqué**   *I looked for*

In all **-gar** verbs (**llegar**) g → gu: **llegué**   *I arrived*

NECAXA vs. PUEBLA

REÑIDO DUELO.

**Un emocionante partido desde el Estadio "Azteca",
cuando se enfrente el Necaxa, el cual no ha recibido goles en 664 minutos,
a los "Camoteros" del Puebla, dispuestos a mantener el superliderato.**

11 DE LA NOCHE.

23:00 HORAS

"¡Torero!, ¡torero!"

BARCELONA
VS.
MILAN

Los italianos, después de vencer
a los "Merengues", ahora
en la "SUPER COPA EUROPEA".
Los barceloneses esperan desquitarse
y vencer al Milán.

DEPORTES

River Plate empata y no pudo llegar al liderato del torneo

Servicios cablegráficos combinados

Buenos Aires — River Plate   ■ Méxic─

FUTBOL EN EL MUNDO

Saprissa líder en fútbol tico

Servicios cablegráficos combinados

San José — El Deporti─
Saprissa consolidó ─l

..utro tema, Medina   los que no han enten─
el sistema", concluyó.

Se acaba el mundo: Diego Maradona está lesionado

NÁPOLES, Italia, 21 de noviembre (AP).— El argenti─
─dona, que hace poco fue sancion─
─prácticas, no ──

Conquista de Copa alienta a Colombia

Los Angeles —(AP)— Las
enseñanzas del técnico argentino   cido.
    "Fue un gol m──

Aluvión de goles en Paraguay

¿GANARON O PERDIERON?

Manténgase al tanto de las victorias de sus equipos
favoritos. Llame a TeleHerald y escuche todos los

Maradona marca su gol número 100 con el Nápoles

AGENCIAS, Roma   mero 100 desd─

In all **-zar** verbs (**comenzar**) z → c: **comencé** *I began*

However, the spelling is normal in other forms: **buscaste, llegó, comenzamos.**

-car	-gar
explicar to explain **sacar** to take out **tocar** to touch; to play (*music*)	**apagar** to put out, turn off **colgar (ue)** to hang **entregar** to hand in, over, deliver **jugar (ue)** to play (*games*) **negar (ie)** to deny **pagar** to pay
-zar	
almorzar (ue) to have lunch **alcanzar** to reach **empezar (ie)** to begin	

In the first-person singular of verbs ending in **-guar** (**averiguar** *to find out*) the **gu** changes to **gü** before **e** to show that the **u** is pronounced: **averigüé** *I found out*, **me santigüé** *I made the sign of the cross*.

C. VERBS WITH Y IN THE PRETERIT

The third-person preterit endings of **caer**, **creer**, **leer**, and **oír** are written **-yó**, **-yeron**. The other preterit forms of these verbs have a written accent on the **í**.

creer: creí, creíste, creyó, creímos, creísteis, creyeron

oír: oí, oíste, oyó, oímos, oísteis, oyeron

Verbs ending in **-uir** have the third-person preterit endings **-yó** and **-yeron**.

concluir: concluí, concluiste, concluyó, concluimos, concluisteis, concluyeron

Cambie los verbos al pretérito.

1. El partido empieza a las seis de la tarde.
2. Los dos equipos llegan al estadio La Bombonera.
3. Los once jugadores de cada equipo entran a la cancha.
4. A los 24 minutos un defensa del otro equipo recoge un tiro de esquina.
5. Lanza un misil y el balón acaricia la red.
6. Mete el balón lejos del golero ante el delirio de los casi 50.000 espectadores.
7. El árbitro no declara un penalty.
8. Al final del primer tiempo quedan empatados a cero.
9. Luego un desastre comienza para nuestro equipo.

A los 24 minutos un defensa del otro equipo recogió un tiro de esquina. Lanzó un misil y el balón acarició la red. Metió el balón lejos del golero ante el delirio de los casi 50.000 espectadores.

10. Nuestro equipo ofrece una patética imagen en el estadio.
11. El enemigo logra la mayor goleada de la historia.
12. Al final del segundo tiempo nuestros jugadores huyen del campo.
13. La máxima estrella del otro equipo marca tres tantos sensacionales.
14. Abraza a sus compañeros.
15. Luego vuelve al centro del campo y saluda al público.
16. El público blande sus pañuelos blancos y grita: «¡Torero!, ¡torero!»
17. Nuestro equipo cae de la gracia de los aficionados.
18. Unos fanáticos persiguen al árbitro en pleno centro de la ciudad.

la cancha (**el campo**) field	**el tiempo** half (*of a soccer game*)
el defensa defender	**empatados a cero** tied 0–0
un tiro de esquina a corner shot	**lograr** to achieve
lanzar to fire, let fly	**la goleada** scoring of many goals
el balón ball	**marcar** to score
acariciar to caress	**el tanto** point (*in scoring*)
la red net	**abrazar** to hug
el golero (**portero, arquero, guardameta**) goalie	**blandir** to wave
el árbitro referee	

The term **fútbol** refers to the game called soccer in the U.S. and is derived from the British word *football*. Mexico has its own national conference of American-style football, called **fútbol americano** or **el fut americano**.

Pronouns after a preposition

para mí for me	**sin nosotros/as** without us
al lado de ti next to you	**hacia vosotros/as** towards you
después de él after him	**tras ellos** behind them
contra ella against her	**cerca de ellas** near them
por usted because of you	**frente a ustedes** facing you
conmigo with me	**contigo** with you

Except for **mí** and **ti***, the prepositional pronouns are the same as the subject pronouns. The prepositions **entre** *between*, **salvo** / **excepto** / **menos** *except*, **según** *according to*, and **hasta** *up to, as far as* take **yo** and **tú** (not **mí** and **ti**): **entre tú y ella, todos excepto tú y yo.** Note also the special forms after **con**—**conmigo** and **contigo**: **Sabes que puedes contar conmigo** *You know you can count on me.*

Prepositional pronouns are used

1. After prepositions and personal **a**.

   —¿**A quién invitaron?**   "Who did they invite?"
   —**A ti, hombre.**   "You, man."

2. To clarify, contrast, or emphasize.

   —¿**Se lo mandaron a Ud.?**   "Did they send it to you?"
   —**No, se lo mandaron a ella.**   "No, they sent it to her."

   —¿**A mí me invitaron?**   "Did they invite *me*?"
   —**Claro, te invitaron a ti, no a mí.** "Of course, they invited *you*, not me."

Traduzca.

1. ALICIA: Who did they invite?
2. CRISTINA: I know that they invited *me*.
3. ALICIA: I want to go with *him*, not with you.
4. CRISTINA: But he wants to go with *me*, not with you.
5. ALICIA: Between you and me, they only invited Guadalupe.
6. CRISTINA: You don't know anything. They invited *me*, not her.
7. ALICIA: Then (**entonces**) I'm not going to the party!

*Ti has no accent mark because there is no other such word in Spanish. **Mí** is matched by **mi** *my*.

Diversión y práctica 3

Países, idiomas y nacionalidades

UN POCO DE GEOGRAFÍA

A. Dime en qué parte de Estados Unidos queda el estado de Kansas. Por ejemplo:

—**El estado de Kansas se halla en el medioeste de los Estados Unidos.**

Minnesota / La Florida / Vermont / Arizona / Nueva Jersey / Indiana / California / Wáshington (estado) / Misisipí

B. Ahora dime dónde se halla el Japón con respecto a China. Por ejemplo:

—**El Japón se halla al este o al noreste de China.**

México y Tejas / Cuba y Puerto Rico / la U.R.S.S. (la Unión Soviética) y Polonia / Chile y Brasil / Panamá y Colombia / España y Francia / Nicaragua y Costa Rica

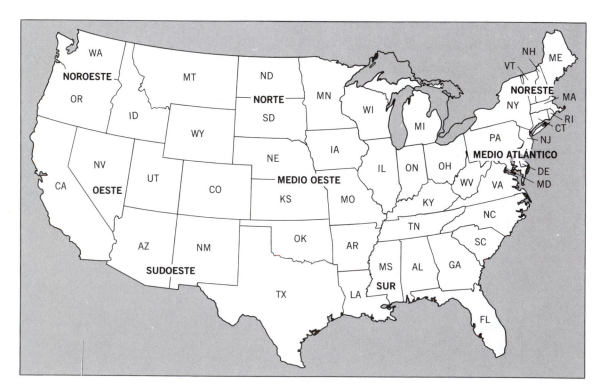

MÉXICO, AMÉRICA CENTRAL Y EL CARIBE

Nacionalidades hispanas		
argentino / a	ecuatoriano / a	paraguayo / a
boliviano / a	español / a	peruano / a
colombiano / a	guatemalteco / a	puertorriqueño / a
costarricense	hondureño / a	salvadoreño / a
cubano / a	mexicano / a	uruguayo / a
chileno / a	nicaragüense	venezolano / a
dominicano / a	panameño/a	

**Algunos países no hispanos y sus habitantes
(y en algunos casos su lengua también)**

Austria — austríaco / a	Irán — iraní
Bélgica — belga	Irlanda — irlandés / a
Checoslovaquia — checoslovaco / a	Israel — israelí
China — chino / a	Noruega — noruego / a
Dinamarca — danés / a	Polonia — polaco / a
Egipto — egipcio / a	Rumania — rumano / a
Grecia — griego / a	Suecia — sueco / a
Holanda — holandés / a	Suiza — suizo / a
Hungría — húngaro / a	U.R.S.S (Unión Soviética) — ruso / a
Irak — iraquí	

Entre las tres mil lenguas del mundo las diez que encabezan la lista en número de hablantes son: *el chino, el inglés, el hindi, el ruso, el español, el árabe, el portugués, el bengalí, el alemán* y *el japonés.*

C. A ver si sabes qué lengua(s) se habla(n) en varios países. Por ejemplo:

—**¿Paraguay?**
—**En Paraguay se hablan español y guaraní.***

Bogotá (Colombia) / el Canadá / Suecia / Portugal / Teherán / Tokio / Viena / El Cairo / Israel / Bucarest / el Reino Unido / el Brasil / San Juan

D. Dime de qué país es Lima la capital. Por ejemplo:

—**Lima es la capital del Perú.**

Asunción / Bagdad / Damasco / Caracas / San José / Ottawa / Pekín / Moscú / Quito / Manila / Ankara / Varsovia / Buenos Aires / Tegucigalpa

*El guaraní es un idioma indígena y casi todos los paraguayos son bilingües.

Unit 12

═══

Verbs irregular in the preterit

 ## A. VERBS WITH *I* IN THE STEM

decir	venir	hacer	querer
dije	vine	hice	quise
dijiste	viniste	hiciste	quisiste
dijo	vino	hizo	quiso
dijimos	vinimos	hicimos	quisimos
dijisteis	vinisteis	hicisteis	quisisteis
dijeron	vinieron	hicieron	quisieron

Note that **dijeron** has no **i** in its ending, unlike the other third-person plural forms.

 ## B. VERBS WITH *J* IN THE STEM

-**ducir** verbs	traer
produje	traje
produjiste	trajiste
produjo	trajo
produjimos	trajimos
produjisteis	trajisteis
produjeron	trajeron

Note that **produjeron** and **trajeron** have no **i** in their endings, unlike most regular third-person plural forms.

C. VERBS WITH *U* IN THE STEM

estar	poder	poner	saber	tener
estuve	pude	puse	supe	tuve
estuviste	pudiste	pusiste	supiste	tuviste
estuvo	pudo	puso	supo	tuvo
estuvimos	pudimos	pusimos	supimos	tuvimos
estuvisteis	pudisteis	pusisteis	supisteis	tuvisteis
estuvieron	pudieron	pusieron	supieron	tuvieron

Andar *to walk, go* is like **estar**: **anduve, anduviste**, etc.

Caber *to fit (into)* is like **saber**: **cupe, cupiste**, etc.

D. OTHER IRREGULAR VERBS

ir, ser	dar	ver
fui	di	vi
fuiste	diste	viste
fue	dio	vio
fuimos	dimos	vimos
fuisteis	disteis	visteis
fueron	dieron	vieron

Ir and **ser** are identical in the preterit. The monosyllabic verb forms **di / dio, vi / vio, fui / fue** require no written accent since they are not matched by any other Spanish word, as are **dé** and **sé**, for example.

E. VERBS WITH *E → I* AND *O → U*

Verbs ending in **-ir** that are stem-changing in the present (pp. 20–21 and p. 37) also have stem changes (e → i, o → u) in the two third-person forms of the preterit.

e → i			o → u
pedir	**sentir**	**reír**	**dormir**
pedí	sentí	reí	dormí
pediste	sentiste	reíste	dormiste
pidió	sintió	rió	durmió
pedimos	sentimos	reímos	dormimos
pedisteis	sentisteis	reísteis	dormisteis
pidieron	sintieron	rieron	durmieron

A las ocho de la mañana el viejo tomó su decisión. . . . y a las diez vino a verme.

Like **pedir** are **competir, despedir, impedir,** and **seguir: competí, despidió, impidieron, seguimos,** etc.

Like **sentir** are **mentir, sugerir: mentí, sugirió,** etc.

Like **reír** is **sonreír: sonreí, sonrió,** etc.

Like **dormir** is **morir: moriste, murió,** etc.

Cambie los verbos subtitulados al pretérito. El primer cambio ya está hecho como ejemplo.

EL PADRINO

Isidro Crespo, el padrino de Rosalía, ___**durmió**___ toda la noche como un ángel. Al amanecer, el nuevo día _____ limpio y
duerme
hermoso en Villavieja de la Sierra. A las ocho de la mañana el viejo
nace

_____ su decisión.
toma

Pero primero _____ . Esa mañana su mujer no _____
desayuna hace
chocolate con churros. Su desayuno _____ en una copa de
consiste
anís y un café con leche en un vaso en el que _____ un cacho de
moja
pan.

A las diez de la mañana el viejo _____ a verme. Él
viene
me _____ a mí, y yo lo _____ a él. Él, tranquilo,
saluda saludo
me _____ pero yo, preocupado, sólo le _____ los dientes.
sonríe veo

•   •   •

Isidro _____ : «_____ la amistad entre Ud. y
dice Muere
yo.» Le _____ yo: «¿Cómo?»
digo

ISIDRO: —Ud. le _____ cartas a Rosalía.

escribe

YO: —¿Yo? Nunca, señor. Le aseguro que ella jamás _____

tiene

carta de mí. No, señor. (Mentalmente me _____ .)

santiguo

Isidro me pregunta: —¿ _____ Ud. con ella alguna vez?

Sale

YO: —No, hombre, no _____ así. (Yo _____ nerviosamente.)

es   río

ISIDRO: —¿Ud. la _____ en alguna ocasión?

ve

YO: —Bueno, quizá una vez. _____ con ella una vez al mer-

Voy

cado. Allí en la plaza la _____ una vez.

veo

El viejo me _____ una explicación. _____ un fuerte

pide   Siento

temblor que me _____ el corazón. Isidro _____ con las

sacude   sigue

preguntas.

ISIDRO: —¿Qué _____ Uds. allí?

hacen

YO: —Hombre, en la plaza no _____ nada. Rosalía _____

pasa   está

allí conmigo una vez no más.

Isidro _____: —Alguien me _____ que Ud. le

insiste   dice

_____ la mano, que hasta la _____ allí.

tocar   abraza

YO: —La mano, nunca. Hombre, por favor. Y tampoco

_____ a nadie en ninguna plaza, nunca, señor.

abrazo

Isidro no _____ discutir más y por el momento no

quiere

_____ concluir la disputa.

podemos

Isidro me _____: —¿Por qué no damos un paseíto ahí por

sugiere

el río?

• • •

Y allí, andando por el río, _____ a una decisión que me

llego

_____ la vida para siempre. _____ la mejor decisión que

cambia   Resulta ser

_____ en esta vida terrenal. _____ casarme con Rosalía.

tomo   Decido

el padrino godfather	**el diente** tooth
al amanecer at dawn	**quizá** perhaps
el churro dough fried and sugared	**sugerir (ie)** to suggest
el anís anise-flavored brandy	**un paseíto** a stroll
	andando walking
mojar to soak, dunk	**casarse** to get married

Unit 13

Imperfect past:
imperfect vs. preterit

A. FORMATION OF THE IMPERFECT

cerrar	vender	salir
cerr aba	vend ía	sal ía
cerr abas	vend ías	sal ías
cerr aba	vend ía	sal ía
cerr ábamos	vend íamos	sal íamos
cerr abais	vend íais	sal íais
cerr aban	vend ían	sal ían

The imperfect indicative of all but three Spanish verbs is formed by adding the person-number endings to the stem. Verbs in **-er** and **-ir** have the same endings. Stem-changing verbs show no stem change in the imperfect (see **cerrar** above). The verbs below are irregular in the imperfect.

ser	ir	ver
era	iba	veía
eras	ibas	veías
era	iba	veía
éramos	íbamos	veíamos
erais	ibais	veíais
eran	iban	veían

B. USES OF THE IMPERFECT

The imperfect tense describes an event as ongoing and unfinished in the past. It expresses neither the beginning nor the ending of an event. It states only that it was going on in the past, at some point or over a period of time. It also describes repeated, customary or habitual events in the past. The imperfect is used

1. As the equivalent of English *was/were going to* + verb.

Íbamos a estudiar para el examen anoche.	We were going to study for the exam last night [when you saw us].
Rosa dijo que iba a ser difícil.	Rosa said it was going to be difficult.

2. As the equivalent of English *used to* + verb, and *would* + verb, often with adverbs that indicate repeated or habitual actions (**generalmente, por lo general, constantemente**).

Practicábamos casi todos los días.	We used to practice almost every day.
Por lo común, el entrenador gritaba sus órdenes y nosotros las seguíamos.	Generally the coach would yell out his orders and we would follow them.

3. All the verbs above, like most verbs, express actions. With non-action or "mental" verbs like **conocer, creer, estar, querer, saber, ser,** and **tener,** the equivalent in English of the Spanish imperfect is the simple past.

Sabíamos que Julio estaba aquí.	We knew that Julio was here.
Julio creía que teníamos un horario perfecto.	Julio thought that we had a perfect schedule.

4. The imperfect is used in a narrative for description in the past.

Eran las once de la mañana. Las campanas ya tocaban a misa mayor. La plaza estaba desierta. El día estaba claro. Brillaba un sol que quemaba. Una mujer vestida de negro cruzaba la plaza lentamente. No sabía quién era.	It was eleven in the morning. The bells were now ringing for High Mass. The square was deserted. The day was clear. The sun was burning bright. A woman dressed in black slowly crossed the square. I didn't know who she was.

C. IMPERFECT/PRETERIT CONTRASTS

1. The imperfect is used with time expressions that indicate repeated action.

Iba a Costa Rica cada año.	He went to Costa Rica every year.
Leía el diario todos los días.	She read the paper every day.

The preterit is used with time expressions that indicate a completed action or series of completed actions.

Fue a Costa Rica ese año.	He went to Costa Rica that year.
Leyó el diario dos veces.	She read the paper twice.

2. The imperfect expresses an event as ongoing at a certain time.

El equipo no es lo que era el año pasado.	The team isn't what it was (used to be) last year.
Aquel año estaba en Nicaragua cuando...	That year he was in Nicaragua when...

The preterit expresses an event as finished at a certain time.

El equipo no es lo que fue el año pasado.	The team isn't what it was (had been) last year.
Aquel año estuvo en Nicaragua dos meses.	That year he was in Nicaragua for two months [he had been there for a time that year].

D. VERBS THAT HAVE A DIFFERENT ENGLISH MEANING IN THE PRETERIT

CONOCER	**¿Tú lo conocías?**	Did you know him?
	¿Dónde lo conociste?	Where did you meet him [i.e., "know" him for the first time]?
SABER	**No sabíamos cómo era el nuevo jefe.**	We didn't know what the new boss was like.
	Pero supimos que no tolera bromas.	But we found out that he doesn't go for practical jokes.
QUERER	**Querían aprender italiano.**	They wanted to learn Italian.
	Quisieron aprender francés y lo lograron.	They wanted (tried, made an effort) to learn French and they succeeded.
PODER	**Concha podía reparar sus propios aparatos. Su marido no podía hacer ese tipo de trabajo.**	Concha could (was able to) repair her own appliances. Her husband couldn't do (was not capable of doing) that kind of work [and thus he never tried].
	Ayer pudo reparar la batidora. Su marido ni pudo cambiar canales en su nuevo vídeo.	Yesterday she was able to repair (succeeded in repairing) the mixer. Her husband couldn't even (failed, was unable to) change channels on their new VCR.

Real Madrid quiso, pero no pudo

13.1 Exprese el verbo entre paréntesis en pretérito o imperfecto, según el caso.

1. Cristóbal Colón (*said*) que el viaje (*was going*) a ser largo.
2. (*We believed*) que (*he knew*) la verdad.
3. El plan (*was*) llegar a las Indias.
4. El día que (*we left*), (*it was raining*) constantemente.
5. El cielo (*was*) gris.
6. (*It wasn't*) mucho frío.
7. Los barcos (*were*) pequeños.
8. Sus hombres (*were waiting*) en el puerto.
9. (*It was*) las dos de la tarde.
10. Colón les (*asked*) si (*they wanted*) ir.
11. A él le (*they asked*) si (*he had*) un mapa bueno.
12. (*He said*) que (*he did have*) uno, y (*they left*) en seguida.
13. Durante todo el viaje (*they didn't see*) ni un solo monstruo.
14. El viaje (*lasted*—**durar**) varios meses y por fin (*they arrived*).
15. (*It was*) un mundo realmente nuevo.
16. Y el viejo mundo (*was going*) a cambiar para siempre.

13.2 Siga como antes.

1. (*I met*) a Alicia en el metro [for the first time].
2. (*She already knew*) a unos amigos míos.
3. (*We had*) amigos mutuos.
4. Pero esta mañana yo (*had* ["got"]) una carta de Carolina.
5. (*She was*) mi amiga.
6. (*She used to write to me*) cada semana.
7. (*She wrote to me*) que su situación (*wasn't*) lo que (*it was* ["had been"]) el verano pasado.
8. (*She was living*) en Haití cuando (*began*) la revolución.
9. (*She used to go there*) cada año.
10. Pero (*she didn't go*) allí este año.
11. (*She worked here*) todo el verano.
12. Pero (*she was unable*) completar su trabajo.

13.3 Use los infinitivos entre paréntesis en pretérito o imperfecto, según el caso.

Cuando yo (estar) en Perú, (decidir) ir a ver Cuzco, antigua capital de los Incas, y Machu Picchu, su fortaleza escondida. (Tomar) el avión en Lima y el viaje (durar) unos setenta minutos. Después de bajar del avión, (sentir) en seguida que no (haber) mucho oxígeno en la atmósfera. (Tener) dificultad en respirar. (Ir) al hotel y (dormir) durante tres horas antes de comenzar el viaje en tren a Machu Picchu. Cuando (salir) a la calle, (hacer) sol, pero (hacer) fresco al mismo tiempo. El cielo (ser) de un azul brillante, y los demás turistas (parecer) alegres y animados por la idea del viaje. Cuando nosotros (salir) del hotel, (ver) a muchos indios que (pasar) por las calles con grandes bultos a sus espaldas. Algunos (traer) llamas para cargar con otros bultos aun más grandes. De repente, un indio (venir) hacia mí y me (preguntar) si (querer) comprarle un poncho de lana. Le (decir) que no, que ya (tener) uno en mi habitación. (Ser) evidente que no me (creer). Mientras tanto, el tren nos (esperar) para llevarnos a la famosa fortaleza de los Incas.

LECTURA II

Read through the selection first. Then complete the exercise on verb forms before re-reading the passage. Questions for comprehension follow.

Un presidente con mucha «salsa»[1]

Carlos Arboleya encarna° como pocos el mito del *self-made man*,   *embodies*
el hombre hecho a sí mismo. Nacido en La Habana, en el seno°   *bosom*
de una familia humilde, es el primer exiliado cubano que preside
un banco en Estados Unidos. Dos veces empezó desde cero y dos
veces le sonrió la fortuna, pero no cree en la suerte.

    Hijo de un asturiano[2] emigrado a Cuba, la muerte de su
padre lo obligó a aceptar un puesto de botones° en el Citibank   *messenger boy*
de La Habana. Tenía pocos años y todo el entusiasmo de un ado-
lescente dispuesto a llegar muy lejos. Por lo pronto, llegó a ser jefe
del departamento fiduciario° del banco. Algún tiempo después era   *trust*
el auditor general del Banco Central de La Habana.

    En esa situación estaba cuando las tropas revolucionarias de
Fidel Castro tomaron la capital de la isla. Arboleya no aceptaba la
nacionalización bancaria impuesta por el nuevo régimen y decidió
exiliarse. Tenía 30 años, una mujer, un hijo de corta edad y 40
dólares en el bolsillo.

No hay nada como un cafecito a las once, el aperitivo de la mañana, y uno de los placeres sublimes que nos esperan en esta vida secular...a veces Miami sabe a café cubano.

No corrían buenos tiempos en Miami. La oferta de mano de trabajo° era abundante y no era fácil encontrar trabajo. Sin éxito solicitó empleo en todos los bancos del Estado. Cuando presentaba su currículo lo rechazaban° porque su calificación profesional era muy alta. O desestimaban° su petición porque carecía de° experiencia.

Encontró por fin su oportunidad en una fábrica de zapatos: 45 dólares a la semana. Se propuso saber más que nadie sobre zapatos. Consiguió llegar a tenedor de libros°, y después a vice-presidente y jefe de contaduría° de la empresa. Entonces un banco de Miami, que había rechazado en su día a Arboleya, lo contrató con el encargo° de proceder a una reorganización integral de la entidad. En poco tiempo lo nombraron vice-presidente ejecutivo. Actualmente[3] preside todas las operaciones de la mayor cadena bancaria de Florida en toda la región sur del Estado.

«Me han noqueado°», dice, «y siempre me he levantado con mayor ímpetu. Se trata de° de aprender por qué te tumbaron y no vuelven a tumbarte[4] otra vez.»

mano . . . workforce

rejected
disregarded / he lacked

bookkeeper
accounting

assignment

they KO'd me
It's a question of

Notas

1. **Salsa** is a term used to indicate current Latin American influence worldwide—spicy and energetic—in music, arts, food, etc.
2. **Asturiano**, inhabitant of Asturias, a region in mountainous northwestern Spain that was home to many hard-working emigrants to the Americas. Many settled in Cuba before the Spanish-American War of 1898, and many more arrived in the years after the resulting Cuban independence.
3. **Actualmente** means *currently, presently*; **en realidad** or **realmente** means *actually* or *really*.
4. **Volver a** + infinitive   *to* + verb + *again*: **No vuelven a tumbarte** *They won't knock you down again.* The **otra vez** at the end adds even more emphasis to the expression.

Prácticas

Vamos a suponer durante unos momentos que usted mismo / a venga a ser el propio Carlos Arboleya / la propia Carlota Arboleya. Y lo que usted tiene que hacer ahora es volver a escribir, pero en *primera* persona, las frases del artículo que lógicamente admiten una forma en 1ª persona. Vamos a comenzar así (por ejemplo):

> Yo, Marcia Hennessy, encarno como pocas el mito de la *self-made woman*, la mujer hecha a sí misma. Nacida en La Habana . . . soy la . . .

Comprensión

1. ¿Dónde nació Arboleya?
2. ¿De dónde era su padre?
3. ¿Por qué buscó Carlos un empleo?
4. ¿Cuál fue su primer trabajo?
5. ¿Cuántos años tenía entonces?
6. ¿Cuántos años tenía cuando vino a Estados Unidos?
7. ¿Era fácil encontrar trabajo en Miami?
8. ¿En dónde trabajó primero?

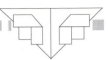

Unit 14

Progressive tenses

A. FORMS OF PROGRESSIVE TENSES

The progressive tenses in Spanish are formed with an auxiliary verb—usually **estar**—plus the present participle of the main verb. Regular present participles are formed with the endings **-ando** and **-iendo**.

-ar	-er	-ir
cantando singing	**bebiendo** drinking	**abriendo** opening

Stem-changing verbs ending in **-ir** have these stem changes: **e → i, o → u**.

sentir (ie)	pedir (i)	dormir (ue)
sintiendo feeling	**pidiendo** asking for	**durmiendo** sleeping

The ending **-iendo** is spelled **-yendo** when added to a stem ending in a vowel.

caer	concluir
cayendo falling	**concluyendo** concluding
leer	oír
leyendo reading	**oyendo** hearing

Other irregular present participles:

decir	reír
diciendo saying, telling	**riendo** laughing
ir	venir
yendo going	**viniendo** coming
poder	
pudiendo being able	

B. USES OF PROGRESSIVE TENSES

The progressive tenses are used to express a graphic unfolding of an action. They emphasize the progressive nature of an event as it is or was going on. The tense of **estar** is determined by the same considerations that regularly determine tense usage (see Unit 13 for uses of the imperfect and the preterit).

—¿**Qué está haciendo Tomás?**	"What is Tomás doing (right now)?"
—**Todavía está limpiando el carro.**	"He's still cleaning the car."
—**Ayer cuando llegaste, ¿qué estaba haciendo Loli?**	"Yesterday when you got there, what was Loli doing?"
—**Cuando llegué, estaba trabajando con la computadora. ¿Y sabes que estuvo trabajando así hasta las tres de la madrugada?**	"When I got there, she was working on the computer. And do you know that she was working on it until three in the morning?"

The progressive constructions are never used to refer to future time or anticipated events, as they often are in English. The simple tenses or **ir a** + infinitive are used instead.

Sale mañana.	He's leaving tomorrow.
Y creo que va a salir a las dos.	And I think he's leaving at two.

C. OTHER AUXILIARY VERBS USED IN PROGRESSIVE CONSTRUCTIONS

Other auxiliary verbs used with the present participle are **continuar** and **seguir** *to keep on, continue.*

Siguen gastando todo su dinero.	They keep on wasting all their money.

Continuábamos practicando todas las tardes.	We kept on practicing every afternoon.

Progressive constructions with **andar, ir,** and **venir** add another dimension to the action.

Anda recogiendo las cosas de los niños.	She's going around picking up the kids' things.
Los políticos venían prometiéndonos estas reformas.	The politicians were (kept) promising us these reforms [they had been continually doing so].

D. PLACEMENT OF OBJECT PRONOUNS

Object pronouns may either precede or follow the progressive constructions with no change in meaning.

Estamos mirándolo ahora. **Lo estamos mirando ahora.**	We are looking at it now.
Su novio sigue llamándola. **Su novio la sigue llamando.**	Her boyfriend keeps on calling her.

14.1 Para cada frase escriba una continuación según el modelo.

> **Yo quiero ver la telenovela** (*soap opera*). → **Y estoy viéndola.**

1. Mi padre quiere vender el carro.
2. Queremos limpiar el garaje.
3. Mercedes quiere leer la novela.
4. Loli quiere completar las tareas.
5. Quiero hacer el trabajo.
6. Inés quiere abrir el regalo.
7. Rosario quiere oír las respuestas.
8. Quieren pedir otro plato.

14.2 Construya oraciones escribiendo el verbo a la derecha en forma progresiva. Utilice todas las expresiones de abajo y traduzca las oraciones. Por ejemplo:

ayer a las siete + mi compañero ya escuchaba música en el estéreo →**Ayer a las siete mi compañero ya estaba escuchando música en el estéreo.** (*Yesterday at seven o'clock my roommate was already listening to music on the stereo.*)

a las tres cuando empezó a llover al mediodía cuando comenzó la clase al atardecer (*dusk*) temprano esta mañana a medianoche cuando sonó el teléfono	+	visitábamos el museo cruzaban los Andes tú regresabas del cine huían de la policía yo buscaba a Emilio esperábamos a Sara ellos veían televisión tomaban un refresco

14.3 Llene los espacios en blanco con el equivalente en español.

LA CURIOSA MUERTE DE SEBASTIÁN RODRÍGUEZ

Durante aquellos primeros meses, cuando el anciano casi no hablaba

o decía muy poco, sabíamos que Sebastián Rodríguez

_____ . Los médicos
       was dying

_____ que Sebastián iba a mejorar. Pero
     kept on telling us

no era así. _____ de algo que no
     He continued suffering

reconocían los médicos.

Desde enero venían _____ que se
      promising us

le iba a mejorar la salud. _____ : «Los
     They continued saying

especialistas andan ahora _____ una cura milagrosa.
     looking for

Pronto la van a encontrar.» Durante todo el verano Sebastián

_____ de lejos los felices días y los
     kept on remembering

dulces aires de sus años jóvenes en Santiago de Cuba.

El viejo _____ :
     kept on thinking

« _____ aquellos aires voy a estar mejor.»
   Breathing (respirar)

Eso no era posible, claro, pero durante todo el invierno

iba _____ un poco la salud. Creíamos por fin
   recovering (recobrar)

que _____ .
     he was going to continue improving

No fue así. Llegó la primavera con sus flores y el pobre Sebastián

murió _____ aún una noche en la playa de Santiago,
   remembering

cuando soplaba una brisa tan limpia y fresca.

Llegó la primavera con sus flores, y el viejo murió, recordando aún una noche en una
playa lejana de Santiago, cuando soplaba una brisa tan limpia y fresca.

Unit 15

Uses of *se*

A. *SE* AS INDEFINITE SUBJECT

The pronoun **se** is used in Spanish with third-person singular verbs to indicate an indefinite subject, i.e., to refer to people in general. English uses a variety of subjects for this meaning: *you, one, people, they.*

—¿**Se puede cenar ahora?**	"Is it possible to have dinner now?"
—No, **ahora no se puede. Es un poquito temprano.**	"No, not now. It's a bit early."
¿Cómo **se dice** *soccer* **en español?**	How do you say *soccer* in Spanish?
Aquí se come de todo.	Here they eat everything.
¿Cómo **se enciende esta luz?**	How do you turn this light on? (How is this light turned on?)
No **se debe hablar así.**	A person (people) shouldn't talk like that.
Si se lee mucho, se aprende mucho.	If one reads a lot, one learns a lot.
Se juega mucho al béisbol en San Pedro de Macorís.	They play baseball a lot in San Pedro de Macorís. (A lot of baseball is played . . . .)

B. PASSIVE *SE*

Se can also signal a passive construction, particularly when an object, rather than a person, is involved.

También se venden entradas en la plaza mayor.	Tickets are also sold on the main square.

Ropa vieja cubanísima se come en Las Vegas

Con
SAMS
ELECTR

¿Se puede medir la opinión pública?

Aquí no se discrimina
Un estudio revela que muchos textos escolares perpetúan, por omi

ya nada
se ve igual
que antes

Se necesitan
más empresas

7-Eleven se vende a japoneses

■ **Se calcula que el trato asciende a**
$1,000 millones.

This construction is regularly used for the passive when no agent is expressed. The grammatical subject (i.e., the thing in question) usually follows the verb.

Se hizo bien el trabajo.	The job was well done.
Se chequeó el agua ayer.	The water was checked yesterday.
Se firmaron todos los cheques esta mañana.	All the checks were signed this morning.
Por fin se reveló la verdad.	Finally the truth was revealed.
Esos libros se publicaron en Barcelona.	Those books were published in Barcelona.

Se constructions are also frequently the equivalent of English constructions with *to get*, *become*, or *"go."*

Se pinchó la llanta.	The tire went flat.
Se caló el motor.	The motor stalled (got flooded).
Se rompieron los vasos en el camino.	The glasses got broken en route.
Se calentó mucho el motor.	The motor got very hot.
Con el tiempo se ensució la alfombra.	With time the carpet became filthy.

C. *SE* CONSTRUCTIONS WITH HUMAN DIRECT OBJECTS

Se constructions may be used with human direct objects, marked, as usual by personal **a**.

> **Se respeta al jefe.** The boss is respected.

If the object is indefinite, personal **a** is omitted.

> **«Se necesitan meseros.»** "Waiters wanted."

A pronoun may replace a specific human object—only **le / les** for males, but either **la / las** or **le / les** for females.

> **Se le detesta.** He is hated.
> **Se les admira.** They (the men) are admired.
>
> **Se la (le) quiere.** She is loved.
> **Se las (les) respeta.** They (the women) are respected.

D. *SE* + INDIRECT OBJECT + VERB

Se constructions (**se** + indirect object pronoun + verb) are also used for unintentional and involuntary events. The indirect-object pronoun indicates the person affected by the event. The subject follows the verb.

> **¡Ay, se me olvidaron las entradas!** Oh, I forgot the tickets!
> **Se le rompió el reloj en la pelea.** His watch got broken in the scuffle.
> **Se le cayó el boli en el pasillo.** She dropped her pen in the hallway.
>
> **Se les murió su padre.** They lost their father.
> **Se nos acabó el café.** We ran out of coffee.
> **¿Dónde se te perdieron las llaves?** Where did you lose your keys?

15.1 Lea el diálogo.

1. —¿Se puede cenar?
2. —No, señora, ahora no se puede. Es un poquito temprano. La cena se sirve a las ocho.
3. —Por favor, es que ayer se me perdió la cartera. Creo que fue aquí.
4. —Se limpió bien el comedor anoche, señora. Ahora no se sabe nada, lo siento mucho.
5. —¿Se me permite buscar? Se me cayó ahí, creo.
6. —No, señora. No se puede entrar al comedor ahora.
7. —Oiga, muchacho, no se debe hablar así. Una tiene derechos. Se vive aquí en una democracia, ¿no?
8. —En este comedor no hay democracia, señora. Se come, se paga y adiós, se acabó, buen viaje.
9. —Se ve que aquí se abusa del cliente, y en un hotel donde se cobran (*charge*) precios de escándalo. Pues, dígame, ¿dónde se venden entradas para los toros?
10. —Está usted en Galicia, señora. Aquí sólo se crían (*raise*) toros sementales (*for breeding*). Para ver a ésos, ni se venden entradas.

15.2 Traduzca.

1. How do you say *hello* in Spanish?
2. You say **Buenos días.**
3. And how does one respond?
4. You repeat **Buenos días.**
5. How do you go from here to the subway station?
6. At the end of this street, you go to the right.
7. How can one finish this translation soon?
8. It's finished now (already).

15.3 Lea estos anuncios y conteste.

1. ¿Qué tipo de mercancía vende el comercio ENRICO?
2. ¿Qué ocurre en una discoteca? ¿Qué hace un portero? ¿Por qué necesitan porteros las discotecas?
3. ¿Qué campo científico tienen que conocer a fondo los traductores que se buscan aquí?
4. ¿Qué hace un botones? ¿Tiene que coser? ¿Qué hace el comercio aquí que precisa un botones? ¿Su edad mínima?
5. ¿Cuántos de estos anuncios ofrecen trabajo relacionado con la comida?
6. ¿Según qué anuncio se dice que van a hablar un poco para llegar a un acuerdo sobre la remuneración?

SE SOLICITA

N A N A

Sepa manejar, trabajo de planta. Comunicarse al 696-18-27 o presentarse en Castilla 261, Col. Alamos

---

HOSTELERÍA

PARA PIZZERIA SE NECESITAN

PIZZEROS COCINEROS

Se requiere personal joven con experiencia. Sueldo a convenir.

Presentarse, para mantener entrevista personal, días 6 y 7 del presente mes, de 4 a 9, en el propio local (plaza de Santo Domingo, esquina calle Preciados).

LABORATORIO FOTOGRAFICO

necesita para incorporación en plantilla

BOTONES

PARA REPARTO

Edad, entre 16 y 18 años. Llamar, de 9 a 14 y de 15.30 a 19, a los teléfonos 250 03 95 y 250 66 44. Señorita Mª José.

ENRICO

MODA HOMBRE

NECESITA

▶ **PERSONA JOVEN** (25-35 años)
Dinámica, para encargado sucursal.

▶ **VENDEDORES/AS** (20-25 años)

Para ambos puestos se requiere experiencia y muy buena presencia.
Teléfono 445 26 04 (Margarita), de 9 a 11 h.

RESPONSABLE LOCAL

DE FAST FOOD

2.000.000 (fijo más variable)
Selecciona empresa en expansión.

Funciones:
- Encargado del local.
- Control y promoción de ventas.
- Control de calidad y consumos.

Se requiere:
- Persona joven con espíritu de superación.
- Dotes de organización y mando.
- Experiencia afín a la del puesto, en cadena de fast food.

Se ofrece:
- Posibilidad de promoción.
- Lugar de trabajo: Madrid.

Interesados enviar curriculum vitae urgentemente al Apdo. de Correos n.º 36.171 Madrid.

DISCOTECA

SOLICITA

PORTERO

Experiencia imprescindible

1.700.000 ptas. anuales

Teléfono 535 20 62. Srta. Anabel

SE NECESITAN

TRADUCTORES E INTÉRPRETES

ESPECIALIZADOS EN MÉDICAS

TODOS LOS IDIOMAS

Escribir con detalles a: Versión, S. C. Oña, 127, 7ª, 1. 28050 Madrid.

Diversión y práctica 4

Fechas, fiestas y adivinanzas

A. Oyendo a tu compañera mencionar una de las fiestas indicadas en la primera columna, tú le dices la fecha correspondiente, o, si ella lo prefiere, puede darte una fecha de la segunda columna, y tú puedes identificar la fiesta.

el Día del Año Nuevo	el primer lunes de septiembre
el Día de la Independencia (EE.UU.)	el 14 de febrero
el Día de Martin Luther King	el 25 de diciembre
el Día de las Elecciones (EE.UU.)	el 31 de octubre
el Día de la Madre	el 1° de enero
el Día de la Raza (de Cristóbal Colón)	el cuarto jueves de noviembre
el Día de San Patricio	el segundo domingo de mayo
la Navidad	el tercer lunes de enero
el Nacimiento de Jorge Wáshington	el primer martes tras el primer lunes de noviembre
el Día del Trabajo (de los Obreros) (EE.UU.)	el 22 de febrero
el Día de los Enamorados (San Valentín)	el segundo lunes de octubre
el Día de Acción de Gracias	el 17 de marzo
la noche cuando los niños andan disfrazados pidiendo caramelos	el 4 de julio

Pero si sabes alguna de éstas de abajo, ya sabes demasiado para esta clase.

el 6 de enero	la Asunción (Virgen de Agosto)
40 días entre febrero y marzo o abril	la Nochebuena
el 15 de agosto	la Cuaresma
el 1° de noviembre	Todos los Santos
el 2 de noviembre	el Día de los Muertos (los Difuntos)
el 12 de diciembre	la Noche Vieja
el 24 de diciembre	el Día de Reyes o Epifanía
el 31 de diciembre	la Virgen de Guadalupe (la Patrona de Hispanoamérica)

B. Otras adivinanzas. Tu compañero describe lo que ocurre y luego tú identificas la ocasión. Y, si quieres, puedes poner alguna original.

> *la Serie Mundial*
> *la Copa Mundial*
> *Noche Vieja*
> *los Juegos Olímpicos*

Hay gran cantidad de fiestas, muchos se divierten y van contando los últimos segundos del último día — 10, 9, 8, 7 . . .

Cada cuatro años el mundo entero decide quién va a ser el campeón de fútbol.

Cada cuatro años hay competición atlética entre numerosas naciones del mundo.

Las ligas mayores, la Nacional y la Americana, disputan el campeonato del béisbol.

Aquí pon tú una original.

C. Más adivinanzas. Aquí tu compañera y tú juegan otro juego de identificación — esta vez de trabajos, oficios y profesiones.

—Doy clases de álgebra.
—**Eres profesor / a de matemáticas.**

—Mi compañero juega primera base y yo patrullo el jardín.
—**Son ustedes peloteros, es decir, juegan al béisbol.**

—Paso toda la noche sudando ante un enorme horno.
—En la cocina preparo comida suculenta.
—Voy de mesa en mesa sirviéndoles a los clientes.
—Conduzco un autobús del municipio.
—Estudio las enfermedades humanas y los modos de curarlas.
—Cuido a los enfermos en mi consultorio y en el hospital.
—Estudio la vida de las plantas.
—Escribo cartas en mi computadora para el jefe de la compañía.
—Defiendo a mis clientes en el tribunal.
—Digo en mi idioma lo que dicen otros en su propio idioma.

Present subjunctive

The subjunctive is a usage or mode of speaking whose verb forms contrast with the forms of the indicative. The indicative tenses may be described as presenting facts more or less objectively. The subjunctive tenses, on the other hand, refer generally to events that are viewed subjectively.

Es bueno que vaya. It is good for him to go ("it is good that he go").

Vaya above is a subjunctive form used because the speaker is expressing a personal or subjective reaction (**es bueno**) to the event in the subordinate clause (**que vaya**).

The subjunctive occurs primarily in subordinate clauses. The English equivalents of subjunctive forms vary and must be determined by context. The tenses and uses of the subjunctive are taken up here and in several future units.

A. REGULAR VERBS

With only six exceptions the present subjunctive is formed on the stem of the first-person singular of the present indicative. Verbs ending in **-ar** replace the **o** with the "opposite" theme (characteristic) vowel **e**. Verbs ending in **-er** and **-ir** replace the **o** with the "opposite" theme vowel **a**.

hablar	comer	vivir
(que) habl e	(que) com a	(que) viv a
habl es	com as	viv as
habl e	com a	viv a
habl emos	com amos	viv amos
habl éis	com áis	viv áis
habl en	com an	viv an

B. STEM-CHANGING VERBS

The stem-changing verbs in Unit 1 show the same changes in the present subjunctive.

cerrar	perder	contar	volver
cierre	pierda	cuente	vuelva
cierres	pierdas	cuentes	vuelvas
cierre	pierda	cuente	vuelva
cerremos	perdamos	contemos	volvamos
cerréis	perdáis	contéis	volváis
cierren	pierdan	cuenten	vuelvan

Exceptions are the first- and second-person plural forms of some stem-changing -ir verbs (pp. 20–21). In these two forms the **e** of the stem changes to **i**, and the **o** of the stem changes to **u**. Verbs like **pedir** (p. 21) have **i** throughout the present subjunctive.

sentir	dormir	pedir
sienta	duerma	pida
sientas	duermas	pidas
sienta	duerma	pida
sintamos	durmamos	pidamos
sintáis	durmáis	pidáis
sientan	duerman	pidan

C. IRREGULAR VERBS

Verbs irregular in the first-person singular of the present indicative (Unit 5) show the same irregularity throughout the present subjunctive.

decir	concluir	conducir
diga	concluya	conduzca
digas	concluyas	conduzcas
diga	concluya	conduzca
digamos	concluyamos	conduzcamos
digáis	concluyáis	conduzcáis
digan	concluyan	conduzcan

Similarly:

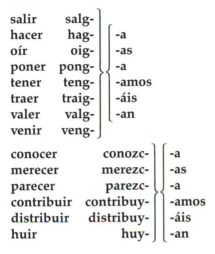

salir	salg-	
hacer	hag-	-a
oír	oig-	-as
poner	pong-	-a
tener	teng-	-amos
traer	traig-	-áis
valer	valg-	-an
venir	veng-	

conocer	conozc-	-a
merecer	merezc-	-as
parecer	parezc-	-a
contribuir	contribuy-	-amos
distribuir	distribuy-	-áis
huir	huy-	-an

D. OTHER IRREGULAR VERBS

Six verbs have irregular stems in the present subjunctive.

dar	estar	haber	ir	saber	ser
dé	esté	haya	vaya	sepa	sea
des	estés	hayas	vayas	sepas	seas
dé	esté	haya	vaya	sepa	sea
demos	estemos	hayamos	vayamos	sepamos	seamos
deis	estéis	hayáis	vayáis	sepáis	seáis
den	estén	hayan	vayan	sepan	sean

Dar has a written accent in the first- and third-person singular, thus distinguishing it in writing from the preposition **de**. **Estar** has a written accent in all forms except the first-person plural. **Caber** *to fit* follows the pattern of **saber**: **quepa**, **quepas**, etc.

E. SPELLING-CHANGING VERBS

The **-er** and **-ir** verbs with spelling changes in the present indicative (Unit 6) show the same changes in the present subjunctive. These spelling changes occur because a given consonant sound in Spanish may be spelled one way before **a**, **o**, and **u**, and another way before **e** and **i**. As already indicated in Unit 6, **ge** / **gi** / **ja** / **jo** / **ju** are spellings for one consonant sound and the indicated vowel. The spellings **gue** / **gui** / **ga** / **go** / **gu** represent another. And **ce** / **ci** / **za** / **zo** / **zu** still another.

1. Thus any verb with a **g** before an **e** or an **i** in the infinitive must change the **g** to **j** before **o** and **a**.

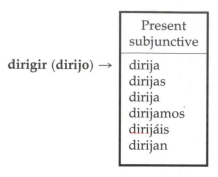

	Present subjunctive
dirigir (dirijo) →	dirija
	dirijas
	dirija
	dirijamos
	dirijáis
	dirijan

2. Similarly, **-guir** verbs change **gu** to **g** before **o** and **a**, and **-cer** verbs change **c** to **z** before **o** and **a**.

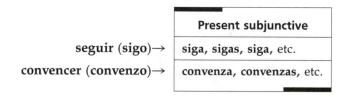

	Present subjunctive
seguir (sigo)→	**siga, sigas, siga,** etc.
convencer (convenzo)→	**convenza, convenzas,** etc.

3. Some verbs ending in **-ar** likewise have spelling changes before the **e** of the present subjunctive.

Infinitive		**Change**	**Present subjunctive**
-car	**buscar (busco)**	c → qu	**busque, busques,** etc.
-gar	**pagar (pago)**	g → gu	**pague, pagues,** etc.
-guar	**averiguar (averiguo)**	gu → gü	**averigüe, averigües,** etc.
-zar	**alcanzar (alcanzo)**	z → c	**alcance, alcances,** etc.

16.1 Con cada infinitivo diga primero la forma del presente de indicativo que corresponde a la persona **yo**. Luego dé la forma correspondiente del presente de subjuntivo. Por ejemplo:

leer → **leo, lea**

1. hablar / contestar / desayunar / preparar
2. comer / vender / creer / asistir / cubrir
3. perder / contar / volver / sentir / dormir
4. pedir / servir / seguir / despedir / conseguir
5. decir / hacer / poner / tener / venir
6. conocer / parecer / conducir / merecer
7. contribuir / distribuir / huir / construir

16.2 Siga igual que antes pero con las formas que corresponden al pronombre indicado.

1. yo—dar / ir / estar / ser / saber / haber
2. ellos—ser / estar / ir / dar / haber / saber
3. nosotros—pedir / sentir / seguir / servir / repetir / dormir

16.3 Identifique cada ejemplo del presente de subjuntivo en los siguientes titulares.

¿Utilizaría usted el sanitario de sus empleados?

¡Visítelo! Es probable que sea deplorable.

Deben ser infalsificables las tarjetas, para evitar que voten los muertos

Temen que haya fraude

Oraciones para que Dios ilumine a Bush

"Hay que ir al museo cuando se necesite ver algo hermoso"

m Landry rompe el silencio
Grave error que Dallas se deshaga de los veteranos

Trabajadores de Villoslada piden en Estrasburgo que se interceda en favor del secuestrado

Alfonso Guerra dice que no hay ninguna razón que justifique que pase un mal momento

Unit 17

Uses of the subjunctive

 A. THE SUBJUNCTIVE AFTER EXPRESSIONS OF EMOTION

> I hope (that) he tells the truth.
> She is sorry (that) they are coming tomorrow.
> We're glad (that) you're with us.

In these sentences the main verb expresses an emotional reaction (hope, sorrow, happiness) to the event in the subordinate clause (telling the truth, coming, being together). The subjunctive is used in Spanish in the subordinate clause, introduced by **que**, whenever the main verb expresses an emotional reaction.

> **Espero que diga la verdad.**
> **Siente que vengan mañana.**
> **Nos alegramos de que estés con nosotros.**

Le duele			It hurts her	
Le disgusta	**que diga eso.**		It annoys her	that he says that.
Le molesta			It bothers her	

Les gusta			They are pleased	
Les sorprende	**que esté mejor.**		They are surprised	that she feels better.
Les alegra			They are happy	

Que must be used in Spanish to introduce the subordinate clause: **Me temo que no vengan.** In English *that* often is omitted: *I fear (that) they're not coming.*

17.1 Traduzca al inglés o al español, según el caso.

1. Dámaso no quiere decirlo pero esperamos que lo diga.
2. *They don't want to go but we hope that they go.*
3. Alonso lo dice y su esposa siente mucho que lo diga.
4. *I repeat it but they are sorry that I repeat it.*
5. Siempre llegan tarde y me irrita que lleguen tarde.
6. *He always comes in late, and it bothers us that he comes in so late.*
7. No quieren hacerlo y no nos sorprende que no lo hagan.
8. *You write to her, and she is pleased that you write to her.*

B. THE SUBJUNCTIVE WITH IMPLIED COMMANDS

> She wants us to leave soon.   They tell us to do it soon.
> We ask her to leave now.   We insist that they do it now.

The subjunctive is used in Spanish after **que** to express what someone wants (tells, asks, etc.) someone else to do.

> **Quiere que salgamos pronto.**   **Nos dicen que lo hagamos pronto.**
> **Le pedimos que salga ahora.**   **Insistimos en que lo hagan ahora.**

An indirect-object pronoun may indicate the subject of the verb in the subjunctive.

> **Nos escribe que vengamos a**   He writes (to) us to come see
> **verlo.**   him.
> **Siempre le digo que regrese**   I always tell her to come back
> **pronto.**   soon.

When communication verbs like **decir** and **escribir** convey information (instead of an indirect command to do something), the subjunctive is not used.

> **Nos escribe que Ana viene**   He writes to us that Ana is coming
> **a verlo.**   to see him.
> **Le dije que Paula regresa**   I told her that Paula is returning
> **pronto.**   soon.

17.2 Traduzca al inglés o al español, según el caso.

1. No quiero hacerlo pero ella prefiere que lo haga.
2. *She doesn't want to do it, but I want her to do it.*
3. Pilar no quiere traerlo pero le decimos que lo traiga.
4. *He doesn't want to sell it, but they tell him to sell it.*
5. No quieren asistir pero les pedimos que asistan.
6. *You don't want to attend, but she prefers you attend.*

7. El niño no quiere comerlo, pero mamá insiste en que lo coma.

8. *I don't want to read it now, but they insist that I read it.*

9. Ella les escribe que Juana no vuelve este verano.

10. *They write to us that they are not returning this year.*

C. THE SUBJUNCTIVE AFTER EXPRESSIONS OF DOUBT

I don't think she'll go.	He denies that it is the truth.
I doubt that she'll go.	He isn't sure it is the truth.

The subjunctive is used in Spanish after expressions of doubt, disbelief, and denial. Such expressions include **no creer que**, **dudar que**, **negar que**, **no estar seguro de que**. The present subjunctive often refers to future as well as present time.

No creo que vaya.	**Niega que sea la verdad.**
Dudo que vaya.	**No está seguro de que sea la verdad.**

The indicative is used after **que** if the event in the subordinate clause is believed to be a fact.

Creo que va.	I believe he's going.
No niega que es la verdad.	She does not deny that it's the truth.
Está seguro de que es la verdad.	He is sure it's true.

17.3 Traduzca al inglés o al español, según el caso.

1. Ella no quiere ir y no creo que vaya.

2. *The children don't want to eat, and Paco doesn't think they'll eat.*

3. Los niños detestan la comida y dudamos que la coman.

4. *Ana María hates the food, and they doubt she'll eat it.*

5. No está seguro de que los papeles lleguen a tiempo.

6. *We are not sure that the book is in the library.*

D. THE SUBJUNCTIVE AFTER IMPERSONAL EXPRESSIONS

Es una lástima que esté aquí.	It's a pity that he is here.
Es muy posible que lo sepa.	It's very possible that he knows it.
Es preciso que estés aquí con anticipación.	It's necessary for you to be here ahead of time.
No es verdad que sea perezosa.	It's not true that she's lazy.

Impersonal expressions (**es** + adjective) are followed by an infinitive if no other subject is indicated: **Es importante salir con anticipación.** With many impersonal expressions + **que** + a subject, the subjunctive is used after **que: Es importante que salgan con anticipación.** Such impersonal expressions that are used with the subjunctive indicate the same concepts already presented: i.e., a reaction, often emotional (**es una lástima que**), an implied wish or command (**es necesario que**), or doubt (**es posible que**).

Es triste		It is sad	
Es terrible	**que crean eso.**	It is terrible	that they believe that (for them to believe that).
Es extraño		It is strange	

Es preferible		It is preferable	
Es conveniente	**que no lo compren ahora.**	It is desirable	for them not to buy it now.
Es mejor		It is better	

Es probable		It is probable	
No es cierto	**que quieran vernos.**	It is not true	that they want to see us.
No es seguro		It is not definite	

Impersonal expressions that indicate certainty or belief are not followed by the subjunctive.

Es evidente		It is evident	
Es verdad	**que no van a ganar.**	It is true	that they are not going to win.
Es cierto		It is certain	

To sum up, the impersonal expressions that are used with the subjunctive express the same ideas that personal verbs used with the subjunctive do: personal or subjective reactions, emotion, implied commands, doubt, disbelief, and denial.

17.4 Traduzca al inglés o al español, según el caso.

1. No quieren visitarnos, por eso, es probable que no nos visiten.

2. *He can't go tomorrow, and it is possible he'll never go.*

3. Yo sé que no les gustan los museos. Es una lástima que no les gusten los museos.

4. *She doesn't like movies (**el cine**), and it's a pity she won't see that film.*

5. Juan Manuel detesta la comida picante; no es verdad que la coma.

6. *My brother likes spicy food, but it's better for him not to eat it.*

7. Es evidente que no hay subjuntivo en esta frase.

8. *It is true that the subjunctive is difficult.*

17.5 Vea el anuncio que ofrece trabajo con la aerolínea Iberia y conteste.

1. ¿Cuál es la mínima estatura requerida para mujeres—primero, en el sistema métrico? ¿ahora en el sistema americano? (*Nota:* un metro = 3.28 *ft.*)

2. ¿Es necesario saber nadar? ¿Cómo lo sabe Ud.?

3. ¿Cuánto tiempo dura el programa de entrenamiento?

4. ¿Le parece excesivo el requisito del conocimiento de idiomas que tiene Iberia? ¿Por qué?

5. ¿Qué pasa si el aspirante sabe otro idioma además del inglés (y el español, claro está)?

6. ¿Puede ser contratado alguien que use gafas? ¿Cómo?

PLAZAS DE TRIPULANTES DE CABINA DE PASAJEROS MASCULINOS Y FEMENINOS (Auxiliares de Vuelo)

La **Compañía** IBERIA Líneas Aéreas de España anuncia la convocatoria de plazas para Tripulantes de Cabina de Pasajeros con contratos eventuales.

El Plazo de admisión de solicitudes finalizará el 23 de Enero 1989.

REQUISITOS:

- Nacionalidad española.
- Adecuada presencia física.
- Edad mínima requerida, 18 años cumplidos al cierre del plazo de presentación de instancias (23 de Enero 1989)
- Estatura: Entre 1,60 y 1,82 metros para mujeres. Entre 1,72 y 1,90 metros para hombres.
- Reunir las condiciones psicofísicas necesarias para el desempeño de las funciones propias de un Tripulante de Cabina de Pasajeros.
- No usar gafas. En caso de necesitar lentes correctoras, usará microlentillas.
- Titulación mínima exigida: B.U.P., F.P. II o equivalente.
- Nadar 100 metros en un tiempo no superior a tres minutos.
- Idiomas: – Imprescindible amplio conocimiento del idioma inglés, hablado y escrito.
  – El conocimiento de los idiomas optativos alemán y/o francés, tendrá especial valoración en el proceso de selección.

Las personas seleccionadas deberán superar un curso de formación de una duración aproximada de un mes.

Vamos a escribir ...2

Presente de subjuntivo

Llene los espacios en blanco con las expresiones indicadas. Y si desea su profesor/a que haga una traducción al inglés también, pues hágala.

ADIÓS, VILLALBA DEL MONTE

Íbamos Ángel y yo a la gran ciudad a buscar fortuna.

NOS DIJERON: — _____ que Uds. _____
<small>It's possible</small> <small>won't find</small>
sitio ni para sentarse.

CONTESTAMOS: —Sí, pero _____ que _____ allí
<small>it's true</small> <small>we aren't going</small>
para sentarnos.

ELLOS: — _____ que Uds. no
<small>We are sorry</small>
_____ quedarse aquí en Villalba del Monte.
<small>want</small>

NOSOTROS: — _____
<small>It's a pity that we have to leave</small>
_____. Pero también _____ que
<small>it's sad</small>
aquí _____ más que del tiempo y de
<small>you don't talk</small>
la cosecha. _____.
<small>It's better for us to leave</small>

ELLOS: —Pues _____.
<small>it doesn't bother us that you are leaving</small>
Adiós, ingratos hijos.

_____ tan pronto.
<small>It pleases us that you are leaving</small>

NOSOTROS: —Cuidado, hombre. _____
<small>It's not true that we want to go</small>

_____. De niños queríamos mucho

a nuestro pueblo. Pero estamos hasta el tope con la vida

aquí. En Villalba hasta se puede morir de aburrimiento.

_____
<small>We want you to understand</small>

97

De niños queríamos mucho a nuestro pueblo. Lo que uno vive de niño no lo olvida nunca.

nuestra situación. ¿_____
What do you suggest that we do
_____ aquí en Villalba?

ELLOS: — _____
We are telling you to go
ahora. _____
We doubt that you are
verdaderos hijos de este pueblo. Tampoco

_____
we think that you are going to have
mucha suerte allá en la capital.

NOSOTROS: — _____.
We believe that we have to leave
_____ lo mejor de nosotros
We don't deny that
_____ aquí en Villalba. El corazón de uno
remains
se queda. Sólo el cuerpo deja atrás al pueblo. Lo que

uno vive de niño no lo olvida nunca. Adiós, Villalba del

Monte.

ELLOS: —Qué va, muchachos, que vamos a llorar nosotros

también. Dennos un abrazo. Buen viaje, y mucha suerte

allá en la capital.

sentarse to sit down	**el aburrimiento** boredom
el tiempo weather	**tampoco** neither
la cosecha harvest	**lo mejor** the best part
cuidado watch out, be careful	**dejar** to leave (behind)
hasta el tope fed up	**qué va** my goodness, what the devil
hasta even	

Reconstrucción

1. ¿Qué quieren hacer los dos jóvenes?
2. ¿Cuál es el consejo que reciben?
3. ¿Por qué creen que tienen que dejar el pueblo?
4. ¿Cuál es la reacción en el pueblo ante la decisión de estos jóvenes?
5. ¿Cómo podemos describir el verdadero sentimiento de los mozos hacia su pueblo?
6. ¿Qué ocurre al final?

Unit 18

Possessives

 ### A. UNSTRESSED POSSESSIVES

my	**mi/mis**	our	**nuestro/a/os/as**
your	**tu/tus**	your	**vuestro/a/os/as**
his		their	
her	**su/sus**	your	**su/sus**
your			
its			

These possessives are used before the noun, which normally receives the emphasis or voice stress. The unstressed possessives agree in number with the noun, not, as in English, with the possessor: **su casa** *their house*, **sus casas** *his houses*. **Nuestro** and **vuestro** also show agreement in gender.

Son mis hermanas.	They are my sisters.
¿Puedo usar tus aretes, María?	Can I wear your earrings, María?
Necesitan nuestra ayuda.	They need our help.
Muchachas, ayudar a vuestro hermanito.	Girls, help your little brother.

 ### B. STRESSED POSSESSIVES

The stressed or long possessives follow the noun: **mío, tuyo, suyo, nuestro, vuestro, suyo**. They each have four forms: **-o/a/os/as** and agree in gender and number with the object possessed, i.e., the noun. They also emphasize the possessor rather than the thing or noun possessed: **un amigo mío** *MY friend*, **una hija suya** *HIS daughter*. They correspond to English *of yours, of theirs*, etc.

Quiero presentarte a un amigo mío.	I'd like to introduce you to a friend of mine.
Esos chicos son unos amigos suyos.	Those boys are friends of hers.

The stressed or long possessive forms are also used in place of nouns.

> los amigos nuestros   our friends → **los nuestros**   ours
> las zapatillas suyas   his running shoes → **las suyas**   his
> el novio suyo   her boyfriend → **el suyo**   hers
> el estéreo tuyo   your stereo → **el tuyo**   yours

The definite article is often omitted after **ser**: **Son suyas** *They're his.*

C. AMBIGUOUS *SU / SUYO*

Context usually makes clear who the possessor is with **su** and **suyo**. If clarification is necessary, definite article + noun + **de** + pronoun is used. This construction is used *only* with **su/s** and **suyo/a/os/as** since the first- and second-person forms are always clear.

—**¿Viniste en el carro de ella?**   "Did you come in her car?"
—**No, vine en el de él.**   "No, I came in *his*."

—**¿Son las hijas de él?**   "Are they his daughters?"
—**No, son las de ella.**   "No, they're *hers*."

D. NEUTER POSSESSIVES

Neuter possessives are formed with **lo** + a stressed form (**lo mío** *what is mine,* **lo tuyo** *what's yours, what belongs to you*) and also with **lo de** + pronoun (**lo de ella, lo de ellos**). Since there are no neuter nouns in Spanish, these **lo** phrases refer to things or ideas in general rather than to specific nouns.

Lo tuyo está encima de la mesa y lo nuestro está aquí cerca de la puerta.   What's yours (your "stuff") is on the table, and ours is here by the door.

Lo suyo vale mucho más.   What belongs to her (what is hers, her things) is worth much more.

18.1 Diga las frases en español.

1. It's her house.
2. They are our children.
3. She's a friend of ours.
4. He's a friend of hers.
5. They are friends of his. [*two ways*]
6. It's my sweater; it's not his.

18.2 Conteste las preguntas, según el modelo.

¿Son las llaves suyas? → **No, tengo las mías aquí.**

1. ¿Es la billetera suya?
2. ¿Es el sombrero suyo?
3. ¿Son las zapatillas suyas?
4. ¿Es la corbata suya?

18.3 Continúe según el modelo.

No es nuestro carro. → **Es el de ellos.**

1. No es nuestra cuenta.
2. No son nuestros boletos.
3. No son nuestras maletas.
4. No es nuestro problema.

18.4 Diga las frases en español.

1. What's mine is worth much more.
2. What's yours [*familiar*] is not important.
3. What's ours is in the car.
4. What belongs to her is by the door.

18.5 Vea estos anuncios de una tienda de abarrotes y conteste.

1. ¿En dónde se tiene que guardar un producto congelado?
2. ¿Qué quiere decir la expresión «colores surtidos»? Explíquenoslo en español.
3. ¿Cómo se explica la diferencia entre una panadería y una pastelería?
4. ¿Qué color identifica la leche totalmente desnatada (sin nada de grasa)?
5. ¿Qué color distingue el envase de la leche que se vende con la mitad de su grasa?
6. ¿Qué quiere decir la palabra «gratis»?
7. La torta francesa se vende aquí en varios sabores. ¿Cuáles son?

PRODUCTOS CONGELADOS

Jamón Ahumado en Lascas

Pollo Frito del Deli

VERDURAS

PANADERÍA

Muffins Extra Grandes .... **4** por
De banana o afrecho. Disponibles en todos los supermercados Publix y Bakeries

Jugo de Naranja

Espárragos Frescos

Central Lechera Asturiana piensa en el ama de casa.
   Para ayudarle en una elección que tiene que hacer cada diá, se han diferenciado con rojo, azul y verde el color de los envases de leche.
   Así podrá Vd. distinguir, sin ninguna duda, la leche que más le gusta, que más le conviene.
● El color rojo es para leche entera con toda su grasa.
● El color azul se ha dado a la nueva leche, con la mitad de su grasa.
● El color verde sigue siendo para la leche desnatada.
   Beba siempre leche de Central Lechera Asturiana. Y distíngala por el color de su envase.

central lechera ASTURIANA

Lasca de Torta Francesa......... c/u **Gratis**
De moca, chocolate, cereza o limón.
(Con su compra de una lascas de 1.29)

Calabaza Fresca

FLORES

Ramos de Flores ....
Para primavera, la Fleurette

Tulipanes ...
Colores Surtidos

Pan Pita en Miniatura ....
Sabores surtidos, Toufayan (Pitet

Pollos Enteros ...
Asados, para microonda, Holly

Manzanas .
Golden Delicious, de

Pimientos Verdes ...
De la Florida (Gree·

Helados o Sorbetes

Unit 19

Demonstratives

this	este, esta	these	estos, estas
that	ese, esa aquel, aquella	those	esos, esas aquellos, aquellas

1. Demonstratives agree in gender and number with the noun they precede: **estos cuadernos** *these notebooks*, **esa toalla** *that towel*. **Ese** and **aquel** may be used at times in everyday Spanish with no difference in meaning. **Aquel**, however, is ordinarily used if the speaker is emphasizing remoteness in time or space.

Aquellos jugadores no son nuestros.	Those players (over there) are not ours.

2. When demonstratives are used in place of nouns they have a written accent on the stressed vowel. The word *one* is often added in English: *this one, that one.* Spanish adds nothing.

Aquel carro es mío.	That car (over there) is mine.
Aquél es mío.	That one (over there) is mine.
Esas revistas no tienen anuncios.	Those magazines don't have any ads.
Ésas no tienen anuncios.	Those don't have any ads.

3. A demonstrative (or a definite article) + adjective can be used in place of a noun.

Me gustan estos zapatos blancos.	I like these white shoes.
Me gustan estos blancos.	I like these white ones.
La toalla amarilla es tuya.	The yellow towel is yours.
La amarilla es tuya.	The yellow one is yours.

4. Neuter demonstratives never change in form: **esto** *this*, **eso/aquello** *that*. They refer to an idea, action, or indefinite object rather than to a specified object, which would be either masculine or feminine.

Esto no lo voy a aceptar. I'm not going to accept this [what you have said or done].

Eso realmente les molesta. That [what was said or done] really bothers them.

Escriba una traducción de la conversación.

1. FÉLIX: These shoes are mine. Those dirty ones are yours.

2. ÓSCAR: These dirty ones are better. Especially when it rains.

3. FÉLIX: I don't believe that. And this dirty T-shirt (**camiseta**) is yours, too.

4. ÓSCAR: That T-shirt is not mine.

5. FÉLIX: It has that aroma I recognize. I thought I forgot to take out (**sacar**) the garbage (**basura**).

6. ÓSCAR: All this doesn't bother me. Whose is that old towel?

7. FÉLIX: These white towels are mine. Those dirty ones are yours.

8. ÓSCAR: I want that clean one.

9. FÉLIX: Oscar, Oscar. This is really impossible.

10. ÓSCAR: What is this? I can't eat this. I want a pizza.

11. FÉLIX: This food is very good. It's better than those pizzas.

12. ÓSCAR: How I wish (**¡Ojalá!**)!

SALUD Y BELLEZA –

Enjuague Bucal
3 59
bot. de 32-oz.
Con fluoruro, Listermint

Gotas para Los Ojos .... bot. de .5-oz.
Clear Eyes

Limpiador para Dentaduras .... pqte. de 60
Potencia máxima, Efferdent

Cebollas Dulces

Gallinitas Cornish .... tamaño 24-oz.
Grado premium, congeladas, Tyson's

Punta de Costillar de Puerco .... lb.
Porción sirloin (Pork Loin Sirloin Roast)

Jamón Curado con Miel

Mangos Frescos
99¢ c/u
Tamaño 12, importados

Comidas para Perros ....
Sabores surtidos, Pedigree

Papel Toalla ...... pqte. de 3-rollos
Big'n Thirsty

TAMAÑOS SURTIDOS, SUPERTRIM OR THICK
PAÑALES HUGGIES

Aceitunas Manzanilla ...
Rellenas, South Shore

Malta Goya .....
Bots. de 7-oz.

Vino Blanco para Cocinar ..
Edmundo

Fideos de Huevo ....
Gruesos o extra gruesos,

V-8
JUGO VEGETAL

Atún Blanco
98¢
lata de 6.5-oz.
En agua o aceite, Star-Kist
(Límite 2 con otras compras de $1 o más excluyendo productos de tabaco y boletos de lotería)

Platanos
29¢ lb.
Deliciosos, importados de Venezuela

Uvas Sin Semillas .... lb. 7
Rojas o negras, Thompson, importadas de Chile

Chayotes Frescos ....

Pan de Muerto
Elaborado con ingredientes de primerísima calidad según nuestra receta tradicional.

Picadillo Limpio
Paquete familiar de 3-lbs. o más
(Menos de 3-lbs. ....
(Beef Ground Chuck)

Fresas Frescas
68¢ pinta

LECTURA III

Read straight through the passage first. Then study the listed examples of preterit and imperfect usage before re-reading the episode. Questions for comprehension follow.

La imposible aventura de un biólogo en el Mato Grosso[1]

Los cuatro miembros de la expedición científica aterrizaron° en una pista° en lo alto de una reserva forestal de la Amazonia boliviana, creyéndola abandonada. Una hora después, tres de ellos murieron acribillados° por narcotraficantes. El único que consiguió escapar con vida fue un biólogo español. Habla el biólogo:

—Bajamos los cuatro de la avioneta°, y el guía y el piloto siguieron por una senda° a ver si había gente. De pronto mi compañero me dice: «Vaya°, se fueron dos y vienen cuatro.»

A unos 70 metros vimos a nuestros amigos que venían seguidos detrás por dos individuos que les encañonaban° con metralletas°. Llevaban escopetas de cartuchos° al hombro.

Se acercaron y yo me dirigí° a ellos en castellano, por darme a conocer°, ya que° tengo aspecto de gringo. Les dije que éramos españoles y que lo que hacíamos era estudiar animales.

Esta escena no duró más de un minuto. El guía hizo un gesto como de tocarse la camisa, y uno de los desconocidos le dijo dos palabras en voz alta en portugués. No sé lo que significaban. Tras esto montó° la metralleta y le disparó° sin mediar nada más°. El piloto salió corriendo hacia atrás, y yo me giré° y el otro compañero se incorporó° de donde estaba sentado y les dijo: «Pero no hagan esto, señores».

Entonces yo salí corriendo y oí detrás mío° otra serie de disparos. Superé° al piloto y nos internamos en la selva siguiendo un caminito. Era un bosque no muy alto pero muy espeso°, con mucha liana° y mucho sotobosque°.

Yo me aparté del camino porque pensé que ellos lo conocían. Antes de salirme miré hacia atrás y vi al piloto que seguía por el camino. Me adentré en la maleza° y me iba liando° continuamente. Al poco decidí tumbarme y quedarme quieto[2]. Oí tres disparos y ya no escuché nada más.

Me quedé inmóvil bajo una maraña° de plantas, comido por insectos. Una hora y media después oí como a unos 50 metros un individuo entraba en el bosque picando° con un machete. Ahí en ese momento me despedí de todo lo que me tenía que despedir. No entendía lo que estaba pasando, no lo asimilaba.—

• • •

El biólogo se quedó allí quieto todo el día y toda la noche. Al alba salió de su escondite° y se encontró el cadáver del piloto tendido° casi en el mismo sitio en el que él había abandonado el

landed
runway

riddled (with bullets)

small plane
path
Well, now

aimed/submachine guns
escopetas . . . *shotguns*
addressed
to make myself known/ since

aimed/shot/right then and there/I turned
stood up

behind me
I overtook
thick
vines/underbrush

thick weeds/I kept getting tangled

thicket

chopping

hiding place
stretched out

camino. Subió a una altura y vio la avioneta quemada. Sobre° la *Around*
una de la tarde escuchó un zumbido. Una avioneta estuvo dando
muchas vueltas°. **dando**... *circling*

—No sabía de quién era esa avioneta. Quería pensar que
eran los míos° y efectivamente[3] así fue. Salí a una zona clara e *my own party*
hice señales con un trapo°. Tardaron un rato en aterrizar. Corrí *a rag (cloth)*
hacia ellos y les dije que nos fuéramos° en seguida. «¡Vámonos, *we should get out of here*
que aquí ha habido un desastre!»

Al despegar° oímos un ruido, así como ratatatá, seco, *taking off*
repetido. El piloto se echó las manos a la cabeza. Miró los ins-
trumentos sin encontrar un fallo°. Con las prisas el cinturón de *malfunction*
seguridad° se había quedado fuera e iba pegando° contra el fuse- *seat belt/banging*
laje.

Notas

1. The Mato Grosso is a half-million square mile plateau (and the name
   of a state) in southwestern Brazil. The plateau extends into adjacent
   Bolivia.
2. **Quieto** means *still, motionless*; **callado/silencioso** means *silent*.
3. **Efectivamente** means *really, actually, in truth*; **eficazmente** means *effec-
   tively*.

Prácticas

Explique el contraste en el uso de los tiempos verbales abajo. (*Review the uses of the
imperfect and preterit in Unit 13 if necessary, to make your contrasts clear.*)

Pretérito	**Imperfecto**
Aterrizaron en una reserva forestal.	La creían abandonada.
Murieron acribillados.	
Uno consiguió escapar con vida.	
Fue el biólogo.	
Dos de ellos siguieron una senda.	Querían ver si había gente.
Vimos a nuestros amigos.	Venían seguidos por dos hombres.
	Los dos les encañonaban.
	Llevaban escopetas al hombro.

Se acercaron.

Yo me dirigí a ellos.

Les dije que . . .   . . . éramos españoles.

                                   Lo que hacíamos era estudiar.

No duró más de un minuto.

El guía hizo un gesto.

Le dijo dos palabras.   Yo no sabía lo que significaban.

Comprensión

1. ¿Dónde tiene lugar esta aventura?
2. ¿Cuántos salieron en la expedición?
3. ¿Cuántos volvieron?
4. ¿Por qué no entendió el biólogo lo que decían los desconocidos?
5. ¿Quién murió primero?
6. ¿Dónde pasó la noche el biólogo?
7. ¿Cómo llamó la atención de los que estaban en la avioneta?
8. ¿Qué ruido los asustó al final?

Unit 20

Verbs like *gustar*

---

convenir (ie) to suit, be suitable

doler (ue) to hurt, ache

encantar to delight, fascinate

faltar to lack, be missing

gustar to please, be pleasing to

hacer falta to need, be lacking

importar to matter

interesar to interest

parecer to seem, appear

preocupar to worry

quedar to remain, be left

tocar to touch; to be one's turn

—¿A usted le gustó la película?	"Did you like the movie?" ("Did the movie please you?")
—Sí, me encantó el final.	"Yes, I loved the ending." ("The ending delighted me.")
—¿Qué te parece esa clase?	"What do you think of that class?" ("How does that class seem to you?")
—A mí me aburre pero a Luz le gusta.	"It bores me, but Luz likes it."
Me duelen los pies.	My feet hurt (me).
A él le preocupa el trabajo.	His job worries him.
Les interesa el cine francés.	They are interested in French films. (French films interest them.)
A ella le conviene ir mañana.	It's to her advantage to go tomorrow. (Going tomorrow suits her.)

Gustar *to be pleasing to* is preceded by an indirect-object pronoun that indicates the person who is, or is not, pleased: **No le gustan las angulas** = *The baby eels* *are not pleasing to him = He does not like baby eels.* What is liked or "does the pleasing" is the subject of the verb. Thus **las angulas** is the subject of **gustar**, which is also plural in order to agree with its subject.

The verbs in the examples above and below are all used like **gustar**. The usual word order is pronoun + verb + subject. As usual, for emphasis or clarity **a** + pronoun or noun can be added.

A aquel tipo no le hace falta nada.	That fellow doesn't need anything. [Nothing is lacking to him.]
No les queda ni un centavo.	They don't have a penny left. [Not a penny remains to them.]
Le toca a ella.	It's her turn. [It "touches" her.]
Me faltan dos libros.	I'm missing two books. [Two books are missing to me.]

20.1 Conteste en español con una oración completa.

1. ¿Te gusta la clase?
2. ¿A quién le toca ahora?
3. ¿Le aburre la película a Víctor?
4. ¿Qué cosa te hace falta?
5. ¿Por qué me miras así? ¿Te duele algo?
6. ¿A Uds. no les preocupan los problemas del mundo?
7. ¿Cuánto dinero nos queda?
8. ¿Le importa a Ignacio lo que andan diciendo?
9. ¿Qué te parecen las ideas de tu mamá?
10. ¿Cuándo les conviene llegar a clase?

20.2 Diga en español.

1. I don't like baby eels.
2. How many pesetas do we have left?
3. We need a dictionary now.
4. She's missing one suitcase.

Diversión y práctica 5

Revelando mi pasado

Lo que tienen que hacer tú y tus compañeros ahora es cambiar entre sí preguntas, respuestas, opiniones y comentarios. Y no necesariamente sólo las sugerencias que se encuentran abajo. Puedes sorprender a tu compañero con una pregunta más bien original. Los dibujos pueden darte unas ideas.

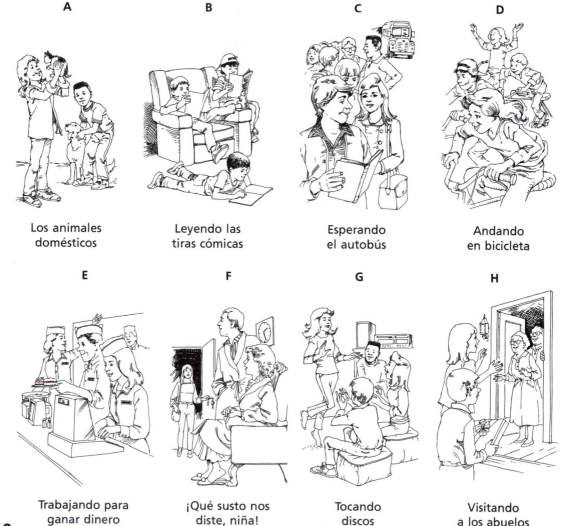

A
Los animales
domésticos

B
Leyendo las
tiras cómicas

C
Esperando
el autobús

D
Andando
en bicicleta

E
Trabajando para
ganar dinero

F
¡Qué susto nos
diste, niña!

G
Tocando
discos

H
Visitando
a los abuelos

1. ¿Dónde vivías cuando eras niño/a?
2. ¿Tenías un perro? ¿Un gato? ¿Cómo se llamaba el animal?
3. ¿Leías las tiras cómicas? ¿Cuál era tu favorita?
4. ¿A qué escuela secundaria fuiste?
5. ¿Te gustaba la escuela secundaria?
6. ¿Qué materias estudiabas? ¿Cuál te gustaba más?
7. ¿Andabas en bicicleta? Si no, ¿cómo ibas de una parte a otra?
8. ¿Trabajabas entonces? ¿Dónde?
9. ¿En el verano qué hacías? ¿Hiciste algún viaje interesante?
10. De noche, ¿a qué hora tenías que volver a casa?
11. ¿Ibas a muchas fiestas? ¿A cuántas cada mes? ¿Una por semana?
12. ¿Aprendiste a bailar? ¿Te gustaban los bailes?
13. ¿Dónde vivían tus abuelos? ¿Lejos o cerca?
14. ¿Cuánto tiempo pasabas con ellos? ¿Los visitabas con frecuencia?
15. ¿Estudiaste español en la escuela secundaria? ¿Hasta qué año?
16. ¿Hacías piñatas? ¿Qué se hace con una piñata?
17. Sus padres, ¿cómo eran? ¿Severos? ¿Tradicionales? ¿Poco exigentes?
18. ¿Practicabas deportes? ¿Cuáles?
19. ¿Escuchabas música? ¿Cuándo?
20. ¿Cómo era el ambiente en tu escuela secundaria? ¿Amistoso? ¿Estricto? Y tú, ¿cómo lo pasabas? ¿Estupendo? ¿Muy mal?

Unit 21

Reflexive pronouns

A. FORMS AND USES

me	myself	nos	ourselves
te	yourself	os	yourselves
se	himself herself yourself itself	se	themselves yourselves

Reflexive pronouns (shown above) are used in reflexive constructions, i.e., those where the direct or indirect object of the verb is identical to the subject.

Yo me afeité.	I shaved (myself).
Yo me afeité la barba.	I shaved my beard.
Usted se lavó.	You washed (yourself).
Usted se lavó el pelo.	You washed your hair.
El niño se lastimó.	The child got hurt (hurt himself).
El niño se lastimó la mano.	The child hurt his hand.
Se secaron.	They dried (themselves) off.
Se secaron los pies.	They dried off their feet.

Reflexive pronouns are omitted in English when the meaning is clear: *She bathed when she got home.* In Spanish, however, they are never omitted if the sentence has a reflexive meaning: **Se bañó cuando llegó a casa**.

B. REFLEXIVE VS. NONREFLEXIVE USAGE

All the verbs above may also be used nonreflexively when the object is something or someone other than the subject, as in the contrasting sentences below.

(Yo)	**Me lavé el pelo.**	I washed my (own) hair.
(Yo)	**Le lavé el pelo.**	I washed her hair.
(Él)	**Se tomó la temperatura.**	He took his (own) temperature.
(Ella)	**Le tomó la temperatura.**	She took his temperature (for him).

English uses a possessive to indicate the person affected by the action or the person whose article of clothing or part of the body it is (*my hair*, *her hair*, *his temperature*). In Spanish the person is indicated by the indirect object.

Se puso la chaqueta.	He put on his (own) jacket.
Le puso la chaqueta.	She put his jacket on (for him).
Se compró un carro.	She bought herself a car.
Me compró un carro.	She bought me a car.
Se quitó la venda.	He took off his (own) bandage.
La enfermera le quitó la venda.	The nurse took off his bandage.

C. RECIPROCAL CONSTRUCTIONS

The reflexive pronouns **nos** and **se** are also used to express reciprocal actions. English equivalents are *each other*, *one another*.

| **Nos vemos los viernes después de clase.** | We see each other Fridays after class. |
| **Se mandan tarjetas de Navidad cada diciembre.** | They send one another Christmas cards every December. |

D. OTHER REFLEXIVE CONSTRUCTIONS

Reflexive pronouns are used in the verbal constructions below. The English equivalents are not reflexive, as indicated.

Antonio se burla de nosotros.	Antonio is making fun of us.
Me di cuenta de que venían en seguida.	I realized they were coming right away.
No se atreve a hacerlo.	She doesn't dare to do it.
¿Nunca te equivocas?	Don't you ever make a mistake?
Se quejan de todo.	They complain about everything.

When **quedarse** means *to stay somewhere*, it must be used reflexively: **Patricia se quedó en Nicaragua durante marzo y abril** *Patricia stayed in Nicaragua during March and April*. Otherwise it may also be used nonreflexively: **Patricia quedó asombrada** *Patricia was astonished*.

Nos vemos en la
Calle ocho
el Domingo,
saboreando el sabroso

y gozando la fiesta cumbre
del Carnaval de Miami

21.1 Haga oraciones completas con el verbo en pretérito. Por ejemplo:

el barbero / afeitarse / y luego / afeitar / a mí→
El barbero se afeitó y luego me afeitó a mí.

1. la madre / bañarse / y luego / bañar / al niño
2. yo / tomarme / la temperatura / y luego / tomar la temperatura / a Jorge
3. ella / ponerse un suéter / y luego / poner un suéter / a su hija
4. el peluquero (*hairdresser*) / lavarse el pelo / y luego / lavar el pelo / a Ud.
5. su papá / comprarse un carro / y luego / comprar un carro / a Leonardo
6. José / quitarse la bufanda (*scarf*) / y luego / quitar la bufanda / a su hijo

21.2 Al español, por favor.

1. I took a bath at seven.
2. I washed my hair, too.
3. I remembered the exam at ten.
4. I put on my jacket.
5. But I made a mistake.
6. I realized the exam was at eight.
7. I went to the infirmary (**la enfermería**).
8. I told the nurse: "I hurt my hand on the bus."
9. She took my temperature.
10. It was normal.
11. I got (**sacar**) a B (**notable**) on the exam.
12. It was easy.

21.3 Igual que antes.

1. Luisa Patiño complained of the heat.
2. She bought herself a fan (**ventilador**).
3. She bathed three times that day.
4. She stayed in the bathtub (**bañera**) all afternoon.
5. Can one (**uno**) drown (**ahogarse**) in a bathtub?

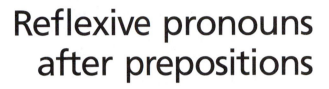

Reflexive pronouns after prepositions

mí mismo/a	myself	**nosotros/as mismos/as**	ourselves
ti mismo/a	yourself	**vosotros/as mismos/as**	yourselves
sí mismo	himself / yourself / itself	**sí mismos**	themselves / yourselves
sí misma	herself / yourself / itself	**sí mismas**	themselves / yourselves

These reflexive pronouns are used primarily after the preposition **a** to add emphasis to a reflexive construction. They are usually followed by **mismo/a/os/as**, depending on the number and gender of the person or persons in question.

Yo lo comprendo pero a veces él no se comprende a sí mismo.	I understand him, but at times he doesn't understand himself.
Ella siempre se habla a sí misma.	She's always talking to herself.
Ellos ni se lo admiten a sí mismos.	They don't even admit it to themselves.

Mí, ti, and **sí** used after the preposition **con** become **conmigo, contigo, consigo. Consigo** is often replaced by **con** + subject pronoun + **mismo**.

Ella se lo lleva consigo misma. Ella se lo lleva con ella misma.	She is taking it with her.
Se lo llevan consigo mismos. Se lo llevan con ellos mismos.	They are taking it with them.
Me lo llevo conmigo mismo.	I'm taking it with me.

The word **mismo** is also used for emphasis in nonreflexive sentences.

Solucioné el problema yo misma.   I solved the problem myself.

Traduzca empleando **a** + objetos reflexivos.

1. She doesn't even understand herself.
2. We don't even understand ourselves.
3. I am always talking to myself.
4. They are always talking to themselves.
5. You know the truth, but you don't want to admit it to yourself.

Vamos a escribir ... 3

Verbos reflexivos y verbos del tipo *gustar*

Escriba la historia de esta aventura de Guillermo Cornejo en su cuaderno. Se emplea aquí una gran parte de los verbos de las unidades 20 y 21, más otros verbos empleados (o no) reflexivamente. Cornejo, escritor de novelas policiacas, y Sonia, la mujer misteriosa a quien Guillermo quiere conocer, se hablan de usted en este primer episodio. Un vocabulario y un cuestionario para prácticas orales o escritas siguen al final.

LA AVENTURA PORTUGUESA
DE GUILLERMO CORNEJO (*episodio 1*)

Two problems worried Cornejo. He needed new ideas for his novels. Also, Guillermo and his girlfriend were no longer writing to each other.

Cornejo remained in Lisbon all summer, living in a small pension. He liked pensions. Especially the pensions that were near a beach. He was fascinated by (**Le encantaban**) the strange characters who stayed (**paraban**) in pensions. They seemed to him natural types for a detective story.

For (during) three weeks he didn't shave and he looked like a television star. After a month he was (**quedó**) so good-looking and mysterious that his girlfriend no longer worried him.

One Tuesday in August he realized that a new guest was in the pension. He found out (**supo**) that she was called Sonia. Sonia was tall, attractive, beautiful, et cetera, et cetera. Also she came dressed in black. Guillermo said to himself: "This I like." But he did not know how to introduce himself to the newcomer.

The next day Sonia changed herself totally into another person. She was going to bathe in the sea. She was wearing very dark sunglasses, elegant beach sandals, and a minibikini that cost thirty dollars a (**el**) square centimeter. She was also carrying a white totebag that shouted in large red letters: "WE SHALL OVERCOME" («**NOSOTRAS VENCEREMOS**»). "How am I going to meet this girl?" Cornejo asked himself.

•   •   •

First he bought himself a new bathing suit. Then one day in the patio Sonia fell down and hurt her foot. She stayed there until Guillermo covered her legs with a blanket. They looked at each other. Then, looking at him directly in his eyes (**a los ojos**), she said: "My foot hurts." Cornejo fell madly in love.

She healed (**Se curó**) rapidly, and Guillermo said to himself: "In affairs of the heart I never make a mistake." "Why don't we see each other tonight?", he asked her. "We can have dinner in a restaurant."

That night a waiter arrived who remembered to say: "What do you find appetizing?" Cornejo asked for veal chops, and the waiter said: "Very good, coming right up (**de acuerdo, vale**)."

•   •   •

Later they strolled along (**por**) the beach. After an hour Sonia dared to speak.

SONIA: "Now it's my turn to speak. But first I have to make a confession. My name is not Sonia."

GUILLERMO: "Names do not interest me."

SONIA: "Men bore me."

These words worried Cornejo.

SONIA: "And you in particular bore me."

Cornejo thought to himself: "It is not to my advantage now to tell her that I love her."

(*continuará*)

no longer **ya no**
Lisbon **Lisboa**
pension **la pensión**
to fascinate **encantarle a uno**
strange characters **tipos raros**
to look like **parecer**
a television star **una estrella de televisión**
good-looking **guapo/a**
to realize **darse cuenta (de)**
guest **huésped/a**
dressed in black **vestido/a de negro**
to introduce **presentar**
newcomer **el(la) recién llegado/a**
the next day **al otro día**
to wear **llevar**
dark **oscuro/a**
sunglasses **las gafas de sol**
beach sandals **las playeras**
square centimeter **centímetro cuadrado**

to carry **traer**
totebag **la bolsa**
to meet **conocer**
bathing suit **el bañador**
to fall down **caerse**
to hurt (oneself) **lastimar(se)**
until **hasta que**
blanket **la manta**
to fall in love **enamorarse**
madly **locamente**
affairs **los asuntos**
to remember **acordarse (de)**
veal chops **chuletas de ternera**
to stroll **pasearse**
to dare **atreverse (a)**
to make a confession **confesar algo**
in particular **en particular**
to be to one's advantage **convenirle a uno**

Cuestionario

1. ¿Dónde pasó el verano Guillermo?
2. ¿Quiénes frecuentaban las pensiones?
3. ¿Qué no hizo Guillermo durante tres semanas?
4. ¿Un día quién llegó a la pensión?
5. ¿Cómo se llamaba esta mujer?
6. ¿Qué traía a la playa?
7. ¿Cómo se lastimó esta mujer?
8. ¿En qué cosas no se equivoca Cornejo?
9. ¿Qué reveló la mujer en la playa?
10. ¿Qué le aburre a esta mujer?

Unit 23

Uses of the indefinite article

A. USES

Su padre es republicano.	Her father is a Republican.
Es un republicano liberal.	He's a liberal Republican.
Ángela es enfermera.	Angela is a nurse.
Es una enfermera muy buena.	She's a very good nurse.
Su madre es católica.	Her mother is a Catholic.
Es una católica devota.	She's a devout Catholic.

The indefinite article **un/una** *a, an,* **unos/unas** *some, several, a few* is omitted before an unmodified noun indicating political affiliation, nationality, profession, or religion: **Dolores es salvadoreña**. *Dolores is a Salvadoran*. But when such nouns are modified, the indefinite article is used: **Dolores es una salvadoreña guapa** *Dolores is a good-looking Salvadoran*.

B. CONTRASTS WITH ENGLISH USAGE

The indefinite article is omitted in Spanish in many other constructions in which it is used in English.

1. Before the numbers **cien** and **mil**.

Nos querían cobrar mil dólares.	They wanted to charge us a thousand dollars.
Y no valía más que cien dólares.	And it was only worth a hundred dollars.

2. After **¡Qué!** in exclamations.

¡Qué desastre!	What a disaster!
¡Qué camisa más vistosa!	What a loud shirt!
¡Qué timo!	What a rip-off!

3. After **como** and **de** when these words mean *as*.

Buscaba empleo como mesero.	He was looking for a job as a waiter.
Trabajó aquí de botones.	He worked here as a messenger boy.

4. After **tal** and before **otro**.

No se hace de tal manera.	You don't do it in such a way (that way).
Aquí prefieren otro modo de hacerlo.	Here they prefer another way to do it.

5. After the prepositions **con** and **sin**, unless the meaning is *one* or *a single one*.

Lo dibujó con lápiz.	He drew it with a pencil.
Le quedaba un solo lápiz.	He had just one pencil left.
No enseña la clase sin corbata.	He won't teach the class without a tie.
Salió para Europa sin una corbata.	He left for Europe without one tie.

6. After **buscar, encontrar, tener,** and **haber**, when the object is referred to in a general or generic way. If the object is identified as one of a specific kind or is modified by an adjective, the article is used.

Siguen buscando casa.	They're still looking for a house.
Buscan una casa grande.	They're looking for a large house.
—**¿No tiene guitarra?**	"Doesn't he have a guitar?"
—**Claro que sí. Tiene una guitarra acústica.**	"Of course he does. He has an acoustic guitar."
—**¿No hay copiadora aquí?**	"Isn't there a copy machine here?"
—**Sí, hay una copiadora nueva en la otra oficina.**	"Yes, there is a new copy machine in the other office."

C. *UNA* → *UN*

Un, not **una**, is often used immediately before singular feminine nouns beginning with stressed **a**.

Stressed a-	Unstressed a-
un <u>a</u>la a wing	**una <u>a</u>buela** a grandmother
un <u>au</u>la a classroom	**una <u>a</u>rtista** an artist (*woman*)

If a word intervenes, **una** remains **una**.

Vimos un águila grande.	We saw a large eagle.
Vimos una hermosa águila.	We saw a beautiful eagle.

The above rule is for feminine nouns only. Feminine adjectives beginning with stressed **a** take **una: una ágil atleta** *an agile athlete* (*woman*), **una ancha avenida** *a wide avenue*.

Complete en español con las palabras indicadas.

1. (*looking for a car*) Sigue _____.
2. (*a big car*) Busca _____.
3. (*a copy machine*) ¿No hay _____ aquí?
4. (*a doctor*) Su padre es _____
5. (*a very good doctor*) Es _____.
6. (*without a hat*) Mi abuela no salía nunca _____.
7. (*a thousand dollars*) Nos cobraron _____.
8. (*What a movie!*) ¡ _____ ! Me emocioné.
9. (*as a nurse*) Magda trabajó aquí _____.
10. (*such a*) No les gusta _____ actitud.
11. (*another*) Quieren _____ bebida, no les gusta ésta.
12. (*a small classroom*) Se reúnen en _____.
13. (*as a guide* [**guía**]) Ese verano dos hombres me emplearon _____.
14. (*a Democrat/a Republican*) Uno era _____ y el otro era _____.
15. (*a hundred dollars*) Cada semana ganaba _____.
16. (*an eagle*) Un día vimos _____.
17. (*a large eagle, with a broken wing* [**ala rota**]) Era _____.
18. (*What a beautiful eagle!*) ¡ _____ !
19. (*a Spaniard/a Catholic*) Manuela es _____ pero no es _____.
20. (*a lawyer/a very sharp* [**astuto**] *lawyer*) Enrique es _____ y además es _____.

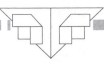

Unit 24

Indefinite and negative words

alguien	someone somebody	**nadie**	no one nobody not anyone
alguno/a/os/as	someone some any	**ninguno/a/os/as**	no one none
algo	something somewhat rather	**nada**	nothing not anything not at all

—**Alguien viene.**	"Someone is coming."
—**No, no viene nadie.**	"No, no one is coming."
Buscaba alguna novela histórica.	He was looking for some historical novel.
No quería ninguna novela romántica.	He didn't want any romantic novel.
—**Esto es algo grave, ¿verdad?**	"This is something serious, isn't it?"
—**No, no es nada importante.**	"No, it's not anything important."

1. The short forms **algún** and **ningún** are used before masculine singular nouns.

Buscaba algún diario en inglés.	He was looking for some newspaper in English.
Pero no tenían ningún diario en inglés.	But they had no newspaper in English.

2. Personal **a** is required before **alguno** and **ninguno** when these forms are used as direct objects referring to persons. The same is true of **alguien** and **nadie**.

—**¿Conoces a alguna de ellas?**	"Do you know any of them?"
—**No, no conozco a ninguna de ellas.**	"No, I don't know any of them."

—¿Viste a alguien en la escalera?   "Did you see anybody on the stairs?"

—No, no vi a nadie.   "No, I didn't see anyone."

3. The forms **ningunos/ningunas** are used before nouns that normally occur in the plural.

No quería usar ningunos zapatos negros.   She didn't want to wear any black shoes.

Aquí no vendemos ningunas tijeras de coser.   We don't sell any sewing scissors here.

Otherwise, **ningún** and **ninguna** are always singular.

Aquí no vendemos ningún diario americano.   We don't sell any American newspapers here.

4. Algo *somewhat, rather* and **no...nada** *not...at all* may be used to qualify adjectives.

La cosa ha quedado algo grave.   The matter has become rather serious.

Esos trajes no son nada típicos de México.   Those suits are not at all typical of Mexico.

•   •   •

también	also / too	tampoco	neither / not...either
o...o	either...or	**ni...ni**	neither...nor

Ella tiene un vídeo y yo voy a comprarme uno también.   She has a VCR, and I'm going to buy one, too.

O van al centro o a la plaza de compras.   They're going either downtown or to the mall.

No voy ni hoy ni mañana.   I'm not going either today or tomorrow.

Tampoco, like **también**, may be used either before or after the word it negates. If it is used after, **ni** may be used before the negated word. The use of **ni** with **tampoco** stresses a repetition of the main clause.

Yo no quiero más. Ella tampoco, ¿verdad? (Tampoco ella, ¿verdad?)   I don't want any more. She doesn't either, does she?

Yo no lo creo, ni ella tampoco (ni lo cree ella tampoco).   I don't believe it, nor does she.

Ni corresponds to *not even*. **Siquiera** adds more emphasis.

Ni (siquiera) tiene estéreo.   He doesn't even have a stereo.

•   •   •

una vez once		**nunca** never	
alguna vez sometime, ever		**jamás** {	never
algún día someday			(not) ever

1. **Una vez** and **alguna vez** refer to an event in the past, **algún día** to one in the future.

Una vez estuvimos en Matamoros.	We were in Matamoros once.
¿Tú fuiste allí alguna vez?	Did you ever go there?
Algún día voy a ir a Atenas.	Someday I'm going to go to Athens.

2. **Jamás** and **nunca** are both equivalent to *never*. **Jamás** is generally more emphatic.

Nunca tenía lo que necesitaba.	He never had what he needed.
Jamás le gustaba lo que le regalaban.	She never liked what they gave her.

Jamás is often used in superlative comparisons.

Es el mejor pelotari que jamás se ha visto.	He's the best jai alai player that there has ever been.

It can be combined with **nunca** for even more emphasis.

¡Nunca jamás!   Never ever again!

Más que nunca means *more than ever*: **Ahora lo desea más que nunca** *Now he wants it more than ever.*

• • •

Nadie nos ayudó. **No nos ayudó nadie.** }	No one helped us.
Tampoco nos atendió nadie. **No nos atendió nadie tampoco.** }	No one took care of us either.
Nunca lo dijo. **No lo dijo nunca.** }	He never said it.
Ninguno lo dijo nunca. **No lo dijo ninguno nunca.** }	No one (none of them) ever said it.

1. Whenever a negative word follows the verb in Spanish, another negative word—often **no**—must precede the verb. Thus double and multiple negatives can and often must be used in the same sentence in Spanish: **No vimos a nadie** *We didn't see anybody.*

2. When a negative word (other than **no** or **ni**) precedes the verb, **no** is not necessary: **Nadie lo vio** *Nobody saw it.*

3. If there are two negatives (other than **no**) in the sentence, one precedes the verb and the other follows it: **Tampoco hizo nada** *He didn't do anything either.*

4. But both must follow the verb if **no** is used in the sentence: **No hizo nada tampoco** *He didn't do anything either.*

24.1 Haga de cada frase una oración negativa.

1. Oyeron algo.
2. Tiene algunos mapas.
3. Busca algún diario en inglés.
4. Alguien viene.
5. Es algo grave.
6. Vimos a alguien en el patio.
7. Conozco a alguna de ellas.
8. Ese traje es algo típico.
9. O van al centro o se quedan aquí.
10. Yo voy también.
11. Una vez estuvimos allí.
12. Algún día lo voy a ver.
13. Alguna de ellas lo conoce.
14. Y ellos también.
15. Salen hoy o mañana.
16. Alguien lo sabe manejar.

24.2 Diga en español.

1. I went to the city to (**para**) look for work.
2. I had nothing.
3. Someone is going to help me.
4. No one helped me.
5. This is something serious (**grave**).
6. But it is not anything important.
7. Were you ever (sometime) hungry?
8. I looked for some job in a factory (**fábrica**).
9. I didn't want any job in a store.
10. What was I going to do? I didn't have any idea.
11. My friend was looking for work, too.
12. I didn't find work, nor did he.
13. Neither he nor I found work.
14. No one helped us either.
15. For us it was never easy.
16. No one ever said it.
17. We don't even understand ourselves.
18. Someday I am going to go back home (**volver a casa**).

Diversión y práctica 6

Más expresiones conversacionales

EXPRESIONES PARA (CASI) CUALQUIER OCASIÓN

A ver.   Let's see.

¡Basta!   That's enough!

¡Bien!   Great!, OK!, Fine! (*also* **¡Está bien!**)

Bueno...   Well..., So..., OK...(*to change the subject*)

¿Cómo te sientes? ¿Mejor?   How do you feel? Better?

Creo que sí.   I think so.

Cuando quieras.   Whenever (you wish). Whatever you say (agreeing to a time).

¡Cuidado!   (Be) careful! Watch out!

De acuerdo.   Fine. I agree.

De nada.   You're welcome. Don't mention it.

Depende.   It depends.

¡Esto es el colmo!   That does it! That's the last straw!

¡Felicidades!   Congratulations. (*also* **¡Felicitaciones!**)

Lo siento.   I'm sorry. (*to apologize, but **not** to express sympathy*)

Me da lo mismo (igual).   It's all the same to me. It doesn't matter. Whatever.

¿Me hace el favor de...?   Would you please...?

¡Menos mal!   It's a good thing. It turned out OK. Thank goodness for that.

¡Mira!   Look!

No es para tanto.   It's not as bad as all that. It's no big deal.

¡No faltaba más!   That does it! That's the last straw!

No hay de qué.   You're welcome. Don't mention it.

No hay (otro) remedio.   There's no other way. There's nothing we can do about it.

¡No me digas!   Don't tell me! Go on! No way!

No vale la pena.   It's not worth the trouble. It's not worth it.

¡Ojalá!   I hope so! Don't I wish!

¡Oye (tú)!/¡Oiga (usted)!   Hey! (*to attract someone's attention*)

Pues...   Well...(*indicating doubt, hesitation or uncertainty*)

¡Por Dios! ¡Dios mío!   My goodness! Wow! (*In Spanish mild references to God and religious figures are not considered profane or impolite.*)

¡Qué barbaridad!   How terrible! How awful!

¡Qué desgracia!   How unfortunate! What bad luck! (**desgracia** = misfortune; **vergüenza** = disgrace, shame, *or* embarrassment)

¿Qué hay de nuevo?   What's up? What's new?

¡Qué lástima!   What a shame! Too bad!

¡Qué lío!   What a mess! What a mix-up!

¡Qué pena!   How sad! I'm sorry! (*to express sympathy, but **not** to apologize*)

¡Qué precioso!   How attractive! How nice!

¡Qué suerte!   How lucky! What a stroke of luck!

¡Qué va!/¡Vaya!   You don't say! Go on! No way!

Tal vez.   Perhaps. Maybe.

¿Te importa mucho?   Does it really matter that much to you?

Ya veremos.   We'll see (how it goes).

Existen en español, como en inglés, expresiones y palabrotas fuertes, vulgares y aun obscenas. Pero no se hagan ilusiones, porque no las vamos a poner aquí. También existen eufemismos como, por ejemplo, los muchos que empiezan con **ca-** o **chi-** (**¡caramba!**, **¡chihuahua!**) que sustituyen a otras palabras más fuertes. Otro ejemplo es **¡miércoles!**.

¿Cómo vas a responder en las siguientes situaciones? ¿Qué vas a decir? (No hay repeticiones—es decir, si ya has dicho una frase, siempre di otra nueva para la situación.)

1. Quieres llamarle la atención a un amigo.
2. Te diriges al empleado de una tienda para llamarle la atención.
3. Te encuentras con tu amiga y quieres saber si tiene algo de nuevo que decirte.
4. Tu amiga Ángela acaba de ganar una beca, o, mejor, la lotería.
5. A tu amigo Marcos se le rompió el brazo haciendo gimnasia.
6. A unos amigos les revelas que sabes dónde hay una gran cantidad de dinero robado. Vas a informar a la policía. Sus amigos tienen miedo pero tú respondes...
7. Alguien sugiere una cosa para saber tu opinión y tú le contestas...
8. Vas a acompañar a unos amigos en un viaje pasado mañana. A ti no te importa la hora de la salida. Dices...
9. En el parque ves a una niña que está a punto de caerse de su bicicleta.
10. Tu profesora te dice que espera que saques una buena nota en el examen. Y tú respondes...
11. Un hombre te agradece alguna información que le diste. Tú respondes...

12. Un compañero te dice algo que no creías posible. Tú le respondes...

13. Vuelves a tu apartmento y te dicen que hubo un incendio. Tú exclamas...

14. Tu compañero te dice que va a abandonar la universidad porque sacó una mala nota en un examen de matemáticas. Tú tratas de consolarlo diciendo...

15. Le dices al compañero que tienes que leer toda una novela en una sola semana para la clase de literatura. Es mucho trabajo, pero...

16. Hay una gran nevada y los caminos están muy malos. Querías volver a tu ciudad para visitar a tus padres, pero decides que no, diciendo...

17. Estás reponiéndote de un ataque de gripe (influenza), y el profesor te saluda y te pregunta...

18. Tu equipo favorito ha perdido un partido bastante importante, tienes la cara un poco triste, y tu amigo te pregunta...

Unit 25

|||||||||||||||||||||||||||||||||||||||||||||||||||||||||||||||||

Other reflexive constructions

A. REFLEXIVES FOR MOVEMENT AND CHANGE OF POSITION

Me acerqué a la ventana.	I moved closer to the window.
Acerqué la silla a la mesa.	I moved the chair closer to the table.
Se levantó temprano.	He got up early.
Levantó al niño.	He picked up the child.
Nos sentamos en la primera fila.	We sat (down) in the first row.
Sentamos a los niños en la segunda fila.	We seated the children in the second row.
Se acostó a las once.	She went to bed at eleven.
Acostó a los niños a las ocho.	She put the children to bed at eight.
Se movieron de un lado al otro.	They moved from one side to the other.
Movieron la cama al otro lado del cuarto.	They moved the bed to the other side of the room.

The transitive verbs above may be used reflexively or not. They take a non-reflexive direct object when the action is done to someone or something else (**Levantó al niño**, **Movieron la cama**) and a reflexive object when the subjects perform the action on or by themselves (**Se levantó**, **Se movieron**).

Some intransitive verbs, i.e., those that do not take direct objects, undergo a shift in meaning or emphasis when used reflexively.

Marcharon por la plaza.	They marched across the square.
Se marcharon ayer temprano.	They left (departed) early yesterday.
Volvió en seguida.	He came back (returned) right away.
Se volvió a la puerta.	He turned around (back) at the door.
Voy al cine.	I'm going to the movies.
Me voy mañana.	I'm leaving (going away) tomorrow.

130

The English equivalents of many of these verbs have an adverb (*close, up, down, around, about, away*).

Se acercó.	*He got close.*	**Se movió.**	*He moved about.*
Se levantó.	*He got up.*	**Se volvió.**	*He turned around.*
Se sentó.	*He sat down.*	**Se fue.**	*He went away.*

Bajar(se) can mean *to get off* (a bus, plane, etc.), *to get out of* (a taxi, car, etc.), or *to come down(stairs)*. When it means to get down from a high place, it is always reflexive: **Se bajaron del árbol**   *They got (climbed) down out of the tree.* **Bajar** can also mean *to bring (take) something down*. **Subir** is used similarly.

Bajaron del taxi.	
Se bajaron del taxi.	They got out of the taxi.
Se bajaron del techo.	They climbed down off the roof.
Bajaron las maletas.	They brought (took) the suitcases down.
Subieron al autobús.	They got on the bus.
Se subieron al techo.	They climbed up on the roof.
Subieron las maletas.	They brought (took) the suitcases up.

B. REFLEXIVES FOR EMOTIONAL INVOLVEMENT AND CHANGE OF CONDITION OR STATUS

In the case of the following reflexive constructions, the subject is someone who is affected, emotionally or otherwise, by an event, or whose condition or status is changed.

Me aburro viendo televisión.	I get bored watching television.
¿No te alegras de verme?	Aren't you glad to see me?
Se asustaron con el ruido.	They were (got) scared by the noise.
Se calmaron tras la discusión.	They calmed down (became calm) after the argument.
Se emocionaron con la noticia.	They were moved by the news.
Se enfermó en marzo.	She got sick in March.
Se enojó conmigo.	She got angry with me. (She got mad at me.)
Se graduaron en junio y se casaron en septiembre.	They graduated in June and got married in September.
Nos ofendimos con el discurso.	We were offended by the speech.
Tú te preocupas demasiado.	You worry too much.

All the verbs above may also be used nonreflexively.

Nos aburre.	It bores us.	**Nos calma.**	He makes us calm (calms us down).
Nos alegra.	She makes us happy.	**Nos enoja.**	He makes us mad.
Nos asusta.	It scares us.	**Nos ofende.**	She offends us.

C. OTHER VERBS IN REFLEXIVE AND NONREFLEXIVE CONSTRUCTIONS

Usually there is a difference in meaning depending on whether a verb is reflexive or not.

Lo negó.	He denied it.
Se negó a prestármelo.	He refused to lend it to me.
Durmió ocho horas.	She slept eight hours. '
Se durmió a las once.	She fell asleep at eleven.
Lo sienten mucho.	They are very sorry about it. (They regret it a lot.)
Se sienten contentos.	They feel happy.

Below are examples of other verbs used in nonreflexive and reflexive constructions.

La enamoró todo el semestre.	He courted her all semester.
Pero ella nunca se enamoró de él.	But she never fell in love with him.
El borracho nos molestó durante todo el partido.	The drunk bothered us during the whole game.
No se molestó en averiguar la verdad.	She didn't bother to find out the truth.
María enteró a todos.	Maria told (informed) everybody.
Eduardo no se enteró de la verdad.	Eduardo didn't find out the truth.
Su salud mejoró un poco.	His health improved a little bit.
Se mejoró un poco.	He got a little bit better. (He improved a little bit.)
El payaso quiere divertir a los niños.	The clown wants to entertain the children.
Los niños siempre se divierten en los circos.	Children always have a good time at circuses.
Olvidó el libro.	He forgot the book.
Se olvidó del disgusto.	He forgot all about the unpleasant event.
Nos disgustó mucho.	She made us very angry.
Se disgustó mucho con nosotros.	She got very angry with us.
El final me sorprendió.	The ending surprised me.
Me sorprendí del final.	I was surprised at the ending.

25.1 Las frases de abajo no contienen ninguna construcción reflexiva. De cada frase haga otra que sea reflexiva, usando el mismo verbo. Y en cualquier tiempo verbal (*in any tense*).

1. Acostó a los niños a las diez.
2. Levantó al niño.
3. Acercaron la mesa a la pared.
4. La maestra sentó a los niños en la última fila.
5. Fue al cine.
6. El árbitro calmó a los jugadores.
7. Esto nos divirtió.
8. Su opinión les preocupó.
9. ¿Te alegró la noticia?
10. Esa película me aburrió.

25.2 Igual que antes. De cada frase haga otra que sea reflexiva.

1. El discurso nos disgustó.
2. Lo negaron.
3. Durmió siete horas.
4. Lo siento mucho.
5. No les molesta nada.
6. Su salud mejoró ayer.
7. Uno de los niños divirtió a los demás.
8. Ella enteró a todo el mundo.

25.3 Exprese las frases en español.

1. (acostarse) I didn't go to bed last night.
2. (volver) I came back this morning at six.
3. (dormirse) I fell asleep in the kitchen.
4. (dormir) I slept three hours.
5. (bajar) My mother came downstairs at nine.
6. (ver / asustarse) She saw me and at first (**al principio**) she was scared.
7. (despertarse) Then I woke up.
8. (levantarse) I got up off the floor (**del piso**).
9. (enojarse) Then she got angry with me.
10. (calmarse) Finally she calmed down.
11. (sentarse) We sat down at the table.
12. (decir / irse) I said: "I'm leaving tomorrow."
13. (sorprenderse) She was surprised at (**de**) my decision.
14. (ofenderse) But she was not offended.
15. (preocuparse) You must not (**Tú no debes**) worry so much.
16. (comprender) We understand each other. [Be sure to supply the appropriate reflexive pronoun.]
17. (sentirse) I feel better now.
18. (ver) Then I saw myself in the mirror (**espejo**). [Be sure to supply the appropriate reflexive pronoun.]

LECTURA IV

Read once straight through these news reports. Then study the aids and exercises before re-reading the passages and noting the use of certain verb constructions. Comprehension questions follow each selection.

NOTICIERO MUNDIAL

Un niño de diez años salva a un bebé que cayó desde un primer piso

San Pedro de Macorís (República Dominicana).[1] El niño Raúl Ripoll Ortega, de diez años, logró salvar a un bebé de un año, cuando éste° cayó al vacío desde una casa de apartamentos, de San Pedro de Macorís.   *the latter*

    Raúl estaba jugando al béisbol con sus amigos cuando de pronto la pelota fue a dar contra° el balcón donde se hallaba el bebé. Raúl se dio cuenta de que el bebé se encontraba suspendido de la barandilla° de un balcón, con una distancia aproximada al suelo de más de diez metros°. Le pareció al niño que a él le tocaba hacer algo para salvar al bebé y se situó debajo del pequeño.   **dar**... *hit*   *railing*   *un metro = 39.37"*

    En ese momento también les dice a sus compañeros que vayan a avisar° a la madre del pequeño, mientras él se pone debajo del balcón. A los pocos instantes el niño caía en sus brazos.   **vayan**... *go warn*

    Por la fuerza con que cayó, ambos rodaron° al suelo, pero no se lastimaron ni recibieron heridas° de ningún tipo. Al poco rato Raúl le entregaba el bebé a su madre sano y salvo°, mientras ésta, con evidentes muestras de nerviosismo, le daba gracias al niño.   *fell tumbling*   *injuries*   *safe and sound*

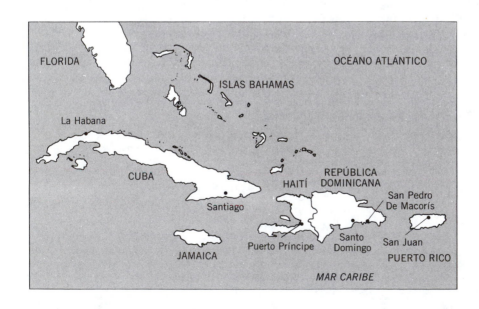

Estaba jugando al béisbol con sus amigos cuando la pelota fue a dar contra el balcón de una casa.

Notas

1. San Pedro de Macorís is a small city in the Dominican Republic, a country which, along with Haiti, occupies a Caribbean island between Cuba and Puerto Rico. San Pedro de Macorís is noted for its contribution to professional baseball, having sent some twenty players to the major leagues.

Comprensión

1. ¿Dónde está San Pedro de Macorís?

2. ¿Cómo se llama el héroe de este acto de valor?

3. ¿En dónde se encontraba el pobre bebé?

4. ¿Qué hizo Raúl para salvar al bebé?

5. ¿Al final Raúl le entrega el bebé a quién?

6. ¿Diez metros son más o menos cuántos pies?

Un toro de más de 450 kilos subió hasta el tercer piso de una casa

Monterrey (México).[1] Julián Marcos, veterano carnicero° de Monterrey (Nuevo León), tuvo que subir el lunes al tercer piso de una casa de la periferia° de aquella localidad, para recuperar su toro de 450 kilos° de peso, que escapó por la ciudad y ascendió, una a una, las escaleras de una casa.

    Perseguido por su dueño y el yerno° de éste, el animal entró en un portal de la calle y subió pese a la estrechez° de las escaleras.

butcher

outskirts
un kilo = 2.2 lbs.

son-in-law
narrowness

Stewart por Oakland y Garrelts por San Francisco

ESTA TARDE ¡PLEYBOL!

Luis Rivera, torpedero de Boston, se encog...
causado por un mal rebote en roletazo bateado...

Bravos cifran esperanzas en jóvenes lanzadores

Viene de la página 5B

cuantos peloteros que hay que observar. Tenemos al joven pitcher John Smoltz. Dicen que es un potencial ganador de 20 juegos. La juventud que tiene. Las

Padres santiguan a los Bravos

ATLANTA (AP) - Andy Benes pitchó ocho innings formidables y los resurgentes Padres de San Diego...

Un squeezplay dio la victoria a Naranjeros ante Tijuana, 6-5

HERMOSILLO, Son., 25 noviembre.— Un por...

Samuel al jardín central de Dodgers

Canseco tras otro 40-40

Beisbol de la Liga del Pacífico

Tomateros ganó en 13 actos a los Venados 4-2 y empató el liderato con Los Mochis

Por ENRIQUE MORALES

MAZATLAN, 13 de no... mbre.— Un total...

NUESTRA PEQUEÑA SERIE MUNDIAL

Campeonato de la Liga de Béisbol del Caribe

Por primera vez en la histo...

Tartabull batea jonrón en victoria de Reales

22 peloteros latinos millonarios

Tartabull conecta 2 jonrones al Detroit

Beisbol del Pacífico

Guillermo Sandoval lanzó para 4 jits en la victoria de Algodoneros

Por ENRIQUE MORALES

las nueve entradas, para que los Algodoneros de Guasave vencieran por 1-0

Jonrones boricuas hunden a RD

PR gana 5-4 y empata 1er lugar

Dodgers aplastan a Mellizos 13-6

Orlando —(UPI)— John Shelby impulsó dos ...
permitió que entraran dos carreras, y el torpedero Doug Baker, dejó pasar otra rodada, y los Dodgers se pusieron en ventaja 9-6. Shelby encontró un hueco por el centro para
das, que incluyeron su jonrón solitario y dos carreras impulsadas. Eddie Murray agregó un vuelacerca. Gary Gaetti ...

En el tercer piso se bañaban dos escolares° que se preparaban para acudir al colegio[2]. Cuando se disponían a salir, se encontraron de frente° con el toro. Llamaron a gritos a sus padres que se hallaban acostados y al principio creyeron que se trataba de[3] una broma°.   *students* *face to face* *joke*

El padre de la familia pese a todo se levantó de la cama, soltando blasfemias, y se dio cuenta de que, efectivamente°, un toro enorme se hallaba al otro lado de la puerta de su domicilio. Durante treinta minutos varias personas forcejearon° con el toro, cubriéndole los ojos, tirándolo del rabo°, y dándole golpes hasta que lograron bajar al animal de nuevo a la calle.   *in fact* *struggled* *tail*

Notas

1. Monterrey is an industrial city in northeastern Mexico.
2. **Colegio** has a variety of meanings in the Hispanic world, ranging from *nursery school* and *kindergarten* to *college dorm*, although it never means *college*. Here it is *high school*.
3. **Tratarse de** *to be a question of*. **Tratar de** + infinitive = *to try to* + verb.

Comprensión

1. ¿Hasta qué piso subió el toro?
2. ¿Quiénes vieron al toro primero?
3. En esta lectura, ¿qué es un colegio? Descríbalo.
4. ¿Al pobre animal le tuvieron que cubrir qué parte anatómica?
5. ¿Cuatro libras (*lbs.*) y media son más o menos cuántos kilos?

Seis niños huyeron de un hogar-escuela para ir de safari a África

Cáceres (España).[1] La aventura de cazar° en África fue el objetivo de seis niños de edades comprendidas entre los 12 y los 15 años, que huyeron con tal fin de un hogar-escuela[2] de Madroñera (Cáceres).   *hunting*

Todos son hijos de agricultores de la zona que cursan sus estudios en un colegio nacional de Madroñera y residen en régimen de pensionistas[3] en el hogar-escuela. Los niños desaparecieron en la mañana del pasado miércoles, después del desayuno. La idea sedujo a numerosos alumnos del colegio, pero sólo seis de ellos se decidieron a dar el paso definitivo para consumar la aventura.

Con unos cientos de pesetas en sus bolsillos, producto de sus ahorros° semanales, los seis chavales° se dijeron que les convenía ir a Cádiz, donde pensaban tomar un barco que iba a llevarlos al continente africano. El país hacia el que encaminaban sus pasos iba a tener una selva al modo tradicional de las películas: espesa naturaleza y grandes animales salvajes. Para mantenerse durante el viaje, una vez agotado° el dinero, iban a robar en los pueblos por los que pasaban.

savings/boys

spent

David Morales, el más pequeño del grupo, reveló que le dolían los pies a pocos kilómetros de Madroñera, y regresó hacia su hogar familiar en Casar de Miajadas. Los otros cinco continuaron la ruta, pasando la noche en un pajar° de Zarza de Montánchez. Por la mañana, después de una noche de nervios y de hambre, el largo viaje les preocupaba a otros dos integrantes del grupo y anunciaron su decisión de volver.

hayloft

Diezmado° a tres el grupo de aventureros, se dirigían a la carretera 630, que iba a llevarlos a Sevilla. Pero agentes de la Guardia Civil[4] localizaron a los expedicionarios en las proximidades de Aldea del Cano, hasta cuyo cuartel° fueron trasladados. Les dieron unos bocadillos° que comieron con gran apetito. Se mostraron descorazonados°. De allí fueron devueltos al hogar-escuela.

Decimated (down)

barracks
sandwiches
disheartened

Notas

1. **Cáceres** is a province in southwestern Spain.
2. **El hogar-escuela** is a public day school, common in rural Spain, that provides room and board on weekdays.
3. **Pensionista** = person receiving room and board.
4. **La Guardia Civil** is the national police force of rural Spain.

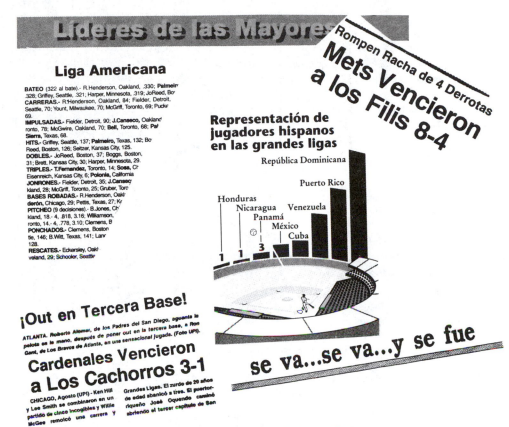

Líderes de las Mayores

Liga Americana

BATEO (322 al bate).- R.Henderson, Oakland, .330; **Palmeir**
.328; Griffey, Seattle, .321; Harper, Minnesota, .319; JoReed, Bo'
CARRERAS.- R.Henderson, Oakland, 84; Fielder, Detroit,
Seattle, 70; Yount, Milwaukee, 70; McGriff, Toronto, 69; Pucke
69.
IMPULSADAS.- Fielder, Detroit, 90; **J.Canseco**, Oakland
ronto, 78; McGwire, Oakland, 70; **Bell**, Toronto, 68; **Pal**
Sierra, Texas, 68.
HITS.- Griffey, Seattle, 137; **Palmeiro**, Texas, 132; Bo'
Reed, Boston, 126; Seitzer, Kansas City, 125.
DOBLES.- JoReed, Boston, 37; Boggs, Boston,
31; Brett, Kansas City, 30; Harper, Minnesota, 29.
TRIPLES.- T.Fernandez, Toronto, 14; **Sosa**, Cr
Eisenreich, Kansas City, 6; **Polonia**, California
69.
JONRONES.- Fielder, Detroit, 35; **J.Cansec'**
kland, 28; McGriff, Toronto, 25; Gruber, Toro
BASES ROBADAS.- R.Henderson, Oakl'
derón, Chicago, 29; Pettis, Texas, 27; K'
PITCHEO (9 decisiones).- B.Jones, Cr'
kland, 18.- 4, .818, 3.16; Williamson,
ronto, 14.- 4, .778, 3.10; Clemens, B
PONCHADOS.- Clemens, Boston
tle, 146; B.Witt, Texas, 141; Lan'
128.
RESCATES.- Eckersley, Oakl'
veland, 29; Schooler, Seattle

Rompen Racha de 4 Derrotas
Mets Vencieron a los Filis 8-4

Representación de jugadores hispanos en las grandes ligas

República Dominicana
Puerto Rico
Honduras
Nicaragua — Venezuela
Panamá
México
Cuba

1   1   3

¡Out en Tercera Base!

ATLANTA. Roberto Alomar, de los Padres del San Diego, aguanta la
pelota en la mano, después de poner out en la tercera base, a Ron
Gant, de Los Bravos de Atlanta, en una sensacional jugada. (Foto UPI).

Cardenales Vencieron a Los Cachorros 3-1

CHICAGO, Agosto (UPI) - Ken Hill
y Lee Smith se combinaron en un
partido de cinco incogibles y Willie
McGee remolcó una carrera y

Grandes Ligas. El zurdo de 20 años
de edad abanicó a tres. El puertor-
riqueño José Oquendo caminó
abriendo el tercer capítulo de San

se va...se va...y se fue

Atléticos conquistó la Serie Mundial
COMPLETARON LA LIMPIA
★ Antes de morir, los Gigantes trataron de salir de su enanismo, pero cayeron 9 carreras a 6 ★

SAN FRANCISCO. 28 de octubre (Reuter).— Los Atléticos de Oakland
vencieron hoy 9-6 a los Gigantes de San Francisco y ganaron la Serie
Mundial de beisbol de 1989 en cuatro juegos.
Los Atléticos ganaron los primeros cuatro cotejos de la Serie Mundial
y su victoria de esta noche sobre los Gigantes en el Clandestick Park.
''antes no ganaron un solo encuentro de la serie.

Oakland capturó su primer campeonato mundial desde 1974 y logró
su primera barrida en una Serie Mundial desde que los Rojos de Cincin
nati vencieron a los Yanquis de Nueva York en 1976.
Los Atléticos han ganado cuatro títulos mundiales en Oakland y nuevo
en la historia de la franquicia.
Pareció que los Atléticos alcanzarían una fácil victoria al comandar

una ventaja de 8-0 luego de cinco entradas, pero los Gigantes no se dieron por vencidos y anotaron dos carreras en la sexta y cuatro anotaciones en la séptima, que puso la pizarra 8-6.
Los espectadores en el estadio Clandestick saltaron de sus asientos y
con coros de "Vamos Gigantes" y el encendido de lámparas de mano,

(CONTINUA EN LA PAGINA 11)

★ Dave Henderson, otra vez el héroe: pegó dos jonrones y un doblete e impulsó 4 anotaciones ★

Comprensión

1. ¿Qué aventura se les ocurrió a los niños cacereños?
2. ¿Cómo iban a viajar de Europa a África?
3. ¿Con cuánto dinero salían?
4. ¿Qué buscaban en África?
5. ¿Qué ocurrió en Aldea del Cano?

Prácticas

A. Estudie y traduzca estas construcciones verbales. Los verbos siguen el orden de su uso en los tres textos.

1. **lograr** + infinitivo   *to succeed in* + *-ing* form of verb
   El niño logró salvar a un bebé.

2. **caer al vacío**   *to fall (through space)*
   Cayó al vacío desde el primer piso.

3. **darse cuenta de**   *to realize*
   Se dio cuenta de la verdad de lo que yo le decía.

4. **encontrarse/hallarse**   *to find oneself, be* (**estar**)
   Nos encontramos en una situación grave.

5. **lastimarse** *to injure, hurt oneself*
No se lastimó cuando se cayó al suelo.

6. **bañarse** *to take a bath*
Se estaban bañando cuando subió el toro.

7. **disponerse a** + infinitivo *to get ready to +
verb*
Ya se disponían a salir a la calle.

8. **tratarse de** (3rd-person sing.) *to be a question
(matter) of*
Al principio creyeron que se trataba de una
broma.

9. **levantarse** *to get up*
¿Te levantaste a las seis?

10. **tirar (de)** *to pull, drag*
Tiraron al toro del rabo.

11. **decidirse a** + infinitivo *to be determined, to
decide to* + verb
Nos decidimos a dar el paso definitivo.

12. **pensar** + infinitivo *to plan, intend to* + verb
Al llegar a Cádiz, pensaban tomar un barco
para África.

13. **mantenerse** *to persevere, support (feed) oneself*
Para mantenerse, pensaban ir robando de
pueblo en pueblo.

14. **dirigirse a** *to go toward, head for*
Se dirigieron a una carretera nacional.

B. Note también el uso del pronombre de complemento indirecto con
estos verbos y traduzca.

1. **parecer** *to seem, appear*
Le pareció que no podía salvar al bebé.

2. **tocarle (a uno)** *to be (someone's) turn, to fall to,
be up (to someone to do something)*
A él le tocaba hacer algo para salvarlo.

3. **cubrir** *cover*
Cubriéndole los ojos, empezaron a forcejear
con el toro.

4. **convenir** *to be appropriate, suitable, "right"; to
be to one's advantage*
Se dijeron que les convenía ir primero a Cádiz.

5. **doler** *to hurt, ache*
¿No te duelen las piernas después de tanto
caminar?

6. **preocupar** *to worry*
Comenzó a preocuparnos un viaje tan largo.

Other noun modifiers

Many noun modifiers distribute, select, and measure rather than describe the nouns they modify.

ambos/as   both
Ambos libros son míos.   Both books are mine
los/las demás   the other(s)
Aquí tienes los demás vasos.   Here are the other glasses.
cada (*m, f*)   each, every
Cada vaso vale tres dólares.   Each glass costs three dollars.

Most such words can replace nouns. Note that with **cada, uno** or **una** replaces the noun.

Ambos son míos.	Both are mine.
Aquí tienes los demás.	Here are the others.
Cada uno vale tres dólares.	Each one costs three dollars.

Here are some additional noun modifiers.

1. **cierto/a/os/as**   certain

Cierta amiga mía me lo dijo.	A certain friend of mine told me.
Ciertos libros no valen lo que cuestan.	Certain books are not worth what they cost.

2. **tal/tales**   such, such a

Tal libro no vale veinte dólares.	Such a book is not worth twenty dollars.
Tales libros cuestan demasiado.	Such books cost too much.

3. **cualquier** (*m, f*)   any, any . . . at all

Cualquier periódico sirve.	Any newspaper will do.
Cualquier marca está bien.	Any brand is all right.

cualquiera (*m, f*)   any, any one, anyone (at all)

Cualquiera de estos periódicos es mejor que los que tienen en su país.	Any one of these newspapers is better than the ones they have in their country.
Cualquiera de esas chicas sabe dónde viven.	Any of those girls knows where they live.
Necesito un televisor nuevo, pero no voy a comprarme cualquiera.	I need a new TV, but I'm not going to buy just any kind (at all).

4. **otro/a/os/as**   another, other, others

¿No tomas otro café?	Aren't you having another coffee?
¿No quieres otro?	Don't you want another one?
¿Tienes las otras cestas?	Do you have the other baskets?
Sí, ya tengo las otras.	Yes, I already have the others.

Otro can be used before or after numbers, **tanto,** and **mucho.**

seis otros libros otros seis libros	six other books
tantas otras cosas otras tantas cosas	so many other things
muchas otras razones otras muchas razones	many other reasons

5. **varios/as**   several, various

Nos sirven varios platos.	They serve us several dishes.

6. **suficiente/s**   enough (meaning *just enough*)

No hay suficientes lavatorios en este estadio.	There aren't enough restrooms in this stadium.

7. **bastante/s**   plenty of, quite a few, quite a bit

—¿Tiene bastantes clientes?	Does he have plenty of customers?
—Sí, tiene bastantes.	Yes, he has quite a few.
Nos ponen bastantes exámenes.	They give us quite a few quizzes.
Se juega al béisbol bastante allí.	Baseball is played quite a bit there.

8. **demasiado/a**   too much; **demasiados/as**   too many

Toma demasiada cerveza.	He drinks too much beer.
Hay demasiados pasajeros para este autobús.	There are too many passengers for this bus.

9. **todo/a** + *singular noun*   every (meaning *universally true*)

Todo ciudadano debe votar.	Every citizen should vote.
Hay crimen en todo sitio.	Crime is everywhere.

todos los/todas las + *plural noun*   every, all the . . . (*limited group rather than universal class*)

Invitó a todos los socios del negocio.	He invited every partner in the business.
Hizo footing todos los días.	She went jogging every day.

Some phrases with **todo**:

todo un día a whole day		**todo el día** all day long
todo un mes an entire month		**toda la tarde** all afternoon long
de todos modos, de todas maneras at any rate, anyway		**en todas partes** everywhere

10. **poco/a** little, not much; **pocos/as** few, not many

Los aficionados tienen poco interés por el partido.	The fans have little interest in the game.
Asistieron muy pocos.	Very few (not very many) attended.

11. Other expressions with noun modifiers

Quiere un poco de mantequilla.	She wants a little (some) butter.
No quiere nada de mantequilla.	She doesn't want any butter.
De algún modo va a ganar.	Somehow he's going to win.
De ninguna manera va a ganar.	By no means is he going to win.
Siempre van a alguna parte en julio.	They always go somewhere in July.
Nunca van a ninguna parte en diciembre.	They never go anywhere in December.

26.1 Complete cada oración con la expresión indicada.

1. (*too much*)   Toma _____ café.
2. (*Both*)   _____ son míos.
3. (*Every*)   _____ individuo quiere ser libre.
4. (*enough*)   No hay _____ lavabos en este edificio.
5. (*plenty of*)   Tiene _____ clientes.
6. (*Few*)   _____ van a ir al partido.
7. (*nowhere*)   No van _____ en enero.
8. (*a little bit of*)   Quiere _____ mantequilla.
9. (*the others*)   ¿Quién tiene _____?
10. (*another*)   ¿No quieres contarme _____ historia?
11. (*many other*)   El abuelo conoce _____ historias.
12. (*such a*)   No puede tomar _____ decisión.

26.2 Complete las frases como antes.

1. (*somehow*)   Van a hacerlo _____.
2. (*somewhere*)   Siempre van _____ en febrero.
3. (*everywhere*)   La veo _____.
4. (*At any rate*)   _____ sé su número de teléfono y puedo localizarla.
5. (*seven other*)   En ese curso tienes que leer _____ dramas.
6. (*In no way*)   _____ van a ganar.
7. (*all afternoon long*)   Vimos telenovelas _____.

8. (*little*)   Los americanos tienen _____ interés por el fútbol internacional.

9. (*an entire week*)   Pasaron _____ pintando la casa.

10. (*every day*)   Escribe un poco _____.

11. (*each*)   No pude decidir porque _____ cuadro (*painting*) era hermoso.

12. (*Each one*)   _____ de los cuadros le encantaba.

26.3   Complete la narración traduciendo las palabras suscritas.

_____ niñas ven la televisión como mi hermanita Juli. Ella
   Few

se puede pasar _____ ante el televisor.
               an entire afternoon

_____ programa vale para Juli en cualquier canal.
      Any

_____ tiene _____ que le interesa. Y hay
    Each one   *something*

_____ canales en nuestra ciudad.
   plenty of

   Juli estudia _____. _____ programas le interesan
             little   *Certain*

más que _____. Según ella, _____ vale
      other ones   *any of these programs*

maś que la gramática española. A veces, durante _____ progra-
                            certain

mas, Juli se duerme. Pero, como en _____ ocasiones,
                         so many other

duerme _____ minutos.
     not many

   Juli se queja: «No hay _____ horas en el día.
                    enough

Hay _____ programas y _____ horas para ver-
      too many   *few*

los todos.» Ella dice: « _____ ciudadano debe tener derecho a ver
           Every

_____ programas de _____ canal.» Una tarde vio
   all the   *each*

_____ programa y dijo: « _____ programa no me gusta.
   some   *Such a*

_____ programas enseñan _____.»
   Such   *too much*

   Los sábados Juli ve _____ programas
                 various

_____.
   all day long

_____

      Each of these programs

18:00	LOS PEQUEÑOS MUPPETS
18:30	COMANDOS HEROICOS
19:00	BATMAN
19:30	LOS PICAPIEDRA
20:00	LOS FELINOS COSMICOS
20:30	SUPERBOY
21:00	LOBO DEL AIRE (B)
22:00	EL CAZADOR (C)
23:00	CAGNEY Y LACEY (C)
	(VIERNES)
24:00	NOTIVISA
0:30	PROGRAMA ESPECIAL ATC
1:00	TELEOPORTUNIDADES

ofrece _____ propaganda. Venden juguetes y
quite a bit of

_____ cosas. Le digo a Juli: «No debes prestar
so many other

atención a _____ anuncios.»
such

_____, ahora no ve _____
At any rate   so much

televisión. La señorita Juli es ya mayor. Es una bonita joven con

_____ oportunidades.
plenty of

Pero queda _____ problema. Y _____ problema no es
a certain   such a

fácil de resolver. Juli no sabe leer.

26.4 Lea estos anuncios de teleprogramas y conteste.

1. ¿En qué canal se emite el programa «*Wild Kingdom*»?
2. ¿Quiénes son las estrellas de *El síndrome de China*?
3. ¿Cómo se llama la película sobre el establecimiento de la dictadura franquista en España en 1939?
4. ¿Cuál es un sinónimo de la palabra «actor» que se emplea aquí?
5. ¿Cuál de estos filmes tiene como tema un misterio familiar?
6. ¿Cómo se titula la película que quiere espantar al público?

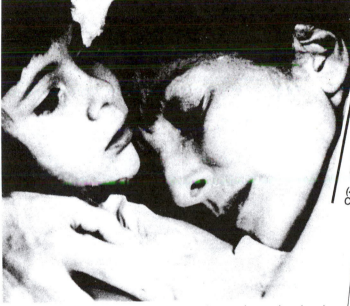

■ *NORMA ALEANDRO en el papel de una madre argentina que tiene el coraje suficiente para buscar la verdad sobre el origen de su hijo adoptado. Esta es una escena de "La Historia Oficial" que presentará Univisión, Canal 41 el miércoles 8 de febrero las ocho de la noche.*

Fin de semana

SABADO 21

9 a.m.
(41) Capitán Centella
(47) Bombay Broadcasting
9:30 a.m.
(41) La Isla del Tesoro
10 a.m.
(41) Tesoro del saber
10:30 a.m.
(41) Capitan Poder
11 a.m.
(41) Reino salvaje
11:30 A.M.
(41) Embajadores de la música
Colombiana, con Arnulfo Briceño

EL CONDE DRÁCULA

Canal Sur   **0.30**

1969 (97 minutos). Director: Jesús Franco. Intérpretes: Christopher Lee, Herbert Lom, Klaus Kinski.

El joven abogado británico Jonathan Winters llega a la mansión del misterioso conde Drácula. Un día descubre una tumba subterránea vacía. Tres hermosas jóvenes vampiras, chupadoras de sangre, aparecen de repente ante el horrorizado Jonathan.

19.30
DOCUMENTAL

Lluvia ácida. La segunda cadena de TVE emite el documental *Lluvia ácida, nubes en azufre*. En este espacio se mostrará la acción destructora de las sustancias desprendidas por la combustión del carbón, la actividad industrial o los automóviles, que alteran gravemente el equilibrio ecológico.

10 MULTICINEMA 1
16:00 COMO ROBAR UN MILLON DE DOLARES
PELICULA COMEDIA CON AUDREY HEPBURN, PETER O'TOOLE Y HUGH GRIFFITH.
18:00 EL SINDROME DE CHINA
PELICULA SUSPENSO Y DRAMA CON JANE FONDA, MICHAEL DOUGLAS Y

RÉQUIEM POR UN CAMPESINO ESPAÑOL

1985 (93 minutos). Director: Francisco Betriu. Intérpretes: Antonio Ferrandis, Fernando Fernan-Gómez, Antonio Banderas.

Versión cinematográfica de la novela de Sender sobre el advenimiento del fascismo.

Unit 27

Present perfect and past perfect indicative

A. PAST PARTICIPLES

Regular past participles are formed by adding -**ado** to the infinitive stem of -**ar** verbs and -**ido** to the stem of -**er** and -**ir** verbs.

	-ado			-ido	
(hablar)	hablado	spoken	(comer)	comido	eaten
(mejorar)	mejorado	improved	(entender)	entendido	understood
(invitar)	invitado	invited	(vivir)	vivido	lived

The past participle of -**er** verbs whose stem ends in a vowel has a written accent: (**traer**) **traído** *brought*, (**caer**) **caído** *fallen*, (**leer**) **leído** *read*.

Oír, **reír**, **sonreír** also take written accents: **oído** *heard*, **reído** *laughed*, **sonreído** *smiled*.

Verbs in -**uir** require no accent mark since / ui / is a diphthong (two vowels pronounced in the same syllable): **construido** *built*, **concluido** *concluded*.

A few verbs have irregular past participles.

(abrir)	abierto	opened	(poner)	puesto	put, set
(cubrir)	cubierto	covered	(resolver)	resuelto	resolved
(decir)	dicho	said	(romper)	roto	broken, torn
(escribir)	escrito	written	(satisfacer)	satisfecho	satisfied
(hacer)	hecho	done, made	(ver)	visto	seen
(morir)	muerto	died	(volver)	vuelto	returned

Verbs based on those above have similarly irregular past participles.

(descubrir)	**descubierto**	discovered
(describir)	**descrito**	described
(deshacer)	**deshecho**	undone, taken apart
(suponer)	**supuesto**	supposed
(devolver)	**devuelto**	returned

Freír *to fry* has two past participles: **freído** / **frito** *fried*. Either may be used after **haber** in perfect tenses (discussed below), but only **frito** is used as an adjective: **papas fritas** *French fries* (literally, *fried potatoes*).

B. USES OF THE PAST PARTICIPLE

1. The auxiliary verb **haber** *to have* is used with a past participle to form six compound tenses; the tense of **haber** used indicates which compound tense. The past participle in **-o** in these cases in invariable. The equivalent in English is the verb *to have* + a past participle.

PRESENT PERFECT	**he hablado**
PAST PERFECT	**había hablado**
FUTURE PERFECT	**habré hablado**
CONDITIONAL PERFECT	**habría hablado**
PRESENT PERFECT SUBJUNCTIVE	**haya hablado**
PAST PERFECT SUBJUNCTIVE	**hubiera hablado**

Only the first two compound tenses above are taken up in this unit.

2. Some past participles have become ordinary nouns.

aficionado fan	**entrada** entrance	**pedido** order
desconocido stranger	**hecho** fact	**puesto** job
despedida farewell	**helado** ice cream	**recién llegado** newcomer
dicho saying	**invitado** guest	**salida** departure, exit
empleado employee	**pecado** sin	**vuelta** change (*money*)

3. Past participles can also function as nouns when a modified noun is omitted.

los carros usados → **los usados** the used ones
las flores cortadas → **las cortadas** the cut ones
el piso amueblado → **el amueblado** the furnished one

4. Past participles are used with **ser** for the passive voice, and with **estar** to indicate resultant condition. These uses are treated in Unit 28.

C. PRESENT PERFECT INDICATIVE

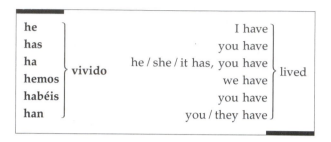

he		I have	
has		you have	
ha	vivido	he / she / it has, you have	lived
hemos		we have	
habéis		you have	
han		you / they have	

The present perfect is formed with the present tense of **haber** + an invariable past participle ending in **-o**. Its use corresponds generally to the same tense in English, i.e., it describes a past event that continues to the present: **Hemos vivido aquí tres años** *We've lived here three years.* Pronoun objects precede the form of **haber**: **No la han visto desde ayer** *They haven't seen her since yesterday.*

D. PAST PERFECT INDICATIVE

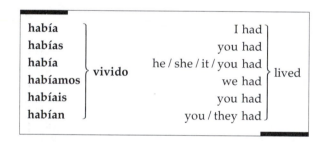

había		I had	
habías		you had	
había	vivido	he / she / it / you had	lived
habíamos		we had	
habíais		you had	
habían		you / they had	

The past perfect is formed with the imperfect tense of **haber** + a past participle. The use of this tense corresponds to its use in English. It describes a past event prior to another point or event in the past: **No la habían visto antes de esta mañana** *They hadn't seen her before this morning.*

27.1 Conteste según el modelo, cambiando el verbo al presente perfecto.

¿Lavó Ud. la ropa? → **No, todavía no la he lavado.**

1. ¿Limpió Ud. el suelo?
2. ¿Pagaron Uds. la cuenta?
3. ¿Mandaron Uds. las fotos?
4. ¿Sirvió Ud. la ensalada?
5. ¿Aprendieron Uds. la lección?
6. ¿Pusiste las flores en agua?
7. ¿Abrió Ud. las ventanas?
8. ¿Viste a tu hermano?

27.2 Conteste según el modelo, expresando el verbo en pluscuamperfecto.

¿No vino Emilio? → **No, a las dos todavía no había venido.**

1. ¿No salió Manuel?
2. ¿No llamó Beatriz?
3. ¿No terminó Pablo?
4. ¿No volvió Rafael?
5. ¿No llegó Pedro?
6. ¿No acabó Raquel?

FUTBOL

COBRAS vs. SANTOS.
Desde Ciudad Juárez, Chihuahua.
En XEW TV, El Canal de las Estrellas.
(SIMULTANEO POR XEW).
12 DEL DIA

FUTBOL AMERICANO PROFESIONAL

"BENGALIES" de CINCINNATI vs.
"CAFES" de CLEVELAND,
en XHGC. que es MAS.
(SIMULTANEO POR XEX)
12 DEL DIA

ROUND CERO

En XEW TV, El Canal de las Estrellas.
2 DE LA TARDE

FUTBOL ESPAÑOL

CELTA vs. REAL MADRID.
Desde el Estadio "Balaidós",
de Vigo, España.
En XEW TV, El Canal de las Estrellas.
(SIMULTANEO POR XEQ)
DOS Y MEDIA DE LA TARDE

TENIS

TORNEO DE MAESTROS.
En XHGC. que es MAS.
Desde Estados Unidos.
3 DE LA TARDE

RITMO VITAL

En XEQ TV, El Canal Cultural de Televisa,
haga ejercicio y póngase en forma
con el dinamismo de los "Aerobics"
8 DE LA MAÑANA

FUTBOL ITALIANO

JUVENTUS vs. SAMPDORIA.
En XHGC. Más acción, desde Italia.
(SIMULTANEO POR XEX)
9 DE LA MAÑANA

ACCION

El programa más completo
con el panorama deportivo, nacional
e internacional.
En XEW TV, El Canal de las Estrellas.
CUATRO Y MEDIA
DE LA TARDE

RESUMEN DE TOROS

En XHTV, Tu Propio Espacio.

ONCE Y MEDIA
DE LA NOCHE

NOTICIERO DEPORTIVO

En XEW TV, El Canal dé las Estrellas.
1 DE LA MAÑANA

MAÑANA LUNES 4:

FUTBOL AMERICANO PROFESIONAL

"BILLS" de BUFALO vs.
"HALCONES MARINOS" de SEATTLE.
En XHTV, Tu Propio Espacio.
(SIMULTANEO POR XEX)
9 DE LA NOCHE

RESUMEN DE BEISBOL DE LAS GRANDES LIGAS

En LA SERIE MUNDIAL, los mejores
jugadas y los momentos de más brillo,
en XHTV, Tu Propio Espacio.
12:15 DE LA NOCHE.

MENTE SANA

Noticias y comentarios
sobre lo que acontece en el deporte
amateur, en XEQ TV, El Canal Cultural
de Televisa.
9 DE LA MAÑANA

27.3 Complete las oraciones con las palabras indicadas.

1. (*guest*) Todavía no había llegado ningún _____ .

2. (*employees*) Los _____ han declarado una huelga general.

3. (*change*) La cajera le dio la _____ .

4. (*saying*) Hay un _____ : «En lunes, ni las gallinas ponen.»

5. (*ice cream*) Aquí tienen _____ variados.

6. (*newcomers*) Extienden una calurosa bienvenida a todos los _____ .

7. (*order*) El negocio no ha recibido ni un solo _____ este mes.

8. (*exit*) ¿Dónde está la _____ ?

9. (*facts*) No nos ha explicado los _____ importantes del asunto.

10. (*used ones*) En este sitio tienen los carros nuevos y ahí están los _____ .

11. (*fans*) El estadio se agitó con la tremenda bronca que soltaron los _____ .

12. (*strangers*) El recién llegado se encontró entre _____ .

Diversión y Práctica 7

Veinte preguntas

Un miembro de la clase piensa en una persona, un lugar, un animal o un objeto. Para empezar, declara sólo **dos cosas**—si es **persona, lugar, animal** u **objeto**, y si es **real** o **imaginario**. Por ejemplo: «Soy hombre y soy imaginario» o «Soy un lugar que existe en el mundo» o «Soy una cosa de la televisión o la literatura». Cada pregunta tiene que contestarse con «Sí» o «No». Otro ejemplo:

   —**Soy una cosa y existo en el mundo.**

   1. —¿Estás en el Hemisferio Occidental?   —No. (*En este caso, es tonto preguntar si la cosa está en el Hemisferio Oriental, porque ahora lo sabes.*)

   2. —¿Estás en Europa?   —No.

   3. —¿Estás en África?   —Sí.

   4. —¿Eres grande?   —Sí.

   5. —¿Eres útil?   —No.

   6. —¿La gente viene a verte?   —Sí.

   7. —¿Los hombres te construyeron?   —Sí.

   8. —¿En tiempos recientes?   —No.

   9. —¿Una pirámide?   —No.

   10. —¿La Esfinge?   —¡¡¡Sí!!! ¡Qué listo eres!

Ahora sigan Uds. con el juego.

Ser and estar + past participles

 **A. PASSIVE VOICE**

La policía identificó a las víctimas. ↓ **Las víctimas fueron identificadas por la policía.**	The police identified the victims. ↓ The victims were identified by the police.
Un físico inventó la bomba. ↓ **La bomba fue inventada por un físico.**	A physicist invented the bomb. ↓ The bomb was invented by a physicist.
Todos lo conocían. ↓ **Era conocido de todos.**	Everyone knew him. ↓ He was known by everyone.

1. The second Spanish sentence of each pair above is an example of the passive voice. A passive sentence is one in which the subject does not act but is acted upon, i.e., the action of the verb falls on the subject (**víctimas**, **bomba**, "**él**").

2. Active sentences, like the first Spanish sentence of each pair above, are rendered passive by making the direct object of the active sentence the subject of the passive sentence.

3. Spanish forms passive sentences with **ser** + a past participle. The participle (**identificadas**, **inventada**, **conocido**) agrees with the subject of the passive sentence. The agent (**la policía**, **un físico**, **todos**) is preceded by the preposition **por**, or by either **por** or **de** in the case of a few verbs such as **admirar**, **conocer**, and **odiar** *to hate*.

4. Use of the passive construction with **ser** is less common in Spanish than the same construction with *to be* in English. Also, certain common English passive constructions become ungrammatical in Spanish if rendered literally as passives. (See section D below.)

5. The **ser** passive is used in Spanish mainly when the agent or doer of the verb's action is expressed: **El libro fue devuelto por el alumno** *The book was returned by the student*.

6. Even here, however, the active voice is preferred to the passive in Spanish: **El alumno devolvió el libro** *The student returned the book.*

B. *SER* PASSIVES WITH INANIMATE SUBJECTS

a) **El motor fue reparado por el mecánico.**	The engine was repaired by the mechanic.
b) **El mecánico reparó el motor.**	The mechanic repaired the engine.
c) **El motor fue reparado.**	The engine was repaired.
d) **Se reparó el motor.**	The engine was repaired.
e) **Repararon el motor.**	They repaired the engine.

1. The first sentence (*a*) is an example of a **ser** passive construction in Spanish. The subject (**motor**) is inanimate, and the agent (**mecánico**) is expressed. This type of passive is seen frequently in journalistic Spanish. In everyday conversation, however, it is more common and preferable to use the active voice (*b*) to say the same thing.

2. The **ser** passive with no agent, illustrated in (*c*), is possible but not as commonly used as the passive reflexive with **se** (*d*), or an active sentence with a third-person plural verb (*e*).

C. *SER* PASSIVES WITH HUMAN SUBJECTS

a) **Los testigos fueron llamados por el juez.**	The witnesses were called by the judge.
b) **El juez llamó a los testigos.**	The judge called the witnesses.
c) **Los testigos fueron llamados.**	The witnesses were called.
d) **Se llamó a los testigos.**	The witnesses were called.
e) **Llamaron a los testigos.**	They called the witnesses.

1. Sentence (*a*) is an example of a **ser** passive construction in Spanish. The subject (**testigos**) is human, and the agent (**el juez**) is expressed. This type of passive is often encountered in newspapers and magazines. In colloquial Spanish, however, it is more common and preferable to use an active sentence (*b*) to say the same thing.

2. The **ser** passive with no agent, illustrated in (*c*), may be used in written Spanish when the subject of a passive sentence (**los testigos**) is being emphasized. In everyday usage, however, it is regularly replaced either by a construction with **se** and personal **a** to mark the human object (**los testigos**), as in (*d*), or by an active sentence with a third-person plural verb, as in (*e*).

D. ENGLISH PASSIVES NOT POSSIBLE AS SPANISH PASSIVES

1.	The girls were seen downtown. They were seen taking a taxi.	**Vieron a las jóvenes en el centro.** **Les vieron tomar un taxi.**
	The man was heard shouting in a loud voice. He was heard speaking to an officer.	**Oyeron al hombre gritar en voz alta.** **Lo oyeron hablar con un agente.**

Verbs of perception like **ver** and **oír** cannot be used in passive constructions in Spanish, as they often are in English. In Spanish an active sentence must be used, as in the examples above.

A more formal **se** construction is also possible here, but it would be used less frequently in everyday language: **Se vio a las jóvenes / Se las (les) vio, Se oyó al hombre / Se le oyó.**

2.	I was given all the money.	**Me dieron todo el dinero.** ↓ **Se me dio todo el dinero.**
	They were told the truth.	**Les dijeron la verdad.** ↓ **Se les dijo la verdad.**
	You were shown the pictures.	**Le enseñaron las fotos.** ↓ **Se le enseñaron las fotos.**

The English examples above all have an indirect object as the subject of passive sentences: *They gave (to) me = I was given*, etc. In Spanish, active verbs must be used to express this: **Me dieron todo el dinero.** Constructions with indefinite **se** are also possible but less common: **Se me dio todo el dinero.**

3.	All the money was given to me by the clerk.	**La empleada me dio todo el dinero.** ↓ **El dinero me lo dio todo la empleada.**
	The truth was told to them by their mother.	**Su madre les dijo la verdad.** ↓ **La verdad se la dijo su madre.**
	The pictures were shown to you by his girlfriend.	**Su novia le enseñó las fotos.** ↓ **Las fotos se las enseñó su novia.**

The English examples above have a direct object as the subject of a passive sentence with the agent expressed: *The truth was told to them by their mother = Their mother told them the truth.* In Spanish an active sentence must be used in such cases: **Su madre les dijo la verdad.** In the examples above, English can emphasize the passive subject by placing it first: *The pictures were shown to you.* . . . In Spanish the same emphasis is supplied by placing the direct object first. The direct-object noun (**fotos**) is then necessarily repeated with a pronoun (**las**): **Las fotos se las enseñó** . . . .

E. *ESTAR* + PAST PARTICIPLE

1.

| El banco fue cerrado. | The bank was closed. |
| El banco estaba cerrado. | |

1. **Ser** + past participle is used for the passive voice, which expresses an action: **El banco fue cerrado** *The bank was closed* (by an employee who locked the door at one o'clock sharp).

Estar + past participle expresses the state of affairs or condition of things resulting from the action which took place: **El banco estaba cerrado** *The bank was closed* (when we got there one minute after one).

Since the English equivalents both have *to be* + past participle, the choice of either **ser** or **estar** must be made from context.

| The errors were marked in red. | **Las faltas fueron marcadas en rojo.**
(action emphasized: She *marked* them in red.) |
| | **Las faltas estaban marcadas en rojo.**
(condition emphasized: When I looked at the paper, I saw errors *marked in red*.) |

2. **Estar** is used with the past participle of a verb of motion to indicate position or posture.

Se inclinó.	She leaned over.
Está inclinada.	She's leaning over.
Se sentaron.	They sat down.
Están sentados.	They are sitting (down).
Se acostó.	He lay down.
Está acostado.	He's lying down.
Se paró.	She stood up.
Está parada.	She's standing up.
Se arrodillaron.	They knelt down.
Están arrodillados.	They are kneeling.

28.1 Cambie las frases a la voz pasiva.

1. Un físico inventó la bomba. (La bomba fue inventada...)
2. Todos los amaban. (Use **de**.)
3. Mi amigo identificó a la víctima.
4. El estudiante devolvió los libros.
5. El mecánico reparó los dos motores.
6. El juez llamó al testigo.
7. El perro comió la chuleta.
8. La niña rompió los juguetes.

28.2 Cambie las frases a la voz activa en pretérito. Por ejemplo:

Los paquetes fueron envueltos por nuestra tía. → **Nuestra tía envolvió los paquetes.**

1. El regalo fue abierto por el niño.
2. La carta fue enviada por un desconocido.
3. El dictador fue odiado por el pueblo hasta su muerte.
4. Las casas fueron construidas por ese arquitecto.
5. El paisaje fue descrito por un viajero.
6. El motor fue desmontado por el mecánico.

28.3 Convierta en construcciones con **se** en pretérito.

1. El motor fue desmontado en quince minutos. (Se desmontó...)
2. Los testigos fueron llamados ante el tribunal.
3. El regalo fue abierto antes de la Navidad.
4. Los trabajos fueron hechos en la computadora.
5. La boda fue celebrada en la capilla.
6. El paquete fue devuelto sin abrir.
7. Los vecinos fueron invitados a la recepción.
8. El dictador fue asesinado en la plaza.
9. El portero fue despedido por negligencia.
10. Los criminales fueron detenidos en el parque.

28.4 Cambie al español.

1. I sat down, and she leaned over to kiss (**besar**) me.
2. Then I was sitting and she was leaning over.
3. I lay down and I went to sleep.
4. My mother said: "He's lying down."
5. They knelt down in the street.
6. When the police arrived, they were still (**aún**) kneeling.

28.5 Al español.

1. I explained it all to them.
2. I was given the money by a stranger.
3. The police thought that the money was given to me by an employee.
4. The lawyer was shown my girlfriend's letter.
5. He was not told the truth.
6. A stranger was seen at the same time.
7. He was heard shouting in a loud voice.
8. In any case, the money was returned to the bank.

28.6 En estos titulares se ve más de un tipo de construcción gramatical que se emplea con sentido pasivo. Estudie las distintas construcciones y explique en ciertos casos la concordancia gramatical que se observa.

Isabela es investigada por el comisario de policía

Nueve récords fueron quebrados

No se tolerará a vendedores ambulantes en el centro de Acapulco, advierten autoridades

Fue asesinado un dirigente petrolero

¿Qué se vende?

Con manifestaciones antigubernamentales fue celebrada la independencia de Checoslovaquia

No se despedirá a mineros ni se venderá el contrato: Gómez Sada

Han sido cesados más de 1,000 funcionarios corruptos

Vamos a escribir... 4

Verbos reflexivos y otras cosas

En una hoja aparte o en su cuaderno siga narrando la historia de esta aventura de Guillermo Cornejo. En la narración de aquí se emplea una buena parte de los verbos reflexivos y otras muchas construcciones recién presentadas. En este segundo episodio Cornejo y la mujer se hablan de **tú**, es decir, se tutean, usando las formas familiares de los pronombres y los verbos (**tú, te, ti, debes,** etc.).

LA AVENTURA PORTUGUESA DE GUILLERMO CORNEJO (*episodio 2*)

Guillermo Cornejo and Sonia were sitting on a Portuguese beach. The sea was high. Great waves were breaking on the rocky shoreline. Cornejo was not able to calm down.

He was not offended by what Sonia had said. He said to himself: "What have I done? I have never made a mistake before, but this time . . . I don't know." During several moments, not **(ni)** one word was said. They looked at each other.

GUILLERMO: "I have fallen in love with you, Sonia."

SONIA: "I am not called 'Sonia'. My name is Natasha. I have come from Transylvania."

GUILLERMO: "Natasha? From Pennsylvania?"

SONIA: "No, Transylvania, from the Carpathian mountains."

Suddenly Natasha was scared.

NATASHA: "It's preferable that I say goodbye to you now. I have suffered too much. I have become tired of this life. Tonight some stranger is going to come up to my room."

GUILLERMO: "Me?"

NATASHA: "No, the count. I refuse to say his name. I never say it. It begins with a D. He has found out where I am. They are going to bring down my body. You must forget me. It is a pity that you won't see me again."

•   •   •

Guillermo was moved by her words. Then he got angry. He had thought about writing a novel called *The Woman Who Wore Black*. And now this. . . . He got close to Natasha.

GUILLERMO: "I have decided to come up to your room. Somehow I feel very strong tonight."

NATASHA: "You have gone mad. You do not know the count. But it is possible for you to protect yourself. It is best for you to eat a lot of garlic."

GUILLERMO: "I don't like garlic. I get sick from too much garlic. Is there no other way?"

NATASHA: "None. You must remember the garlic. Thirty cloves are enough. Raw."

Guillermo was thinking: "It is doubtful that I'll kiss her tonight. They must eat a lot of garlic in Transylvania."

GUILLERMO: "When can we get married?"

NATASHA: "There is a saying: 'Better late than never.' " (**Más vale tarde que nunca.**)

GUILLERMO: "I have heard it before. I am not sure it is true."

•   •   •

They got up. Cornejo had calmed down. They left. They stopped at the door of the pension.

GUILLERMO: "Do you want something to drink?"

NATASHA: "No, I feel very sad. I am rich. I travel everywhere, but I am sad. You must come up to my room at midnight. The moon is full, but no one is going to see you."

Guillermo thought: "Someone is going to smell me." He bought himself a whole string of garlic. He went up to his room. He lay down. He went to sleep. He slept until eleven-thirty. Then he woke up trembling: "God help me!"

(continuará)

sea **el mar**	to be moved by **emocionarse con**
wave **la ola**	to get angry **enojarse**
to break **romper(se)**	to think about **pensar en**
shoreline **la orilla**	to wear black **vestir de negro**
rocky **rocoso/a**	to get close **acercarse**
to calm down **calmarse**	to decide to **decidirse a**
to be offended by **sentirse ofendido por**	to feel + *adj* **sentirse +** *adj*
to make a mistake **equivocarse**	to go mad **volverse loco/a**
to fall in love with **enamorarse de**	to protect oneself **protegerse**
to be called (named) **llamarse**	garlic **el ajo**
Transylvania **Transilvania**	to get sick **enfermarse**
Pennsylvania **Pensilvania**	to remember **acordarse (de)**
Carpathian mountains **los montes Cárpatos**	clove (of garlic) **el diente**
to be scared **asustarse**	raw **crudo/a**
to say goodbye to **despedirse de**	doubtful **dudoso/a**
to become tired **cansarse**	to get married **casarse**
room **la habitación**	to leave **marcharse**
count **el conde**	to stop **parar(se)**
to refuse to **negarse a**	to smell **oler**
to find out **enterarse (de)**	string (*of garlic*) **la ristra**
body (corpse) **el cadáver**	trembling **temblando**
to forget **olvidarse (de)**	God help me! **¡Dios me ayude!**

Cuestionario

1. ¿Dónde comienza este episodio?

2. ¿De dónde ha venido Sonia/Natasha?

3. ¿Por qué quiere despedirse de Cornejo?

4. ¿Por qué tiene tanto miedo?

5. ¿Cómo se llama el conde?

6. ¿Qué se decide a hacer Cornejo?

7. ¿Cómo es posible protegerse del conde?

8. ¿Cómo se siente Natasha?

9. ¿Por qué no quiere nada de beber?

10. ¿Hasta qué hora durmió Cornejo?

Unit 29

Uses of the definite article

A. USES

The definite article (**el** / **la** / **los** / **las**) is used in Spanish in a number of cases in which it is not used in English.

1. Before nouns used in a generic or general sense.

La gasolina es tan cara.	Gas is so expensive
Les gusta el cine.	They like movies.
El fútbol es muy popular allí.	Soccer is very popular there.

2. Before people's titles (**señor**, **doctora**, **profesora**, etc., but not **don**, **doña**) when the person is not directly addressed.

Deseo hablar con la doctora Molina.	I want to speak to Dr. Molina.
Buenos días, doctora Molina.	Good morning, Dr. Molina.
¿Dónde está el profesor Arévalo?	Where is Professor Arévalo?
Hasta luego, profesor Arévalo.	So long, Professor Arévalo.

3. Before a specified amount or quantity that indicates a rate.

Se venden a noventa centavos la docena.	They sell for ninety cents a dozen.
Ese biquini cuesta diez dólares el centímetro cuadrado.	That bikini costs ten dollars a square centimeter.
Allí les pagan cuatro dólares la hora.	They pay them four dollars an hour there.

4. Before names of languages.

El japonés no es fácil.	Japanese is not easy.
Tampoco es fácil el chino.	Chinese is not easy either.

But after the prepositions **de** and **en** and verbs of speaking, learning, reading, writing, and the like, the article is usually omitted unless the verb or language is modified.

Estudia ruso ahora pero ya habla polaco.	He is studying Russian now, but he already speaks Polish.

No comprende (el) sueco.	She doesn't understand Swedish.
Las señales están escritas en francés.	The signs are written in French.
Tienen que preparar una lección de latín.	They have to prepare a Latin lesson.
Habla perfectamente el catalán.	He speaks Catalan perfectly.
No entiende nada del griego que se habla ahora en Grecia aunque había estudiado el griego antiguo.	He doesn't understand a bit of the Greek spoken today in Greece even though he had studied ancient Greek.

5. With a day of the week, the article is the equivalent of *on* or *every* (in the plural).

Viene el sábado.	She's coming on Saturday.
Salen los sábados.	They go out every Saturday.
Pero hoy no es sábado.	But today isn't Saturday.

6. With clothing, personal belongings, parts of the body.

Se le perdió el llavero.	He lost his key case.
Se quitaron los guantes.	They took off their gloves.
Tiene las manos sucias.	His hands are dirty.
Levantó los brazos.	She raised her arms.
Les cortó el pelo.	She cut their hair.
Se me quedó el paraguas.	I forgot my umbrella.

To avoid ambiguity a possessive is used: **Dejó tu paraguas en el coche** *He left your umbrella in the car.*

7. With expressions of time modified by **próximo** *next* (for future), **siguiente** *following* (for past), **pasado** *last*, and similar adjectives.

la semana pasada	last week
la semana próxima	next week
el año pasado	last year
el año que viene	next year
el mes entrante	next (the coming) month
al día siguiente	on the following day

B. *LA → EL*

El, not **la**, is used immediately before singular feminine nouns beginning with a stressed **a** for phonetic reasons: **el agua** *the water*, **el águila** *the eagle*, **el alma** *the soul*, **el aula** *the classroom*. However, the gender of the noun does not change.

El agua está contaminada.	The water is polluted.
Las aguas internacionales comienzan más o menos aquí.	The international waters begin more or less here.
El alma humana, ¿quién la puede explicar?	The human soul, who can explain it?
El drama trata de las almas perdidas.	The drama deals with lost souls.

29.1 Complete la frase con un artículo definido, si el sentido lo exige (*requires*).

1. Aquí tienes _____ agua.
2. Mañana es _____ jueves.
3. Voy a Tegucigalpa _____ martes.
4. _____ pescado es caro hoy.
5. Cuesta más que _____ carne.
6. _____ águila devoró tres salmones.
7. Ana se puso _____ zapatillas.
8. _____ paz es lo que desean.
9. Les gusta _____ helado.
10. Hay partidos de fútbol casi todos _____ días.
11. Está escrito en _____ hebreo.
12. Catalina todavía tiene _____ pelo largo.
13. Doctor, me duele _____ garganta.
14. _____ señora de Arjona lo espera en este momento.
15. Habla bastante bien _____ catalán.
16. Les pagan seis dólares _____ hora.

29.2 Igual que antes.

1. A Cornejo le gustan _____ playas portuguesas.
2. En Colombia sí se entiende lo que es _____ café.
3. _____ doctora Ortiz está en el consultorio.
4. _____ doña Alicia enseña _____ español como lengua extranjera.
5. _____ domingos estudiamos todo _____ día.
6. _____ chino no es tan difícil como el coreano.
7. Las naranjas se venden a cien pesetas _____ docena.
8. La tela cuesta cuarenta pesos _____ metro cuadrado.
9. Prefiere sobre todo _____ vinos de la ribera del Duero.
10. _____ presidente y _____ señora Gutiérrez veranearon en Canarias.
11. Los bogotanos saben cómo debe ser _____ café.
12. Tiene _____ manos grasientas porque ha estado trabajando en el motor del carro.

Future and conditional tenses

A. FUTURE TENSE

entrar	comprender	recibir
entrar é	comprender é	recibir é
entrar ás	comprender ás	recibir ás
entrar á	comprender á	recibir á
entrar emos	comprender emos	recibir emos
entrar éis	comprender éis	recibir éis
entrar án	comprender án	recibir án

The future tense is formed with the infinitive + endings that are the same for every verb. The twelve exceptions to this pattern are given below.

Voice stress is on the final syllable in every form except the first-person plural, also the only form that does not have a written accent.

The English equivalent of this tense is *will* or *'ll* + verb.

Tú lo comprenderás.	You'll understand it.
Entraremos si nos dejan.	We'll go in if they let us.

B. CONDITIONAL TENSE

JUAR, JUAR,
EL DUO DINAMICO VOLARA
HASTA MI GUARIDA,
DONDE EL SEÑUELO
ESTA LISTO... ES EL FIN
DE BATMAN Y EL JOVEN
MARAVILLA.

entrar	comprender	recibir
entrar ía	comprender ía	recibir ía
entrar ías	comprender ías	recibir ías
entrar ía	comprender ía	recibir ía
entrar íamos	comprender íamos	recibir íamos
entrar íais	comprender íais	recibir íais
entrar ían	comprender ían	recibir ían

The conditional tense is formed with the infinitive + endings that are the same for every verb. The twelve verbs with irregular stems in the future have those same shortened stems in the conditional and are presented below.

Voice stress falls on the first vowel of the ending throughout the conditional. This **í** takes a written accent in every person to show that it is a separate syllable rather than part of a diphthong.

The English equivalent of the conditional is *would* or *'d* + verb.

Tú no lo comprenderías.	You wouldn't understand it.
Les gustaría recibirlo pronto.	They would like to receive it soon.

C. VERBS WITH IRREGULAR FUTURE AND CONDITIONAL STEMS

Twelve verbs have shortened stems in the future and conditional. The stem in each case is the same for both tenses and only the stems are irregular. The personal endings are identical to those presented above.

	Infinitive	Stem	Future Endings	Conditional Endings
-r- stems	caber	cabr-		
	haber	habr-		
	poder	podr-		
	querer	querr-		
	saber	sabr-	-é	-ía
			-ás	-ías
-dr- stems	poner	pondr-	-á	-ía
	salir	saldr-	-emos	-íamos
	tener	tendr-	-éis	-íais
	valer	valdr-	-án	-ían
	venir	vendr-		
two shortened stems	decir	dir-		
	hacer	har-		

The future and conditional of **hay** are **habrá** *there will be* and **habría** *there would be*.

No habrá suficientes sillas.	There won't be enough chairs.
Hay demasiados alumnos. No cabrán en esta aula.	There are too many students. They won't fit in this classroom.
Con veinte sillas más, habría bastantes.	With twenty more chairs, there would be plenty.
Todo el mundo podrá sentarse.	Everybody will be able to sit down.
El profesor no querrá dar su conferencia aquí.	The professor will not want to give his talk here.
No tendría espacio ni para respirar.	He wouldn't even have room to breathe.

Mis compañeros no sabrán qué hacer.	My friends won't know what to do.
¿Qué haremos? ¿Qué dirán los invitados?	What will we do? What will the guests say?

Verbs derived from those above are similarly irregular: **contener—contendré**, **contendrás**, etc.; **contendría**, **contendrías**, etc.

D. USES OF THE FUTURE AND CONDITIONAL

Dice que lo hará.	She says that she will do it.
Dijo que lo haría.	She said that she would do it.

The English equivalents of these tenses are regularly *will* or *'ll* + verb for the future, and *would* or *'d* + verb for the conditional. Other uses and substitutions for these tenses are the following:

1. **Ir a** + infinitive is commonly used in everyday spoken Spanish instead of the future tense:

Voy a verlo mañana.	I'll see him tomorrow. (I'm going to see him tomorrow.)

2. The present tense is used in Spanish for predicting events, or the intent to do something, in the near future. English uses a progressive construction or *will* + verb.

Salimos mañana.	We are leaving tomorrow. We'll leave tomorrow.
Vuelven esta noche.	They are coming back tonight. They will come back tonight.

3. **Querer**, not the future, is the equivalent of English *will* in questions when *will* means *to be willing*, as in making requests.

¿Nos quiere acompañar?	Will you come with us?
¿Quiere ayudarlos?	Will he help them?
¡No, no quiero hacerlo!	No, I won't do it!

4. In questions that ask for advice or instructions, the present tense, not the future, is used in Spanish where the English equivalent is *shall* or *should* + verb.

¿Abro la ventana?	Shall I open the window?
¿Lo hago ahora o después?	Should I do it now or later?

5. When *would* means *used to* and refers to repeated or habitual actions in the past, the imperfect tense, not the conditional, is used in Spanish.

Siempre acompañaba a la abuela a misa.	He would always go to Mass with his grandmother.
Los domingos siempre comíamos arroz con pollo y flan de postre.	On Sundays we would always have rice and chicken, with custard for dessert.

6. The future tense is also used in Spanish to express conjecture or probability about present and future events. English uses *must* and a variety of expressions.

Serán las dos ya.	It must be two o'clock already. / It's probably two o'clock now.
¿Cuándo vendrá el doctor?	When do you suppose the doctor is coming?
¿Dónde estará ahora?	Where can he be now? / I wonder where he is now?
¿Quién será?	Who could it be? / Who do you suppose it is?

The conditional is also used for conjecture about past events.

¿Qué hora sería cuando llegó?	What time do you suppose it was when he arrived?
¿Y dónde estaría antes?	And where could he have been before? / And I wonder where he was before?
Serían las cuatro cuando lo vi.	It must have been four when I saw him.

The addition of adverbs like **quizás** *perhaps*, **a lo mejor** *maybe, most likely*, and **probablemente** *probably* is possible in the sentences above. They intensify the idea of probability and conjecture.

30.1 Cambie la frase al futuro. Luego repita la frase usando cada infinitivo en la misma forma del futuro.

1. Saben algo.   (tener / valer / decir / hacer / comprar / ver) (Sabrán algo. / Tendrán algo . . .)
2. No me dice nada.   (mandar / explicar / dar / entregar / ofrecer)
3. Entramos pronto.   (salir / venir / marcharse / acostarse / subir)
4. Yo llego a las dos.   (ir / salir / despertarse / venir / vestirse)

30.2 Repita el **30.1** cambiando esta vez al condicional.

    1. Saben algo. (Sabrían algo...)

30.3 Cambie cada oración, (1) al futuro, y (2) a una construcción con **ir a**.

    ¿Dónde está el libro? → **¿Dónde estará el libro?, ¿Dónde va a estar el libro?**

    1. Me llevan a la estación.
    2. El autobús sale a las tres.
    3. Es mi amigo.
    4. Tengo problemas.

    5. Lo ponemos ahí.
    6. Sales mañana.
    7. No me dejas nada.
    8. Arreglan el motor.

30.4 Conteste usando el futuro.

    ¿Vamos a verte hoy? → **No, pero Uds. me verán mañana.**

    1. ¿Ellos van a hacerlo hoy?
    2. ¿Tú vas a salir hoy?
    3. ¿Usted se pone el nuevo suéter hoy?
    4. ¿Vas a comprarlo hoy?

    5. ¿Usted va a tener tiempo hoy?
    6. ¿Lorenzo va a venir hoy?
    7. ¿Esto vale mucho hoy?
    8. ¿Hay tiempo para hacerlo hoy?

30.5 Escriba en castellano.

    1. My friend Ramiro says that he will help me.
    2. But last week he said that he wouldn't help me.
    3. I said: "Ramiro, will you help me?"
    4. Nobody wants to help me.
    5. Ramiro says: "I am leaving today, but I am coming back early on Friday."
    6. Today is Friday. He has not arrived. Where do you suppose he is?
    7. It's probably six o'clock now.
    8. What would you do?
    9. I will not get angry (**enojarse**) with him.
   10. I wonder who knows (who can "possibly" know). (Don't translate "possibly.")

Diversión y Práctica 8

Señales, avisos y letreros

Explica en español las señales, los avisos y los letreros que se encuentran abajo. Busca las palabras en el vocabulario si es necesario.

REFRIGERADO
HOY 5'45—8y 10'45
ESTRENO
MAYORES DE 18 AÑOS

NO SE RESPONDE
DE OBJETOS QUE
NO SE ENTREGUEN

AVISO
SE PROHIBE HACERSE CARICIAS
LOS ADULTOS Y SENTAR LOS
NIÑOS EN EL MOSTRADOR. GRACIAS

TOLERADO MENORES

IMPARES   PARES

CARTELES, NO

DOBLE
CIRCULACION

PROHIBIDA VUELTA
A LA IZQUIERDA

CERRADO

SALIDA   ENTRADA

CIRCUNVALACION

ENTRADA
DE CARNET

SE RUEGA
NO TIRAR BASURAS

PROHIBIDO
SEGUIR DE FRENTE

SE ALQUILA
LOCAL 750 m^2

APARCAMIENTO
VIGILADO 5 PTAS

PULSAR
EL BOTON

SE PROHIBE
ESCUPIR

SEMÁFORO

CEDA
EL
PASO

RECEPCION

TIRE   EMPUJE

FOTOCÓPIAS
EN EL ACTO

ES PELIGROSO
ASOMARSE

Usted commands / tú commands

A. *USTED* COMMANDS

Oiga, por favor, dígame dónde se venden estampillas (sellos).	Listen, please tell me where stamps are sold.
Para mandar una carta vaya al correo.	To mail a letter go to the post office.
Siga todo derecho por esta misma calle hasta el final.	Go on straight ahead along this same street to the end.
Luego doble a la izquierda y siga andando tres cuadras.	Then turn left and keep walking three blocks.
Ahí busque una parada de autobuses.	Look for a bus stop there.
Tome un autobús verde cón el número 26.	Catch a green bus with the number 26.
Bájese en la Quinta Avenida. Vuelva a la derecha y cruce al parque al otro lado.	Get off on Fifth Avenue. Turn to the right and cross over to the park on the other side.
Siéntese y quédese ahí sentado durante un rato.	Sit down and stay sitting there for a while.
Disfrute ahí de la tranquilidad. Pida un refresco.	Enjoy the peace and quiet there. Order a soft drink.
Bébalo. Pero no lo beba de una vez.	Drink it. But don't drink it all at once.
Pregúntele a alguien dónde queda el correo.	Ask someone where the post office is.
Cómpreme tres estampillas para correo aéreo. Gracias.	Buy me three airmail stamps. Thanks.
De nada, vale.	You're welcome. That's OK.

Usted / **ustedes** command forms are identical to the present-subjunctive forms for **usted** / **ustedes**.

Vuelva a la derecha y vaya al parque al otro lado. Siéntese y quédese ahí un rato. Disfrute de la tranquilidad. Pregúntele a alguien dónde queda el correo.

1. Just as with the present subjunctive, **-ar** verbs take the vowel **e**, and **-er** and **-ir** verbs take the vowel **a**. Plural commands end in **-n**.

mirar	leer	venir
mire (Ud.)	lea (Ud.)	venga (Ud.)
miren (Uds.)	lean (Uds.)	vengan (Uds.)

2. Stem changes in vowels and consonants, spelling changes, and irregular forms are without exception the same as those found in present-subjunctive forms.

jugar	tocar	salir	dar
juegue (Ud.)	toque (Ud.)	salga (Ud.)	dé (Ud.)
jueguen (Uds.)	toquen (Uds.)	salgan (Uds.)	den (Uds.)

3. Negative commands are preceded by **no**: **No juegue aquí**.

4. Object pronouns and reflexive forms follow and are attached to affirmative commands. A written accent is required in such cases on the stressed vowel of the verb form.

Repítamelo, por favor.	Repeat it to me, please.
Repítanselo, por favor.	Repeat it to him, please.
Acuérdese (Ud.) de nosotros.	Remember us.
Acuérdense (Uds.) de mí.	Remember me.

5. Object pronouns and reflexive forms precede the verb and are written separately in negative commands. Thus written accents are not required in negative commands.

No se lo escriba ahora.	Don't write to him now.
No me lo pida Ud.	Don't ask me for it.
No se sienten aquí.	Don't sit here.
No se levante Ud. todavía.	Don't get up yet.

6. The use of the subject pronouns **Ud.** / **Uds.** with commands is normally optional (**Siéntese aquí** / **Siéntese Ud. aquí** *Sit down here*), although the subject pronouns can add courtesy and / or emphasis.

31.1 Conteste con un mandato (command).

¿Lo llamo ahora? → **Sí, llámelo.**

1. ¿Lo hago ahora?	**4.** ¿Lo traduzco ahora?
2. ¿Lo devuelvo ahora?	**5.** ¿Lo escribo ahora?
3. ¿Lo traigo ahora?	**6.** ¿Lo muestro ahora?

31.2 Cambie a la forma negativa.

Dígamelo. → **No me lo diga.**

1. Léamelo.	**5.** Pregúntenoslo.	**9.** Acuéstese.
2. Ciérrelas.	**6.** Háblenme.	**10.** Súbase.
3. Mándeselo.	**7.** Váyanse.	
4. Siéntense.	**8.** Ábralos.	

B. *TÚ* COMMANDS

Óyeme, Marisa, dime qué hago con esta carta.	Hey, Marisa, tell me what I'm to do with this letter.
No la eches al buzón de la esquina. Ve al correo.	Don't mail it in the box on the corner. Go to the post office.
Sigue esta calle al final y cruza al otro lado de la plaza.	Follow this street to the end and cross over to the other side of the square.
Para un momento. Busca la parada de taxis.	Stop for a moment. Look for the taxi stand.
Toma un taxi. Súbete al primero que veas.	Take a taxi. Get in the first one you see.
Pregúntale al taxista dónde está el correo.	Ask the taxi driver where the post office is.
Pídele que te lleve allí.	Ask him to take you there.
Disfruta del largo viaje que harás por la ciudad.	Enjoy the long trip you'll make around the city.
Págale lo que debes.	Pay him what you owe.
No le des una propina demasiado grande.	Don't give him too big a tip.

1. Except for a handful of common verbs, affirmative **tú** commands are identical to the third-person singular of the present indicative: **Habla / Come / Escribe.**

2. Verbs with shortened stems for **tú** commands.

(decir) di	(hacer) haz	(ir) ve	(poner) pon
(salir) sal	(ser) sé	(tener) ten	(venir) ven

3. Negative **tú** commands without exception are identical to the second-person singular of the present subjunctive.

No lo comas	No le escribas.	No hables.
No lo hagas.	No seas así.	No te vayas.

4. Placement of object pronouns with **tú** commands is the same as with **usted** commands. A written accent is necessary if the stressed syllable is third or fourth from the end.

Pídele el dinero.	Ask him for the money.
Pídeselo.	Ask him for it.

5. Over most of the Spanish-speaking world, the plural command forms for **ustedes** are used for the plural of **tú** commands. The familiar plural **vosotros** commands are not used in this book.

31.3 Responda Ud. a la oración con un mandato afirmativo de **tú**, según el modelo.

Clara no hace su cama. → **Clara, haz tu cama.**

1. Elisa no viene en seguida.
2. Eloísa no se pone el abrigo.
3. Benjamín no toma la leche.
4. Paco no tiene paciencia.
5. Gustavo no se sienta.
6. Héctor no nos deja en paz.
7. Pepe no dice la verdad.
8. Blanca no va a la puerta.
9. Concha no hace sus tareas.
10. Rufina no es amistosa.
11. Juan no escribe su trabajo.
12. Jesús no sale a las dos.

31.4 Conteste con un mandato negativo de **tú**, según el modelo.

¿Lo hago aquí? → **No, no lo hagas aquí.**

1. ¿Lo traigo ahora?
2. ¿Me siento ahora?
3. ¿Vengo a la una?
4. ¿Me voy ahora?
5. ¿Le doy el libro?
6. ¿Se lo digo a él?
7. ¿Salgo ahora?
8. ¿Lo pongo aquí?
9. ¿Lo leo ahora?
10. ¿Se lo explico ahora?
11. ¿Se lo entrego ahora?
12. ¿Le vendo mi carro?

31.5 ¿Cuántos mandatos se hallan aquí en estos anuncios? ¿Cuántos son de **tú**? ¿Cuántos son de **usted**? ¿Cuántos son negativos? Cuidado, que se no le escape ni uno.

LECTURA V

Read straight through these "Letters to the Editor" first. The number of verbs used reflexively illustrates the importance of this construction in Spanish. Then study the aids and exercises that follow before re-reading the letters more carefully. Your instructor may ask you to use certain of these reflexives in other sentences.

Cartas al director

Estimado señor:

El motivo° de mi carta es señalar algo que se oye en las conversaciones de casi todos los españoles: la programación desastrosa, pobre y chabacana° que se nos ofrece diariamente en nuestra Televisión estatal.

No me propongo en este caso hablar sobre la programación en general, sino sobre un programa en concreto: ¡Amor! ¡Amor!

Dicho programa es no sólo de una absoluta falta de buen gusto sino que[1] además no tiene ninguna gracia°. No sólo se revela como ridículo y denigrante° sino que provoca una total y absoluta vergüenza ajena° por los/las concursantes°, la presentadora y el señor con el traje de corazón rojo que, dicho sea de paso[2], es todo un poema°.

¿A qué tipo de mente se le ocurre que con semejante programa se puede mitigar la soledad y relacionar a la gente°?

Es patético ver la cara de la señorita elegida de turno cuando, al ser presentada, se acerca a su galán. Éste la observa como a un jamón de mercado, mientras la señorita presentadora no se avergüenza de preguntarle: «¿Te gusta?», como si se tratara de una mula de feria°. Parece un mercado de piezas de recambio° de segunda mano.

Tanto las preguntas como las respuestas[3] son de una vulgaridad atroz: «¿Qué haces antes de acostarte?», «En el amor, ¿te pones activa o pasiva?», y una larga lista de sandeces° por el estilo°.

Y, como remate°, el premio es una noche con un/una famoso/a más bien de segunda categoría°. Una especie de noche de amor, pero a lo basto°. En fin, parece, más que nada, la tómbola de los Hermanos Cachichi[4], sólo que en lugar de un oso de peluche°, te toca un señor/señora.

Hay mucha gente que tiene que quedarse en su casa y no se aprovecha de más distracción que la televisión (que pagamos todos[5]), y no creo que sea mucho pedir que pongan cosas más serias un viernes por la noche.

Genoveva Aguilar Martín[6]

reason

trashy

it's not even funny
demeaning
sense of shame in others/
contestants
a real clown

get people together

market/spare parts

idiotic remarks
of that kind

final touch
rather second rate
in a cheap way
teddy bear

Notas

1. **Pero** and **sino** mean *but*. **Sino** is used to express a contrast to a prior negative: **No hablo sobre los otros programas sino sobre éste. Sino que** is used when such a sentence has two clauses: **No sólo es ridículo sino que provoca vergüenza. Pero** is used everywhere else.
2. **dicho sea de paso** *let it be said, I might say in passing.*

Madrid. Plaza de la Moncloa, no lejos del distrito céntrico de la capital.

3. **tanto ... como ...**: **Tanto las preguntas como las respuestas** *Both the questions and the answers.*

4. **La tómbola** is a spin-the-wheel raffle or a game of chance present at any local summer fiesta in Spain, usually for the benefit of some charity. The prizes are often trinkets and items of very small value, and from the **Cachichi** brothers one could expect to win very little (**cacho** = *small piece, crumb*; **cachivache** = *piece of junk*).

5. **que pagamos todos** *that we all pay for* (much television in Spain is state subsidized).

6. The signer of the letter, like all Hispanics, has three names: **Genoveva** (her given name), **Aguilar** (her family name—father's last name), and **Martín** (her mother's maiden name).

Estimado Sr. Director:

Me siento obligada a escribirle para que usted se entere de lo que usted mismo anuncia en su digno periódico. Me refiero concretamente a la empresa Toujours Jolie, que anuncia un sistema revolucionario para perder peso, justo° en las zonas más gruesas del cuerpo, (1) sin pasar hambre, (2) sin pastillas°, (3) sin molestias y (4) en poco tiempo.

Pues bien, señor, esto es, sin más ni más[1], un camelo°.

exactly

pills

fraud

Los pobres inocentes que hemos caído[2] en esta trampa°, lle- *trap*
vados por nuestro narcisismo y nuestras ganas de estar guapetes[3],
hemos descubierto que, a cambio de un dineral°, se nos ofrece lo *large sum of money*
siguiente:

Pasar hambre como en los peores tiempos de la posguerra[4];

Verse obligado a tomar vitaminas para no desfallecer° y *pass out*
laxantes° para no reventar°; *laxatives/burst*

Sufrir largas esperas sin derecho al pataleo[5];

Verse literalmente vendados como momias° y sometidos a *wrapped up like mummies*
temperaturas francamente polares; y este triste espectáculo: ¡los
chorros° del mágico líquido adelgazante°! que corren sobre brazos *streams/slenderizing*
y piernas, produciéndose gigantescos charcos° en el suelo. *puddles*

Contra todas las mínimas normas de sanidad° y buena *health*
convivencia°, cada quince minutos aparece una empleada que, *coexistence*
armada con cubo°, fregona° y mala uva[6], se dedica a secar los *bucket/mop*
charcos que se extienden a los pies de los tutankamones[7] maso-
quistas.

En resumen, un absoluto fraude que debe denunciarse, en
vez de anunciarse, desde estas páginas, para evitar que muchos
gorditos inviertan° ilusión y dinero en él. *invest*

Epifanía Carrión Chillida

Notas

1. **sin más ni más** *without beating about the bush.*
2. **Los pobres inocentes que hemos caído** *We poor innocent victims who have fallen.* The verb form **hemos** (literally, *we have*) shows that the writer is including herself among the victims.
3. **estar guapetes** *to look nice.* The diminutive suffix **-ete** adds a humorous or self-deprecating touch to the writer's adjective describing the way the deceived customers would like to appear. She says **estar guapetes** *to look kind of nice,* not **ser guapo** *to be (really) good-looking.*

   Diminutive suffixes are a characteristic feature of colloquial Spanish. They denote small size or youth, and also express affection and a wide range of attitudes on the part of the speaker. The most common are **-ito** and **-cito**: **chica/chiquita, pobre/pobrecito.**
4. **La posguerra** = 1940s, after the Spanish Civil War (1936–1939).
5. **sin derecho al pataleo** *without the right to complain at all.* **Pataleo** is the noise caused by the stamping of feet to show annoyance and disapproval at meetings and public events.
6. **mala uva** *ill-tempered, in a bad mood* (literally, *"bad grape"*): **Siempre entra con mala uva** *She always comes in with a chip on her shoulder.*
7. **tutankamones** = people wrapped up like the mummy of the Egyptian Pharoah Tutankhamen.

Prácticas

A. Primero traduzca estas frases que traen ejemplos de una construcción con **se**.

1. Es algo que se oye en la conversación hoy.
2. La programación que se nos ofrece no es muy buena.
3. ¿Así se puede mitigar la soledad (*loneliness*) de la gente?
4. ¿Así se puede relacionar a la gente?
5. A cambio de mucho dinero se nos ofrece lo siguiente.
6. Corrió mucha agua, produciéndose gigantescos charcos.
7. Es un fraude que debe denunciarse en vez de anunciarse.

B. Ahora estudie y traduzca estos otros ejemplos de construcciones reflexivas. Los verbos de abajo siguen el orden de su uso en las dos cartas.

1. **proponerse** + infinitivo   *to intend (propose) to + verb*
   Me propongo hablar sobre un programa en concreto.

2. **se le ocurre (a uno)**   *it (an idea) occurs (to one)*
   ¿A quién se le ocurre semejante (tal) idea?

3. **avergonzarse de**   *to be embarrassed (ashamed) to*
   La señorita no se avergüenza de hacer preguntas vulgares.

4. **aprovecharse de**   *to take advantage, avail onself of*
   No se aprovechan de más distracción que la televisión.

5. **sentirse** + adjetivo   *to feel* + adjective
   Me siento obligada a escribirle.

6. **enterarse de**   *to become aware of, find out about*
   Ustedes deben enterarse de lo que realmente sucede aquí.

7. **verse**   *to be, find oneself* (in a situation)
   Nos vimos obligados a tomar vitaminas.

8. **dedicarse a** + infinitivo   *to go about, devote oneself to* + verb
   La empleada se dedicaba a secar los charcos.

9. **extenderse**   *to spread, stretch out*
   Los charcos se extienden por todo el piso.

Unit 32

Adjectives

A. ADJECTIVE FORMS

1. Adjectives with a masculine singular form ending in **-o** have a feminine singular in **-a**: **un cuadro hermoso, una pintura hermosa.**

2. Adjectives of nationality that end in a consonant add **-a** in the feminine: **español/española, alemán/alemana, francés/francesa.**

3. Adjectives that end in a consonant, **-e**, or **-ista** have the same form for both masculine and feminine.

un obrero joven	**una estudiante joven**
un libro verde	**una casa verde**
un político idealista	**una mujer idealista**

4. Comparative adjective forms ending in **-or** (**mejor**, **peor**, **mayor**, **menor**) also have only one form for both masculine and feminine.

un carro mejor	**una bicicleta mejor**
mi hermano menor	**mi hermana menor**

5. Adjectives ending in a vowel have a plural in **-s**: **largo/larga/largos/largas, alegre/alegres, francesa/francesas, pesimista/pesimistas.**

6. Adjectives ending in a consonant have a plural in **-es**: **francés/franceses, capaz/capaces, joven/jóvenes, peor/peores.**

7. **Bueno** and **malo** become **buen** and **mal** before a masculine singular noun. **Grande** becomes **gran** before masculine and feminine singular nouns and often means *impressive* or *great* in that position.

un buen viaje	**un mal sueño**
un gran descubrimiento	**una gran exploración**
los grandes misterios	

8. Several other noun modifiers drop final **-o** before masculine singular nouns.

algún día	**ningún ruido**
el primer capítulo	**el tercer piso**

B. ADJECTIVES THAT FOLLOW NOUNS

The following categories of adjectives follow the noun they modify:

1. Color, shape, condition, and material

una nube gris	a gray cloud
una ventana redonda	a round window
un camino inseguro	an unsafe road
una orilla rocosa	a rocky shore

2. Technical, scientific, and formal classifications

un aparato electrónico	an electronic appliance
un estudio botánico	a botanical study
el derecho internacional	international law
las alianzas militares	military alliances
el déficit federal	the federal deficit
una campaña publicitaria	a publicity campaign

3. Religion, nationality, political affiliation, and personal/moral/social attributes

la iglesia metodista	the Methodist church
la naciones iberoamericanas	the Latin American nations
la constitución rusa	the Russian constitution
una aerolínea colombiana	a Colombian airline
un congresista republicano	a Republican congressman
los derechos humanos	human rights
un hombre cruel	a cruel man

4. Past participles used as adjectives

la fe perdida	the lost faith
un circuito cerrado	a closed circuit

5. Modified adjectives of almost any kind.

Era un hombre poco inteligente.	He was not a very intelligent man.
Vivían bajo un sistema demasiado opresivo.	They lived under an excessively oppressive system.
¡Qué postre más rico!	What a delicious dessert!

C. ADJECTIVES THAT PRECEDE NOUNS

The following types of adjectives regularly precede the noun they modify:

1. Adjectives that the speaker believes express an inherent and obvious characteristic of the object or person described. The speaker is expressing a personal point of view that this noun and this adjective naturally belong together.

Ese hermoso cuadro lo pintó el ilustre artista Joan Miró.	The famous artist Joan Miró painted that beautiful picture.
Nos encanta el sereno paisaje de aquí.	We love the peaceful countryside here.
Van a tocar el famoso Concierto en Do que compuso el brillante músico de Salzburgo.	They're going to play the famous Concerto in C that the brilliant musician from Salzburg composed.

But if the speaker is merely stating what he/she believes is an objective fact rather than a judgment or opinion, the adjective follows the noun, thus merely distinguishing it from others of its class.

Sí, es un cuadro hermoso, pero ha pintado otros mejores.	Yes, it is a beautiful painting, but he's painted other better ones.
Por aquí hay mucha industria. No existe un paisaje sereno.	There is a lot of industry around here. There's no peaceful landscape to be found.
¿No te gusta? Es una novela famosa. Y de un escritor conocido.	Don't you like it? It's a famous novel. And by a well-known author.

2. Adjectives that express a degree of intensity or extremes are ordinarily placed before the noun: **mejor/peor**, **perfecto/pésimo**, **excelente/desastroso**, **maravilloso/terrible**, and the like.

el peor partido de la temporada	the worst game of the season
una magnífica película	a magnificent movie
un increíble desastre	an incredible disaster
una verdadera oportunidad	a real opportunity
una pésima idea	a rotten idea
una fuerte sensación	a strong feeling
un tremendo terremoto	a tremendous earthquake
peligrosas condiciones	dangerous conditions

Exclamations with **¡Qué!** fall in this category. The adjective typically precedes the noun in this construction.

¡Qué rico postre!	What a delicious dessert!
¡Qué fantástico gol!	What a fantastic goal!

D. TWO OR MORE ADJECTIVES

The placement of two or more adjectives that modify one noun basically follows the pattern of usage already explained above.

1. Descriptive adjectives that classify or specify (section B above) follow the noun and are connected by **y** (**e**).

una lucha económica y política	an economic and political struggle

una tarde gris y lluviosa	a gray, rainy afternoon
una charla amena e interesante	a pleasant, interesting talk

2. Adjectives that enhance in a subjective or emotional manner (section C above) may both precede the noun.

una grave y terrible sensación	a grave, terrible feeling
un ambicioso y creativo proyecto	an ambitious, creative plan
la creciente y peligrosa inflación	the growing, dangerous inflation

3. If one adjective is more subjective, it may precede the noun, and the other descriptive adjective follows the noun. The first adjective gives the speaker's opinion; the second, an indisputable fact.

un conocido artista puertorriqueño	a well-known Puerto Rican artist
los sabrosos bizcochos colombianos	the delicious Colombian pastries

4. If two descriptive adjectives without **y** follow a noun, the more differentiating and restrictive adjective comes last.

el arte mexicano contemporáneo	contemporary [not colonial] Mexican art
el arte contemporáneo mexicano	Mexican [not Peruvian] contemporary art

E. CHANGE OF MEANING ACCORDING TO POSITION

The meaning of certain adjectives depends on whether they are used before or after the noun they modify. The adjectives below are among the more common ones that have a basically descriptive meaning when they come after the noun, and a more subjective or numerical/quantitative meaning when they come before the noun.

After the Noun	Before the Noun
antiguo	
old, ancient	former
Vimos unas fortalezas antiguas.	No vieron la antigua capital de los incas.
We saw some old fortresses.	They didn't see the former capital of the Incas.

grande	
big	great
Es un hombre grande.	Es un gran hombre.
He is a big man.	He is a great man.

nuevo

new	another
Ya tiene un puesto nuevo. He now has a new job.	**Cambió la situación y ahora trabaja en un nuevo puesto.** The situation changed, and he now works at another job.

mayor

older / oldest	greater / greatest, larger / largest
Conocimos a su hija mayor. We met her oldest daughter.	**Ganó la mayor parte de los votos.** She won most of the vote.

menor

younger / youngest	less / least, smaller / smallest
Paco es el nieto menor. Paco is the youngest grandchild.	**Tomó el poder sin la menor resistencia.** He took power without the slightest resistance.

pobre

not rich	unfortunate
Es un hombre pobre. He is a poor man.	**El pobre hombre murió a los tres días.** The poor (unfortunate) man died in three days.

único

unique	only
Utilizaron un método único. They used a unique method.	**Fue el único modo.** It was the only way.

triste

not happy	dismal, hopeless
Es una joven triste. She is an unhappy (sad) young woman.	**Qué triste final.** What a sad ending.

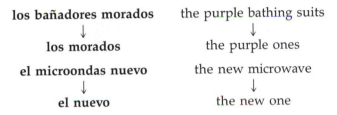

viejo	
not young	**former**
Me saludó una señora vieja. An elderly lady said hello to me.	**Rita era una vieja amiga mía del colegio.** Rita was an old school friend of mine.

F. ADJECTIVES USED AS NOUNS

Adjectives may function as nouns when the modified noun is left out. English adds the word *one*. Spanish adds nothing.

los bañadores morados	the purple bathing suits
↓	↓
los morados	the purple ones
el microondas nuevo	the new microwave
↓	↓
el nuevo	the new one

32.1 Describa el sustantivo con la forma correcta de los adjetivos entre paréntesis.

1. una estudiante   (dominicano / alegre / joven / alto / diligente)
2. los estudiantes   (amable / joven / feliz / triste / capaz)
3. la música   (francés / moderno / español / medieval / brasileño)
4. las ciudades   (grande / pequeño / viejo / interesante / alemán)
5. una chaqueta   (azul / amarillo / verde / blanco / gris / rojo)

32.2 ¿Dónde quiere Ud. colocar el adjetivo? No olvide que en algunos casos depende de su actitud hacia lo que se dice. Por eso, puede haber (*there can be*) a veces dos respuestas.

Un famoso artista vino a nuestra fiesta. (The speaker is giving his subjective opinion.)
Miró es un artista famoso. (The speaker is making an objective statement to differentiate this artist from others who are not famous.)

Así en éste, como en otros ejercicios aquí, puede parecer a veces imposible hacer una frase incorrecta. Pero aun así es posible que su profesor/a le pida a Ud. una explicación lógica para justificar su respuesta.

1. (amarilla) Ha comprado una _____ chaqueta _____ .
2. (chilenos) Aquí se venden _____ vinos _____ .
3. (comercial) Busca empleo en el _____ mundo _____ .
4. (desastrosa) Nos hemos metido en una _____ situación _____ .
5. (mexicana) Les gusta la _____ cerveza _____ .
6. (gran/grande) Fuimos a ver un _____ circo _____ .
7. (terrible) Para nosotros era una _____ tragedia _____ .
8. (práctico) Gerardo es un _____ muchacho _____ .
9. (peruanas) Van a asistir unas _____ estudiantes _____ .
10. (trágico) El drama tenía un _____ final _____ .

Ybor City, Tampa, Florida. José Martí (1853–1895) llegó en 1891 y tras sus discursos famosos, la pequeña ciudad se convirtió en un conocido centro revolucionario en contra de la opresión española en Cuba. El apóstol Martí murió luchando contra los españoles. Este patriota y gran escritor cubano se reconoce universalmente como el padre de su país.

11. (escandalosos)   Los _____ programas _____ que ponen ahora me dan rabia.

12. (buen/o)   Paco es un _____ chico _____ .

13. (barato)   Éste no es un _____ suéter _____ .

14. (estupendo)   En la televisión pública ponen _____ programas _____ .

15. (magnífica)   Para ella era una _____ oportunidad _____ .

16. (emocionante)   Celia Cruz cantó su _____ versión _____ de *La Guantanamera*.

32.3   No pare aquí. ¡Hay más! Siga como antes.

1. (tercer)   Viven en el _____ piso _____ .

2. (rocosa)   La Tierra del Fuego presenta una _____ orilla _____ .

3. (famoso)   Antes de la película *Amadeus*, Salieri no era un _____ compositor _____ .

4. (grises)   Encima de nosotros había _____ nubes _____ .

5. (primer/o)   Han leído el _____ capítulo _____ ya.

6. (mejor) *Las Meninas* es el _____ cuadro _____ que jamás se ha pintado en la historia del arte.

7. (Redonda) Se denominaron los Caballeros de la _____ Tabla _____ .

8. (egoísta) Todos sabemos que es una _____ persona _____ .

9. (gran/grande) *El Quijote* es una _____ obra _____ .

10. (insegura) Tuvieron que llegar por una _____ carretera _____ .

11. (militares) Se estrellaron dos _____ aviones _____ .

12. (peor) Fue el _____ partido de la temporada.

13. (injusta) Les parece una _____ tarifa _____ .

14. (verdadera) Entendían que era una _____ oportunidad _____ .

15. (electrónicos) Aquí venden _____ equipos _____ .

16. (pobre) Perdió la casa en el incendio. ¡Qué _____ hombre _____ !

32.4 ¿Dónde quiere Ud. colocar los adjetivos? Recuerde que a veces existen dos respuestas posibles y lógicas. En ese caso, ¿puede defender su solución?

1. (valenciano, joven) Vicente Martínez Ybor era un _____ emigrado _____ .

2. (tabaquera) A los 35 años dirigía una _____ fábrica _____ .

3. (oeste) Fundó Ybor City en la _____ costa _____ de la Florida.

4. (tremendo) Un _____ incendio _____ destruyó toda su industria.

5. (compatriota, viejo) Pensó en un _____ amigo _____ .

6. (algún/o, gran/grande) Él creía que Tampa sería _____ día _____ una _____ ciudad _____ .

7. (hispanos, primeros) Ybor City se convirtió en uno de los _____ núcleos _____ .

8. (revolucionario, conocido) Pronto llegó a ser un _____ centro _____ en contra de la opresión española en Cuba.

9. (floridiana, pequeña) El apóstol José Martí llegó en 1891 a la _____ ciudad _____ .

10. (famosos, varios) En Ybor City dio _____ discursos _____ .

11. (cubanos, pequeñas, tabaqueras, afilados) Poco después muchos _____ exiliados _____ cambiaron sus _____ cuchillas _____ por _____ machetes _____ .

32.5 Una vez más. ¿Hace falta la conjunción **y**?

1. (política, económica) Se entregaron a una _____ lucha _____ .

2. (cubana, sabrosa) Nos dieron una _____ comida _____ .

3. (puertorriqueña, conocida) Nos presentaron una _____ artista _____ .

4. (terrible, grave) Se le ocurrió a ella una _____ premonición _____ .

5. (moderna, americana) Estudiamos la _____ historia _____ .

6. (clásica, romana) Saben algo de la _____ arquitectura _____ .

32.6 Diga en español.

1. He is not a big man.

2. But he is a great man.

3. He lost his former job.

4. Esteban was his oldest son.

5. Carlota was his youngest daughter.

6. They were his only children.

7. Esteban was an old friend of mine.

8. He was my only friend.

9. Carlota is now an unhappy old woman.

10. What a sad story!

32.7 Lea el anuncio y conteste.

1. ¿Cuál sería el propósito de una «venta almacén»?
2. Según la empresa, ¿cómo son estos precios especiales que se ofrecen ahora al comprador?
3. ¿Qué productos sugiere la expresión «imagen y sonido»?
4. ¿Cuáles son los medios de pagar que acepta este comercio?
5. ¿Qué productos en venta son para instalar en la cocina?
6. Explique en español lo que quiere decir la frase: «No se admiten devoluciones».
7. Explique igualmente la expresión «Sólo por 8 días».

Desde mañana, sábado 28
Domingo abierto de 10 a 8

Sólo por 8 días

Gram VENTA ALMACEN
ELECTRODOMESTICOS·IMAGEN Y SONIDO

A PRECIOS INCREIBLES

Artículos nuevos de las principales marcas a eliminar de nuestro surtido

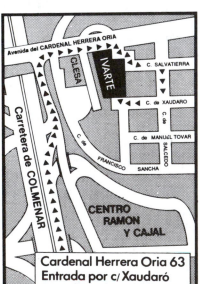

Cardenal Herrera Oria 63
Entrada por c/ Xaudaró

- 200 frigoríficos
- 200 lavadoras
- 100 lavavajillas
- 500 compactos musicales
- 1300 radiocassettes
- 400 cadenas HI·FI
- 350 vídeos/cámaras
- 700 televisores
- 500 hornos/encimeras
- 150 microondas
- 1000 cámaras fotográficas y accesorios

Y....cientos de pequeños electrodomésticos

Pago en efectivo o con Tarjeta de Compras de Galerías
Lléveselo usted mismo
No se admiten devoluciones

ABIERTO DE 10 A 20 h.
No cerramos a mediodía

Galerías Preciados

GALERIAS

The neuter article *lo*

A. NEUTER *LO* WITH ADJECTIVES AND ADJECTIVE PHRASES

La mejor parte de la película es el final. **Lo mejor de la película es el final.**	The best part of the movie is the ending.
La cosa difícil es llegar a un acuerdo. **Lo difícil es llegar a un acuerdo.**	The difficult thing is to reach an agreement.
El aspecto inquietante es su actitud. **Lo inquietante es su actitud.**	The disturbing aspect is his attitude.

1. The neuter article **lo** is used with an adjective to describe a certain aspect or quality of something: **Lo peor del asunto** *The worst thing about the matter*. The adjective is always masculine singular in form. English equivalents have the words *part*, *thing*, *aspect*, and the like.

2. Abstract notions and ideas may likewise be expressed with **lo** + adjective. English equivalents use expressions with words like *things* and *what is*.

Le gustan las cosas nuevas. **Le gusta lo nuevo.**	She likes new things. She likes what is new.
Pero compra las cosas baratas. **Pero compra lo barato.**	But she buys cheap stuff. But she buys what is cheap.

3. Phrases with **lo de** are used to refer to situations and ideas. English equivalents include *the matter of*, *the affair of*, *the incident of*.

Se niega a discutir lo de anoche.

He refuses to discuss
- the business about last night.
- that incident of last night.
- what went on last night.

B. OTHER USES OF *LO*

1. When **lo** + adjective is followed by **que** and **ser** or **estar**, the adjective must agree with the subject of the verb. The English equivalent is *how* + adjective: **No sabes lo dulce que es** *You don't know how sweet it is*.

Nunca nos dijo lo difíciles que eran los exámenes.	He never told us how difficult the tests were.
No me di cuenta de lo cara que está la gasolina.	I didn't realize how expensive gasoline is.

2. Spanish expresses adverbial superlative phrases with neuter **lo** as follows:

$$\text{lo} + \left\{ \begin{array}{l} \textbf{mejor} \\ \textbf{peor} \\ \textbf{más} + \text{adverb} \\ \textbf{menos} + \text{adverb} \end{array} \right\} + \textbf{posible}\,/\,\textbf{que} + \textbf{poder}$$

Ayer mi abuela conducía su carro lo más rápido posible.	Yesterday my grandmother was driving her car as fast as possible.
Un policía la siguió lo mejor que pudo.	A policeman followed her the best he could.
Hoy ella conduce su carro lo menos rápido posible.	Today she drives her car as slowly as possible.

3. Set phrases with **lo**:

a lo mejor	maybe	**por lo común**	usually
por lo general	in general	**por lo visto**	apparently

4. Lo + **que** is used as a neuter relative pronoun in Spanish to refer to something indefinite in a general sense. The English equivalent is *what*: **Tienen lo que quieren** *They have what they want*.

If the idea referred to is explicitly stated in a clause, **lo cual** or **lo que** is used. The English equivalent is *which*: **Los alemanes ganaron la Copa, lo cual (lo que) no nos sorprende** *The Germans won the Cup, which doesn't surprise us*.

33.1 Haga otra oración con **lo** + adjetivo.

1. La parte difícil es creerlo.
2. El peor aspecto es su actitud.
3. La cosa no entendida es cómo ganó el premio.
4. La cosa incomprensible aquí es poder estudiar en el extranjero.
5. A ella le gustan todas las cosas españolas.
6. A esos niños les encantan las cosas militares.

33.2 Haga frases con **lo de**.

1. ¿Has oído lo que pasó anoche?
2. No comprendo lo que ocurrió ayer.
3. No explicarán el asunto del incendio.
4. No le apetece a mi tío Alejandro eso de comer menos.

33.3 Haga frases según el modelo.

Son difíciles. → **Ud. no sabe lo difíciles que son.**

1. Son absurdos.
2. Son sabrosas.
3. Son elegantes.
4. Son buenas.

33.4 Haga frases según el modelo.

Conduce muy rápido. → **Conduce lo más rápido posible.**

1. Se levanta muy temprano.
2. Se acuesta bastante tarde.
3. Come menos.
4. Lo hace mejor.

33.5 Cambie al español.

1. I have what I want.
2. Apparently she did not receive what she ordered (**pedir**).
3. Usually they lose, which doesn't surprise me.
4. In general, I know what I need.
5. But maybe she doesn't know what she wants.

33.6 ¿Cuántas veces se emplea una construcción con **lo** neutro en estos titulares? ¿Qué diferencias se notan aquí en el uso de este pronombre?

LO PELIGROSO DEL SIDA ES NO SABER NADA DE EL

Algunos expertos esperan lo peor

Lo latino está de moda

MONSTRUOS VIVOS, TERROR EN VIVO

Llegar al fin del mundo, es más fácil de lo que piensas.

PARQUE DE ATRACCIONES

LO NUNCA VISTO

Lo nunca visto. Ya verás lo que te espera en el Parque. Ahora hay un montón de nuevas Atracciones. Excitantes, emocionantes, espeluznantes... ¡lo nunca visto! Vente y verás.

Nápoles ante Génova, lo mejor en el fut italiano

Reconocer lo pasado

El humor: de lo gracioso a lo enfermizo

Diversión y práctica 9

Buscando sitios y pidiendo información

Yo me encuentro en la plaza central de esta ciudad por primera vez en mi vida. Tengo que hacer algunas compras y atender algunos compromisos. Éstos están indicados abajo. Le digo a la primera persona que encuentro lo que quiero comprar y lo que quiero hacer. Él me dice adónde tengo que ir y qué tengo que hacer, pero me hace algunas preguntas también. No tengo planeados muy bien mis quehaceres y, por eso, sigo volviendo por el mismo territorio de la ciudad. Tengo que hacerle preguntas a cada persona que encuentro.

Sigan el modelo. Por ejemplo:

Poner un pleito (*a lawsuit*).

    —Oye, tengo que consultar un abogado. ¿Hay un abogado aquí en la plaza o cerca de aquí?
    —Sí. Cómo no. Tienes que cruzar la plaza y, a la derecha, entrar en la Avenida Borges. Después de pasar la esquina de la Diagonal Rómulo Gallegos, el primer edificio que encuentras a la derecha es el despacho del Licenciado Noriega, uno de los mejores abogados de la ciudad. ¿Por qué quieres consultar un abogado?
    —Quiero poner un pleito contra mi vecino.
    —¿Tu vecino? ¿Qué te ha hecho?
    —¡Cortó uno de mis árboles sin mi permiso!

Ahora sigue tú así con los compañeros con cada una de las frases de abajo.

1. Hablar con un cura para confesarme.
2. Comprar aspirinas para mi dolor de cabeza.
3. Cambiar un cheque para pagar al abogado.
4. Conseguir un plano de la ciudad para encontrar los sitios yo mismo/a.
5. Comprar chuletas de cerdo para llevárselas a mi amigo.
6. Comprar pan para acompañar las chuletas.
7. Denunciar un crimen que he visto.
8. Mandarles una carta a mis familiares.
9. Comprar libros para mis cursos en la Universidad.
10. Comprar herramientas de construcción, carpintería y plomería en caso de que suspenda en la Universidad.
11. Comprar globos para mi sobrino que está esperándome en el parque.
12. Comprar un pasaje de avión para volver a mi propio país.

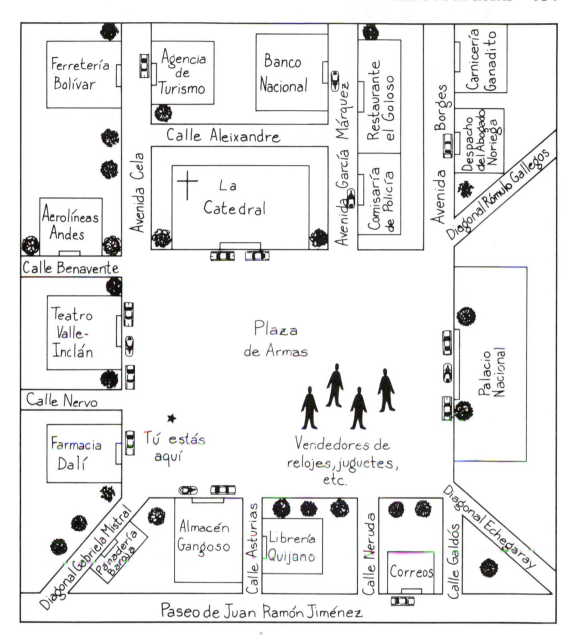

Unit 34

Para and *por*

A. USES OF *PARA*

MEANING	ENGLISH EQUIVALENTS	EXAMPLES
PURPOSE	*for*	**¿Para qué lo quieres?** What do you want it for?
	in order to	**Lo quería para mostrárselo.** I wanted it in order to show it to him.
DIRECTION / DESTINATION (in space or time)	*for*	**¿Para dónde van?** Where are they headed? **Para el correo.** For the post office.
	toward	**Caminaban para (hacia) el correo.** They were walking toward the post office.
	by	**Lo completarán para el martes.** They will complete it by Tuesday.
INTENDED RECIPIENT	*for*	**Esta rosa es para ti.** This rose is for you.
EMPLOYMENT	*for*	**Trabaja para su hermano.** He works for his brother (as an employee).
COMPARISON	*for*	**Para buenas películas no hay como este canal.** For good movies, there's no channel like this one.
	considering	**Para lo poco que hace, gana mucho.** Considering how little he does, he earns a lot.

B. USES OF *POR*

MEANING	ENGLISH EQUIVALENTS	EXAMPLES
REASON	*why*	**¿Por qué lo quieres?** Why do you want it? (**¿Por qué?** is used in a simple request for information, implying no disagreement on the part of the speaker, unlike **¿Para qué?**, which often does have that implication.)
AGENT	*by*	**Fue construido por mi tío.** It was built by my uncle.
RATE	*by / per*	**Pagan por hora.** They pay by the hour. **Ciento treinta kilómetros por hora** 130 kilometers an hour
EXCHANGE	*for*	**Me dieron mil dólares por el auto.** They gave me a thousand dollars for the car.
GENERAL LOCATION	*around*	**Trabajan por aquí.** They are working around here.
ROUTE or PASSAGE (in space)	*by way of / through / along*, etc.	**Van a ir por Jalisco.** They are going to go by way of (through, via) Jalisco. **Andábamos por la playa.** We walked along the beach. **Voy a pasar por tu apartamento a las siete.** I'm going to come by your apartment at seven.
APPROXIMATE TIME (passage of time)	*for* *in*	**Trabajó aquí por (durante) varios meses.** He worked here for several months. **Nos visita por la tarde.** She visits us in the afternoon.
CHOICE (in favor of)	*for*	**Votó por Vargas Llosa.** He voted for Vargas Llosa.
CAUSE	*because of*	**Hago esto por ti, no por tu padre.** I'm doing this because of you, not your father.
MOTIVE	*for, for the sake of*	**Hazlo por mí.** Do it for me. Do it for my sake.
SUBSTITUTION	*for / in place of*	**Iré por ti.** I'll go for you (in your place). **Trabajó ayer por su hermano.** He worked for (in place of) his brother yesterday.

SOLICITUD PARA LA TARJETA DE BIBLIOTECA
BIBLIOTECA PUBLICA DE LOS ANGELES
(ENGLISH – OTHER SIDE)

SOLAMENTE PARA USO OFICIAL

```
O [ ] [ ] [ ] [ ] [ ]
  CAT.   CLASS    AGENCY
```
_____   _____
        DATE   CLERK

Esta solicitud es un contrato; léala con cuidado. El solicitante adulto tiene que presentar identificación con esta solicitud que con-
cuerde con el nombre y dirección escritos en la solicitud. La identificación puede ser una licencia de manejar, el registro de votante,
una identificación del banco, una identificación del empleo o una carta con marca postal que tenga su dirección actual. La solicitud
de un niño tiene que tener la firma de un padre o guardián.

PRESENTE LA SOLICITUD COMPLETA A LA MESA DE REGISTROS

PARA COMPLETARSE POR EL SOLICITANTE

APELLIDO   [_____]

NOMBRE   [_____]

INICIAL   [__]

DIRECCION   [_____]

CIUDAD   [_____]   ESTADO [____]

ZONA POSTAL   [_____]

CODIGO DE AREA   [_____]   TELEFONO [_____]

APELLIDO DE SOLTERA DE SU MADRE   [_____]

Deseo pedir préstamo de la Biblioteca Pública de Los Angeles. Consiento a observar todas las reglas de la biblioteca y ser responsable por todos
los materiales prestados con mi tarjeta, con o sin mi consentimiento. También consiento pagar cualquier multa u otros cobros por retorno atrasado o daño hecho a los materiales de la biblioteca.

FIRMA _____
        EL SOLICITANTE NECESITA FIRMAR EN PERSONA

BIBLIOTECA PUBLICA DE LOS ANGELES
TARJETA TEMPORAL DE BIBLIOTECA

Fecha de vencimiento de esta tarjeta

Nombre del usuario
(Capitalize apellido, nombre)

Firma del usuario

(Esto es la traducción de lo que esta escrito en el verso.
Por favor firme donde dice Patron's Signature).

INFORMACION GENERAL

Su tarjeta de biblioteca, temporal o permanente, se tiene que presentar cada vez que pide préstamo de la biblioteca. Esta tarjeta se
puede usar en todas las sucursales de la Biblioteca Pública de Los
Angeles, sea una biblioteca vecindaria, una biblioteca ambulante o
la Biblioteca Central. Notifique a la biblioteca si pierde su tarjeta o
cambia de dirección. Si pierde su tarjeta temporal, no se pueden
prestar materiales hasta que reciba su tarjeta permanente. Multas
o cobros seran impuestos por materiales vencidos o dañados. Su
ingreso en el Sistema de la Biblioteca Pública de Los Angeles le au-
toriza para pedir préstamo de otras bibliotecas en el sur de California. Pregunte al personal de la biblioteca para más información.

At times a context is necessary to determine the meaning of **por**: **Haré esto por
ti** means either *I'll do this in your place* or *I'll do this for your sake.*
There are a great many fixed expressions with **por**.

por consiguiente	consequently	**por lo tanto**	therefore
por eso	therefore	**por lo visto**	apparently
por fin	finally, at last	**por mi parte**	as for me
por lo demás	as for the rest	**por si acaso**	just in case
por lo menos	at least	**por supuesto**	of course

En telefonía celular...
La mejor opción está por llegar. ¡ **Espérela !**

╱╲╱╲ **TELMEX**

Compound prepositions with **por** usually indicate direction and movement.

por encima de	*over*	**Saltó por encima de (sobre) la silla.** He jumped over the chair.
por debajo de	*under*	**Corrió por debajo de la mesa.** It ran under the table.
por delante de	*in front of*	**Pasó por delante de tu casa.** She passed in front of your house.
por detrás de	*in back of,* *behind*	**Lo persiguieron por detrás de la casa.** They chased him behind the house.

34.1 ¿**Para** o **por**? Si caben las dos preposiciones, explique por qué.

1. Fue descubierto _____ un físico.
2. _____ un niño de diez años es muy fuerte.
3. Lo harán _____ mañana sábado.
4. Este paquete es _____ usted.
5. _____ hacerlo bien hay que hacerlo despacio.
6. Dieron un paseo _____ la plaza central.
7. ¿_____ qué sirve este aparato?
8. Lo despidieron _____ hacer mal su trabajo.
9. _____ crear problemas entre buenos amigos no hay como tú.
10. Es una casa construida _____ un músico famoso.
11. El ladrón se escapó _____ detrás del garaje.
12. Nos pagaban treinta pesos _____ hora.
13. Volamos _____ encima de los Andes.
14. Lo enviaron _____ correo aéreo.

34.2 Convierta lo siguiente en frases con **para** o **por**.

1. Lo voy a hacer debido al honor de la familia.
2. Cornejo caminaba a lo largo de la playa.
3. Esta tarde ella va a trabajar en tu lugar.
4. Es una película interesante debido a sus escenas dramáticas.
5. Lo hizo en mi favor.

6. Esto lo voy a hacer a fin de ayudarte.
7. El drama es sorprendente debido al asesinato en la escena final.
8. Venían andando hacia la farmacia.
9. No asiste a clase a causa de su enfermedad.
10. Ellas trabajaron ahí durante varios meses.
11. Hoy no van a partir debido al mal tiempo.
12. Son regalos destinados a mi suegra.
13. No puedo hablar en lugar de ella.
14. Todo será preparado antes del lunes a más tardar.
15. Les dio veinte dólares a cambio de su cassette.
16. Los niños juegan cerca de aquí.
17. Ella siempre nos visita en la mañana.
18. Van a volver vía Caracas.
19. Hay problemas en todas partes.
20. Considerando lo poco que hace, le pagan bien.
21. ¿A qué propósito me ha traído esto?
22. Alrededor de (*around*) julio y agosto se van de vacaciones.

34.3 Diga en español.

1. At least she knows the truth.
2. As for me, I don't want to participate.
3. It is better for us to leave now, just in case.
4. She felt better in the afternoon.
5. For that reason it is impossible for her to go now.
6. Why can't he speak French?
7. Why do you want to learn a language like Quechua?
8. Apparently you know nothing about Peru.

Uses of the infinitive and accompanying pronouns

A. VERB + INFINITIVE

Esperan		They hope	
Saben		They know how	
Pueden		They can	
Necesitan	hacerlo.	They need	to do it.
Piensan		They intend	
Prefieren		They prefer	
Deciden		They decide	
Van		They are going	
Vienen		They are coming	
Aprenden		They are learning	
Empiezan	a hacerlo.	They are beginning	to do it.
Nos enseñan		They teach us	
Nos ayudan		They help us	
Nos invitan		They invite us	
Acaban	de hacerlo.	They have finished doing it. / They have just done it.	
Dejaron	de hacerlo.	They stopped doing it.	

1. In verb + infinitive constructions some Spanish verbs take a preposition and some do not. They must be learned individually.

Deben ayudarla.	They must help her.
Parecen conocerlo.	They seem to know him.
Tratan de ayudarla.	They are trying to help her.
Insisten en ayudarla.	They insist on helping her.
Sueña con ganarse un premio.	He dreams about winning a prize.

2. Hay, **había**, etc., and **tener** take **que** before an infinitive.

Había (hubo) que estar en forma.	It was necessary to be in shape.
El equipo tenía que practicar más.	The team had to practice more.

3. Seguir / **continuar** *to keep on, continue* do not take infinitives but **-ndo** participles.

Seguimos (continuamos) tratando de resolverlo.	We keep on trying to solve it. / We continue to try to solve it.

4. In many verb + infinitive constructions, object pronouns may either be placed before helping verbs like **poder**, **deber**, **querer**, **ir a**, and **acabar de**, or after the infinitive.

Me lo pueden vender. **Pueden vendérmelo.**	They can sell it to me.
Se lo van a explicar. **Van a explicárselo.**	They are going to explain it to her.
Se debe hacer ahora. **Debe hacerse ahora.**	It must be done now.
Me acababa de acostar. **Acababa de acostarme.**	I had just gone to bed.

In other verb + infinitive constructions, object pronouns are placed only after the infinitive when the helping verb is reflexive or when it takes the prepositions **con**, **en** or **por**.

Se niega a decirlo.	She refuses to say it.
Se acordó de mandarlo.	He remembered to send it.
Se trata de darles una explicación.	It's a matter of giving them an explanation.
Soñé con ganarla.	I dreamt about winning it.
Insistió en pagármelo.	She insisted on paying me for it.
Se esfuerzan por aprenderlos de memoria.	They're making an effort to memorize them.

B. VERBS OF PERCEPTION AND INFLUENCE + INFINITIVE

Los vi salir.	I saw them go out.
Y los oí entrar.	And I heard them come in.

1. Verbs of perception like **ver**, **mirar**, **oír**, and **escuchar** can take both a direct object and an infinitive. The direct object of the perception verb is the subject of the infinitive.

Oímos cantar a Celia Cruz.	We heard Celia Cruz sing.
La oímos cantar en México.	We heard her sing in Mexico.

However, if the infinitive has its *own* direct object, the perception verb takes an *indirect object* (**la** → **le**).

> **Le oímos cantar una canción conmovedora.**   We heard her sing a moving song.

2. Two verbs of influence (**hacer** *to make*, **dejar** *to let*) are used exactly the same way.

> **Los hice trabajar.**   I made them work.
>
> **Les hice lavar las ventanas.**   I made them wash the windows.

3. However, most verbs of influence take an indirect object and an infinitive.

> **Les impidió volver.**   He kept them from coming back.
>
> **Les impidió encontrar los documentos.**   He kept them from finding the documents.

$$\text{Les} \begin{cases} \textbf{aconsejó} \\ \textbf{permitió} \\ \textbf{mandó} \end{cases} \textbf{volver.} \qquad \begin{cases} \text{He advised} \\ \text{He allowed} \\ \text{He ordered} \end{cases} \text{them to return.}$$

C. OTHER USES OF THE INFINITIVE

1. The infinitive is used as a noun with and without the definite article. The English equivalent is often the *-ing* form of the verb.

> **Ver es creer.**   Seeing is believing.
>
> **(El) ganar la medalla de oro es sumamente difícil.**   Winning the gold medal is extremely difficult.

2. The infinitive is the only form of the verb used after a preposition.

> **antes de llegar**   before arriving
>
> **después de salir**   after leaving

3. **Al** + infinitive expresses an action going on at the time of the main verb.

> **Al llegar al aeropuerto buscamos a nuestros amigos.**   Upon arriving (when we arrived) at the airport, we looked for our friends.

4. Adjectival phrases with **de** + infinitive are used to modify nouns.

> **el derecho de votar**   the right to vote
>
> **la decisión de ir**   the decision to go
>
> **el modo de hacerlo**   the way to do it
>
> **la voluntad de ganar**   the will to win

5. Other adjectival phrases with **de** + infinitive:

$$\text{Es algo} \begin{cases} \textbf{fácil} \\ \textbf{difícil} \\ \textbf{posible} \\ \textbf{imposible} \end{cases} \textbf{de hacer.} \qquad \text{It's something} \begin{cases} \text{easy} \\ \text{difficult} \\ \text{possible} \\ \text{impossible} \end{cases} \text{to do.}$$

6. Para + infinitive is used to express purpose.

Es un buen sitio para nadar.	It's a good place for swimming.
Hacemos esto para no fracasar.	We are doing this in order not to fail.
No tiene lo necesario para hacer paella.	She doesn't have what is needed to make paella.
Para correr olas, esta playa no vale.	This beach is no good for surfing.

35.1 Haga oraciones completas. A veces no usará ninguna palabra de la tercera columna. Hay varias posibilidades en cada caso.

el camarero	insistir	a	ir a Londres
el mecánico	acabar	con	ver la televisión
el atleta	soñar	de	hacer paella
mis hijos	deber	en	ganar una medalla
nosotros	querer	por	reparar el motor
el cocinero	ponerse	que	poner la mesa
María	tener		viajar por España
mi compañero	tratar		tocar la guitarra

35.2 Exprese los sustantivos (*nouns*) como pronombres.

Ella vio ganar la Copa Mundial a los alemanes → **Ella les vio ganarla.**

1. Oí entrar a mis padres.
2. Hicieron esperar a los viajeros.
3. Se niega a decir la verdad.
4. Insiste en explicar sus problemas.
5. Esperan comprar la casa.
6. Se trata de quitarles la Copa a los argentinos.
7. Dejó pasar la aduana a los turistas americanos.
8. Aconsejó salir al desconocido.
9. Vi al ladrón robar el coche.
10. Se puso a cantar coplas amorosas.
11. Me acordé de cerrar bien la puerta.
12. Mi papá siempre ha soñado con ganar la lotería.

35.3 Traduzca notando el uso del infinitivo.

1. This is difficult to explain.
2. I felt like (**tener ganas de**) going away.
3. At times I like to be alone in order to be able to think.
4. What (**cuál**) is the best way to do this?
5. I decided to go to a provincial city (**ciudad de provincias**) in August.
6. A friend tried to give me advice (**consejos**).
7. Doing this in August is madness (**locura**).
8. He advised me to go to a beach.
9. He continued to give me advice.

¿Es que se ha ido todo el mundo? Parece que nadie quiere despertarse. Para encontrar la paz en agosto uno tiene que ir a una ciudad de tierra adentro. Te aconsejo hacer el viaje a Jaén, Teruel o Badajoz.

10. But I intend to go tomorrow.
11. My friend began to laugh (**reírse**). Seeing is believing.
12. He saw me leave at seven in the morning.
13. Upon arriving, I went to walk around the square.
14. It was a Sunday in (**de**) August, 10:30 in (**de**) the morning.
15. I went to sit down in the Plaza de la Soledad. Total silence.
16. No one seems to want to wake up.
17. I begin to think: a neutron bomb (**una bomba de neutrones**).
18. The people disappear (**desaparecer**). The houses stay (**quedarse**).
19. After leaving the square, I saw two men cross the street.
20. They were talking in a low voice (**en voz baja**). In order not to break (**romper**) the silence?
21. Upon seeing me, they stopped talking.
22. But they told me: "To eat well, it is necessary to go to the Mesón de Manuela."
23. To begin the battle (**la batalla**) against the heat, some women were throwing (**echar**) water on the sidewalks (**a las aceras**).
24. I decided to stay here the whole month.
25. In order to find peace (**la paz**) and calm (**la calma**) in August, you must go to an inland city (**ciudad de tierra adentro**).
26. I advise you to go to Jaén or Teruel or Badajoz or to any other one (**cualquier otra**).
27. The decision to go is yours.
28. You are going to find tranquility (**la tranquilidad**).

35.4 Identifique cada infinitivo en estos titulares. Observe, estudie y explique el uso del infinitivo en cada caso.

Tiburones como el perro... se le pegan las pulgas

El árbitro hizo ganar al Necaxa 2-0

Cocinar es cosa de hombres

Los aerobics también hacen engordar

Manos **Unidas**
CAMPAÑA CONTRA EL HAMBRE

Infórmate de la situación actual del Tercer Mundo
Haz que se conozcan las causas de esta realidad
Coopera con tu trabajo, tu tiempo, tu dinero...

**COMPARTIR
ES HACER JUSTICIA**

*Usted tiene que
aprender a decir 'no*

**Rompió el Savile Club su regla de
no conversar durante el desayuno**

Mueren tres al chocar aviones

ENFERMEDAD FACIL DE PREVENIR

Pero apostar
puede no ser
recomendable

Un hombre dispara contra un grupo
de jóvenes porque no le dejaban dormir

La forma
más segura
de morir

Trabajar demasiado puede ser mortal

Unit 36

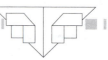

Adverbs

A. ADVERBS OF MANNER

Era una herida grave.	It was a serious wound.
↓	↓
Fue herido gravemente.	He was seriously wounded.
Dio una respuesta rápida.	She gave a quick answer.
↓	↓
Respondió rápidamente.	She answered quickly.

1. To form an adverb of manner, the suffix **-mente** is added to the feminine singular of adjectives ending in **-o**, and directly to the end of other adjectives: **perfecto** → **perfectamente** *perfectly*, **feliz** → **felizmente** *happily*, **amable** → **amablemente** *nicely, in a kindly way*. The English equivalent has *-ly*. Written accent marks on the adjective are kept on the adverb: **fácil** → **fácilmente** *easily*. Sometimes **con** + the corresponding noun is a synonym: **con cariño** = **cariñosamente** *affectionately*, **con cuidado** = **cuidadosamente** *carefully*.

2. Adverbs in **-mente** are regularly placed immediately after the verb in Spanish: **Lo ha olvidado completamente.** In English the corresponding *-ly* adverb is often placed after an auxiliary verb: *He has completely forgotten it*. If there are two or more consecutive **-mente** adverbs, the **-mente** is used only on the last adverb: **Hizo su trabajo rápida y eficazmente** *She did her work rapidly and efficiently*.

3. Other adverbs of manner:

alto	high	**gratis**	free, without charge
bajo	low	**mal**	poorly, badly
bien	well	**mejor**	better
despacio	slowly	**peor**	worse

—¿**Cómo trabaja ahora?**	"How does he work now?"
—**Trabaja mejor que yo.**	"He works better than I do."
—**Debería volar más alto.**	"He should fly higher."
—**Sí, está volando muy bajo.**	"Yes, he's flying very low."

B. ADVERBS OF PLACE

aquí here **ahí / allí** there	**arriba** up, upstairs **abajo** down, downstairs
cerca near(by) **lejos** far (away)	**adentro** inside **afuera** outside
adelante in front, forward **encima** on top, over, on one's person	**enfrente** in front, opposite **atrás** back, in the back

1. Other adverbs of place are **acá** *here* and **allá** *there*: **Ven acá** *Come here*; **¿No los ve allá?** *Don't you see them (over) there?* They are often intensified with **más: Está más allá** *It is farther over there*. They are virtually synonymous with **aquí** and **allí**, respectively, although **acá** is preferred in many South American countries such as Argentina.

2. Direction and motion are expressed with **hacia, para,** and other phrases.

Voló hacia (para) arriba.	It flew up(ward).
Flotó hacia (para) abajo.	It floated down(ward).
Saltó hacia (para) atrás.	It jumped back(ward).
Caminaba calle arriba.	She was walking up the street.
Corría calle abajo.	He was running down the street.

C. ADVERBS OF TIME

antes before, earlier	**temprano** early
aún still, yet	**todavía** still, yet
después after, later	**todavía no** not yet, still not
luego then, later	**ya** already, now
tarde late	**ya no** no longer, not anymore

1. Notice how **ya** differs in meaning when it is negative: **Ya está en Madrid** *He's already in Madrid*, **Ya no está en Madrid** *He's no longer in Madrid*. In other cases **ya** means *now* or *right away*: **¡Hazlo ya!** *Do it right away!* **Ya** is also used when asking when to begin to do something.

—**Escríbame estas dos cartas, por favor.**	"Write these two letters for me, please."
—**¿Ya?**	"Right now?"
—**Sí, las necesito cuanto antes.**	"Yes, I need them as soon as possible."

2. Aún and **ya** are never used right after an auxiliary verb, as their equivalents often are in English.

Aún estaba estudiando a las tres.	He was still studying at three o'clock.
Estaba estudiando aún a las tres.	
Ya está trabajando y se graduó hace dos días.	He is already working, and he graduated two days ago.

D. ADVERBS OF EXTENT AND ADJECTIVE QUALIFIERS

algo somewhat, rather	**mucho** a lot
bastante quite, enough	**muy** very
demasiado too, too much	**poco** little, not much
más more	**tan** so
menos less	**tanto** so much

Many adverbs of extent are also used to qualify adjectives.

Come demasiado.	He eats too much.
Es demasiado gordo.	He's too fat.
Ha hecho bastante.	She's done enough (quite a bit).
Es bastante ambiciosa.	She's quite (pretty) ambitious.
Estudian muy poco.	They study very little.
Son poco estudiosos.	They're not very studious.

In a few cases the corresponding adjective qualifier is a shortened form of the adverb or a related word.

Ha crecido tanto.	He's grown so much.
Ya es tan alto que casi no cabe en mi carro.	He's already so tall that he hardly fits in my car.
Trabaja mucho.	She works hard (a lot).
Es muy trabajadora.	She's very hard-working.

Very little is either **muy poco** or **poquísimo**. However, *very much* can only be expressed by **muchísimo**.

Toca la guitarra muy poco.
Toca la guitarra poquísimo.⎱   He plays the guitar very little.

Antes la tocaba muchísimo.   Before he played it a great deal.

36.1 Cambie la frase adverbial a un adverbio con **-mente**.

Ha esperado con paciencia. → **Ha esperado pacientemente.**

1. Lo ha aceptado con dificultad.
2. Hemos practicado con intensidad.
3. Aceptaron la decisión con tristeza.
4. Los saludó con alegría.
5. Elaboró su plan con inteligencia.
6. Construyó el modelo con cuidado.

36.2 Cambie esta escena al español, prestando atención a los adverbios.

1. My grandmother tries to drive slowly (*not with* **-mente** *this time*).
2. The policeman said: "You were flying (**volar**) too low."
3. She: "You seem very friendly."
4. He: "You do not seem very intelligent."
5. Here comes the judge (**juez**).
6. The judge: "We see each other frequently."
7. She: "Too much."
8. The judge: "Why were you going so fast?"
9. She: "I was going up the street moderately (*moderate* = **moderado**). A bird (**pájaro**) flew upward, in front of the car. It gave me a scare (**susto**)."
10. The judge: "The policeman says you were going at 90 miles (**millas**) an (*per*) hour."
11. She: "He was not very friendly. Also he was too far away."
12. The judge: "No, he was quite nearby."
13. She: "Earlier I had to pay a fine (**multa**)."
14. The judge: "I have already heard enough."
15. My grandmother no longer has her license (**carné** / **permiso de conducir**).
16. She is still in jail (**encarcelada**).
17. She is inside.
18. The car is outside.

Vamos a escribir ...5

Infinitivos, mandatos y otras cosas

Siga contando la historia de la aventura portuguesa de Guillermo Cornejo en su cuaderno. En este capítulo se incluye un repaso de numerosas construcciones recién estudiadas.

LA AVENTURA PORTUGUESA DE GUILLERMO CORNEJO
(episodio 3 y final)

On waking up, Cornejo said to himself: "The good thing is that I am still alive. And after eating so much raw garlic. I need to go to the bathroom."

He had to go to the end of the hallway. A man was inside. Guillermo saw him come out. As (**al**) he got close to Cornejo, the man jumped backward. The smell of the garlic was very strong. The man looked at Guillermo furiously and headed for his room.

•   •   •

Cornejo knew what he had to do. It was the only way to help Natasha. Now or never. As (**al**) he reached the door, he was thinking about black pajamas.

CORNEJO: Knock, knock! (**¡Tun tun!**)
NATASHA: "Who's there?" (**¿Quién es?**)
CORNEJO: "The president of the republic of Transylvania. For heaven's sake,

Natasha, open the door! Let me come in."

NATASHA: "Close the door. Sit down. Not on the bed. Don't say anything. Don't do anything."

CORNEJO: "Why am I here? Tell me the truth."

•   •   •

Then Guillermo heard something. Outside, he saw a bat. It was flying high over the pension. Then it flew downward.

NATASHA: "Close the window. Hurry. Listen to me. It is now twelve o'clock. The worst part has arrived. Will you help me?"

CORNEJO: "I will do it for you. Let me help."

NATASHA: "Upon entering, the count will try to give you an embrace. Believe me, it will be your last embrace."

CORNEJO: "But what shall I do? What shall I say to him? 'Good evening, sir (**Buenas noches, caballero**), and welcome to Natasha's bedroom?'"

Suddenly, in front of the window, they saw him enter. Like an apparition. Miraculously (**milagrosamente**). Cornejo liked the black cape with its red lining (**forro**). He thought that he would ask him where he bought it.

•   •   •

Then the count smiled. Good heavens, thought Guillermo, on seeing his teeth.

CORNEJO: "Pardon me, but just in case you want it, I know the name of a good dentist here in Lisbon."

With his arms raised, the count came for Guillermo. Natasha screamed. The cape opened. The smell of garlic was intense. The count fell backward, breaking the window.

Cornejo ran toward the window. The bat! He saw it fly upward. It flew in back of a huge cloud. Then the full moon disappeared behind the clouds.

•   •   •

Guillermo and Natasha embraced. Then they kissed...

CORNEJO: "The garlic doesn't bother you?"

NATASHA: "On the contrary (**al contrario**), my dear."

Outside, in the garden, a nightingale began to sing.

to be alive **estar vivo/a**	embrace **el abrazo**
bathroom **el lavabo, el wáter**	welcome **bienvenido**
to the end of **al fondo (final) de**	apparition **la aparición**
hallway **el pasillo**	miraculous **milagroso/a**
to get close to **acercarse a**	cape **la capa**
to jump **saltar**	good heavens **Dios mío**
smell **el olor**	just in case **por si acaso**
to head for **irse para**	to embrace **abrazar**
pajamas **los pijamas** (*also* **piyamas**)	bother **molestar**
for heaven's sake **por el amor de Dios**	my dear **amor mío**
bat **el murciélago**	nightingale **el ruiseñor**
to hurry **apurarse**	

Cuestionario

1. ¿Qué tomó Cornejo antes de acostarse?
2. ¿Qué cosa provocó al hombre que salía del wáter?
3. ¿Por qué no abrió Natasha la puerta en seguida?
4. ¿Qué vio Cornejo volar por encima de la pensión?
5. ¿A qué hora llegó el conde?
6. ¿Qué peligro hay en un abrazo del conde?
7. ¿De qué manera entró al cuarto el conde?
8. ¿Cómo sabemos que le gustó mucho a Cornejo la capa del conde?
9. ¿Qué aspecto físico del conde le impresionó a Cornejo?
10. ¿Por dónde cayó el conde?
11. ¿Qué vio Guillermo fuera de la ventana?
12. ¿Qué ocurre al final?

Unit 37

Comparison

A. REGULAR COMPARATIVE FORMS

> **tan ... como**   as ... as
> **tanto / a ... como**   as much ... as
> **tantos / as ... como**   as many ... as

1. Tan / tanto ... como expresses equivalence and compares equal things. **Tan** is used with adjectives and adverbs. **Tanto / a / os / as** agrees with the noun it modifies.

Es tan alto como su padre.	He's as tall as his father.
No corre tan rápido como su hermano.	He doesn't run as fast as his brother (does).
Ella tiene tantos pares de zapatos como Imelda.	She has as many pairs of shoes as Imelda (does).

> **más (...) que**   more (...) than
> **menos (...) que**   less / fewer (...) than

2. Más *more* and **menos** *less* are used to express unequal comparisons. They may be used alone or with nouns, adjectives, and adverbs.

Han ganado más partidos que nosotros.	They've won more games than we have.
Rafael es más inteligente que su jefe.	Rafael is more intelligent than his boss.
Corre más rápido que el delantero titular.	He runs faster than the first-team forward.
Sí, pero juega menos intensamente que él.	Yes, but he plays less intensely than he does.

3. The definite article + **más / menos** expresses the superlative: **Adriana es la menos ambiciosa de su familia** *Adriana is the least ambitious one in her family.* Note also that **de** (not **en**) is used after the superlative.

4. **Más que** means *only* in a negative sentence.

Cómpralo. No cuesta más que tres dólares.	
Cómpralo. Cuesta sólo tres dólares.	Buy it. It costs only three dollars.

5. **Más (menos) de** means *more (less) than* before numbers and expressions of amounts or quantities.

Hoy ha trabajado más de diez horas.	Today she has worked more than ten hours.
Ese hombre controla más de la mitad de las acciones.	That man controls more than half the shares.
Compuso la obra en menos de seis semanas.	He composed the work in less than six weeks.
Hizo muchas compras y no le quedan más que tres dólares.	She bought quite a bit and has only three dollars left [exactly three].
Hizo muchas compras. Comenzó con cien dólares y ahora le quedan menos de cinco.	He bought quite a bit. He started with a hundred dollars, and now he has less than five left [he's not sure how much—maybe three or four].

B. IRREGULAR COMPARATIVE FORMS

mejor	better, best	**peor**	worse, worst
mayor	bigger, biggest / older, oldest	**menor**	smaller, smallest / younger, youngest

Mayor and **menor** may be used to indicate a person's age, as well as size.

Aurora es mayor que su hermana Matilde.	
Aurora es más vieja que su hermana Matilde.	Aurora is older than her sister Matilde.

Some speakers prefer the first sentence above regardless of the sisters' ages since they often wish to avoid the word **viejo** *old* when speaking of people.

Felisa es la menor de las hijas.	
Felisa es la más joven de las hijas.	Felisa is the younger (youngest) of the daughters.

Note that unlike formal English, there is no difference in Spanish between comparative (two) and superlative (three or more). In the two sentences above there could be two, three or more daughters.

C. *DE LO QUE* = *THAN*

Creíamos que aquella familia era pobre.
We believed that family was poor.

Pero aquella familia es más pobre de lo que creíamos.
But that family is poorer than (what) we believed.

Pensaba que su esposo era poco ambicioso.
She thought her husband was not very ambitious.

Pero es aun menos ambicioso de lo que pensaba.
But he's even less ambitious than (what) she thought.

When a whole clause is the point of comparison, the clause is introduced by **lo que**, and **de** is the equivalent of *than*.

Trabaja mucho más de lo que sospechaban.	She works much harder than they suspected.

If the main verb is repeated in the second part of the sentence, **de lo que** must be used.

Juanito come más que su papá.	Juanito eats more than his dad.
Juanito come más de lo que come su papá.	Juanito eats more than his dad (eats).

D. ABSOLUTE SUPERLATIVE

El postre estaba muy rico. **El postre estaba riquísimo.**	The dessert was very delicious.
El examen fue sumamente difícil. **El examen fue dificilísimo.**	The exam was extremely difficult.

1. The absolute superlative is used to lend a degree of intensity (*extremely, very, exceptionally*) to adjectives and adverbs without really comparing them to anything in particular. Spanish uses either an adverb (**muy, sumamente,** etc.) before the adjective or adds the suffix **-ísimo** / **a** / **os** / **as.** This can be done with adverbs, too: **Puede correr rapidísimo** *He can run extremely fast.* The use of **muy,** etc., is more common in ordinary conversation, the **-ísimo** superlative in more formal language and writing.

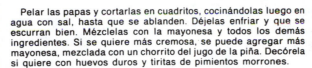

Reta de la Semana

GOYA

ENSALADA DE CAMARONES ESTILO GOYA

4 lbs. de papas
3 tazas de camarones jumbo GOYA
1 lata de pimientos morrones GOYA
1 lata de guisantes GOYA escurridos
1 lata de piña en trocitos
1 1/2 taza de mayonesa
1/2 taza de aceitunas rellenas GOYA
Sal GOYA a gusto

Pelar las papas y cortarlas en cuadritos, cocinándolas luego en agua con sal, hasta que se ablanden. Déjelas enfriar y que se escurran bien. Mézclelas con la mayonesa y todos los demás ingredientes. Si se quiere más cremosa, se puede agregar más mayonesa, mezclada con un chorrito del jugo de la piña. Decórela si quiere con huevos duros y tiritas de pimientos morrones.

Es un plato riquísimo e ideal para una fiesta, o el almuerzo del domingo. ¡Sírvalo con pan de miga tostado!

2. Forms ending in a vowel drop the vowel: **lento → lentísimo.** Forms ending in a consonant just add -ísimo: **fácil → facilísimo.** Note also that the written accent on **-ísimo** replaces the one on the stem (**fácil**). Three final consonants show a spelling change: (z → c) **veloz → velocísimo,** (g → gu) **largo → larguísimo,** (c → qu) **rico → riquísimo.**

E. *EL MISMO QUE*

Vienen los mismos invitados que antes.	The same guests as before are coming.
Su respuesta es la misma que di yo.	His answer is the same one that I gave.
Este examen es el mismo que dio el año pasado.	This exam is the same one he gave last year.

1. El mismo que means *the same as,* **Mismo / a / os / as** agrees with the noun it modifies (**las mismas camisas** *the same shirts*) or the noun it replaces (**las mismas** *the same ones*).

2. Lo mismo que means *the same way* or *the same thing* (in general).

Los trato lo mismo que siempre.	I treat them the same as always.
Sigues haciendo lo mismo.	You keep on doing the same thing.
Me lo explicó lo mismo que tú, pero todavía no comprendo.	He explained it to me the same way you did (the same as you), but I still don't understand.

F. *IGUAL A, IGUAL QUE*

Tú eres igual a tu papá.   You're just like your dad.
 «De tal palo, tal astilla.»   "A chip off the old block."

Esta computadora es igual a la This computer is just like yours,
 tuya, ¿no?   isn't it?

Gana un salario igual que el de He earns a salary the same
 un abogado o un médico.   as a lawyer's or a doctor's.

1. Ser igual a means *to be (just) like*: **Son iguales a los míos** *They are just like mine*.

2. Igual que and **el mismo que** are similar in meaning to **igual a**; however, **igual** follows the noun.

Recibió
{
el mismo aviso que tú.
un aviso igual al tuyo.
un aviso igual que el tuyo.
}
  He received
{
the same notice you did.
a notice just like yours.
}

3. Igual que and **lo mismo que** are also interchangeable as adverbs; they correspond to English *the same way (as)* or *just like*.

Mi prima habla
{
igual que
lo mismo que
}
tú. My cousin talks
{
the same way
just like
}
you do.

37.1 Haga una comparación con **tan(to)...como.**

En la Copa Mundial Diego Maradona marcó cuatro goles, pero Hugo Sánchez marcó cuatro goles también. → **Hugo Sánchez marcó tantos goles como Diego Maradona.**
Tú cocinas bastante, pero yo cocino bastante también. → **Yo cocino tanto como tú.**

1. Los cubanos juegan bastante al béisbol, pero los dominicanos juegan bastante también.
2. Mi tío hace muchos viajes de negocios, pero mi amigo hace muchos también.
3. Stephen King escribe muchas novelas, pero Danielle Steele escribe muchas también.
4. Los japoneses hacen miles de autos, pero los americanos hacemos miles también.
5. Tú eres muy alta, pero tu hermana es muy alta también.

37.2 Conteste diciendo la verdad en una oración completa.

¿Dónde cuesta más vivir, en Houston o en Tokio? → **Cuesta más vivir en Tokio que en Houston.**

1. ¿Cuál ciudad es más grande. Seattle o Los Ángeles?
2. ¿Quién bateó más jonrones, Babe Ruth o Hank Aaron?
3. ¿En cuál país se habla más el francés, en Canadá o en Estados Unidos?
4. ¿Cuál cuesta menos, un Mercedes-Benz o un Yugo?
5. ¿Quién es más alto, usted o Michael Jordan?
6. ¿Quién contribuyó más a la música rock, Elvis o Madonna?
7. ¿Cuál de estos países ganará más medallas en la próxima Olimpiada, Alemania o Estados Unidos?
8. ¿Quién es el mejor mariscal de campo, Joe Montana o Dan Marino?

37.3 Añada una frase siguiendo el modelo.

Yo pagué diez dólares. → **Mi amigo pagó más de diez.**

1. Yo gané cincuenta dólares en la lotería.
2. Yo tuve cuatro cartas ayer.
3. Yo comí la mitad de una pizza.
4. Yo contribuí cien dólares.

37.4 Convierta la frase en otra de semejante sentido.

Sólo cuesta cuarenta y nueve centavos. → **No cuesta más que cuarenta y nueve centavos.**

1. Sólo mide diez pulgadas.
2. Van a venir a la boda sólo veinte invitados.
3. Sólo ha vivido aquí cinco meses.
4. En ese bar venden cerveza exclusivamente.
5. No sueña con ninguna otra cosa. Sueña con tener auto propio.

37.5 Combine las oraciones según el modelo.

Parecía caro. Pero no era muy caro. → **Era menos caro de lo que parecía.**

1. Pensaba que era muy difícil. Y era aun más difícil.
2. Creía que su esposo era poco ambicioso. Pero era aun menos ambicioso.
3. Creía que el partido iba a durar mucho tiempo. Y el partido sí duró aun más tiempo.
4. Es necesario que los jugadores jueguen duro. Pero juegan demasiado duro.

37.6 Cambie la oración a otra con el mismo sentido. A veces hay dos o tres respuestas posibles.

Maneja como tú. → **Maneja igual que tú.** o **Maneja lo mismo que tú.**
La comida estaba muy rica. → **La comida estaba riquísima.**

1. Estaban sumamente cansados.
2. Trabaja de sol a sol igual que tú.
3. A él le gustan las salsas picantes lo mismo que a ti.
4. Es excepcionalmente grande.
5. El examen fue extremadamente difícil.
6. Es una actriz super famosa.

LECTURA VI

Read through the passage first. It contains examples of (1) modified nouns—many with two modifiers, (2) **para** *and* **por**, *and (3) neuter* **lo**. *Then go through the exercises before re-reading the passage. Questions for comprehension follow.*

Estamos para fiestas[1]

Agosto, septiembre . . . va acabando° el año agrícola. Con el tiempo la naturaleza dará un espectáculo agónico° de brillantes colores. Después, todo se vuelve° gris. La vida se extingue.

    Desde los tiempos más remotos el ciclo anual de las estaciones, el ciclo de sembrar y cosechar°, de morir y renacer, ha representado algo mágico y ritual para el hombre del campo.

    Estamos en un pueblo de la alta meseta castellana. Hecha la recolección de cereales°, terminada la vendimia°, ocurre en el pueblo un paréntesis en la monótona vida diaria. Se reúnen las familias. Los que han nacido aquí acuden de dondequiera que estén°. Regresan los emigrados. La vida del pueblo gira en torno a° un ritual que apenas ha cambiado por los siglos.

    Es un ritual colectivo, una ruidosa celebración humana. Ocurre de norte a sur, en todos los rincones de esta gran piel de toro[2] que es España. Y no sólo allí, sino en cualquier país hispano o latino. Somos un pueblo ritual, dice el mexicano Octavio Paz.

    Esta celebración de la vida, un caluroso grito que clama° a los cielos, se llama fiesta. Desde San Juan°, y el solsticio de verano[3], hasta Todos Los Santos° a principios de noviembre, el arte de la fiesta se conserva intacto.

    En parte, la fiesta es una explosión, una viva manifestación popular por el pueblo. En la calle no para nadie. Después de los encierros[4] y la suelta de vaquillas[5], hay jotas y fandangos[6] y otros bailes tradicionales, en los más vistosos° trajes típicos. Tras el desfile° de cabezudos[7], dragones y gigantes, vienen gaiteros y chistularis, y saltarines[8] que voltejean° al tam-tam del tambor°. Más tarde será hora de bailar sevillanas.

    Ante la iglesia, en máscaras terribles e imaginativas, luchan el Bien y el Mal, las Virtudes y los Pecados°. El castillo de fuegos artificiales° echa centellas° y desaparece en una gran humareda° explosiva. Y una vez más, salen a la calle las peñas[9] de mozos y mozas, interpretando, a modo muy suyo, otra escandalosa canción popular. Con los brazos levantados, pasean culebreando[10] por angostas° calles medievales. La calle es un agitado río humano.

    La fiesta es dramática y religiosa. En la cima° de ese monte ahí se ve un pequeño santuario°. Es la ermita° donde siglos atrás descubrieron enterrada° la imagen del santo protector del pueblo. Ahora vienen llegando los romeros°, por un paisaje convertido en puro teatro. Desde la Navidad y el solsticio de invierno, por Carnaval[11] y Semana Santa, hasta el jueves del Corpus[12], el calendario religioso se mezcla con ritos casi prehistóricos.

is gradually ending
dying
turns

sowing and reaping

grain harvest/grape harvest

de . . . *from wherever they may be*

gira . . . *revolves around*

cries loudly
June 24
All Saints' Day

showy
parade
cartwheel/drum

sins
fireworks/sparks/cloud of smoke

narrow
top
shrine/abandoned chapel
buried
pilgrims

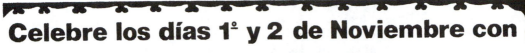

Celebre los días 1º y 2 de Noviembre con

y calaveritas en

EL MOLINO

...su pastelería

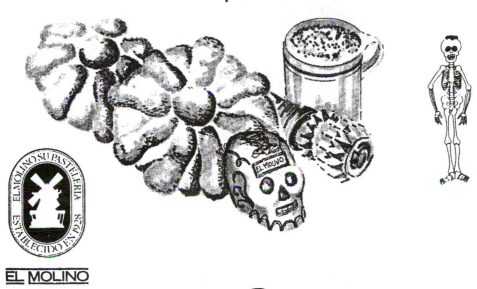

EL MOLINO

NARANJAS, LIMAS Y LIMONES, TODOS A COYOACAN A COMER COLACIONES, EN COYOACAN ES FIESTA TRADICIONAL

DICIEMBRE EN COYOACAN ES FIESTA POPULAR

La Delegación Coyoacán, a través de la Subdelegación de Acción Social y la Subdirección de Servicios Culturales y Turísticos, lo invita a concursar con UNA PASTORELA TRADICIONAL, bajo las siguientes

BASES:

1. Podrán participar en este concurso los grupos de barrios, colonias o escuelas que organicen pastoreras tradicionales no profesionales.
2. El concurso se llevará a cabo en el Foro "Ana María Hernández", sito en Pacífico No. 181, esq. Fernández Leal, Barrio de la Concepción, del 4 al 13 de diciembre, de 16:00 a 20:00 horas.
3. Cada pastorela tendrá una hora treinta minutos para presentarse, y la fecha del concurso le será asignada al inscribirse.

Delicioso pan con esqueletito

La fiesta puede ser expiatoria° y brutal. El animal mítico y simbólico ha sido siempre el toro. Usted lo ve ahí amarrado° en la plaza. Su sangre está en la calle.   *for atonement* / *tied (to a post)*

Muy poco de todo esto se conserva en la gran ciudad. Allí la gente olvida sus tradiciones para crear otras. Desaparece la mitología.

El forastero°, si viene, será amablemente recibido. Pero si no entiende de estas cosas, sólo cree que no ha visto jamás tanta gente borracha. Vuelve a casa para decir que ha visto una calle llena de mozos que bebían a morro° botellas de cava° catalán. Claro, una parte de la fiesta es la juerga° amistosa. El forastero se da cuenta de que en la fiesta las gentes se manifiestan como quieren. Espontáneamente. Lo insólito° resulta normal.   *stranger* / *straight from the bottle/ champagne/partying* / *unusual*

Quizá en sus correrías° el viajero ha notado, dolorosamente, cómo el español puede exhibir poco aprecio por lo español. Esto no es evidente en el delirio del momento que se llama fiesta. Bajo el cálido sol de agosto todos gritan su indivisible humanidad.   *travels*

Pues vamos ahí para la plaza, señor. ¿No quiere tomar una copa° con nosotros? Estamos en fiestas.   *drink*

Notas

1. **Estamos para fiestas**   *We're in the mood for* fiestas, *We're ready for* fiestas.
2. **Piel de toro**   *bull's hide*: the ancient Greek geographer Strabo described the Iberian peninsula's land mass as having the outline of a bull's hide stretched out to dry in the sun.
3. **Solsticio de verano**   *summer solstice* (about June 21, when the sun peaks over the equator and summer officially begins in the northern hemisphere).
4. **El encierro**   running of the bulls along a barricaded route to a pen.
5. **La suelta de vaquillas**   releasing young heifers to run down and often trample the local youth.

Después del encierro de los toros bravos, los mozos gozan corriendo por la plaza en la suelta de vaquillas.

6. **Jotas, fandangos, sevillanas** dances and songs typical of various regions of Spain.
7. **Cabezudos** wear enormous heads depicting historic or comic figures.
8. **Gaiteros y chistularis** *bagpipe and flute players*; **saltarines** *acrobatic dancers* (popular features of many local fiestas).
9. **Las peñas** groups from a specific parish or barrio.

Tras el desfile de cabezudos, dragones y gigantes, vienen gaiteros y chistularis, y saltarines que voltejean al tam-tam del tambor.

10. **Pasean culebreando** *they move past as if tracing the figure of an S* (**culebra** = *snake*).
11. **Carnaval** revelry preceding Lent.
12. **El Corpus** feast day after Pentecost in June.

Prácticas

A. Observe y estudie la colocación de adjetivos en las frases de abajo.*

1) **un adjetivo colocado tras el sustantivo**

el año agrícola · fuegos artificiales
un espectáculo agónico · el santo protector
los tiempos más remotos · el calendario religioso
el ciclo anual · ritos casi prehistóricos
un ritual colectivo · tanta gente borracha
cualquier país hispano · cava catalán
un pueblo ritual · la juerga amistosa
otros bailes tradicionales

2) **un adjetivo colocado antes** (Fíjese cómo en dos casos sigue una frase adjetival con **de**.)

brillantes colores · puro teatro
esta gran piel de toro · la gran ciudad
un caluroso grito · el cálido sol de agosto
un pequeño santuario · su indivisible humanidad

*Review the placement of adjectives in Unit 32 if necessary; remember that the more subjective or enhancing of two adjectives may precede the noun, while the more descriptive/objective adjective follows the noun.

Y una vez más, salen a la calle las peñas de mozos y mozas, interpretando, a modo muy suyo, otra escandalosa canción popular. Con los brazos levantados, pasean culebreando, y la calle es un agitado río humano.

3) **dos adjetivos**

algo mágico y ritual	máscaras terribles e imaginativas
la alta meseta castellana	una gran humareda explosiva
la monótona vida diaria	otra escandalosa canción popular
una ruidosa celebración humana	angostas calles medievales
una viva manifestación popular	un agitado río humano
los más vistosos trajes típicos	el animal mítico y simbólico

B. Estudie también estas frases con ejemplos de **para/por** (incluidos dos casos del uso de **lo** neutro).

apenas ha cambiado por los siglos	olvida sus tradiciones para crear otras
una manifestación por el pueblo	vuelve a casa para decírselo a sus amigos
pasean culebreando por angostas calles	lo insólito resulta normal
vienen llegando por un paisaje	exhiben poco aprecio por lo español
desde la Navidad, por Carnaval y hasta el Corpus	vamos ahí para la plaza

Comprensión

1. ¿En qué época del año ocurren la mayoría de las fiestas?
2. ¿Qué son los cabezudos?
3. «La fiesta es en la calle. La calle es la fiesta.» ¿Qué quiere decir esto?
4. ¿Qué cosas ocurren en la calle?
5. ¿Son legales los fuegos artificiales donde vive Ud.?
6. ¿Por qué desaparecen estas tradiciones en las ciudades grandes?

Unit 38

Present perfect subjunctive

Present perfect subjunctive forms:

haya hecho	hayamos hecho
hayas hecho	hayáis hecho
haya hecho	hayan hecho

Espero		I hope	
Siento	que lo haya hecho.	I'm sorry	that he has done it.
No creo		I don't believe	that he did it.
Dudo		I doubt	

1. The present perfect subjunctive is formed with the present subjunctive of **haber** + a past participle. This tense is the subjunctive counterpart of the present perfect and preterit indicative tenses and is used in subordinate clauses in which the subjunctive is required. The usual English equivalents of the present perfect subjunctive are *have done/did, have come/came, have left/left*, etc.

Present subjunctive		
Es posible que vengan hoy.	It is possible	they are coming today.
		they will come today.
		for them to come today.
Present perfect subjunctive		
Es posible que hayan venido antes.	It is possible	they have come earlier.
		they came earlier.
Present subjunctive		
Es una lástima que se vayan ahora.	It is a pity	they are leaving now.
		they will leave now.
		for them to leave now.
Present perfect subjunctive		
Es una lástima que se hayan ido tan pronto.	It is a pity	they have left so soon.
		they left so soon.

2. The present perfect subjunctive is used after:

a) expressions of emotion

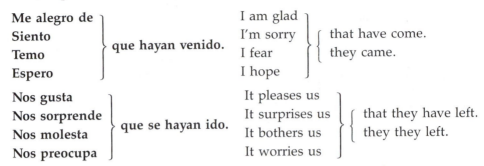

Me alegro de		I am glad	
Siento	que hayan venido.	I'm sorry	that have come.
Temo		I fear	they came.
Espero		I hope	

Nos gusta		It pleases us	
Nos sorprende	que se hayan ido.	It surprises us	that they have left.
Nos molesta		It bothers us	they they left.
Nos preocupa		It worries us	

b) expressions of doubt

No creen		They don't believe	
Dudan	que haya llegado.	They doubt	he has arrived.
No están seguros de		They are not sure	he arrived.
Niegan		They deny	

But the indicative is used if the event in the subordinate clause is believed to be a fact.

Creen	que ha llegado.	They believe	he has arrived.
Están seguros de	que llegó.	They are positive	he arrived.
No niegan		They don't deny	

c) impersonal expressions

Es probable		It is probable	
No es verdad	que no me haya querido nunca.	It is not true	she never loved me.
Es mejor		It is best	she has never loved me.
Es triste		It is sad	

Such impersonal expressions are used with the subjunctive because they present the same concepts the verbs above do: emotion and doubt. However, impersonal expressions that indicate certainty or belief are followed by the indicative.

Es cierto		It is certain	
Es verdad	que siempre lo ha querido (lo quería).	It is true	she has always loved him.
Es evidente		It is evident	she always loved him.

38.1 Cambie las oraciones del indicativo al perfecto del subjuntivo, según el modelo.

Es verdad que vinieron ayer (posible) → **Es posible que hayan venido ayer.**

1. Creo que ha ido al concierto. (no creo)
2. Sé que ganó la lotería. (me alegro de)
3. Están seguros de que ha llegado a la universidad. (dudan)
4. Es cierto que murió en el accidente. (es triste)
5. Saben que ha encontrado el dinero. (esperan)
6. Afirmamos que han pagado la deuda. (negamos)

38.2 Cambie las oraciones al inglés o al español, según el caso.

1. Felipe no quería confesarlo, pero esperamos que lo haya confesado.
2. *He didn't want to go, but we hope that he went.*
3. Los niños detestaban la comida y dudamos que la hayan comido.
4. *Her friend denies that she found the money.*
5. No deseaban ir a Cancún y es probable que no hayan ido.
6. *Aurelio bought two cars last year. It is strange (**extraño**) that he bought two cars last year.*
7. Usted no nos ayudó y nos disgusta que no nos haya ayudado.
8. *You didn't get angry (**enojarse**) with him, and it pleases us you didn't get angry.*

Diversión y práctica 10

Anuncios clasificados

Lee los anuncios clasificados que siguen abajo y contesta las preguntas correspondientes. Busca las palabras en el vocabulario si es necesario.

1

> **$25 EXAM.** Conductor o aprendizaje. 2do gratis. Lince, Lima. Horacio López. Hra. $10. Instructor(a) **468-5632**.

2

> **SE OFRECE CLASES PRIVADAS DE INGLÉS** con una experta. Horas flexibles. Precios razonables. Llame **82-96-93**.

1. ¿Qué quiere hacer la persona que toma el examen? ¿Cuánto cuesta el segundo examen?
2. ¿Cuándo son las clases de inglés? ¿Cuestan mucho?

3

> **PRÉSTAMOS**
>
> **VISA–MASTERCARD.** Obtenga su tarjeta sin importar su pasado crédito. Esta tarjeta **VISA** está 95% aprobada y es lo que Ud. esperaba. **No requiere salario mínimo.** Llame ahora: Tels: **851-6734**, 24 hrs o escriba a EL PALACIO DEL CRÉDITO. Apto. 773, Montevideo, Uru.

4

> **SE SOLICITA PERSONAL** con conocimientos en plomería y electricidad para instalación de equipo doméstico, triturador de desperdicios. Favor llamar **39-42-12**.

3. ¿Puedes obtener esta tarjeta de crédito si todavía tienes muchas deudas? ¿Cuánto dinero tienes que ganar para obtener la tarjeta?
4. ¿Qué servicios instala o repara un plomero? ¿Dónde en la casa se encuentra un triturador de desperdicios? ¿Para qué sirve?

5

SE SOLICITA persona responsable
y honesta para trabajo general
casa y cocinar. **Dormir en
colocación.** Referencias
indispensables y papeles en orden.
Domingos libres. $150 semanales.
Día Sr. Cervantes, 234-7834
Noche 234-9079

6

JÓVENES

COMIENCE EL AÑO NUEVO
CON $375 SEMANALES
PROMEDIO PARA COMENZAR.
Se requiere buena presencia,
Escuela Superior, poder comenzar
inmediatamente y deseos de
superarse. Entrenamiento
completo por la Compañía. Para
entrevista pasar adecuadamente
vestido de 9–11 AM de lunes a
jueves. Edif. Banco de la
Mancha, Ofic. 743, Reina (frente
Teatro HAMETE BENENGELI)

5. ¿Qué significa «Dormir en colocación»? (También se dice «Dormir en el trabajo».) ¿La persona tiene que trabajar todos los días? ¿Puede aceptar el trabajo si no ha tenido ese trabajo antes? ¿Cómo lo sabes?

6. ¿Cuánto puedes ganar al mes si consigues este trabajo? ¿Al año? ¿Cuáles son los requisitos? ¿Qué pasa si no tienes experiencia?

7

SECRETARIA EJECUTIVA para
Corredor de Seguros. Bachillerato
o Grado Asociado en Secretarial,
Bilingüe. Que pueda trabajar con
mínimo de supervisión. Salario
de acuerdo a cualificación. Si
cualifica, envíe résumé al:
Apartado 438, Estación Toboso.

8

ENTRENAMIENTO DE perros a
domicilio. 21 años experiencia.
Servicio toda la ciudad. Llamar
a Sancho **16-05-16**.

7. ¿Cuáles son los requisitos de este trabajo? ¿Cuánto dinero puedes ganar? ¿Qué son «los seguros»?

8. ¿Qué hace la persona que anuncia? ¿Para qué sirve este trabajo? ¿Adónde tienes que llevar a tu perro?

9

> **VENDO CABALLOS** o yeguas de paseo o paso fino, mansos, lindos, domados profesionalmente. A precios bien baratos. Para más información favor de llamar al **421-7686** día, **421-3881** noche y hablar con el Sr. Clavileño. Si quiere entrar en el deporte del caballo lo ayudamos con todo para que todos en su familia lo disfruten.

10

> **¡REGALO! BUEN HOGAR** linda gatita, aprox. 8 meses. Tabby Gris, ojos verdes. Esterilizada, vacunada. Inf. **34-82-95**.

9. ¿Cuál es la diferencia entre un caballo y una yegua? ¿Son estos animales fieros —es decir, difíciles de domar (entrenar)? ¿Cuál es otra ventaja de este servicio?

10. ¿Por qué ha sido esterilizada esta gata? ¿Por qué vacunada? ¿Cuánto cuesta el animal?

11

> **OPORTUNIDAD ÚNICA** para todas las novias del 1992. Alquiler de traje de novia y fino tocado (enagua y velo incluidos) $450. Oferta aplica a todos nuestros estilos, incluyendo los nuevos. Si te casas en algún momento este año, apresúrate y separa tu ajuar. Oferta expira el 31 de enero. Inf. 214-4397. Hablar con María Tórnez.

12

> **PARA HOMBRES** solos se alquilan habs. amuebladas, agua, luz, sitio familiar. Calle Gobernador, Núm. 5, cerca Centro Judicial, Barataria.

11. ¿Qué ofrecen a las novias del 92? ¿Qué van a hacer las novias con el traje después de llevarlo puesto? ¿La oferta vale por todo al año?

12. ¿Qué significa «habs.»? ¿Qué ambiente tiene este lugar? ¿Qué hay en el sitio?

13

ARGAMASILLA DE ALBA. Hab. amuebl., dama trabaje fuera. 6000 pts. semanal. No independiente y no fume. Interesadas llamar día al Sr. Carrasco. **35-76-00**.

14

CARPINTERÍA

SE HACEN TRABAJOS de carpintería, albañilería, electricidad, plomería y se pintan casas. Precios razonables. Llamar a **546-8003**, hablar con Ginés.

13. ¿Qué tipo de inquilina busca el dueño de esta casa? ¿La inquilina esperada tendrá que traer su propia cama y una mesa, etc.?

14. ¿Qué quiere y puede hacer la persona que anuncia su trabajo? ¿Cobra mucho por sus servicios? ¿En qué cuartos de la casa se hacen trabajos de plomería?

15

MUDANZAS ROCINANTE:

Estimados gratis. Nuestros precios son incomparables. ¡Yo amo mucho mi trabajo! Inf. **745-8992**

15. ¿Qué trabajo hace Rocinante? ¿Cómo sabes cuánto va a cobrar antes de hacer el trabajo? ¿Te gustaría contratar a Rocinante? ¿Por qué o por qué no?

Conjunctions always followed by the subjunctive

a menos que	unless	**en caso de que**	in case
antes de que	before	**para que**	so that
con tal que	provided	**sin que**	without

No lo hago
{ **a menos que** / **antes de que** / **para que** / **con tal que** / **en caso de que** } **vengan.**

I'm not doing it { unless / before / so that / provided / in case } they come.

Y ya lo entiendo sin que me lo expliques.

And I already understand it without your explaining it to me.

The six conjunctions above begin subordinate clauses that refer to unaccomplished or hypothetical events. The verb in such clauses is in the subjunctive.

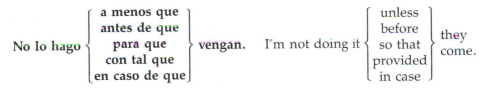

GROLIER, S.A.
SALUDA AL
PUEBLO Y GOBIERNO
DE COSTA RICA
CON MOTIVO
DE LA
CELEBRACION DE

100 AÑOS DE DEMOCRACIA
Y HACE VOTOS
PARA QUE ESTE PAIS
SIGA SIENDO EJEMPLO
DE LIBERTAD Y PAZ

V E N E N O

**Encuentre Los Venenos
En Su Hogar
Antes De Que
Su Niño Lo Haga**

Consejos Para Primeros Auxilios

Veneno Ingerido

Si la persona está consciente y puede tragar:

1. Si la substancia ingerida es un producto doméstico, dilúyase la ingestion con sorbos de leche o agua.
2. No provoque el vómito a menos que sea recomendado por personal médico.
3. Llame al Centro de Venenos LACMA, al médico de la sala de urgencias del hospital o privado para obtener más información referente al tratamiento.

Veneno Inhalado

1. Retire a la persona del foco venenoso.
2. Si está consciente, siente a la persona con la cabeza y los hombros hacia arriba.
3. Si está inconsciente, déle respiración artificial y pida ayuda paramédica.

Contacto de los Ojos con el Veneno

1. Separe los párpados y lave el ojo con suavidad y despacio con agua.
2. Quítese los lentes, si los tiene.
3. Continúe el lavado del ojo durante 10 a 15 minutos. Lávelo de la nariz hacia el extremo del ojo.
4. Llame al Centro de Venenos LACMA, al médico de la sala de urgencias del hospital o privado, referente al tratamiento.

Contacto de la Piel con el Veneno

1. Lave la zona de contacto con agua corriente durante unos 10 o 15 minutos.
2. Llame al Centro de Venenos LACMA, al médico de la sala de urgencias del hospital o privado para mayor información referente al tratamiento.

If there is no change of subject, the infinitive should be used after the three corresponding prepositions **antes de**, **para**, and **sin**.

CHANGE OF SUBJECT

Quieren mostrárnoslo antes de que salgamos.

They want to show it to us before **we** go out.

NO CHANGE OF SUBJECT

Quieren mostrárnoslo antes de salir.

They want to show it to us before going out (before **they** go out).

39.1 Acabe la frase con la forma correcta del verbo indicado.

1. (explicar)   No me marcho hoy sin que ella me lo _____ .

2. (acompañar)   No nos marchamos hoy a menos que ella nos _____ .

3. (entender)   Estoy explicándolo para que Ud. lo _____ .

4. (venir)   Quiere ir con nosotros con tal que _____ tú también.

5. (llamar)   En caso de que _____ Joaquina, dile que no estoy.

6. (oír)   Está gritando para que _____ todos.

7. (decir)   No lo voy a hacer a menos que tú me lo _____ .

8. (llover)   Tenemos que acabar antes de que _____ .

39.2 Complete las oraciones con la frase entre paréntesis.

1. Ella no va a venir (*unless you are here*).
2. No va a comprarlo (*unless it is cheap*).
3. Sí, quiere comprarlo (*provided it is not expensive*).
4. Voy a comprarlo (*before he sees it*).
5. Tenemos que comprarlo (*without his seeing it*).
6. Yo sé lo que pasó (*without her telling it to me*).
7. A ti te lo voy a decir (*in case you don't know it*).
8. Te lo explico a ti (*so that you'll understand*).

39.3 Cambie al español.

1. Give me the money so that I can buy it.
2. Here is the money to buy it.
3. I'll buy it before I leave.
4. I'll buy it before you leave.
5. I buy things without explaining it to him.
6. He already knows this without my explaining it to him.

Unit 40

Indicative vs. subjunctive in time clauses

cuando when	**mientras** as long as, while
después (de) que after	**en cuanto** ⎱ as soon as
hasta que until	**tan pronto como** ⎰

Se lo diremos { **cuando** / **después que** / **en cuanto** / **tan pronto como** } **llegue.**   We will tell him { when / after / as soon as / as soon as } he comes.

No haremos nada { **hasta que** / **mientras** } **esté aquí.**   We won't do anything { until / as long as } he is here.

1. The six conjunctions of time above are followed by the subjunctive when they refer to an event that has not taken place: **Se lo daré cuando lo vea** *I'll give it to him when I see him.*

2. They are followed by the indicative when they refer to past or present (habitual) events.

Le di su cheque cuando lo vi.	I gave him his check when I saw him.
Siempre se lo doy cuando lo veo.	I always give it to him when I see him.
Compró un diario después de que salió.	She bought a newspaper after she went out.
Por lo general compra un diario después de que sale.	Generally she buys a newspaper after she goes out.

3. The subject often follows the verb in subordinate clauses.

Jugarán en el patio hasta que suene la campana de la iglesia.	They'll play in the patio until the church bell rings.

Como Hacer Una Llamada

Es importante que sus hijos aprendan a distinguir entre una llamada local y una de larga distancia. Llamar a alguien que vive lejos cuesta más dinero. Por eso hay que explicarles que la mayoría de las llamadas que uno hace son a personas que viven cerca. También, si habla uno por más tiempo, puede resultar más costoso.

Asegúrese de que sus hijos aprendan su número telefónico, con el código de área. Explíqueles cuándo necesitan marcar el código de área y cuándo no. Recuérdeles que no es necesario marcar el código de área cuando se hace una llamada a un lugar dentro del mismo código de área.

¡Estos Números Cuestan Más!

Hay algunos números telefónicos especiales a los que se llama para averiguar programas de televisión, los resultados del beisbol, la hora, y otra información. Estos números, que comienzan con el **976** o **900**, cuestan más, así como llamar a la operadora **(O)**, también a información **(411)**, y todos los que comiencen con el número uno **(1)**.

Cuando sus hijos llamen, es recomendable que sea con el permiso de usted. No deje que ocupen por mucho tiempo la línea telefónica, ya que otra persona podría estar tratando de llamar. Además, las llamadas largas podrían costar más, y a nadie le gustan las sorpresas en su cuenta de teléfono.

4. If there is no change of subject the prepositions **después de** and **hasta** plus an infinitive may be used instead of the subjunctive.

SUBJUNCTIVE

Voy a preguntárselo después de que vuelvan.	I'm going to ask them after they get back.

INFINITIVE

Voy a prepararlo después de volver.	I'm going to prepare it after I get back (coming back).

5. The time conjunction **antes de que** *before* is not included here with the other time conjunctions because it is *always* followed by the subjunctive.

Por lo general compra un diario antes de que llegue el autobús.	Generally she buys a newspaper before the bus arrives.

40.1 Complete la frase utilizando la forma propia del infinitivo.

1. (llegar)   Va a darme el cheque cuando _____ .
2. (salir)   Siempre compra un diario cuando _____ .
3. (terminar)   Se quedó en la fiesta hasta que _____ .
4. (venir)   Nos dirá lo que pasó tan pronto como _____ su madre.
5. (levantarse)   Siempre se afeita después de _____ .
6. (ver)   Ayer me saludó en español cuando me _____ .
7. (llegar)   Dile a Mario que me llame después de que _____ a Miami.
8. (acabar)   No estará contento mientras no _____ su proyecto.

40.2 Póngalo todo en castellano.

1. Pardon me, gentlemen, but when you finish (**terminar de**) eating, you always pay.
2. As soon as the bill arrives, we will pay.
3. We will pay when our friend returns from the restroom (**cuarto de caballeros**).
4. After he returns, we will be able to pay.
5. As soon as we see him, you will have the money.
6. We won't be able to pay as long as he is not here.
7. We won't leave until we pay.
8. No one is going to leave until the police get here (arrive).
9. And no one left until the police got there.

Unit 41

More on prepositions

 ### A. MEANINGS OF VARIOUS COMMON PREPOSITIONS

> **delante de**   in front of
> **ante**   before, in the presence of

Había muchos estudiantes delante de la biblioteca.	There were many students in front of the library.
Se presentó la evidencia ante el tribunal.	The evidence was introduced before the court.
El tema de esta obra es el hombre ante Dios.	The theme of this work is man in the presence of God.

CON COMBAT, DONDE VIVEN ES DONDE MUEREN.

LAS CUCARACHAS ENTRAN EN LAS CAJITAS DE COMBAT Y SE LLEVAN EL CEBO MORTAL DE VUELTA A LAS PAREDES EN DONDE VIVEN.

¡ALLI, MUCHAS OTRAS CUCARACHAS COMPARTEN EL VENENO... Y MUEREN!

hasta up to, as far as	
desde from	

Hasta el momento no han resuelto nada.	Up to ('til) now they haven't solved anything.
El metro no va hasta el estadio.	The subway doesn't go as far as the stadium.
El autobús que vas a tomar sale desde aquí.	The bus you are going to take leaves from here.
Desde ahora no van a poder usar mi equipo.	From now on they are not going to be able to use my equipment.

debajo de under, underneath (*literal*)	
bajo under (*figurative*)	

Vio un ratón debajo de la mesa.	He saw a mouse under the table.
Bajo la nueva administración va a perder su puesto.	Under the new administration, he's going to lose his job.

sobre over, about (concerning)	
encima de on, on top of	

Uno voló sobre el nido del cuco.	One flew over the cuckoo's nest.
Sobre ese asunto no van a decir nada.	On (concerning) that matter they are not going to say anything.
Deja la cinta encima del televisor.	Leave the tape on the TV.
¿No es peligroso dejar cintas encima del televisor?	Isn't it dangerous to leave tapes on top of the TV?

B. ENGLISH/SPANISH CONTRASTS IN THE USE OF PREPOSITIONS

1. The following Spanish constructions and their English equivalents take a preposition before a complement. The prepositions do not correspond.

Se enamoró de ella.	He fell in love with her.
Se rieron de mí.	They laughed at me.
Se despidió de nosotros.	She said goodbye to us.
Esto trata de la selección nacional.	This deals with (is a matter of) the national team.

Eso depende de ti.	That depends on you.
Cuentan contigo.	They're counting on you.
Dice que sueña conmigo.	She says she dreams about me.
Se preocupan mucho por ti.	They're very worried about you.
Consiste en tres partes.	It consists of three parts.
Fuimos los últimos en llegar.	We were the last to arrive.

2. The Spanish constructions below have a preposition before a complement.

Se oponen a mi decisión.	They oppose my decision.
Se casó con su hermanastra.	He married his stepsister.
No nos dábamos cuenta de eso.	We didn't realize that.
Ha dejado de beber.	She's stopped drinking.
¿Te acuerdas de ella?	Do you remember her?
Se olvidó de su familia.	She forgot her family.
Trataron de ayudarla.	They tried to help her.
Fíjese en esos detalles.	Notice those details.

3. Verbs of motion take the preposition **a** to indicate purpose and destination.

Han llegado a Asunción.	They have arrived in Asunción.
Se cayó al agua.	He fell into the water.
Se marcharon a (para) París.	They left for Paris.
Bajó a (para) saludarnos.	He came downstairs (in order) to greet us.

4. The use of two-word verbs in English (verb + preposition / adverb / particle) has no real parallel in Spanish. Where, for example, English uses one verb plus different adverbs (*go down, go in, go on, go out, go up*), Spanish uses five different verbs (**bajar, entrar, seguir, salir, subir**) with no adverbs.

Lo miró.	He looked at it.
Lo buscó.	He looked for it.
Lo bajaron.	They took (brought) it down.
Lo sacaron.	They took it out.
Volvió.	She came (went) back.
Entró.	She came (went) in.
Subimos al tren.	We got on the train.
Salimos de la casa.	We got out of the house.
Se levantó.	He got (stood) up.
Se fue.	He went away.
Se puso los zapatos.	She put on her shoes.
Nos aguanta.	She puts up with us.
Encendí la luz.	I turned the light on.
Apagué la luz.	I turned the light off.

Diga en español lo que sigue. Cuidado con las preposiciones y los adverbios.

1. Yesterday I was in front of the library.
2. I was going to look for a novel.
3. A novel about love and revolution.

La novela que buscas está ahora en la librería. Ahí la ves, encima del mostrador. El autor cuenta contigo. Quiere que tú la compres.

4. I looked at the titles.
5. One novel is called *Amor y revolución.*
6. I took it out.
7. I went up to my room to read it.
8. I turned the light on. I lay down.
9. This book deals with strange people.
10. A man dreams of marrying his stepsister.
11. He fell in love with her.
12. Under the law he couldn't marry her.
13. Under the circumstances it was impossible.
14. Then he left for Veracruz.
15. He waited for her a year.
16. She never arrived in Veracruz.
17. She forgot him.
18. He threw (**tirar**) himself into the sea.
19. From the first page you realize the truth.
20. I read as far as the third chapter (**capítulo**).
21. I stopped reading.
22. The book consists of many chapters.
23. The author counts on your patience.
24. He depends on your good will (**voluntad**).
25. He wants us to buy this book.
26. This novel is now at the bookstore.
27. On top of the counter (**mostrador**).
28. The author is laughing at the critics (**críticos**).

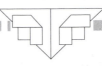

Useful lexical equivalents

Miami sabe a café cubano

saber to know [*facts*]	**conocer** to know [*be familiar/acquainted with people, things, etc.*]
saber + *infinitive* to know how + *infinitive*	
saber (a) to taste (like)	

Sé que Walter sabe algo de francés. I know that Walter knows some French.

Conoce unos verbos franceses. He is familiar with (knows) a few French verbs.

Conoce muy bien París. He knows Paris really well.

Conoce a una familia francesa. He knows a French family.

Sabe los nombres de todos los hijos y los nietos también. He knows the names of all the children and the grandchildren as well.

Sabe hacer un suflé estupendo. He knows how to make a tremendous soufflé.

¿A qué sabe su suflé? What does his soufflé taste like?

Sabe muy bien si te gusta un suflé que sabe a queso limburgués. It tastes very good if you like a soufflé that tastes like Limburger cheese.

conozca el auto de sus sueños...

asistir to attend	**atender** to look after, take care of
perder to miss, lose, waste	**cumplir con** to carry out, fulfill, comply with

No asistió a la reunión.	He did not attend the meeting.
Ha perdido todas las reuniones de este mes.	He has missed all the meetings this month.
Tenía la dirección, pero la perdió.	He had the address, but he lost it.
Uno no debería perder el tiempo así.	One should not waste time like that.
Me atendieron muy bien mientras estuve en Granada.	They took good care of me while I was in Granada.
No cumple con sus deberes.	He doesn't fulfill his obligations.

tener éxito   to be successful; to succeed
suceder   to occur, happen
lograr   to succeed, achieve
lograr + *infinitive*   to succeed in + *present participle*

Tuvo mucho éxito en Nueva York.	She was very successful in New York.
¿Y qué sucedió en Londres?	And what happened in London?
También logró un gran éxito allí.	She also achieved great success there.
Lograron desarmar la bomba.	They succeeded in defusing the bomb.

---

ponerse to become, get [*temporary condition—thus used with adjectives*]

hacerse to become, get [*achieve/attain a certain state or position through effort—thus used with either adjectives or nouns*]

llegar a ser to get to be, to become [*after a period of time*]

En esa época se ponía deprimida con frecuencia.	In those days she often became depressed.
Pero a pesar de eso, se hizo una bailadora rica y famosa.	But in spite of that she became a rich and famous dancer.
En efecto, llegó a ser primera bailarina en el Bolshoi de Moscú.	In fact, she became (got to be) prima ballerina in Moscow's Bolshoi company.

---

disfrutar (de) to enjoy

gozar (de) to enjoy

Rosa goza (disfruta) mucho corriendo maratones.	Rosa enjoys running marathons.
Rosa goza (disfruta) mucho de correr maratones.	
Goza el sabor de Santo Domingo. Disfruta bailando el merengue. Visita la primera universidad de América.	Enjoy the flavor of Santo Domingo. Enjoy dancing the merengue. Visit the first university in America.
Deseamos disfrutar (gozar) del sol cuando vamos de vacaciones.	We want to enjoy the sun when we go on vacation.
De lo que goza (disfruta) Jorge es de un bistec con un montón de papas fritas.	What Jorge enjoys is a steak with lots of French fries.

> **querer/desear**   to want, to wish
> **querer**   to love

No quiere (desea) casarse ahora.	He doesn't want to get married now.
Quiere mucho a la abuela.	She loves her grandmother very much.

> **preguntar**   to ask (*for information*)
> **pedir**   to ask for (*something from someone*)
> **hacer una pregunta**   to ask a question
> **preguntar por**   to ask for/about (*someone, something, etc.*)

Me preguntó dónde había estado.	He asked me where I had been.
Nos pidió más ayuda.	He asked us for more help.
Tengo que hacerte tres preguntas.	I have to ask you three questions.
Preguntó por ti.	{ He asked for you [to see you]. { He asked about you.

---

dejar to leave (behind)
dejar de + *infinitive* to stop (doing something); to fail (to do something)
dejar caer to drop (*usually on purpose*)

Lo dejaron aquí.	They left it here.
Por fin, dejó de fumar.	He finally stopped smoking.
No deje de depositar el cheque mañana mismo.	Don't fail (be sure) to deposit the check tomorrow for sure.
El ladrón dejó caer la pistola.	The robber dropped his gun [*on purpose*].

---

ponerse a + *infinitive* to begin; to go about (doing something)
volver a + *infinitive* to do (something) again

Se pusieron a limpiar el suelo.	They began to clean the floor.
Anoche volví a leer la propuesta. **Anoche leí la propuesta otra vez.**	Last night I read the proposal again.

---

porque [+ *clause*] because [+ *clause*]
a causa de, por [+ *noun or infinitive*] because of
debido a [+ *noun or infinitive*] due to [+ *noun or gerund*]

Ganaron porque no jugaron limpio.	They won because they didn't play fair.
Perdimos a causa de (por, debido a) los penales.	We lost because of (due to) the penalties.

Escriba estas cartas en español.

Dear Mom,

Up to now I have enjoyed playing baseball in the winter. I enjoy playing in Venezuela, too. They said the experience would be good.

But we lost again last night. And I missed the team meeting (**reunión del equipo**) yesterday. They asked for me, somebody said.

Walter is my roommate here, the outfielder (**jardinero**) from Cheraw. Walter knows how to cook. He also knows some (**algo de**) Spanish, thank heaven (**gracias a Dios**). He attends classes. And he knows how to make

Las llamadas «ligas del invierno» de Centro y Sudamérica. Aquí se juega el béisbol profesional a un nivel muy alto.

chicken and rice (rice with chicken). It tastes very good even though it tastes like butter (**mantequilla**) instead of olive oil (**aceite de oliva**).

But I miss (**extrañar**) you all, Mom. All the time. I don't know what to say. I believe I am going to leave the team.

Your son who loves you,

Rogelio

Dear Dorita,

José María called again. You know him. He was asking about you. I asked him a question. Then he dropped a bomb. He said he wants to marry you. He says he loves you.

He was very successful in Madrid. And he achieved great success in Barcelona, too. He is going to become famous. He never stops talking about his successes. He enjoys talking about himself (**sí mismo**). Because of all this, he has become very boring (**aburrido**). Anyway, he asked me for your address.

But I know him, Dorita. Leave him. I say this from the bottom of my heart (**de todo corazón**).

Your good friend,

Consuelo

Diversión y práctica 11

Leyendo el diario

Lee los siguientes trozos del diario e indica si lo que dicen las oraciones que siguen es «cierto» o «falso».

En 1989 se presentó en la televisión norteamericana un programa llamado *Los más buscados de América* o America's Most Wanted. En el programa se relató la historia de un hombre de Nueva Jersey que 18 años antes había matado a toda su familia. Desde entonces el asesino había eludido la justicia. En el programa se presentó una fotografía del hombre de 1971 y una maqueta o imagen de cómo podría ser hoy. Un público de 22 millones vieron el programa. Esa misma noche el FBI recibió más de 300 llamadas. Dos semanas después, el asesino fue detenido por la policía en el estado de Virginia, donde era un agente de seguros muy respetado por sus vecinos.

1. En Estados Unidos el número de televidentes es enorme.
2. Al verdadero criminal no lo encontraron.
3. El FBI sólo investiga los robos de bancos.
4. La policía no pudo arrestar al hombre porque había pasado demasiado tiempo.
5. En este informe sí se cumplió con la justicia.

La desesperada práctica de almacenar gasolina, que algunos ciudadanos iniciaron en días pasados al anticiparse un alza en el precio del combustible, resulta sumamente peligrosa. El Servicio de Bomberos advirtió ayer sobre el peligro del almacenamiento, que está reglamentado por ley. Pedro Mataincendios, jefe, indicó que «para el almacenaje de gasolina se utilizarán envases debidamente aprobados y con la rotulación adecuada donde se identifique el producto almacenado». Además se prohíbe la venta de gasolina en envases que no estén debidamente aprobados, así como «el depósito, manejo o uso de gasolina en exceso de cinco galones en el interior de viviendas, o en exceso de 10 galones en el interior de cualquier otro edificio sin haberse obtenido el correspondiente permiso».

1. Algunos ciudadanos creen que la gasolina va a estar muy barata.
2. Almacenar gasolina no es buena idea porque no es seguro.

3. Se puede almacenar gasolina en cualquier cosa.

4. Tienes que poner algo escrito en el envase de gasolina para que todos sepan que es gasolina.

5. No se debería almacenar 10 galones de gasolina en una casa particular.

11:30 AM   BANDOLERO — Canal 12
Dos desesperados de Texas escapan a México con una rehén, pero se encuentran en territorio de bandidos. Situaciones adultas y violencia. Con Dean Martin y James Stewart.

12:30 PM   EL ENDEMONIADO — Canal 4
Un exorcista trata de resolver la misteriosa ola de fuegos que aterroriza una escuela de niñas en Massachusetts. Violencia. Con James Farentino y Harrison Ford.

2:00 PM   ¿QUIÉN ES HARRY CRUMB? — Canal 9
El intrépido investigador a través de un caso de secuestro no sabe que su suerte tonta es su mejor aliada. Lenguaje fuerte. Con John Candy.

7:00 PM   ASESINO EN EL ESPEJO — Canal 16
Hermanas idénticas, y aunque una de ellas ha asesinado a su marido y al de la hermana, no se puede saber cuál fue. Drama con Ann Jillian y Jessica Walter.

10:00 PM   CAZAFANTASMAS II — Canal 22
Los tipos que salvaron al mundo de las fuerzas demoníacas vuelven a juntarse cuando unos poderes sobrenaturales amenazan con destruir a Nueva York. Situaciones maduras y lenguaje fuerte. Con Dan Akroyd y Sigourney Weaver.

---

1. Los criminales van a México solos.

2. El exorcista amenaza a las niñas de la escuela.

3. El investigador es un poco tonto, pero no le causa dificultades.

4. Cada una de las dos hermanas mata a su propio esposo.

5. Los hombres tratan de salvar a la ciudad de Nueva York de unas fuerzas monstruosas.

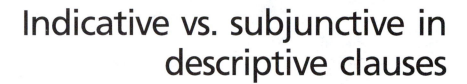

Unit 43

Indicative vs. subjunctive in descriptive clauses

A descriptive or adjective clause is a subordinate clause that modifies a noun or pronoun. The noun or pronoun, like *man* in the following sentence, is called the "antecedent."

Main Clause	Descriptive Clause
I know a man	who eats pistachio nuts in bed.

A. THE ANTECEDENT IS A NEGATIVE EXPRESSION— USE THE SUBJUNCTIVE.

SUBJUNCTIVE	INDICATIVE
Negative Antecedent	**Antecedent Exists**
No hay nada que le guste.	**Aquí hay algo que le gusta.**
There is nothing he likes.	Here is something he likes.
No conozco a nadie que hable catalán.	**Aquí viene una señora que habla catalán.**
I don't know anyone who speaks Catalan.	Here comes a lady who speaks Catalan.
Aquí no tienen libros que vayan acompañados de programas de computadora.	**Aquí venden muchos libros que van acompañados de programas de computadora.**
Here they don't have any books that have computer programs with them.	Here they sell lots of books that have computer programs with them.

FUTUROS PERROS-GUIA BUSCAN FAMILIA

La **Organización Nacional de Ciegos** tiene prevista la implantación de su Escuela de Perros-Guía en la zona Noroeste de Madrid.

La instrucción de estos perros, que se inicia desde el primer mes de vida, ha de realizarse durante el primer año en un núcleo familiar donde reciban cariño y atención.

Todas aquellas familias que residan en las localidades de la zona Noroeste de Madrid y que deseen colaborar en la educación de los cachorros, pueden dirigirse a los teléfonos 734 85 89 y 734 74 50 de la O.N.C.E., donde se les ampliará esta información.

B. THE ANTECEDENT IS A PERSON OR THING UNSPECIFIED IN THE SPEAKER'S MIND— USE THE SUBJUNCTIVE.

SUBJUNCTIVE	INDICATIVE
Antecedent Not Specific in Speaker's Mind	**Antecedent Is Specific in Speaker's Mind**
Necesito un vuelo que salga temprano.	**Déme el vuelo que sale temprano.**
I need a flight that leaves early.	Give me the flight that leaves early.
El niño que no traiga su anorak en esta excursión va a tener mucho frío.	**¿Dónde está el niño que no trajo su anorak?**
The child who doesn't bring his hooded jacket on this outing is going to be very cold.	Where is the child who didn't bring his hooded jacket?
Los que vuelen en el Concorde van a gastar bastante.	**Mi tío, que vuela a menudo en el Concorde, gasta bastante.**
Those who fly on the Concorde will spend plenty.	My uncle, who flies regularly on the Concorde, spends a bundle.
El que quiera comprar temprano encontrará muchas tiendas todavía cerradas.	**El que compra temprano puede escoger.**
Whoever wants to shop early will find a lot of stores still closed.	The one who shops early can choose.

C. THE CLAUSE REFERS TO SITUATIONS, PLACES, PERSONS, ETC., UNDETERMINED AND UNSPECIFIED IN THE SPEAKER'S MIND—USE THE SUBJUNCTIVE.

SUBJUNCTIVE	INDICATIVE
Clause Represents Something Unspecified In the Future	**Clause Represents Something Specific In the Present or Past**
Llenaré el formulario como me digan.	**Lleno el formulario como me dicen.**
I will fill out the form whichever way (however) they tell me.	I fill out the form just the way they tell me to.
Van a ofrecernos lo que tengan.	**Nos ofrecen lo que tienen.**
They will offer us whatever they have.	They offer us what they have.
Nos va a decir lo que sepa del crimen.	**Nos ha dicho lo que sabe del crimen.**
He is going to tell us whatever he knows about the crime.	He's told us what he knows about the crime.
Quiere trabajar donde tengan los mejores beneficios marginales.	**Trabaja aquí, donde tienen los mejores beneficios marginales.**
She wants to work wherever they have the best fringe benefits.	She works here where they have the best fringe benefits.

43.1 Sustituya lo subrayado por las palabras entre paréntesis. Cambie lo que haya que cambiar. Por ejemplo:

(ningún carro) Hay <u>un carro</u> que nunca tiene problemas. → **No hay ningún carro que nunca tenga problemas.**

1. (nadie) Hay <u>una persona</u> aquí que ha ido al Ecuador.
2. (aquí hay) <u>Buscamos</u> un almacén que venda microondas.
3. (no tiene ninguna) El vecino <u>tiene una herramienta</u> que podemos usar.
4. (algo) No hay <u>nada</u> en la lección que no entendamos.
5. (ningún) Conozco a <u>varios</u> chicos que son miembros del club.
6. (una persona) No hay <u>nadie</u> aquí que fume.
7. (nadie) Vive aquí <u>una señora</u> que ha ganado la lotería.
8. (algunos) No van a visitar <u>ningún</u> sitio que me interese.

43.2 Complete la frase con la forma apropiada del infinitivo.

1. (saber) ¿Conoce Ud. a alguien que _____ la dirección?
2. (poner) No le gustaba la película que ellos _____ anoche.
3. (ir) Conozco a un fanático que _____ a todos los partidos sin falta.
4. (ir) No conozco a nadie que _____ a todos los partidos sin falta.
5. (servir) Aquí no se vende nada que nos _____ .

6. (explicar)   Esperan encontrar un manual que _____ cómo funciona la impresora.

7. (explicar)   Ya tienen un libro que lo _____ todo.

8. (levantarse)   Los que _____ tarde mañana van a perder el tren que va a Machu Picchu.

9. (llegar)   Los turistas que _____ esta mañana están descansando ya.

10. (pasar)   Los turistas que _____ demasiado tiempo en el bar esta noche no podrán levantarse temprano mañana para ir a las ruinas.

11. (gustar)   Aquí hay una cosa que le va a _____ mucho.

12. (gustar)   Pruebe Ud. cualquier cosa que le _____ .

43.3 Traduzca.

1. I see a woman who wants to dance with you, señor.

2. There is no one here who wants to dance with me.

3. Is there anybody here who knows how to dance the lambada?

4. No, but there is one person here who knows how to dance the merengue.

LECTURA VII

Read the article, noting the constructions illustrated and their use: participles, verb tenses, numbers and dates, reflexives, prepositions, and infinitives. Review and comprehension exercises based on the reading follow.

Mientras el cuerpo aguante...[1]

En las carreteras españolas hay aún[2] 350.000 ejemplares del Seat 600[3] en funcionamiento, pese a que° en 1972 dejaron de fabricar este coche. A José Ortiz de Echagüe, primer presidente de Seat, le dieron la orden de motorizar a los españoles, y a fe° supo cumplirla.

    En mayo de 1957 salió el primer coche y, según los sociólogos, con el seiscientos España pasó del siglo XIX al XX. Ha servido para hacer peregrinaciones° a Lourdes y escapadas a los cines porno de Biarritz[4]. Fue el coche más vendido en Finlandia durante tres años consecutivos. Ha sido picadero° de una generación de españoles expertos a la fuerza° en gimnasias amatorias y hogar provisional para otros que no tenían techo. Ahora se está convirtiendo en el primer coche-kleenex—usar y tirar—de la historia del automovilismo español.

    El seiscientos lo diseñó un italiano, Dante Giacossa, padre de casi todos los coches de la Fiat. Se concibió como un utilitario[5] de fácil manejo°, mecánicamente simple pero resistente° y de poco consumo°, cualidades que lo pusieron al alcance° de los bolsillos y las habilidades de conducción de los españoles de los años cincuenta. No todos se quedaron en España. Las primeras exportaciones fueron a Colombia. Se hizo famoso en Alemania y Holanda, y fracasó en Francia. En España había cola° de cuatro años para adquirirlo.

    El 600 tenía muy repartidos° virtudes y vicios. Es cierto que en caso de golpe la barra de dirección° clavaba el volante° en el pecho del conductor. Pero las averías° se podían arreglar en herrerías y fraguas°, ventaja nada desdeñable° en tiempos en que escaseaban° los talleres. El depósito de gasolina delantero suponía tremendo riesgo, pero era poco exigente en carburantes° y admitía cualquier líquido parecido a la gasolina.

despite the fact that

truly

pilgrimages

bachelor pad
a... *of necessity*

easy to drive / durable
fuel consumption / within reach

line (waiting period)

well-distributed
steering column / steering wheel / breakdowns
machine shops/by no means unimportant / were scarce
poco... *not very demanding in fuel*

«Viajábamos mucho mi señora y yo, sobre todo en los veranos. Salíamos por la carretera de Valencia y a lo mejor volvíamos un mes después por la de La Coruña.»

Típica quizá es la historia del Seat 600 M-482.817°, que cumple más de 23 años. Se encuentra en perfecto uso de sus cualidades mecánicas, aunque es verdad que sufre de los naturales efectos de tan avanzada edad. En su laboriosa vida, en manos de cuatro distintos dueños, ha recorrido un número difícilmente calculable de kilómetros.

 °license plate number (M = Madrid)

En contadas° ocasiones ha dejado tirados° a sus conductores. Tirado, lo que se dice tirado[6], quedó Jaime Ferrer hace un año. «Fui a sentarme, cedió° todo el piso y quedé literalmente sobre el asfalto. Menos mal que no se rompió del todo[7] y le busqué solución metiendo una barra de hierro. Así sigue.»

 °rare / stranded

 °gave way

La madrileña que lo compró primero es Aurora Fernández. No quiere confesar su edad pero acabada la guerra[8] aprendió a conducir con un Ford T.

«Nosotros habíamos tenido chófer de toda la vida, pero al acabar la guerra no podía ser y tuve que aprender a conducir yo misma. Lo hice sola, practicando. Hemos tenido el Ford T y un Opel General, pero a mí la Seat me parece muy buena marca. Los 600 los compraba, les hacía° 25.000 ó 30.000 kilómetros y tan pronto como empezaba a fallar° algo los vendía.»

 °put

 °fail (break down)

Así pasó este ejemplar° de que hablamos, en 1973, a los siete años de su edad, a manos de Amancio Cabezón, hoy taxista jubilado y vecino de Madrid.

 °example (i.e., individual car)

«Yo sólo puedo hablar bien de él. No nos dejó nunca en la carretera como otros. Lo usábamos mucho mi señora y yo, sobre todo los veranos. Salíamos por la carretera de Valencia y a lo mejor volvíamos un mes después por la de La Coruña. Lo pinté yo mismo, de mano.»

Según Jaime Ferrer, el tercer dueño, «mi mujer acababa de sacarse el carné[9] y vimos un anuncio en el *Segunda Mano*. Nos costó 20.000 pesetas. ¿El viaje más largo? Pues al hipermercado. Más lejos no, porque se calentaba mucho el motor. Por lo demás°, no *As for the rest* andaba mal. El que me lo vendió me regaló todos los repuestos°, *spare parts* un carburador, un delco°, cilindros. En fin, llevábamos otro coche *battery / an extra car* encima°. Otra cosa era cambiar las piezas. Una vez pinché° y no *besides / I had a flat* había manera de sacar la rueda°. Estaba literalmente pegada° al *wheel / stuck (frozen)* tambor del freno°. Nunca la habían desmontado. La sacamos a *brake drum* mazazos[10].»

Una amiga de la familia, Elisa Becerril, es desde hace dos meses la feliz propietaria de este esforzado° vehículo. *tough*

«Me lo regalaron. Bueno, pusimos° que era una venta de *we agreed* 5.000 pesetas. Lo tengo en una fábrica de lácteos° en la que tra- *dairy products* bajo. Me entreno con él para sacarme el carné. Doy vueltas por° *I drive around* el aparcamiento de la fábrica hasta que se calienta. Me examino° *I'll take my test* en un par de meses.»

«¿De qué color es el coche? No sé, es un color indefinido, tirando a gris°. El original lo desconozco. ¿No te lo han dicho los *kind of grayish* anteriores dueños?»

Notas

1. **Mientras el cuerpo aguante**   *As long as the body holds out.*
2. **Aún** bears a written accent whenever it means **todavía** *still* or follows the verb. Elsewhere **aun** (without an accent) has the same meaning as **hasta/incluso** *even.*
3. **Seat 600**   make of automobile first mass-produced in Spain in the 1950s. Similar to the Italian Fiat, the 600 model was a low-cost **mini-coche** built in Barcelona and designed to be economical to run.
4. **Biarritz**   city in southwestern France on the Bay of Biscay.
5. **Un (coche) utilitario**   a small car built to be practical and useful without regard for looks or fancy design.
6. **Tirado, lo que se dice tirado**   *stranded, what you can really call being stranded.*
7. **Menos mal que no se rompió del todo**   *Thank goodness it wasn't completely broken.*
8. **Acabada la guerra = cuando acabó la guerra** (i.e., the Spanish Civil War, 1936–1939).
9. **Sacarse el carné**   *to get one's driver's license.* **Carné** refers not only to a driver's license but to any ID card in general.
10. **A mazazos**   *by means of hammer blows* (**mazo** *mallet, hammer*). The suffix **-azo** on certain nouns often conveys a meaning similar to *a blow with . . . , a blast with . . . ,* and the like:

frenos	*brakes*	**frenazo**	*jamming on the brakes*
puerta	*door*	**portazo**	*slamming the door*
puño	*fist*	**puñetazo**	*blow with the fist*

¡EL GRAN CAMPANAZO!
del 1 al 17 de Febrero
"Más de cien artículos en 3x2"

Sopas normales MAGGI
64
LLEVE 3 Y PAGUE 2

Juego de Estrellas: un exitazo

Como equipo principiante en la NBA, Miami ha tenido sus altas y bajas, más de lo último que de lo primero.

PELOTAZOS

un acuerdo con su lanzador zurdo Allan Anderson, renovarán el lunes su contrato por una cantidad estimada en $300,000, pero el agente ·' lanzador dijo que lo alargará lo

---

At other times, the suffixes **-azo/-aza**, **-ote/-ota**, **-ón/-ona** are used to indicate large size, at times with a derogatory meaning:

silla	*chair*	**sillón**	*armchair*
perro	*dog*	**perrazo**	*big (ugly/ferocious) dog*
palabra	*word*	**palabrota**	*swear word*

Ejercicios de Repaso

A. En estas frases paralelas note Ud. la diferencia o la semejanza en el uso de las palabras subrayadas. Tal vez en un caso u otro se le ocurra a Ud. usarlas en otras frases más bien originales, o traducirlas.

1. (a) pese a que en 1972 dejaron de fabricar este coche
   (b) a pesar de que en 1972 cesaron de fabricar este coche
2. (a) la orden de motorizar a los españoles
   (b) el orden cronológico / el orden público
3. (a) durante tres años consecutivos
   (b) durante tres años seguidos
4. (a) un italiano diseñó el seiscientos
   (b) el seiscientos lo diseñó un italiano
5. (a) se concibió como un coche utilitario
   (b) fue concebido como un coche utilitario
   (c) lo concibieron como un coche utilitario
6. (a) no todos se quedaron en España
   (b) no todos permanecieron en España
7. (a) se hizo famoso en Alemania
   (b) llegó a ser famoso en Alemania

8. (*a*) es cierto que clavaba el volante en el pecho del conductor
   (*b*) hoy no es cierto que clave el volante en el pecho del conductor

9. (*a*) una ventaja nada desdeñable
   (*b*) una ventaja de ningún modo desdeñable

10. (*a*) un depósito de gasolina delantero
    (*b*) un depósito de gasolina trasero

11. (*a*) es verdad que sufre de los efectos
    (*b*) no es verdad que sufra de los efectos

12. (*a*) se encuentra en perfecto uso
    (*b*) se halla en perfecto uso

13. (*a*) en manos de cuatro distintos dueños
    (*b*) en manos de cuatro dueños diferentes

14. (*a*) acabada la guerra aprendió a conducir
    (*b*) cuando acabó la guerra aprendió a conducir
    (*c*) al acabar la guerra aprendió a conducir

15. (*a*) tan pronto como empezaba a fallar algo lo vendía
    (*b*) tan pronto como empiece a fallar algo lo voy a vender

16. (*a*) ella acaba de (*has just*) sacarse el carné
    (*b*) ella acababa de (*had just*) sacarse el carné

17. (*a*) Elisa es desde hace dos meses la feliz propietaria
    (*b*) hace dos meses que Elisa es la feliz propietaria

18. (*a*) me entreno con él para...
    (*b*) practico con él para...

B. Diga en español estas fechas y números.

1492	siglo XII	500	2.700
1898	siglo XVIII	868	4.860
1939	siglo XIX	60.000	350.000
1992	siglo XX	1.004	7.000.000

C. Exprese en español.

1. When the war was over, I had to learn to drive.
2. I did it alone, I myself.
3. After three months, I got my driver's license.
4. Then I bought myself a 600.
5. It never left me on the highway.
6. I would sell each car as soon as something started to break down.
7. My longest trip? Well, to the supermarket because the engine used to get hot.
8. What color was my car?
9. It is difficult for me to describe it. Sort of grayish, I think.
10. A family friend has been the new owner of the 600 for two months.

D. Comprensión

1. Explique con sus propias palabras lo que quiere decir la expresión «motorizar a las españolas».
2. Exprese también lo que quiere decir el autor con la curiosa frase «coche-kleenex».
3. ¿De dónde vino el diseño del 600?
4. ¿Cuánto tiempo había que esperar para adquirir un 600?
5. ¿En qué país fracasó el 600?
6. ¿Cuántos kilómetros ha recorrido el 600 cuya historia se detalla en el artículo?
7. Si ponemos por caso que el cambio de un dólar vale ahora cien pesetas, ¿cuántos dólares son 20.000 pts.?
8. ¿Qué quiere decir la expresión un coche «utilitario»?

Lea los anuncios y explique o conteste en español.

1. ¿Cuál es el juego de palabras en «¡Ahorra, o nunca!»
2. ¿Qué quiere decir el término aquí «reposesiones» (autos reposesionados)?
3. ¿Qué ocurre en una subasta?

4. Un aviso ofrece el consejo de convertir en ganancia propia la pérdida de otro. Explique cómo puede resultar esto.
5. ¿Por qué es importante una inspección de seguridad?

ESPECIAL DE CAMBIO DE ACEITE

Incluye:
• Hasta 5 Cuartos De Galon De Aceite
• Filtro Adicional

ESPECIAL DE TUNE-UP

Incluye:
• 4 Bujias
• Ajuste De Tiempo
• Inpeccion De Mangueras
• Inspeccion De Seguridad En 25 Puntos.

LUN.-VIER.
9-8
SABADO
9-6

¡Sí! Somos el único SUPER CENTRO
de camiones usados
en Nueva Jersey de

MACK TRUCKS, INC.

**2nd. St. & Central Ave. (P.O. Box 626)
Kearny, New Jersey 07032**

Tenemos para la venta
camiones de todas
marcas, años y modelos.

Sí, sabemos de lo que hablamos cuando hablamos de camiones usados de cualquier marca o tamaño.

¡¡NUEVA VENTA DEL GERENTE!!

¡Estamos Empeñados En Superar Todas Las Marcas De Ventas En Febrero!!

• ¡ENORME EXISTENCIAS!
• ¡INCENTIVOS ESPECIALES PARA CLIENTES!
• ¡MAGNIFICOS PRECIOS!

¡AHORRA, O NUNCA!

APURESE, OFERTA LIMITADA

¡LOS PRECIOS MAS BAJOS!

Traiganos La Mejor Oferta y Si La Nuestra
No Es Mas Baja... ¡Le Regalamos 100 Galones de Gasolina!†

SUBASTA

SABADO
FEB. 24
1:00 p.m.

68 Autos De Modelo Reciente

Bajo techo llueva o truene

ALMACEN DE REPOSESIONES
SE ACEPTAN OFERTAS DIARIAMENTE

Aprobación inmediata de ofertas y entrega instantánea de vehículos. Convierta la perdida de otro en su ganancia.

ABIERTO AL PUBLICO

ABIERTO PARA INSPECCION DIARIAMENTE 9 A 5
$500 Depósito en efectivo para cada auto que compra

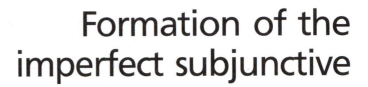

Unit 44

Formation of the imperfect subjunctive

Infinitive	Third-Person Plural Preterit Indicative		Imperfect Subjunctive	
pasar	pasar-on	→	pasar-a	pasár-amos
			pasar-as	pasar-ais
			pasar-a	pasar-an
entender	entendier-on	→	entendier-a	entendiér-amos
			entendier-as	entendier-ais
			entendier-a	entendier-an
escribir	escribier-on	→	escribier-a	escribiér-amos
			escribier-as	escribier-ais
			escribier-a	escribier-an

The imperfect subjunctive is formed by replacing the ending **-on** of the **ellos** form of the preterit indicative with the endings **-a**, **-as**, **-a**, **-amos**, **-ais**, **-an**. Thus any irregularity in the preterit is also found throughout the imperfect subjunctive. (Note that the first-person plural form has a written accent.)

Examples of stem-changing and other irregular verbs follow.

Infinitive	Preterit Base Form	Imperfect Subjunctive
pedir	pidieron	pidiera, pidieras, etc.
sentir	sintieron	sintiera, sintieras, etc.
servir	sirvieron	sirviera, sirvieras, etc.
seguir	siguieron	siguiera, siguieras, etc.
reír	rieron	riera, rieras, etc.
repetir	repitieron	repitiera, repitieras, etc.
dormir	durmieron	durmiera, durmieras, etc.

morir	murieron	muriera, murieras, etc.
creer	creyeron	creyera, creyeras, etc.
oír	oyeron	oyera, oyeras, etc.
leer	leyeron	leyera, leyeras, etc.
caer	cayeron	cayera, cayeras, etc.
-uir	construyeron	construyera, construyeras, etc.
	incluyeron	incluyera, incluyeras, etc.
dar	dieron	diera, dieras, etc.
ver	vieron	viera, vieras, etc.
ser	fueron	fuera, fueras, etc.
ir	fueron	fuera, fueras, etc.
decir	dijeron	dijera, dijeras, etc.
traer	trajeron	trajera, trajeras, etc.
-ducir	produjeron	produjera, produjeras, etc.
	tradujeron	tradujera, tradujeras, etc.
querer	quisieron	quisiera, quisieras, etc.
hacer	hicieron	hiciera, hicieras, etc.
venir	vinieron	viniera, vinieras, etc.
andar	anduvieron	anduviera, anduvieras, etc.
estar	estuvieron	estuviera, estuvieras, etc.
tener	tuvieron	tuviera, tuvieras, etc.
haber	hubieron	hubiera, hubieras, etc.
poder	pudieron	pudiera, pudieras, etc.
poner	pusieron	pusiera, pusieras, etc.
saber	supieron	supiera, supieras, etc.

In Spanish America most speakers use these **-ra** forms for the imperfect subjunctive. In Spain both these **-ra** forms and alternate forms in **-se, -ses, -se, -semos, -seis, -sen** are used. The two forms are generally equivalent in meaning. Examples of the **-se** form follow.

hablase	hablásemos	escribiese	escribiésemos
hablases	hablaseis	escribieses	escribieseis
hablase	hablasen	escribiese	escribiesen

pidiese	pidiésemos	dijese	dijésemos
pidieses	pidieseis	dijeses	dijeseis
pidiese	pidiesen	dijese	dijesen

44.1 Para cada infinitivo dé la forma indicada (**-ra, -ras,** etc.) del imperfecto del subjuntivo.

  1. (yo)   pasar / escribir / hacer / creer / escuchar
  2. (tú)   tomar / conducir / beber / vivir / pedir
  3. (ella)   oír / leer / dar / perder / cerrar

4. (ustedes)   sentir / encender / caer / creer / decir
5. (nosotros)   reír / destruir / traer / producir / poder
6. (ellos)   saber / poner / estar / tener / querer
7. (él)   seguir / pedir / dormir / repetir / morir / servir

44.2 Complete cada frase con la forma conveniente del imperfecto del subjuntivo (**-ra**, etc.).

1. Era posible que la novia no (**presentarse**) a la boda.
2. Era también probable que el novio no (**asistir**) tampoco.
3. Era lamentable que los novios (**ser**) dos personas tan frívolas.
4. Era curioso que los dos (**ser**) personas poco serias.
5. El padre de la novia quería que el novio (**trabajar**) para su compañía.
6. Quería que él (**aceptar**) un puesto en Los Ángeles.
7. La madre del novio quería que la pareja (**vivir**) en San Antonio.
8. Era imposible que todos (**llegar**) a un acuerdo.
9. Los abuelos les escribieron que (**venir**) a vivir con ellos.
10. Luego la novia le pidió al novio que (**escribir**) una carta al padre de ella.
11. Quería que él le (**explicar**) la situación a su padre.
12. Parecía mejor que Plácido, el novio, y Reposo, la novia, no (**casarse**) jamás.
13. Era triste que (**pasar**) tanto tiempo en peleas.
14. Francamente yo dudaba que los jóvenes (**ir**) a casarse.
15. Las dos madres esperaban que sus hijos no (**verse**) durante por lo menos un mes entero.
16. Yo les propuse a los enamorados que (**salir**) en un viaje de novios para no volver jamás.
17. Yo les dije que (**irse**) en seguida.
18. Pero negaron que (**estar**) enamorados.
19. Yo no creía que ellos me (**decir**) la verdad.
20. Yo quería que la pareja (**encontrar**) felicidad y contento.
21. No estaba seguro de que ellos (**poder**) encontrar la paz.
22. Pidieron que yo (**callarme**) de una vez.
23. Luego se marcharon para París sin que lo (**saber**) nadie.
24. Llegaron a la ciudad de los enamorados antes de que yo (**darme cuenta**) de que habían partido.
25. Le pidieron a un pastor protestante que los (**casar**) bajo el Arco de Triunfo.
26. Iban a estar contentos mientras (**quedarse**) allí tan solitos.
27. Parecía probable que (**estar**) alegres con tal que no los (**visitar**) sus padres.
28. Yo les conté esta historia para que Uds. (**aprender**) algo del imperfecto del subjuntivo.
29. Si Uds. (**leer**) todo esto en voz alta, eso sí sería bueno.
30. Pero aceptaríamos su decisión si Uds. no (**querer**) hacerlo, porque no queremos molestar a nadie, especialmente ahora y en esta parte del libro.

Unit 45

Uses of the imperfect subjunctive

A. TENSE EQUIVALENTS

The imperfect subjunctive is essentially the subjunctive counterpart of the imperfect indicative and conditional tenses.

Present / Future	Present Subjunctive	
Juan va. **Juan irá.**	**No creo que vaya.** I don't think	he is going. he will go.

Preterit / Present Perfect	Present Perfect Subjunctive	
Juan fue. **Juan ha ido.**	**No creo que haya ido.** I don't think	he went. he has gone.

Imperfect / Conditional	Imperfect Subjunctive	
Juan iba. **Juan iría.**	**No creía que fuera.** I didn't think	he was going. he would go.

B. USAGE

The imperfect subjunctive is used for past events in subordinate clauses that require the subjunctive.

260

Present Time Frame	Past Time Frame
Temo que no les guste.	**Temía que no les gustara.**
I'm afraid they don't like it.	I was afraid they didn't like it.
Quiere que jueguen afuera.	**Quería que jugaran afuera.**
She wants them to play outside.	She wanted them to play outside.
Me sorprende que no vayan.	**Me sorprendió que no fueran.**
It surprises me they aren't going.	It surprised me that they weren't going.

The imperfect subjunctive is used after:

1. Expressions of emotion like **alegrarse de, esperar, temer,** etc.

Esperábamos que viniera. { We hoped he was coming.
{ We hoped he would come.

Nos gustaba que aprendiera tanto. We were pleased { he was learning so much.
{ he would learn so much.

Sentíamos que no pudieran ir. We were sorry { they were not able to go.
{ they could not (would not be able to) go.

2. Expressions of doubt like **dudar, no creer, no estar seguro de,** and **negar**.

Dudaban que dijera la verdad. They doubted that he would tell the truth.

Negaron que estuviera allí. They denied that he was there.

3. Implied commands with verbs like **querer, decir,** and **pedir**.

Quería que salieran pronto. She wanted them to leave soon.

Le pedí que hablara más despacio. I asked him to speak more slowly.

Insistieron en que pagáramos en seguida. They insisted we pay at once.

4. Many impersonal expressions (excluding those of belief and certainty like **es cierto** and **es verdad**).

Era preferible que destruyeran los recibos. It was preferable for them to destroy their receipts.

No era verdad que lo supiera. It was not true that he knew it.

Era preciso que estuviera allí un poco temprano. It was necessary for her to be there a little bit early.

Era posible que quisieran pasar más tiempo en Cancún. It was possible they would want to spend more time in Cancún.

Era triste que lo creyeras. It was sad that you believed it.

5. Conjunctions that always require the subjunctive.

Lo trajeron para que lo vieras primero. They brought it so that you might see it first.

Me lo dio sin que se lo pidiera.	She gave it to me without my asking her for it.
Estaban discutiendo antes de que vinieras.	They were arguing before you came.

6. Unspecified and negative antecedents.

Buscábamos un vuelo que hiciera escala en Centro América.	We were looking for a flight that made a stop in Central America.
No vi a nadie que tuviera aspecto sospechoso.	I didn't see anyone who looked suspicious.

45.1 Cambie al pasado, según el ejemplo.

Es probable que lo crea. → **Era (fue) probable que lo creyera**.

1. No creo que vaya.
2. Javier niega que sean espías.
3. No es verdad que sepamos hacerlo.
4. Espero que me lo den en seguida.
5. Es preciso que estén en la reunión.
6. Siempre me lo da sin que yo se lo pida.
7. Es dudoso que compren una cosa dañada.
8. Dudo que diga la verdad.
9. No veo a nadie que los conozca.
10. Es triste que crean eso.
11. Es preferible que los niños no jueguen en el camino.
12. Hace todo el trabajo antes de que lleguen.
13. Es posible que quieran ir.
14. Busco un vuelo que salga temprano.
15. Lo traigo para que lo veas tú.
16. Quiere que hablen depacio.
17. Temo que no les guste.
18. Pide que le contesten más pronto.
19. Sentimos que no puedan ir.
20. Nos sorprende que aprendan tanto.
21. ¿Quieres que los niños salgan a jugar?
22. Me dicen que no sea tan soso.
23. Nos dice que tengamos más cuidado.
24. ¿Te alegras de que no haya más preguntas?

45.2 Complete con una forma del infinitivo. A veces hay más de una forma aceptable.

1. (ir)   Es posible que Martín no _____ .
2. (ir)   Era dudoso que Miguel _____ .
3. (recitar)   Nos pide que _____ más rápido.
4. (recitar)   Les pidió que _____ rapidísimo.
5. (leer)   Era imposible que nosotros lo _____ todo tan rápido.
6. (saber)   Era ridículo exigir que yo lo _____ todo.
7. (llegar)   Era absurdo que _____ el tren tan tarde.
8. (llegar)   Era verdad que el tren siempre _____ tarde.

   9. (hacer)   Era cierto que ellos no lo _____ a tiempo.

   10. (hacer)   Querían que yo lo _____ a tiempo.

   11. (completar)   Era preciso que ellos _____ el proyecto para hoy.

   12. (venir)   Era necesario hacerlo antes de que _____ el jefe.

   13. (saber)   Lo hicieron sin que lo _____ su madre.

   14. (estar)   Negaron que ellos mismos _____ allí.

   15. (estar)   No negaron que ellos _____ allí.

   16. (estar)   Yo creía que ellos _____ allí.

   17. (estar)   Yo no creía que ellos _____ allí.

   18. (saber)   Lo hacen sin que lo _____ su padre.

   19. (tener)   Buscan un apartamento que _____ tres dormitorios.

   20. (gozar)   Encontraron un apartamento que _____ de una enorme sala de estar.

45.3 Cambie al inglés o al español, según el caso.

   1. Querían ir más tarde pero yo les dije que fueran ahora.

   2. *I wanted to take three suitcases, but they told me to take one.*

   3. Lo hicieron. Nunca creí que lo hicieran.

   4. *I wrote the letter. They never believed I would write it.*

   5. Tenían tanto miedo. Negaron que tuvieran tanto miedo.

   6. *I was really afraid, but I denied that I was so afraid.*

   7. Me dio veinte dólares a pesar de que le pedí que me diera diez.

   8. *I contributed fifteen dollars although they asked me to contribute forty.*

   9. Ocupaban un apartamento de lujo pero buscaba otro que tuviera más espacio.

   10. *She was living in the country, but it was necessary for her to live in the city.*

   11. Dijo que él tenía que llamarla antes de que ella lo llamara a él.

   12. *I lost my mother's keys. I had to find them before she found out (knew it).*

   13. La quería mucho. Parecía imposible que pudiera vivir sin ella.

   14. *She loved him very much. It was impossible for her to live without him.*

   15. No tenían nada. Les envié dinero para que vinieran a verme.

   16. *He often slept until 10:30. I had to yell in order for him to wake up.*

Escribiendo una carta

Todos tenemos que escribir cartas de vez en cuando si no soportamos el costo cada vez máz elevado del teléfono. Ahora bien, una breve comunicación escrita en español y de cualquier índole es la orden del día. Puede ser una misiva emocionante al novio despedido, una explicación a las autoridades policiales de tu súbita ausencia de la ciudad y de su jurisdicción, o lo que sea. Por ejemplo:

Querido tío Ignacio,

¿Qué tal está? ¿Cómo encuentra la vida ahí en esa comunidad de jubilados? Supongo que con tanto sol se siente más joven y, se espera, más generoso. Para decirlo tal como es, voy a confesar francamente que aquí en la universidad hay un pequeño problema. Para la inspección anual de mi auto viejo y las reparaciones me quieren cobrar $200. Sólo usted, querido tío, me puede ayudar. Le agradezco toda su ayuda en años pasados, y pienso ir a visitarle cuanto antes.

Reciba un abrazo cariñoso de su sobrino, que siempre recuerda la inmensa paciencia y generosidad que le ha mostrado,

Roberto

Ahora escribe una carta de unos diez renglones (diez líneas) a tu novio (o novia), quien está en tu ciudad natal, no aquí en la universidad. La carta puede ser de «despedida» o de «puro amor». Por ejemplo:

Querido amigo...,

Es muy difícil escribirte esta carta porque, como sabes, no estamos juntos y...

o posiblemente

Mi amor,

Sin ti la vida aquí es un enorme vacío sin sentido que casi no aguanto. Pero en dos semanas más...

O, si prefieres, la carta a la policía indicada antes.

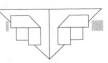

Unit 46

Clauses with *si*, *como si*, and *aunque*

A. *SI*-CLAUSES IN THE INDICATIVE

Si viene, lo veremos.	If he comes, we will see him.
Si tenemos el dinero, lo compraremos.	If we have the money, we will buy it.
Si llueve, no iremos.	If it rains, we won't go.
Si lo sabe, nos lo dirá.	If she knows it, she will tell us.
Si necesitas algo, me lo dices.	If you need something, you tell me.

The **si**-clauses above express something that may or may not happen: **Si él viene** (he may come, he may not), **Si lo tenemos** (we may have it, we may not). The events introduced by **si** here are possible. In present or future time, they may or may not occur in the speaker's mind. When the idea of possibility is present, the tense in the **si**-clause is in the indicative.

Si tú me querías, no lo sabía.	If you loved me, I didn't know it. [Possibly you loved me, possibly you didn't.]

B. *SI*-CLAUSES IN THE SUBJUNCTIVE

Si viniera, lo veríamos.	If he came, we would see him.
Si tuviéramos el dinero, lo compraríamos.	If we had the money, we would buy it.
Si lloviera, no iríamos.	If it rained, we wouldn't go.
Si lo supiera, nos lo diría.	If she knew it, she would tell us.
Si necesitara algo, te lo diría.	If I needed something, I would tell you.

1. The **si**-clauses above are in the imperfect subjunctive. A **si**-clause in this tense expresses something that contradicts facts, now or in the future. **Si viniera** *If he came* means that the speaker thinks that either he won't come or it is highly

unlikely that he will. **Si tuviéramos el dinero** *If we had the money* means that we do not have the money, but if we did.... **Si lo supiera** *If he knew it* means that he doesn't know it, but if he did.... Thus this type of sentence is called "contrary-to-fact."

2. When the main clause is in the conditional, the **si**-clause is usually in the imperfect subjunctive.

3. The examples above refer to *present or future time*, as does the following sentence.

> **Si lo hiciera ahora mismo / mañana, le darían un poco extra.** *If he did it right now / tomorrow, they would give him a little extra.*

This sentence can be stated in *past time*, using the *past perfect* subjunctive in the **si**-clause and the *conditional perfect* in the main clause.

> **Si lo hubiera hecho ayer, le habrían dado un poco extra.** *If he had done it yesterday, they would have given him a little extra.*

Notice again that this is a contrary-to-fact sentence because he did *not* do it yesterday.

The past perfect subjunctive is formed with the imperfect subjunctive of **haber** (**hubiera, hubieras,** etc.) plus a past participle. The English equivalent is *had* + past participle. The past perfect subjunctive is the subjunctive counter-part of the past perfect indicative. It is used in subordinate clauses requiring the subjunctive in which the meaning is *had* + past participle: **Si hubiera venido . . .** *If he had come. . . .*

The conditional perfect is formed with the conditional of **haber** (**habría**, **habrías**, etc.) plus a past participle. The English equivalent is *would have* + past participle: **Lo habríamos visto** *We would have seen him.*

The future perfect is formed with the future of **haber** (**habré**, **habrás**, etc.) plus a past participle. The English equivalent is *will have* + past participle: **Lo habremos visto** *We'll have seen it.*

These tenses are not stressed in this book.

C. *COMO SI* *AS IF*

Como si-clauses are always in the subjunctive since they describe a situation that is unreal, hypothetical, and "contrary-to-fact."

Ella te habla como si te conociera bien.	She talks to you as if she knew you well [but she doesn't].
Me habla como si fuera mi padre.	He talks to me as if he were my father [but he isn't].

D. *AUNQUE* *ALTHOUGH / EVEN THOUGH / EVEN IF*

Aunque trabajan muchas horas, no ganan mucho.	Although (even though) they work a lot of hours, they don't earn very much.
Aunque trabajen muchas horas, no ganarán mucho.	Even if they work a lot of hours, they won't earn very much.
Aunque trabajaran todos los días de la semana, no ganarían mucho.	Even if they worked every day of the week, they would not earn very much.

When a fact is stated in a subordinate clause beginning with **aunque** (= *although, even though*), the verb is in the indicative.

Aunque llovió toda la tarde, no cancelaron el partido.	Although it rained all afternoon, they didn't cancel the game.
Aunque tienes un título, todavía no tienes empleo.	Even though you have your degree, you still don't have a job.

When a hypothetical statement is made in a subordinate clause beginning with **aunque** (= *even if*), the verb is in the subjunctive.

Aunque hubiera llovido toda la tarde, no habrían cancelado el partido.	Even if it had rained all afternoon, they wouldn't have canceled the game.
Aunque tuviera un título, no tendría empleo con este paro.	Even if he had his degree, he wouldn't have a job with this unemployment.

El autobús sigue siendo un medio de transporte muy usado en varios países hispanos. El autobús pone al alcance del viajero aun el pueblo más remoto. ¿Y quién sabe qué aventura le puede ocurrir?

Aunque tenga un título, no tendrá empleo con este paro.	Even if he has (gets) a degree, he won't have a job with this unemployment.

46.1 Cambie la oración a otra que exprese algo contrario a la realidad. Por ejemplo:

Si viene, lo veremos.→**Si viniera, lo veríamos.**

1. Si lo sabe, se lo dirá a ella.
2. Cancelan el partido si llueve.
3. Si puedo trabajar horas extras, le doy algo a él.
4. Si tú vas conmigo, podemos prosperar juntos.
5. Si practicamos más, ganaremos.
6. Si tú me lo dices, no se lo repito a nadie.

7. Si se lo doy a ellos, no saben aprovecharlo.
8. Si estoy en casa el miércoles, pueden llamarme por la mañana.

46.2 Cambie la oración a otra que exprese una idea opuesta a la realidad. Por ejemplo:

Aunque soy su amigo, no me gusta su actitud. *Although I am his friend, I don't like his attitude.* → **Aunque fuera su amigo, no me gustaría su actitud.** *Even if I were his friend, I wouldn't like his attitude.*

1. Aunque tengo suficiente dinero, no lo compro ahora.
2. Aunque ponen todas las luces, no se ve nada desde aquí.
3. Aunque David es vegetariano, come huevos y pescado.
4. Aunque escribe toda la noche, no mejora su ensayo para la clase de inglés.
5. Aunque ganan muchos partidos, no merecen el título de campeones.
6. Aunque llueve constantemente, no hay suficiente agua.

46.3 Traduzca al español.
1. If I had to say *Stop the bus* in Spanish, what would I say?
2. If I travel in Mexico this summer, I am going to say **Pare el camión.**
3. If Julie were going to Mexico, she too would say **Pare el camión.**
4. But **camión** means *truck* in other countries.
5. Believe me, if you are in Mexico, use the word **camión.**
6. Well, I would say **guagua** if I were from the Caribbean (**el Caribe**) or the Canary Islands (**las Islas Canarias**).
7. What word would I use if I were in Spain?
8. If you're in Spain, you won't be on a bus.
9. Yes, but how is it said in Spain?
10. If you spoke Spanish, you would ask: "Where does one take **el autobús?**"
11. Then what is an **autocar**?
12. In Spain it is a very big **autobús**, very comfortable (**cómodo**), that makes long trips.
13. But in certain Latin countries, an **autobús** is an **autocar.**
14. I find myself confused (**confundido / a, perplejo / a**).
15. It does not surprise me that you find yourself confused.
16. If I were you, I would go to Colombia or Peru or Uruguay, where one often says **el bus** or **el ómnibus.**
17. Even if I live a thousand years, I'll never forget it.
18. Even if I lived a thousand years, I'd never forget it.
19. Even if she arrives on time, we won't have enough time.
20. Even if she had arrived on time, we wouldn't have had enough time.

Unit 47

Nosotros commands and other uses of the subjunctive

A. *NOSOTROS* COMMANDS

Let's + verb is expressed in two ways.

Vamos a + Infinitive	Nosotros-Form of Present Subjunctive	*Let's* + *Verb*
Vamos a salir.	Salgamos.	Let's go outside.
Vamos a hacerlo.	Hagámoslo.	Let's do it.
Vamos a sentarnos en un círculo.	Sentémonos en un círculo.	Let's sit in a circle.

1. Only context determines whether **Vamos a hablar** means *Let's talk* or *We are going to talk*.

2. However, for the negative command with **nosotros** only the subjunctive is used. **No lo hagamos** means *Let's not do it*. **No vamos a hacerlo** means only *We are not going to do it*.

3. Pronoun objects are placed as with other commands. They are attached to affirmative commands (**Digámoselo** *Let's tell (it to) him*) and placed before as separate words with negative commands (**No se lo digamos** *Let's not tell (it to) him*).

4. The final **-s** of the **nosotros** subjunctive form is omitted when the reflexive **nos** is added: **Levantémonos temprano** *Let's get up early*. However, it is present when **nos** precedes the verb: **No nos levantemos temprano** *Let's not get up early*.

5. Also, one **s** is omitted when the **nosotros** subjunctive form precedes **-selo/la**, etc.: **Digamos** + **se** + **lo** = **Digámoselo**.

6. The subjunctive form **vayamos** is never used as an affirmative **nosotros** command. *Let's go* is only **Vamos** or **Vámonos**. However, *Let's not go* is **No vayamos** or **No nos vayamos**.

47.1 Diga en español lo que sigue. Dé las dos formas de los mandatos afirmativos. Por ejemplo:

Let's see →**Veamos / Vamos a ver.**

1. Let's eat.
2. Let's not sit down.
3. Let's not do it now.
4. Let's go in (**entrar**).
5. Let's invite her.

6. Let's go upstairs.
7. Let's not go.
8. Let's go!
9. Let's not sit (down) here.
10. Let's leave it.

B. USE OF THE SUBJUNCTIVE IN MAIN CLAUSES

1. Ojalá (que) *I wish, I hope* is always followed by the subjunctive.

Ojalá pudiera venir mañana.	I wish she could come tomorrow.
Ojalá pueda venir mañana.	I hope she can come tomorrow.
Ojalá que pudiéramos ganar, pero no hay esperanza.	I wish we could win, but it's hopeless.
Ojalá que no se haya perdido.	I hope she hasn't gotten lost.
Ojalá que hubieran ganado.	I wish they had won.

Once again the past subjunctive is "contrary-to-fact," expressing something that is not true or is not likely to be so (English *wish*). The present subjunctive expresses something that may happen (English *hope*).

2. Tal vez and **quizá/quizás** *perhaps, maybe* are followed by the subjunctive to express uncertainty.

Tal vez lleguen ahora.	Perhaps they are arriving now [but I'm not sure].
Quizás comiencen a las tres.	Maybe they'll start at three [who knows?].
Tal vez no lo haya vendido todavía.	Maybe he hasn't sold it yet [I have no idea].

The indicative is used to indicate a fair degree of certainty on the part of the speaker.

Quizá lo sabe. Perhaps he knows [I bet he does].

3. The **-ra** forms of the imperfect subjunctive of **deber**, **poder**, and **querer** are used to make polite requests and statements.

Quisieran hablar con usted, señor.	They would like to speak with you, sir.
Debieras hablar con tu consejera.	You (really) should speak with your advisor.
¿Pudiera Ud. indicarme la guagua de la universidad?	Could you (please) point out the bus that goes to the University?

47.2 Conteste con *ojalá*, según los ejemplos.

¿Vendrá tu amigo pronto?
Una respuesta posible es: **No sé. Ojalá (que) venga pronto.** (*I don't know. I hope he comes soon.*). Existe la posibilidad. Pero si no es probable, la respuesta correcta es: **Ojalá (que) viniera pronto, pero lo dudo.** (*I wish he would come soon, but I doubt it*).

1. ¿Volverá pronto tu amigo? (¿Qué piensa Ud.?)
2. ¿Cuesta la excursión más de cien dólares?
3. ¿Va a ganar tu equipo?
4. ¿Ya se van los invitados?

47.3 Exprese en español.

1. You (really) ought to finish your work now.
2. Could you (please) help me now?
3. We would like to know when the plane arrives.

Unit 48

Relative pronouns

que	that, which, who, whom
quien / **quienes**	who, whom
el que / **la que** / **los que** / **las que**	which, who, whom
el cual / **la cual** / **los cuales** / **las cuales**	which, who, whom
cuyo / **cuya** / **cuyos** / **cuyas**	whose (*noun modifier*)

1. Relative pronouns connect descriptive or adjective clauses with the nouns or pronouns they modify. Relative pronouns in English include *that*, *which*, *who*, and *whom*. Spanish relative pronouns are **que**, **quien**, **el que**, and **el cual**, with their corresponding variants as seen in the box above. (**Cuyo**, a relative adjective, is discussed in section D below.)

2. Relative pronouns are often omitted in English, but they are never omitted in Spanish: **la joven con quien estudiaste** *the girl you studied with*.

3. Prepositions always precede relative pronouns in Spanish, which is not the case in conversational English.

la cosa de que me quejaba	the thing I was complaining about
el amigo con quien (con el que) viajo	the friend I am traveling with
los hombres para quienes trabaja	the men he works for

A. *QUE*

Que is the most common relative pronoun in Spanish. It can refer to either objects or persons.

El policía que vino al apartamento nos hizo muchas preguntas.	The policeman who came to the apartment asked us a lot of questions.
El hombre que tú viste salir era un policía.	The man (that, who) you saw come out was a policeman.
La casa que querían comprar es muy pequeña.	The house (that) they wanted to buy is too small.

273

Informaciones telefónicas

En estas páginas usted encontrará la información necesaria para aprovechar al máximo su servicio telefónico. Si usted tiene dificultad para comunicarse en inglés con alguien en la compañía de teléfonos, trataremos de que una persona que hable español lo ayude. O alguna persona que usted conozca y que hable inglés, podrá ayudarlo a discutir con nosotros cualquier asunto relacionado con su servicio telefónico.

Números que pueden servirle
El "0" para la operadora.

Servicio de reparaciones
La New York Telephone se ocupa de su servicio telefónico local, el cuál incluye llevar, a usted, el tono de marcar y la línea de acceso a las cadenas locales y de larga distancia. Si usted tiene problemas en su línea, tales como falta de tono de marcar, interferencias, cortes en la comunicación o imposibilidad de completar una llamada o de recibirla, llame al servicio de reparaciones al **611**. Muchas veces, aunque no sea nada aparente, como el disco o el cordón roto, el problema puede estar en el teléfono. Si usted llama al servicio de reparaciones, un técnico probará su línea y tratará de determinar dónde está dicho problema y le aconsejará de acuerdo con él.

La New York Telephone ya no repara teléfonos. Si usted alquila su teléfono llame al suplidor de aparatos telefónicos.
Si usted compró su teléfono, revise la garantía para saber cómo repararlo.

La Telefónica

Si usted desea obtener servicio telefónico en la ciudad de New York, por primera vez, llame al **430-1281** entre 9 a.m. a 5 p.m. de lunes a viernes. Todos los empleados de La Telefónica hablan español y, además de tomar su orden, le contestarán las preguntas que usted quiera hacer acerca de su nuevo servicio telefónico.

Pedidos de emergencia
Por la noche, durante los fines de semana o días de fiesta en que nuestras centros de servicio están cerrados, si usted tiene una situación de emergencia (que no sea reparación) en relación con el servicio telefónico o una queja que requiera atención inmediata, llame sin cargo al **1 800 722-2300.**

Números de teléfonos importantes

Centro de control de envenenamientos ...	**764-7667**
Centro de reportes de abuso infantil y maltrato (sin cargo)	**1 800 342-3720**
Línea de ayuda en casos de violación	**267-7273**
Emergencia para escapes de gas Con Edison	**683-8830**
Emergencia en el servicio de agua	**966-7500**
Medicaid	**594-3050**
Licencias matrimoniales ...	**269-2900**
Cupones de alimentos	**1 718 237-7371**
Pasaportes Oficina	**541-7700**
Registro de nacimientos y muertes	**619-4530**
Línea rápida para víctimas de crímenes	**577-7777**
Línea de asistencia para víctimas de maltrato en el hogar	**1 800 942-6908**

Conozco a dos profesores que juegan al tenis todos los sábados.

I know two professors who play tennis every Saturday.

El apartamento en que vivían quedaba muy lejos del recinto.

The apartment they were living in was too far from campus.

B. *QUIEN / QUIENES*

This pronoun refers only to persons. One of its most frequent uses is after prepositions. Personal **a** precedes **quien** used as a direct object.

El agente a quien llamamos nunca respondió.	The salesman we called never answered.
Es un anciano por quien tengo muchísimo respeto.	He's an old man for whom I feel a great deal of respect.
Mis compañeros, quienes (que) son todos colombianos, insistían en hablar inglés durante el viaje.	My friends, who are all Colombian, insisted on speaking English during the trip.
Su tía, quien (que) no parece muy amable, nos invitó a la boda.	Her aunt, who doesn't seem very friendly, invited us to the wedding.

Note that in the last two examples above, the descriptive or adjective clause is separated from the main clause by commas (or in speech, by pauses), since it is not considered an essential part of the statement. In such cases either **quien/es** or **que** may be used as the subject *who* of the adjective clause.

But if the adjective clause is considered integral and essential to the sentence's meaning, it is not set off from the main clause by pauses, and only **que** can be used as the subject *who*. A frequent error is the use of **quien** for *who* as subject in sentences such as these.

El hombre que nos dirigió la palabra hoy me ofreció el puesto.	The man who spoke to us today offered me the job.
Ahí está la joven que ganó la medalla.	There's the young girl who won the medal.

C. *EL QUE / EL CUAL*

El que (**la que**, etc.) and **el cual** (**la cual**, etc.) refer to persons and objects. They agree in number and gender with the noun they refer to. They are used after prepositions with the meaning *which* or *whom*. **El que** and **el cual** thus alternate with **que** and **quien** and are often used in descriptive clauses set off by commas. Note that the following three sentences all mean exactly the same thing, the last being the most common.

Ahí ves la maquinaria con que van a excavar el terreno.

Ahí ves la maquinaria con la cual van a excavar el terreno.

Ahí ves la maquinaria con la que van a excavar el terreno.

There you see the machinery with which they are going to excavate the site.*

---

*Note that after the one-word prepositions **a**, **con**, **de**, and **en**, the relative pronoun **que** alone can be used when referring to things: **El apartamento en que vivían quedaba muy lejos del recinto** *The apartment they were living in was very far from campus.*

More examples:

El cañón por el que (por el cual) caminábamos era hondo y estrecho.	The canyon through which we were walking was deep and narrow.
El fútbol americano, sobre el cual (sobre el que) no sé casi nada, es un deporte muy televisado en EE.UU.	American football, about which I know almost nothing, is a sport widely televised in the U.S.
La familia de Arturo, a la que (a la cual) habíamos conocido antes, iba a veranear en el Mar de Cortés.	Arturo's family, whom we had met earlier, was going to vacation on the Sea of Cortez.
Fueron a visitar la ciudad de Antigua, cerca de la cual (cerca de la que) vieron el lago de Atitlán.	They went to visit the city of Antigua, near which they also saw Lake Atitlán.
Nuestra ruta nos llevaba hasta las minas de sal de Zipaquirá, dentro de las que (dentro de las cuales) hay una iglesia subterránea.	Our route took us as far as the salt mines of Zipaquirá, inside of which there is a subterranean church.

D. *CUYO*

Cuyo *whose* is a relative adjective. It agrees with the following noun and is used only in descriptive clauses. The word *whose* in questions is always **¿De quién/es?**.

Mi amigo, cuya biblioteca personal es enorme, va a vender unos quinientos tomos.	My friend, whose personal library is enormous, is going to sell about five hundred volumes.
La chica cuyo padre ganó la lotería está en nuestra residencia.	The girl whose father won the lottery is in our dorm.
¿De quién es la maleta?	Whose suitcase is it?

E. *EL QUE* = *THE ONE WHO, THAT*

El que (**la que**, etc.) is used with the meaning *the one(s) who / the one(s) that* to introduce a noun clause: **el que me gusta** *the one that I like*, **las que prefiere él** *the ones that he prefers*.

Los que se levantan temprano son los que llegan primero.	The ones (those) who get up early are the ones who get there first.
El que más se queja es el que más se beneficia.	The one who complains most is the one who benefits the most.

Las extraordinarias naves de la Catedral de Sal están hechas de las galerías de una antigua mina de sal. Esta mina en Zipaquirá, Colombia, cerca de Bogotá, aún hoy continúa en producción.

48.1 Llene los espacios en blanco con **que, quien, quienes,** o **cuyo**.

1. Aquí viene el cartero, _____ nunca tiene cartas para mí.
2. Ahora sabemos el nombre de la mujer _____ te llamó.
3. Mariano es el joven con _____ vamos a Toronto este verano.
4. El estudiante a _____ le diste los papeles los perdió.
5. Aquéllas son las muchachas de _____ estábamos hablando.
6. La celebración _____ iba a comenzar el jueves se ha cancelado.
7. No entiendo el plan de _____ me hablaste anoche.
8. Ahí está el apartamento en _____ vivíamos antes.

9. La gobernadora es una mujer por _____ tenemos mucho respeto.

10. No sé los nombres de los profesores de _____ siempre se quejan los estudiantes.

11. Aquí hay una herramienta con _____ puedes ajustar el carburador.

12. Quiero asistir a una universidad _____ equipo de fútbol siempre juegue en un «bowl».

48.2 ¿Cómo se dice en español?

1. We have a bookstore whose prices are outrageous (**un escándalo**).

2. And they sold me a book whose pages are torn.

3. Whose book is this?

4. She is a woman whose name is impossible to pronounce.

5. The one who eats first eats best.

6. Those who register (**matricularse**) early get (**sacar**) the best courses (**clases**).

7. Who's the one who did this?

8. They say that those who sit in front get (**sacar**) better grades (**notas**).

9. Those who live in glass houses (**casas de cristal**) should not throw stones (**tirar piedras**).

10. He who laughs last (**el último**) laughs best.

48.3 Complete el espacio en blanco con las formas correspondientes de el que y el cual.

1. Ahí está la guagua detrás de _____ viajamos tres horas.

2. Ella vivió en la Riviera muchos años, después de _____ pasó a vivir en un sanatorio para pobres.

3. Estudié en Salamanca tres veranos, al fin de _____ hablaba muy bien el español.

4. En el hospital tuve cinco o seis enfermeras, entre _____ tres eran monjas.

5. Tienes que seguir andando hasta la segunda bocacalle, a la izquierda de _____ encuentras el edificio que buscas.

6. El accidente ocurrió ahí cerca de ese árbol, debajo de _____ están jugando unos niños.

LECTURA VIII

*Read the passage, noting the constructions illustrated: clauses with **si** and **aunque**, participles, reflexives, infinitives, and relative pronouns. Review and comprehension exercises based on the reading follow.*

«Caravana de mujeres»

(enero de 198–)

> Se necesitan mujeres entre 20 y 40 años con fines matrimoniales para pueblo del Pirineo[1] aragonés.

El anuncio de arriba, que costó quince duros°, apareció un día en un periódico de Huesca[2]. El pueblo indicado en el anuncio es Plan, en el valle de Gistau (Huesca), una pequeña población de 750 habitantes en la que durante años muchos hombres y algunas mujeres se han ido quedando solos con los padres. Las chicas casaderas°, mientras tanto, se fueron a trabajar a Huesca o a Barbastro. En los pueblos cercanos ocurre igual, o es que las mozas tienen novio de fuera. Así es el caso de Pili, de 20 años, que trabaja en hostelería° en Ainsa, un pueblo a 40 kilómetros, y piensa que «en el valle hay chicas que se casarían aquí si los mozos les dijeran algo». Ella no acepta la excusa de la timidez de los lugareños°, porque «yo, si un chico me gustara, se lo diría descaradamente°».

    En todo caso, se han quedado en Plan en estas fechas 142 solteros, todos recios° miembros de la raza pirenaica, acostumbrados a los 14 grados bajo cero° en el duro invierno que azota° esta región montañosa.

    —Mosén[3], con este frío es muy difícil pecar° contra el sexto° . . .

    —Pues . . . sí,—contesta el párroco° del valle de Gistau, que vive exactamente en Plan.

    Bromas aparte°, pueden ser brutales los inviernos de aquí. El último pueblo señalizado° antes de llegar a Plan se llama Sin, como avisando de qué va la fiesta allá arriba[4]. La ruta Sin–Plan transcurre° por varios túneles con estalactitas de hielo y conduce a una planicie° que ha dado nombre al pueblo de esta historia, que comenzó una gélida° noche de enero en el bar del pueblo.

    Un grupo de solteros se entretiene viendo la película *Caravana de mujeres* (en inglés *Westward the Women*), y se les ocurre imitar a los protagonistas de la película y hacer un llamamiento a las mozas casaderas de la provincia, con vistas a modificar su estado civil.

*15 **duros** = 75 **pesetas***

of an age to marry

hotels and tourism

villagers
boldly

robust
= 7° Fahrenheit /
* punishes*
to sin / sixth
(commandment) /
parish priest
all joking aside
identified on a road sign

passes
plain
frigid

La ruta transcurre por varios túneles y conduce a una planicie que ha dado nombre al pueblo de esta historia, que comenzó una gélida noche de enero en el bar del pueblo.

«Aunque no podíamos mandar a Robert Taylor a recoger chicas», explica un soltero de 44 años, de profesión carpintero, «pues si subieran 10 ó 20* a los carnavales, bueno sería.»

Según Pepe, el secretario del Ayuntamiento°, que no busca novia porque ya la tiene en Huesca, «Con lo que nos planeamos aquí, no cabe° hacer un paralelismo en plan rapto de las sabinas[5] y decir que así se fundó Roma con algo semejante, porque como aquí vamos de° cultos y civilizados, no vamos a ir a secuestrarlas al pueblo de al lado.»

town hall

it isn't right

porque... *since here we behave like*

(febrero de 198–)

Dos semanas después apenas° creían lo que pasaba. La noticia había salido en las televisiones y medios de comunicación de todo el mundo. Solteras del mundo entero y periodistas de Europa y América bloquearon durante todo el día el teléfono 50-60-48 de Huesca. Incluso° se puso en contacto con ellos una viuda° zaragozana[6] que residía en París. Nadie sospechaba la repercusión de la propuesta de los recios pirenaicos.

scarcely

even/widow

Ante la avalancha de llamadas la soltería° de Plan tuvo que establecer en el bar un cuartel general de recepción de candidatas. El transeúnte° podía oír a Mariano, que trabaja en la ganadería°, anotando datos y en contacto ahora con Canarias[7]: «Candelaria, ¿cuánto mides? ¿Uno y pico?[8] ¿Y cuánto es el pico?»

all the bachelors

passer-by/cattle farming

Pero no se trataba de atractivo físico, insistían los solteros, sino de otras cualidades más duraderas° y más importantes. Para todas las candidatas, que serían trasladadas a Plan en autocares°

lasting

buses

---

*Between numerals, the word **o** *or* takes a written accent to avoid confusion with the number 0: **10 ó 20** *ten or twenty.*

pagados por el Ayuntamiento, y alojadas en las casas del pueblo, se daría una gran fiesta, comida y orquesta incluidas.

En medio de todo esto, acostándose prácticamente el último y disfrutando como salsa de todos los guisos°, está el mosén, que lleva en el pueblo más de 13 años y parece tener poca actividad profesional. Celebró la última boda hace año y medio[9], y responde a la pregunta de cuál es el sacramento que administra con más frecuencia diciendo: «La extremaunción°». Está dispuesto a celebrar las bodas que vengan, aunque «si a los cuatro días° se van a tirar los platos a la cabeza, pues no merece la pena.»

cooked dishes

last rites
after four days

(mayo de 199-)

Los pasados días 29 y 30 de abril se celebró la Quinta Caravana o Fiesta de los Solteros de Plan, a la que asistieron unas 100 mujeres. En estos años se han celebrado 33 matrimonios y han nacido varios hijos. El panorama ha cambiado en el valle de Gistau, y más concretamente en Plan. «Se ha creado ilusión° por luchar y seguir adelante», declara José María Fantova, autor, con Luis Roger, del libro *Plan: tal como fue*°. El libro recoge paso a paso cómo nació la primera caravana y los acontecimientos posteriores. Han copiado la experiencia en Cataluña[10], en otros pueblos de Aragón y Castilla, en Canadá, Suiza y Austria.

enthusiasm

Plan: the Way It Was

El pueblo ha pasado de tener unas rústicas fondas[11] a un hotel con 20 plazas, un restaurante, farmacia, comercios y otros servicios, como un pabellón de fiestas°. Antes los niños del valle tenían que acudir a una escuela de Boltaña, a 47 kilómetros. Se sentían desarraigados° y había fracaso° escolar. Pero ahora ha cambiado todo eso y Plan ha conseguido su propia escuela «Valle de Gistau».

entertainment center

uprooted/failure

Según el nuevo presidente de la Asociación de Solteros del Valle de Gistau, «Plan es hoy diferente. Hasta° los típicos pesimistas que nos auguraban° todo tipo de fracasos han tenido que cambiar su bola de cristal.»Y aun el propio párroco° de Plan ha encontrado en una de las caravanas una ama de llaves° que lo cuide.

Even
predicted
the priest himself
ama... *housekeeper*

Notas

1. **Pirineo**   Pyrenees mountains, which separate Spain from France.
2. **Huesca**   northern province and its capital in the upper Aragon region along the central Pyrenees.
3. **Mosén**   title (from Catalán) given to clergy in northern Aragon (similar to English *monsignor*).
4. **como avisando...allá arriba**   *as if giving notice about the way things are going (what the party's like) farther on up the road.*
5. **en plan rapto de las sabinas**   a reference to the kidnapping of the Sabine women from central Italy by the founders of Rome to help populate the city.
6. **zaragozana**   from Zaragoza, capital of the region of Aragón.
7. **Canarias**   Spanish islands off the northwest coast of Africa.
8. **¿Cuánto mides? ¿Uno y pico?**   *How tall are you? A little bit over one (meter)?*

9. **hace año y medio** *a year-and-a-half ago.* **Hace** + time expression means *ago* when the main verb is in the past: **Vivió aquí hace diez años** *He lived here ten years ago.* **Que** is often used when the time expression is said first: **Hace diez años que vivió aquí.**

10. **Cataluña**   region of northeastern Spain, where Catalan is spoken.

11. **fonda**   modest boarding house, found often in small towns or villages.

Ejercicios de repaso

A. Observe la semejanza o el contraste entre las expresiones subrayadas. Quizá se le ocurra a su profesor/a exigir que se hagan nuevas frases usando algunas de éstas.

1. (*a*) <u>ante</u> la avalancha de llamadas
   (*b*) <u>antes de</u> llegar a Plan
   (*c*) <u>antes</u> tenían que acudir a una escuela de Boltaña

2. (*a*) si <u>suben</u> 10 ó 20, <u>será</u> bueno
   (*b*) si <u>subieran</u> 10 ó 20, <u>sería</u> bueno

3. (*a*) se les <u>ocurre</u> imitar a los protagonistas
   (*b*) en los pueblos cercanos <u>ocurre</u> igual

4. (*a*) <u>aunque</u> (*although*) no podíamos mandar a Robert Taylor
   (*b*) <u>aunque</u> (*even if*) pudiéramos mandar a Robert Taylor

5. (*a*) <u>disfrutando de</u> todos los guisos
   (*b*) <u>gozando de</u> todos los guisos

6. (*a*) <u>lleva</u> en el pueblo más de 13 años
   (*b*) <u>hace</u> más de 13 años <u>que está</u> (ha estado) en el pueblo

7. (*a*) <u>a</u> los cuatro días
   (*b*) <u>después de</u> cuatro días

8. (*a*) <u>se celebró</u> la Quinta Caravana
   (*b*) <u>celebraron</u> la Quinta Caravana

9. (*a*) <u>no cabe hacer</u> un paralelismo
   (*b*) <u>no conviene hacer</u> una comparación

10. (*a*) <u>apenas</u> creían lo que pasaba
    (*b*) <u>casi no</u> creían lo que ocurría (sucedía)

11. (*a*) la Quinta Fiesta, <u>a la que</u> asistieron unas 100 mujeres
    (*b*) la Quinta Fiesta, <u>a la cual</u> asistieron unas 100 mujeres

12. (*a*) ilusión <u>por</u> seguir adelante
    (*b*) ilusión <u>de</u> seguir adelante

13. (*a*) <u>han copiado</u> la experiencia
    (*b*) <u>se ha copiado</u> la experiencia
    (*c*) la experiencia <u>ha sido copiada</u>

14. (*a*) <u>hasta</u> los típicos pesimistas
    (*b*) <u>incluso</u> los típicos pesimistas
    (*c*) <u>aun</u> el propio párroco

B. ¿Cómo se expresa en español?

1. The village is called Plan.

2. The girls of Plan have their own plan: leave Plan behind (abandon Plan).

3. In order to reach Plan, one must go from Sin to Plan.

4. The route Sin–Plan leads to a village of 142 timid bachelors.

5. The parish priest celebrated the last wedding here a year and a half ago.

6. But one cold January evening the single men are in the bar watching television.

7. An idea occurs to them.

8. They put an ad in a Huesca newspaper.

9. Two weeks later they scarcely believed what was happening.

10. If they all came, there would be a fiesta.

11. But if they're going to throw dishes at each other after four days, well, it's not worth the trouble.

12. Pili says if she liked a boy, she would tell him.

13. If he were not so timid, I would marry him.

14. Last April 30 the Fifth **Caravana** took place, which many attended.

15. Even the pessimists have had to change their crystal ball.

C. Comprensión

1. ¿Cómo se titula en español la película tratada en la lectura?
2. ¿Dónde está Plan?
3. ¿Qué cadena montañosa queda al norte de Plan?
4. ¿Por qué no ha crecido la población?
5. ¿Por qué no celebró muchas bodas el párroco?
6. ¿Qué clase de gente normalmente recibe la extremaunción?
7. ¿Por qué tiene sus dudas el párroco?
8. En la película, ¿qué iba a hacer Robert Taylor por los solteros de California?
9. ¿Por qué se sentían desarraigados los niños de Plan?
10. ¿En qué aspectos ha cambiado el panorama hoy en Plan?

REGULAR VERBS

ENDING	**-ar**
INFINITIVE	hablar
PRESENT PARTICIPLE	hablando
PAST PARTICIPLE	hablado
PRESENT	hablo, hablas, habla, hablamos, habláis, hablan
IMPERFECT	hablaba, hablabas, hablaba, hablábamos, hablabais, hablaban
PRETERIT	hablé, hablaste, habló, hablamos, hablasteis, hablaron
FUTURE	hablaré, hablarás, hablará, hablaremos, hablaréis, hablarán
CONDITIONAL	hablaría, hablarías, hablaría, hablaríamos, hablaríais, hablarían
PR. SUBJUNCTIVE	hable, hables, hable, hablemos, habléis, hablen
IMPERFECT SUBJ.	hablara, hablaras, hablara, habláramos, hablarais, hablaran
	hablase, hablases, hablase, hablásemos, hablaseis, hablasen
PRESENT PERFECT	he, has, ha, hemos, habéis, han + hablado
PAST PERFECT	había, habías, había, habíamos, habíais, habían + hablado
FUTURE PERFECT	habré, habrás, habrá, habremos, habréis, habrán + hablado
COND. PERFECT	habría, habrías, habría, habríamos, habríais, habrían + hablado
PR. PERFECT SUBJ.	haya, hayas, haya, hayamos, hayáis, hayan + hablado
PAST PERFECT SUBJ.	hubiera, hubieras, hubiera, hubiéramos, hubierais, hubieran + hablado
	hubiese, hubieses, hubiese, hubiésemos, hubieseis, hubiesen + hablado
tú COMMANDS	habla, no hables
vosotros COMMANDS	hablad, no habléis

ENDING	**-er**
INFINITIVE	comer
PRESENT PARTICIPLE	comiendo
PAST PARTICIPLE	comido
PRESENT	como, comes, come, comemos, coméis, comen
IMPERFECT	comía, comías, comía, comíamos, comíais, comían
PRETERIT	comí, comiste, comió, comimos, comisteis, comieron
FUTURE	comeré, comerás, comerá, comeremos, comeréis, comerán
CONDITIONAL	comería, comerías, comería, comeríamos, comeríais, comerían
PR. SUBJUNCTIVE	coma, comas, coma, comamos, comáis, coman
IMPERFECT SUBJ.	comiera, comieras, comiera, comiéramos, comierais, comieran
	comiese, comieses, comiese, comiésemos, comieseis, comiesen
PRESENT PERFECT	he, has, ha, hemos, habéis, han + comido

PAST PERFECT	había, habías, había, habíamos, habíais, habían + comido
FUTURE PERFECT	habré, habrás, habrá, habremos, habréis, habrán + comido
COND. PERFECT	habría, habrías, habría, habríamos, habríais, habrían + comido
PR. PERFECT SUBJ.	haya, hayas, haya, hayamos, hayáis, hayan + comido
PAST PERFECT SUBJ.	hubiera, hubieras, hubiera, hubiéramos, hubierais, hubieran + comido
	hubiese, hubieses, hubiese, hubiésemos, hubieseis, hubiesen + comido
tú COMMANDS	come, no comas
vosotros COMMANDS	comed, no comáis

ENDING	**-ir**
INFINITIVE	vivir
PRESENT PARTICIPLE	viviendo
PAST PARTICIPLE	vivido
PRESENT	vivo, vives, vive, vivimos, vivís, viven
IMPERFECT	vivía, vivías, vivía, vivíamos, vivíais, vivían
PRETERIT	viví, viviste, vivió, vivimos, vivisteis, vivieron
FUTURE	viviré, vivirás, vivirá, viviremos, viviréis, vivirán
CONDITIONAL	viviría, vivirías, viviría, viviríamos, viviríais, vivirían
PR. SUBJUNCTIVE	viva, vivas, viva, vivamos, viváis, vivan
IMPERFECT SUBJ.	viviera, vivieras, viviera, viviéramos, vivierais, vivieran
	viviese, vivieses, viviese, viviésemos, vivieseis, viviesen
PRESENT PERFECT	he, has, ha, hemos, habéis, han + vivido
PAST PERFECT	había, habías, había, habíamos, habíais, habían + vivido
FUTURE PERFECT	habré, habrás, habrá, habremos, habréis, habrán + vivido
COND. PERFECT	habría, habrías, habría, habríamos, habríais, habrían + vivido
PR. PERFECT SUBJ.	haya, hayas, haya, hayamos, hayáis, hayan + vivido
PAST PERFECT SUBJ.	hubiera, hubieras, hubiera, hubiéramos, hubierais, hubieran + vivido
	hubiese, hubieses, hubiese, hubiésemos, hubieseis, hubiesen + vivido
tú COMMANDS	vive, no vivas
vosotros COMMANDS	vivid, no viváis

IRREGULAR VERBS

The following verb irregularities are indicated in both Vocabularies by a bracketed number that corresponds to the numbered groups below. Only the tenses containing irregularities are listed. All forms containing irregularities are printed in **boldface**. At the end of each group is a list of all verbs of the group that have been used in this book. Note: **tú** commands are listed only when they are different from the third-person singular of the present tense.

Spelling changes

These changes occur in the spelling alone; the sounds remain the same.

1 c → qu (*before* e)

INFINITIVE	buscar
PRETERIT	**busqué**, buscaste, buscó, buscamos, buscasteis, buscaron
PR. SUBJUNCTIVE	**busque, busques, busque, busquemos, busquéis, busquen**

Also acercar, colocar, chocar, dedicarse, equivocarse, explicar, fabricar, marcar, pecar, picar, remolcar, roncar, sacar, secar, tocar

2 g → j (*before* o *and* a)

INFINITIVES coger
             dirigir

PRESENT **cojo**, coges, coge, cogemos, cogéis, cogen
          dirijo, diriges, dirige, dirigimos, dirigís, dirigen

PR. SUBJUNCTIVE **coja, cojas, coja, cojamos, cojáis, cojan**
         dirija, dirijas, dirija, dirijamos, dirijáis, dirijan

Also corregir, elegir, escoger, exigir, fingir, proteger, recoger

3 g → gu (*before* e)

INFINITIVE llegar

PRETERIT **llegué**, llegaste, llegó, llegamos, llegasteis, llegaron

PR. SUBJUNCTIVE **llegue, llegues, llegue, lleguemos, lleguéis, lleguen**

Also agregar, ahogarse, alargar, apagar, cargar, colgar, desarraigar, despegar, encargar, entregar, fustigar, jugar, mitigar, negar, pegar, plegar, rogar, tragar

4 gu → g (*before* o *and* a)

INFINITIVE distinguir

PRESENT **distingo**, distingues, distingue, distinguimos, distinguís, distinguen

PR. SUBJUNCTIVE **distinga, distingas, distinga, distingamos, distingáis, distingan**

Also conseguir, perseguir, seguir

5 z → c (*before* e)

INFINITIVE cruzar

PRETERIT **crucé**, cruzaste, cruzó, cruzamos, cruzasteis, cruzaron

PR. SUBJUNCTIVE **cruce, cruces, cruce, crucemos, crucéis, crucen**

Also abrazar, alcanzar, almorzar, amenazar, aterrizar, aterrorizar, avanzar, avergonzarse, cazar, comenzar, deslizar, empezar, esforzarse, especializarse, gozar, lanzar, realizar, rechazar, señalizar, tropezar, utilizar

6 c → z (*before* o *and* a)

INFINITIVE vencer

PRESENT **venzo**, vences, vence, vencemos, vencéis, vencen

PR. SUBJUNCTIVE **venza, venzas, venza, venzamos, venzáis, venzan**

Also convencer

7 c → z (*before* c)

INFINITIVES conocer
           conducir

PRESENT **conozco**, conoces, conoce, conocemos, conocéis, conocen
        conduzco, conduces, conduce, conducimos, conducís, conducen

PR. SUBJUNCTIVE **conozca**, **conozcas**, **conozcas**, **conozcamos**, **conozcáis**, **conozcan**
conduzca, **conduzcas**, **conduzca**, **conduzcamos**, **conduzcáis**, **conduzcan**

Also acontecer, agradecer, aparecer, apetecer, carecer, crecer, desfallecer, merecer, nacer, obedecer, ofrecer, parecer, permanecer, pertenecer, prevalecer, producir, reconocer, seducir, traducir

8 u → ü (*before* e)

INFINITIVE averiguar

PRETERIT **averigüé**, averiguaste, averiguó, averiguamos, averiguasteis, averiguaron

PR. SUBJUNCTIVE **averigüe**, **averigües**, **averigüe**, **averigüemos**, **averigüéis**, **averigüen**

Also santiguar

Stem changes

9 e → ie

INFINITIVES cerrar
perder

PRESENT **cierro**, **cierras**, **cierra**, cerramos, cerráis, **cierran**
pierdo, **pierdes**, **pierde**, perdemos, perdéis, **pierden**

PR. SUBJUNCTIVE **cierre**, **cierres**, **cierre**, cerremos, cerréis, **cierren**
pierda, **pierdas**, **pierda**, perdamos, perdáis, **pierdan**

Also alentar, apretar, ascender, atender, atentar, calentar, comenzar, confesar, despegar, despertar, empezar, encender, entender, helar, negar, pensar, plegar, quebrar, reventar, sentar, temblar, tropezar

10 e → ie, e → i

INFINITIVE sentir

PRESENT PARTICIPLE **sintiendo**

PRESENT **siento**, **sientes**, **siente**, sentimos, sentís, **sienten**

PRETERIT sentí, sentiste, **sintió**, sentimos, sentisteis, **sintieron**

PR. SUBJUNCTIVE **sienta**, **sientas**, **sienta**, **sintamos**, **sintáis**, **sientan**

IMPERFECT SUBJ. **sintiera**, **sintieras**, **sintiera**, **sintiéramos**, **sintierais**, **sintieran**
sintiese, **sintieses**, **sintiese**, **sintiésemos**, **sintieseis**, **sintiesen**

Also advertir, consentir, convertirse, divertir, herir, ingerir, mentir, preferir, referirse, requerir, sugerir

11 e → i, e → i

INFINITIVE pedir

PRESENT PARTICIPLE **pidiendo**

PRESENT **pido**, **pides**, **pide**, pedimos, pedís, **piden**

PRETERIT pedí, pediste, **pidió**, pedimos, pedisteis, **pidieron**

PR. SUBJUNCTIVE **pida**, **pidas**, **pida**, **pidamos**, **pidáis**, **pidan**

IMPERFECT SUBJ. **pidiera**, **pidieras**, **pidiera**, **pidiéramos**, **pidierais**, **pidieran**
pidiese, **pidieses**, **pidiese**, **pidiésemos**, **pidieseis**, **pidiesen**

Also competir, concebir, conseguir, corregir, elegir, despedir, impedir, medir, perseguir, repetir, seguir, vestir

12 o → ue

INFINITIVES   contar
            volver

PRESENT   **cuento**, **cuentas**, **cuenta**, contamos, contáis, **cuentan**
           vuelvo, **vuelves**, **vuelve**, volvemos, volvéis, **vuelven**

PR. SUBJUNCTIVE   **cuente**, **cuentes**, **cuente**, contemos, contáis, **cuenten**
           vuelva, **vuelvas**, **vuelva**, volvamos, volváis, **vuelvan**

Also absolver, acordarse, acostar, almorzar, apostar, aprobar, avergonzar, colgar, concordar, costar, devolver, doler, encontrar, envolver, esforzarse, llover, morder, mostrar, mover, probar, promover, recordar, resolver, rodar, rogar, soltar, sonar, soñar, tronar, volar (**Avergonzar** has a dieresis on the **u** of **ue**: **avergüenzo**, **avergüenzas**, etc.)

13 o → ue, o → u

INFINITIVE   dormir

PRESENT PARTICIPLE   **durmiendo**

PRESENT   **duermo**, **duermes**, **duerme**, dormimos, dormís, **duermen**

PRETERIT   dormí, dormiste, **durmió**, dormimos, dormisteis, **durmieron**

PR. SUBJUNCTIVE   **duerma**, **duermas**, **duerma**, **durmamos**, **durmáis**, **duerman**

IMPERFECT SUBJ.   **durmiera**, **durmieras**, **durmiera**, **durmiéramos**, **durmierais**, **durmieran**
          durmiese, **durmieses**, **durmiese**, **durmiésemos**, **durmieseis**, **durmiesen**

Also morir (*see also* [48] **muerto**)

14 u → ue

INFINITIVE   jugar

PRESENT   **juega**, **juegas**, **juega**, jugamos, jugáis, **juegan**

PR. SUBJUNCTIVE   **juegue**, **juegues**, **juegue**, juguemos, juguéis, **jueguen**

15 o → hue

INFINITIVE   oler

PRESENT   **huelo**, **hueles**, **huele**, olemos, oléis, **huelen**

PR. SUBJUNCTIVE   **huela**, **huelas**, **huela**, olamos, oláis, **huelan**

Other Irregularities

16   adquirir

PRESENT   **adquiero**, **adquieres**, **adquiere**, adquirimos, adquirís, **adquieren**

PR. SUBJUNCTIVE   **adquiera**, **adquieras**, **adquiera**, adquiramos, adquiráis, **adquieran**

17   agradecer

PRESENT   **agradezco**, agradeces, agradece, agradecemos, agradecéis, agradecen

PR. SUBJUNCTIVE   **agradezca**, **agradezcas**, **agradezca**, **agradezcamos**, **agradezcáis**, **agradezcan**

Also acontecer, aparecer, apetecer, carecer, crecer, desfallecer, merecer, obedecer, ofrecer, parecer, permanecer, pertenecer, prevalecer

18   andar

PRETERIT   **anduve, anduviste, anduvo, anduvimos, anduvisteis, anduvieron**
IMPERFECT SUBJ.   **anduviera, anduvieras, anduviera, anduviéramos, anduvierais, anduvieran
anduviese,** *etc.*

19   caber

PRESENT   **quepo**, cabes, cabe, cabemos, cabéis, caben
PR. SUBJUNCTIVE   **quepa, quepas, quepa, quepamos, quepáis, quepan**
PRETERIT   **cupe, cupiste, cupo, cupimos, cupisteis, cupieron**
IMPERFECT SUBJ.   **cupiera, cupieras, cupiera, cupiéramos, cupierais, cupieran
cupiese,** *etc.*
FUTURE   **cabré, cabrás, cabrá, cabremos, cabréis, cabrán**
CONDITIONAL   **cabría, cabrías, cabría, cabríamos, cabríais, cabrían**

20   caer

PRESENT PARTICIPLE   **cayendo**
PRESENT   **caigo**, caes, cae, caemos, caéis, caen
PR. SUBJUNCTIVE   **caiga, caigas, caiga, caigamos, caigáis, caigan**
PRETERIT   caí, caíste, **cayó**, caímos, caísteis, **cayeron**
IMPERFECT SUBJ.   **cayera, cayeras, cayera, cayéramos, cayerais, cayeran
cayese,** *etc.*

21   concluir

PRESENT PARTICIPLE   **concluyendo**
PRESENT   **concluyo, concluyes, concluye**, concluimos, concluís, **concluyen**
PR. SUBJUNCTIVE   **concluya, concluyas, concluya, concluyamos, concluyáis, concluyan**
PRETERIT   concluí, concluiste, **concluyó**, concluimos, concluisteis, **concluyeron**
IMPERFECT SUBJ.   **concluyera, concluyeras, concluyera, concluyéramos, concluyerais, concluyeran
concluyese,** *etc.*

     Also construir, contribuir, destruir, diluir, distribuir, huir, incluir

22   conducir

PRESENT   **conduzco**, conduces, conduce, conducimos, conducís, conducen
PR. SUBJUNCTIVE   **conduzca, conduzcas, conduzca, conduzcamos, conduzcáis, conduzcan**
PRETERIT   **conduje, condujiste, condujo, condujimos, condujisteis, condujeron**
IMPERFECT SUBJ.   **condujera, condujeras, condujera, condujéramos, condujerais, condujeran
condujese,** *etc.*

     Also introducir, producir, seducir, traducir

23   confiar

PRESENT   **confío, confías, confía**, confiamos, confiáis, **confían**
PR. SUBJUNCTIVE   **confíe, confíes, confíe**, confiemos, confiéis, **confíen**

     Also ampliar, criarse, enfriar, enviar, liarse

24	conocer

PRESENT **conozco**, conoces, conoce, conocemos, conocéis, conocen
PR. SUBJUNCTIVE **conozca**, **conozcas**, **conozca**, **conozcamos**, **conozcáis**, **conozcan**
    Also desconocer, reconocer

25	continuar

PRESENT **continúo**, **continúas**, **continúa**, continuamos, continuáis, **continúan**
PR. SUBJUNCTIVE **continúe**, **continúes**, **continúe**, continuemos, continuéis, **continúen**
    Also graduarse

26	creer

PRESENT PARTICIPLE **creyendo**
PRETERIT creí, **creíste**, **creyó**, **creímos**, **creísteis**, **creyeron**
IMPERFECT SUBJ. **creyera**, **creyeras**, **creyera**, **creyéramos**, **creyerais**, **creyeran**
    creyese, *etc.*
    Also leer, poseer

27	dar

PRESENT **doy**, das, da, damos, dais, dan
PR. SUBJUNCTIVE **dé**, des, **dé**, demos, deis, den
PRETERIT **di**, **diste**, **dio**, **dimos**, **disteis**, **dieron**
IMPERFECT SUBJ. **diera**, **dieras**, **diera**, **diéramos**, **dierais**, **dieran**
    diese, *etc.*

28	decir

PRESENT PARTICIPLE **diciendo**
PAST PARTICIPLE **dicho**
PRESENT **digo**, **dices**, **dice**, **decimos**, **decís**, **dicen**
PR. SUBJUNCTIVE **diga**, **digas**, **diga**, **digamos**, **digáis**, **digan**
PRETERIT **dije**, **dijiste**, **dijo**, **dijimos**, **dijisteis**, **dijeron**
IMPERFECT SUBJ. **dijera**, **dijeras**, **dijera**, **dijéramos**, **dijerais**, **dijeran**
    dijese, *etc.*
FUTURE **diré**, **dirás**, **dirá**, **diremos**, **diréis**, **dirán**
CONDITIONAL **diría**, **dirías**, **diría**, **diríamos**, **diríais**, **dirían**
tú COMMAND **di**

29	estar

PRESENT **estoy**, **estás**, **está**, estamos, estáis, **están**
PR. SUBJUNCTIVE **esté**, **estés**, **esté**, estemos, estéis, **estén**
PRETERIT **estuve**, **estuviste**, **estuvo**, **estuvimos**, **estuvisteis**, **estuvieron**
IMPERFECT SUBJ. **estuviera**, **estuvieras**, **estuviera**, **estuviéramos**, **estuvierais**, **estuvieran**
    estuviese, *etc.*

30   haber

PRESENT	**he, has, ha, hemos,** habéis, **han**
PR. SUBJUNCTIVE	**haya, hayas, haya, hayamos, hayáis, hayan**
PRETERIT	**hube, hubiste, hubo, hubimos, hubisteis, hubieron**
IMPERFECT SUBJ.	**hubiera, hubieras, hubiera, hubiéramos, hubierais, hubieran hubiese,** *etc.*
FUTURE	**habré, habrás, habrá, habremos, habréis, habrán**
CONDITIONAL	**habría, habrías, habría, habríamos, habríais, habrían**
tú COMMAND	**hé**

31   hacer

PAST PARTICIPLE	**hecho**
PRESENT	**hago,** haces, hace, hacemos, hacéis, hacen
PR. SUBJUNCTIVE	**haga, hagas, haga, hagamos, hagáis, hagan**
PRETERIT	**hice, hiciste, hizo, hicimos, hicisteis, hicieron**
IMPERFECT SUBJ.	**hiciera, hicieras, hiciera, hiciéramos, hicierais, hicieran hiciese,** *etc.*
FUTURE	**haré, harás, hará, haremos, haréis, harán**
CONDITIONAL	**haría, harías, haría, haríamos, haríais, harían**
tú COMMAND	**haz**

Also deshacer

32   ir

PRESENT PARTICIPLE	**yendo**
PRESENT	**voy, vas, va, vamos, vais, van**
PR. SUBJUNCTIVE	**vaya, vayas, vaya, vayamos, vayáis, vayan**
IMPERFECT	**iba, ibas, iba, íbamos, ibais, iban**
PRETERIT	**fui, fuiste, fue, fuimos, fuisteis, fueron**
IMPERFECT SUBJ.	**fuera, fueras, fuera, fuéramos, fuerais, fueran fuese,** *etc.*
tú COMMAND	**ve**

33   nacer

PRESENT	**nazco,** naces, nace, nacemos, nacéis, nacen
PR. SUBJUNCTIVE	**nazca, nazcas, nazca, nazcamos, nazcáis, nazcan**

34   oír

PRESENT PARTICIPLE	**oyendo**
PRESENT	**oigo, oyes, oye, oímos,** oís, **oyen**
PR. SUBJUNCTIVE	**oiga, oigas, oiga, oigamos, oigáis, oigan**
PRETERIT	oí, **oíste, oyó, oímos, oísteis, oyeron**
IMPERFECT SUBJ.	**oyera, oyeras, oyera, oyéramos, oyerais, oyeran oyese,** *etc.*

35	poder

PRESENT PARTICIPLE	**pudiendo**
PRESENT	**puedo**, **puedes**, **puede**, podemos, podéis, **pueden**
PR. SUBJUNCTIVE	**pueda**, **puedas**, **pueda**, podamos, podáis, **puedan**
PRETERIT	**pude**, **pudiste**, **pudo**, **pudimos**, **pudisteis**, **pudieron**
IMPERFECT SUBJ.	**pudiera**, **pudieras**, **pudiera**, **pudiéramos**, **pudierais**, **pudieran** **pudiese**, *etc.*
FUTURE	**podré**, **podrás**, **podrá**, **podremos**, **podréis**, **podrán**
CONDITIONAL	**podría**, **podrías**, **podría**, **podríamos**, **podríais**, **podrían**

36	poner

PAST PARTICIPLE	**puesto**
PRESENT	**pongo**, pones, pone, ponemos, ponéis, ponen
PR. SUBJUNCTIVE	**ponga**, **pongas**, **ponga**, **pongamos**, **pongáis**, **pongan**
PRETERIT	**puse**, **pusiste**, **puso**, **pusimos**, **pusisteis**, **pusieron**
IMPERFECT SUBJ.	**pusiera**, **pusieras**, **pusiera**, **pusiéramos**, **pusierais**, **pusieran** **pusiese**, *etc.*
FUTURE	**pondré**, **pondrás**, **pondrá**, **pondremos**, **pondréis**, **pondrán**
CONDITIONAL	**pondría**, **pondrías**, **pondría**, **pondríamos**, **pondríais**, **pondrían**
tú COMMAND	**pon**

Also componer, descomponer, disponer, exponer, imponer, oponerse, proponer, reponerse, suponer

37	querer

PRESENT	**quiero**, **quieres**, **quiere**, queremos, queréis, **quieren**
PR. SUBJUNCTIVE	**quiera**, **quieras**, **quiera**, queramos, queráis, **quieran**
PRETERIT	**quise**, **quisiste**, **quiso**, **quisimos**, **quisisteis**, **quisieron**
IMPERFECT SUBJ.	**quisiera**, **quisieras**, **quisiera**, **quisiéramos**, **quisierais**, **quisieran** **quisiese**, *etc.*
FUTURE	**querré**, **querrás**, **querrá**, **querremos**, **querréis**, **querrán**
CONDITIONAL	**querría**, **querrías**, **querría**, **querríamos**, **querríais**, **querrían**

38	reír

PRESENT PARTICIPLE	**riendo**
PRESENT	**río**, **ríes**, **ríe**, **reímos**, **reísteis**, **ríen**
PR. SUBJUNCTIVE	**ría**, **rías**, **ría**, **riamos**, **riáis**, **rían**
PRETERIT	reí, **reíste**, **rió**, **reímos**, **reísteis**, **rieron**
IMPERFECT SUBJ.	**riera**, **rieras**, **riera**, **riéramos**, **rierais**, **rieran** **riese**, *etc.*

Also freír (*see also* [48] **frito**), sonreír

39	reunir

PRESENT	**reúno**, **reúnes**, **reúne**, reunimos, reunís, **reúnen**
PR. SUBJUNCTIVE	**reúna**, **reúnas**, **reúna**, reunamos, reunáis, **reúnan**

40		saber
PRESENT	**sé**, sabes, sabe, sabemos, sabéis, saben
PR. SUBJUNCTIVE	**sepa, sepas, sepa, sepamos, sepáis, sepan**
PRETERIT	**supe, supiste, supo, supimos, supisteis, supieron**
IMPERFECT SUBJ.	**supiera, supieras, supiera, supiéramos, supierais, supieran supiese**, *etc.*
FUTURE	**sabré, sabrás, sabrá, sabremos, sabréis, sabrán**
CONDITIONAL	**sabría, sabrías, sabría, sabríamos, sabríais, sabrían**

41		salir
PRESENT	**salgo**, sales, sale, salimos, salís, salen
PR. SUBJUNCTIVE	**salga, salgas, salga, salgamos, salgáis, salgan**
FUTURE	**saldré, saldrás, saldrá, saldremos, saldréis, saldrán**
CONDITIONAL	**saldría, saldrías, saldría, saldríamos, saldríais, saldrían**
tú COMMAND	**sal**

42		ser
PRESENT	**soy, eres, es, somos, sois, son**
PR. SUBJUNCTIVE	**sea, seas, sea, seamos, seáis, sean**
IMPERFECT	**era, eras, era, éramos, erais, eran**
PRETERIT	**fui, fuiste, fue, fuimos, fuisteis, fueron**
IMPERFECT SUBJ.	**fuera, fueras, fuera, fuéramos, fuerais, fueran fuese**, *etc.*
tú COMMAND	**sé**

43		tener
PRESENT	**tengo, tienes, tiene**, tenemos, tenéis, **tienen**
PR. SUBJUNCTIVE	**tenga, tengas, tenga, tengamos, tengáis, tengan**
PRETERIT	**tuve, tuviste, tuvo, tuvimos, tuvisteis, tuvieron**
IMPERFECT SUBJ.	**tuviera, tuvieras, tuviera, tuviéramos, tuvierais, tuvieran tuviese**, *etc.*
FUTURE	**tendré, tendrás, tendrá, tendremos, tendréis, tendrán**
CONDITIONAL	**tendría, tendrías, tendría, tendríamos, tendríais, tendrían**
tú COMMAND	**ten**

Also contener, detener, entretener, obtener

44		traer
PRESENT PARTICIPLE	**trayendo**
PRESENT	**traigo**, traes, trae, traemos, traéis, traen
PR. SUBJUNCTIVE	**traiga, traigas, traiga, traigamos, traigáis, traigan**
PRETERIT	**traje, trajiste, trajo, trajimos, trajisteis, trajeron**
IMPERFECT SUBJ.	**trajera, trajeras, trajera, trajéramos, trajerais, trajeran trajese**, *etc.*

Also atraer, distraer

45	valer

PRESENT **valgo**, vales, vale, valemos, valéis, valen
PR. SUBJUNCTIVE **valga, valgas, valga, valgamos, valgáis, valgan**
FUTURE **valdré, valdrás, valdrá, valdremos, valdréis, valdrán**
CONDITIONAL **valdría, valdrías, valdría, valdríamos, valdríais, valdrían**

46	venir

PRESENT PARTICIPLE **viniendo**
PRESENT **vengo, vienes, viene**, venimos, venís, **vienen**
PR. SUBJUNCTIVE **venga, vengas, venga, vengamos, vengáis, vengan**
PRETERIT **vine, viniste, vino, vinimos, vinisteis, vinieron**
IMPERFECT SUBJ. **viniera, vinieras, viniera, viniéramos, vinierais, vinieran viniese,** *etc.*
FUTURE **vendré, vendrás, vendrá, vendremos, vendréis, vendrán**
CONDITIONAL **vendría, vendrías, vendría, vendríamos, vendríais, vendrían**
tú COMMAND **ven**

Also convenir, prevenir

47	ver

PAST PARTICIPLE **visto**
PRESENT **veo**, ves, ve, vemos, veis, ven
PR. SUBJUNCTIVE **vea, veas, vea, veamos, veáis, vean**
IMPERFECT **veía, veías, veía, veíamos, veíais, veían**
PRETERIT **vi**, viste, **vio**, vimos, visteis, vieron

48 Irregular Past Participles

abrir—abierto
absolver—absuelto (*also* **resolver**)
cubrir—cubierto (*also* **descubrir**)
decir—dicho
disolver—disuelto
escribir—escrito (*also* **describir, inscribir, prescribir, suscribir**)
freír—frito
hacer—hecho (*also* **deshacer**)
imprimir—impreso
morir—muerto
poner—puesto (*also* **componer, descomponer, disponer, exponer, imponer, oponerse, proponer, reponerse, suponer**)
romper—roto
ver—visto
volver—vuelto (*also* **devolver, envolver**)

Vocabularies

The following types of words have been omitted from these vocabularies: (1) easily recognizable cognates (Spanish to English only); (2) obvious derived forms, such as diminutives (unless the meaning is significantly different from the base form), superlatives, and adverbs ending in -**mente** if the adjective is listed; (3) most high-frequency structure words, such as articles, prepositions, pronouns, etc.; (4) regular past participles of listed infinitives unless they have a different meaning as nouns and adjectives; (5) individual verb forms; (6) other common words that a second-year student would reasonably be expected to know.

The gender of masculine nouns ending in -**o** is not listed, nor of feminine nouns ending in -**a**, -**ción**, and -**d**.

All verb irregularities are indicated in parentheses after the verb. The bracketed number indicates the verb group as listed in the preceding Verb Tables. When there are two stem changes, the first is for the present tense and the second for the preterit: **pedir** (**i, i**) [11], **dormir** (**ue, u**) [13]. Other irregularities are also indicated: **andar** (*irr*) [18], **hacer** (*irr*) [31], etc. Verbs with stem changes in addition to other irregularities are listed this way: **decir** (**i**; *irr*) [28], **venir** (**ie**; *irr*) [46]. Spelling changes are indicated: **buscar** (**qu**) [1], **dirigir** (**j**) [2], **cruzar** (**c**) [5]. When both form and spelling irregularities are listed, they are separated by a semicolon: **almorzar** (**ue; c**) [12; 5], **agradecer** (*irr*; **z**) [17; 7].

Prepositional usage is given after verbs—without parentheses if the verb is commonly used with the preposition and a following element—**dirigirse a**—and with parentheses if the verb can be used alone—**casarse** (**con**).

Idioms and common phrases are cross-referenced under their principal words. A dash represents a repetition of the key word: **pronto: de—** *suddenly*.

Proper nouns and cultural, historical, and geographical items explained in footnotes are for the most part not included in this vocabulary.

It should be noted that words appearing in illustrations, advertisements, newspaper headlines, photo captions, etc. have been included in the Spanish–English vocabulary.

The following abbreviations are used:

abbrev	abbreviation	*m*	masculine
adj	adjective	*n*	noun
adv	adverb	*pl*	plural
aux	auxiliary	*pp*	past participle
conj	conjunction	*pr p*	present participle
dim	diminutive	*prep*	preposition
f	feminine	*pro*	pronoun
imp	imperative	*sing*	singular
inf	infinitive	*Sp Am*	Spanish America
intr	intransitive	*tr*	transitive
irr	irregular	*v*	verb

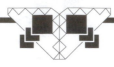
A

a través de through, across; in the course of

abajo below, down; downstairs; **río—** downstream

abandonar to leave, abandon

abarrotes *m pl*: **tienda de—** grocery store (*Mexico, Central America, Andean countries*)

ablandar to soften

abogado / a lawyer

abrazar (c) [5] to hug, embrace

abrazo embrace, hug

abrigo coat (*outer*)

abrir [48] to open

abuela grandmother

abuelo grandfather; *pl* grandparents

aburrido bored

aburrir to bore; **—se** to get, be bored

abuso infantil child abuse

acabar to finish, end; **—de** + *inf* to have just + *pp*, to finish + *pr p*; **—se** to end, run out, be used up

acariciar to caress

acaso: por si— just in case

acceso access

acción action, **Día de—de Gracias** Thanksgiving Day; **acciones** *pl* shares (*stock market*)

aceite *m* oil

aceituna olive

acera sidewalk

acerca de about, concerning

acercarse (qu)(a) [1] to get near (to), go up (to), approach

acontecer (*irr; z*) [17; 7] to happen

acontecimiento event

acordarse (ue) (de) [12] to remember

acostar (ue) [12] to lay down, put to bed, **—se** to lie down, to go to bed

acribillado riddled

acto act, action; inning (*baseball*); **en el—** at once, right away, immediately, on the spot

actual current, presentday; **—mente** currently, nowadays

acudir to go, come, run, hurry, hasten

acuerdo agreement; **de—** agreed, OK

adecuado suitable, adequate

adelante forward, ahead; **en—** from now on; **de 15 años en—** 15 and older

adelgazante slenderizing

además besides, furthermore, moreover; **—de** in addition to

adentrarse to go into

adentro inside

adherido (a) participating (in), involved (in)

adivinanza guess, riddle

admisión *f* acceptance, admission

admitir to admit; to accept; to allow

adquirir (ie) [16] to acquire

aduana customs, customs point

advenimiento coming, advent

advertir (ie, i) [10] to warn

aéreo *adj* air

aerolínea airline

afeitar to shave

aficionado fan (*sports*)

afilado sharp(ened)

afín (a) similar (to)

afrecho bran

afuera outside

agente *m* agent, officer; **—de seguros** insurance agent

agónico dying

agotado exhausted, spent

agradecer (*irr; z*) [17; 7] to thank, be grateful for, to appreciate

agregar (gu) [3] to add

agrio bitter, sour

agrícola *adj* agricultural

aguantar to put up with, bear, endure; to last, hold out

águila eagle

ahogarse (gu) [3] to drown, suffocate

ahorrar to save

ahorros *pl* savings

ahumado smoked

ajeno alien, foreign, characteristic of others

ajo garlic

ajuar *m* trousseau, bride's outfit

ajustarse (a) to adjust (to)

ajuste *m* adjustment

ala wing

alargar (gu) [3] to lengthen, increase, extend

alba dawn

albañilería masonry

alcance *m* reach; **al—de** within reach of

alcanzar (c) [5] to reach, attain

aledaño (a) neighboring, next (to)

alegrar to gladden, make happy; **—se** to be glad, happy

alemán / a German

alentar (ie) [9] to encourage

alfombra rug, carpet

algo *pro* something, anything; *adv* somewhat, rather, a bit

algodón *m* cotton

alguien someone, somebody

alguno some, any; somebody

aliado *n* ally

alimentos *pl* food

almacén *m* warehouse; store

almacenaje *m* storage

almacenamiento storage; hoarding

almacenar to store; to put in storage; to hoard

almeja clam

almorzar (ue; c) [12; 5] to have lunch

almuerzo lunch

alojado *pp of* **alojar** to house, give lodging to

alquilar to rent

alquiler *m* rent(al)

alrededor (de) around; **—es** *m pl* environs, surrounding neighborhood

alta: **en voz—** out loud

alterar to change, alter

alterno alternate, alternating; **clases —as** classes meeting every other day

alto high, tall

aluvión *m* flood, outpouring

alza rise

ama owner, mistress; **—de casa** housewife; **—de llaves** housekeeper

amable friendly, nice, kind

amanecer *m* dawn

amar to love

amarillo yellow

amarrado *pp of* **amarrar** to tie

ambiente *m* atmosphere, environment

ambos both

ambulante itinerant, walking; **biblioteca—** library on wheels

amenazar (c) [5] to threaten

ameno pleasant

amistoso friendly

amnistía amnesty

amor *m* love

ampliar (irr) [23] to amplify, enlarge, widen, extend

amplio ample, wide

amueblado *pp of* **amueblar** to furnish

anaranjado orange (*color*)

anciano old

ancho wide, broad

andaluz Andalusian (*from southern Spain*)

andar (irr) [18] to go, walk (around)

angelino *resident of Los Angeles, California*

angosto narrow

angula baby eel

animado animated; **dibujos —s** cartoons (*movies, television*)

anís *m* anise-flavored brandy

anoche last night

anomalía anomaly

anorak *m* hooded jacket

anotación note; run (*baseball*)

anotar to jot down; **—una carrera** to score a run (*baseball*)

ante before, in the presence of, in front of

antes before, earlier; **— de que** before: **cuanto—** as soon as possible

anticipación: **con—** in advance, ahead of time

antigubernamental *adj* anti-government

antiguo old, ancient

anunciar to announce; to advertise

anuncio ad(vertisement), commercial *n*

año year

añoranza longing, nostalgia

apagar (gu) [3] to put out; to turn off, out

aparato appliance, machine

aparcamiento parking lot

aparecer (irr; z) [17; 7] to appear

apartado de correos post office box

apartarse to separate, stand back, aside; to move back, aside

apellido last (family) name; **—de soltera** maiden name

apenas scarcely

aperitivo apéritif (*drink*)

apertura opening

apetecer (irr; z) [17; 7] to appeal, be appetizing

apetitoso appetizing

aplastar to smash, crush

aportar to provide, present, bring

apostar (ue) [12] to bet

apoyo support

aprecio appreciation

aprender to learn

aprendizaje *m* apprenticeship, act of learning; **examen de—** examination for learner's permit

apresurar(se) to hurry, hasten

apretar (ie) [9] to press, squeeze

aprobar (ue) [12] to approve; to pass (*examination*)

aprovechar to take advantage of, make use of **—se (de)** to take advantage of, avail oneself of

apto. *abbrev for* **apartado**

apunte *m* class note

apurarse to hurry (*Sp Am*); to worry (*Spain*)

aquí mismo right here

aragonés / a Aragonese (*from Aragón, a region of northeastern Spain*)

árbitro umpire; referee

arete *m* earring

arquero goalkeeper

arquitectónico architectural

arreglar to arrange, put in order; to fix, repair

arriba above, up; upstairs; **río—** upstream

arrodillarse to kneel

arrojar to throw

arroz *m* rice

artificiales: **fuegos—** fireworks

as *m* ace

asar to roast

ascender (ie)(a) [9] to ascend; to amount (to)

ascenso ascent, rise

asegurar to assure; **—se (de)** to make sure (of)

aseos *pl* toilets, restrooms

asesinar to murder

asesinato murder

asesino murderer

asesoramiento advice

asiento seat; location

asilo asylum

asistencia attendance, presence; assistance

asistir (a) to attend

asomarse to lean out (*of a window*), over (*a railing*); to appear

asombrado astonished, amazed

aspirante *m, f* applicant, candidate

astilla chip, splinter; **De tal palo, tal—** A chip off the old block

astuto astute, sharp, clever

asunción assumption; ascent; **Asunción** *capital of Paraguay*

asunto matter, affair

asustar to frighten, scare

atardecer *m* dusk

atender (ie) [9] to look after, take care of

atentado violent crime; attempt on someone's life

atentar (ie) [9] to attempt; **—contra la vida de alguien** to endanger someone's life

atento attentive

aterrizar (c) [5] to land

aterrorizar (c) [5] to terrify, frighten, terrorize

atónito dumbfounded, astonished

atraer (*irr*) [44] to attract

atrás back, in the back

atrasado late, overdue, behind (*time*)

atreverse (a) to dare (to)

atroz atrocious

atún *m* tuna

aula classroom

aumentar to increase

aun even

aún still, yet

aunque although, even though, even if

ausencia absence

autocar *m* interurban bus

autónomo self-governing

auxiliar *m, f* assistant; attendant

auxilio aid, help

avanzar (c) [5] to advance

ave *f* bird, fowl, *pl* poultry

avergonzarse (üe;c) (**de**) [12; 5] to be ashamed (of), embarrassed (at, to)

avería breakdown, damage

averiguar (ü) [8] to ascertain, find out, verify

avión *m* airplane

avioneta small plane

avisar to inform, warn, let (someone) know

aviso notice, warning, announcement

ayuda aid, help

ayudante *m, f* assistant

ayudar to help

ayuntamiento town hall, city hall

azotar to punish, lash

azúcar *m* sugar

azufre *m* sulphur

azul blue

azulejo blue jay; ceramic tile

B

bacalao codfish

bachillerato high-school diploma; course of study leading to high-school diploma

Badajoz *city near Portugal in southwestern Spain*

bailador / a dancer

bailar to dance

baile *m* dance

bajar to take, bring down (stairs), lower; **—(se)** to go, come down; to get off, out (*of a vehicle*)

bajo short (stature), low; under; **—techo** indoors

balear to gun down, shoot down

balón *m* ball

bancario *adj* bank(ing)

bandolero bandit

bañador *m* bathing suit

bañar to bathe

bañera bathtub

barandilla railing

barato cheap

barcelonés / a *from Barcelona (Spain)*

barco boat

barra bar, rod; **—de dirección** steering column

barrera first row of seats (*bullring*); barrier, fence

barrio neighborhood, district

base *f* basis, foundation

bastante plenty of, quite a bit; *pl* plenty of, quite a few

bastar to suffice, be enough, sufficient

basto: a lo— coarsely, in a gross or vulgar way

bastón *m* stick, cane

basura garbage, trash

batear to bat, hit (*baseball*)

batido whipped (*food*)

batidora mixer

baúl *m* trunk (*for clothing*)

beber to drink; **—a morro** to drink straight from the bottle

bebida drink, beverage

beca scholarship

béisbol *m* baseball

belleza beauty

beneficiarse (de) to make use (of); to benefit (from)

beneficio benefit; **—s marginales** fringe benefits

bengalí *adj* Bengal; *m* Bengali (*a language of India and Bangladesh*)

besar to kiss

besugo bream, snapper (*fish*)

biblioteca library; **— ambulante** library on wheels

bien *mn* good; *pl* possessions, property; **salir** (*irr*) **—** [41] to win, pass (*a test, course, etc.*); to come out OK

bienvenida *n* welcome; **bienvenido** *adj* welcome

billete *m* ticket (*Spain*)

billetera wallet, billfold

birreactor: avión— twin-engine plane

birria barbecue (*Mexico*)

bizcocho pastry

blanco white

blandir to brandish

blasfemia oath, swearword

blusa blouse

bobo fool

bocacalle *f* intersection

bocadillo sandwich

boda wedding

bodegón *m* inexpensive restaurant

bogotano inhabitant of Bogotá (*capital of Colombia*)

bola ball

boleto ticket (*Sp Am*)

boli *shortened form of* **bolígrafo** ballpoint pen

bolsa bag, totebag

bolsillo pocket

bollo roll (bun)

bombero fireman

bombonera candy box; cozy little place

bono voucher; **—bus** bus pass, bus ticket

boquerón *m* anchovy

bordelés *from Bordeaux (France);* **salsa bordelesa** *sauce based based on red wine and shallots*

bordo: a— on board

boricua *m, f* Puerto Rican

borracho drunk; **tarta —a** whiskey cake

bosque *m* woods

botón *m* button

botones *m sing* bellboy, messenger boy

brazo arm

breve brief, short

brillo shine, luster, brilliance

brindar to offer; to toast

broma joke

bronca row, scrap, fight, fuss, uproar, rumpus

bucal: enjuague— *m* mouthwash

bufanda scarf

bujía spark plug

búlgaro Bulgarian

bulto bundle, package

B.U.P. = Bachillerato Unificado Polivalente "Unified Multipurpose Degree Program" (*national school curriculum of Spain*)

Burdeos Bordeaux (*France*)

burlarse de to make fun of

buscar (qu) [1] to look for, search

buzón *m* mailbox (*outside*)

C

caballero knight, gentleman, horseman; **cuarto de —s** men's room

caballo horse

caber (*irr*) [19] to fit

cabeza head

cabezudo *n person wearing immense head in parade*

cachivache *m* piece of junk

cacho piece, slice

cachorro cub

cada each, every; **—vez más** more and more; **—vez que** whenever, every time that

cadena chain; **—Hi-Fi** stereo system

caer (*irr*) [20] to fall; **—al vacío** to fall out (*of a window, for example*); **—(se)** to fall (down); **dejar—** to drop

café *m* coffee; *adj* brown; **— cortado** coffee with milk

caja box, container; cash register

cajero / a cashier

calabaza pumpkin

calamar *m* squid

calarse to get flooded

calavera skull

caldo broth

calentar (**ie**) [9] to heat

calidad quality

cálido hot

caliente hot

calmar to calm down (*tr*); **—se** to calm down (*intr*)

calor *m* heat; **tener—** (**ie**; *irr*) [43] to be hot

caluroso warm, hot

callado quiet, silent

callarse to be quiet

calle *f* street

camarero waiter

camarón *m* shrimp (*Sp Am*)

cambiar to change; to cash (*check*)

cambio change

camelo fraud

camino road, highway

camión *m* truck; bus (*Mexico*)

camisa shirt

camiseta T-shirt

campana bell

campanazo loud ringing of a bell

campaña campaign

campeón *m* champion

campeonato championship

campesino farmer, peasant

campo field; countryside **—de pruebas** proving ground; **mariscal de—** quarterback

canal *m* channel (*television*)

Canarias *Spanish islands off the northwest coast of Africa*

canasta basket

cangrejo crab

cansado tired

cansar to tire; **—se** to get tired

cantar to sing

caño pipe

capacitación training

capaz capable

capilla chapel

capítulo chapter

Caracas *capital of Venezuela*

caramelo caramel; hard candy

carbón *m* coal

carburante *m* fuel

cardenal *m* cardinal (*church official; bird*)

carecer (*irr*; **z**) **de** [17; 7] to lack

cargador loader, packer

cargar (**gu**) [3] to load, carry

cargo: sin— free of charge

Caribe *m* Caribbean

caricia caress

cariño affection

cariñoso affectionate

Carnaval *m* Mardi Gras

carne *f* meat

carné (*also* **carnet**) *m* driver's license, ID card; **sacarse (qu)** [1] **el—** to get one's driver's license

carnero ram (*male sheep*)

carnicería meat market, butcher shop

carnicero butcher

carnitas *pl meats, peppers, sauce, etc., served in tacos (Mexico)*

caro expensive

carrera race, career; run (*baseball*)

carretera highway

carta letter

cartel *m* poster
cartera large wallet, purse
cartero mailman
cartucho cartridge; **escopeta de —s** shotgun
casa: ama de— housewife
casadero of an age to marry
casarse (con) to marry, get married
casero homemade, domestic
casi almost
caso: en—de que in case: **en todo—** in any case; **poner por—** to take as an example
castellano Spanish, Castilian
castillo castle
castrista *adj for Fidel Castro*
catalán Catalan (*Romance language of northeastern Spain*)
cava *m* champagne
cazador *m* hunter
cazafantasmas *m sing* "ghostbuster"
cazar (c) [5] to hunt
cazuela casserole; clay dish
cebo bait
cebolla onion
ceder to give way, give in, yield, retreat; **—el paso** to yield (*right of way*)
C.E.E. = Comunidad Económica Europea *European Economic Community*
cena supper, dinner
cenar to eat supper, dinner
centella spark
central *f* main office, main factory, *etc.*
centro center, downtown
cerca (de) near, close (to)
cercano nearby
cerdo pig
cereza cherry
cero zero
cerrar (ie) [9] to close, shut
cerveza beer
cesar to cease, stop, quit; to fire (*from a job*)
cesta basket
ceviche *m fish marinated in lime juice*
ciego blind
cien one hundred
científico *adj* scientific; *n* scientist
ciento one hundred

cierre *m* closing; zipper, snap
cierto certain, sure, true
cifra number, digit
cifrar esperanzas en to place one's hopes on
cima top, summit
cine *m* movies, movie theater
cinematográfico *adj* movie, film
cinta ribbon, tape (*adhesive, magnetic*)
cinturón *m* belt; **—de seguridad** seat belt
circulación circulation, traffic
circunvalación ring-road, perimeter road, bypass
cita date, appointment
citar to cite, mention; to incite
ciudad city
ciudadano citizen
clamar to cry (out)
claro *adj* clear, light; *sentence introducer* of course
clavar to pierce, nail
cliente *m, f* customer
cobrador *m* ticket taker
cobrar to charge; to collect
cobro charge, collection
cocido *stew of meat, vegetables, and beans, served as three separate courses*
cocina kitchen; cooking
cocinar to cook
cocinero / a cook
código de área area code
coger (j) [2] to pick up, grab
cola line, queue
colaborar to collaborate, work together
colación offering of sweet snacks (*Mexico*)
colegio school (*various types throughout the Hispanic world*)
colgar (ue; gu) [12; 3] to hang (*tr*)
colocación placing, locating; location
colocar (qu) [1] to place, locate
Colón Columbus
colonia colony; city district (*Mexico, Caribbean*)
colores surtidos assorted colors
combustible *m* fuel
comedor *m* dining room; dining hall, cafeteria (*institution*)

comenzar (ie; c) [9; 5] to begin, start
comercio business, commerce, trade; business establishment
cometa *m* comet; *f* kite
comida food; meal
comisaría commissary; office, headquarters
comisario commissioner; head, chief
como: tan pronto— as soon as
cómo no of course, why not
cómodo comfortable
compacto musical compact-disk player
compartir to share
competencia competition, competence
competir (i, i) [11] to compete
complementario complemental, complementary
complemento: —directo direct object
completo complete; full, booked
componer (*irr*) [36, 48] to compose
compra purchase; **ir de —s** to go shopping; **tarjeta de —s** department store credit card
comprador / a buyer; shopper
comprar to buy
comprender to understand; to comprise
comprendido comprising
compromiso obligation, duty, commitment; compromise
común common; **por lo—** generally, usually, ordinarily
comunicarse (qu) con [1] to call, talk to (*on telephone*)
con with; **—tal que** provided (that)
concebir (i, i) [11] to conceive
concluir (*irr*) [21] to conclude
concordancia agreement
concordar(ue) [12] to agree
concursante *m, f* contestant
concursar to participate in a contest
concurso contest, competition
conde *m* count (*nobleman*)
conducción driving
conducir (*irr*; **z**) [22; 7] to

drive; to lead; **permiso de—** driver's license

conductor *m* driver

conejo rabbit

conferencia talk, lecture

confesar (**ie**) [9] to confess

confiar (*irr*) [23] to trust

confundido confused

confuso confusing

congelado frozen (*usually food*)

congresista *m, f* congressman / congresswoman

conmovedor moving (*emotional*)

conocer (*irr*; **z**) [24; 7] to know, be acquainted with; to meet (become acquainted) with; **dar** (*irr*) [27] **a—** to make known

conquista conquest

conquistar to conquer, defeat; to win

consciente conscious

conseguir (**i, i; g**) [11; 4] to get, achieve; **—** + *inf* to succeed in + *pr p*

consejería advisory council, organization

consejero adviser

consejo word of advice; **—s** advice

consentimiento consent

consentir (**ie, i**) [10] to consent

conserva preserved (pickled) food; jam, preserves

conservador *mn, adj* conservative

consiguiente: por— consequently

consomé *m* broth

constar de to consist of

construir (*irr*) [21] to build, construct

consultorio doctor's office

consumar to consummate

consumo consumption

contaduría accounting

contagiarse (**de**) to be(come) influenced, infected (by)

contar (**ue**) [12] to relate, tell; to count; **—con** to count, rely on

contener (**ie**; *irr*) [43] to contain

contestar to answer

continuar (*irr*) [25] to continue

contra against; **dar** (*irr*) [27] **—** to strike, hit, run into

contratar to hire, employ

contribuir (*irr*) [21] to contribute

convencer (**z**) [6] to convince

conveniente desirable, right, suitable, best

convenir (*irr*) [46] to be desirable, suitable, to one's advantage; to agree

convertirse (**ie, i**) **en** [10] to turn into

convivencia coexistence

convocatoria announcement, notice of a meeting

conyugal conjugal (*pertaining to a married couple*)

coñac *m* brandy; cognac

copa cup, trophy; wineglass; **—Mundial** World Cup (*soccer*); **tomar una—** to have a drink

copla song, ditty

coraje *m* courage, fighting spirit; anger

corazón *m* heart

corbata necktie

cordero lamb

corrector / a corrective

corredor *m* broker; runner

corregir (**i, i; j**) [11; 2] to correct

correo post office; mail, mail service; **apartado de —s** post office box

correr to run; **—olas** to surf

correría trip, excursion; **—s** travels

corriente: agua— running water

cortado: café— coffee "cut" with milk

cortar to cut

corte *m* cut, cutting; interruption, break; *f* court (*of law*)

corto short; small; **un hijo de —a edad** a young son

cosecha harvest

cosechar to reap, harvest

coser to sew

costar (**ue**) [12] to cost

costero coastal

costilla rib; cutlet, chop

costillar *m* ribs, rib cage

costoso costly, expensive

costumbre *f* custom

cotidiano daily, everyday

Coyoacán *district* (**colonia**) of *Mexico City*

crecer (*irr*; **z**) [17; 7] to grow (*intr*)

creciente growing

creer (*irr*) [26] to believe, think

crema cream; cream soup

cremoso creamy

criarse (*irr*) [23] to be raised; to grow (up)

criollo *native Hispanic American*

cristal *m* glass

crucigrama *m* crossword puzzle

crudo raw

Cruz, Celia *contemporary Cuban-American singer of salsa*

cruzar (**c**) [5] to cross; **—se con** to run across

cuaderno notebook

cuadra city block; stable

cuadrado *adj* square

cuadrito small cube

cuadro square; picture, painting

cuál what, which

cualquier any (at all)

cualquiera *m,f* any, any one, anyone (at all)

cuando when; **de vez en—** now and then, from time to time

cuanto: —antes as soon as possible; **en—** as soon as; **en— a** as for, with regard to

Cuaresma Lent

cuartel *m* headquarters, barracks; **sin—** merciless

cuarto quarter, one-fourth

cubierto table place setting

cubo bucket

cubrir [48] to cover

cucaracha cockroach

cuchilla knife

cuenta bill, account; **darse—de** (*irr*) [27] to realize

cuero leather, skin

cuerpo body

cuidado care; ¡**—!** Watch out!, Be careful!; **tener—** (**ie**; *irr*) [43] to be careful

cuidadoso careful

cuidar (de) to care for, take care of

culebrear to move as if tracing the figure of an S

culto cultured, educated

cumbre *f* peak, top

cumpleaños *m sing* birthday

cumplir (con) to carry out, fulfill, comply (with) **—años** to be, turn . . . (*years old*)

cupón *m* **de alimentos** food stamp

cura *m* priest; *f* cure

cursar to take courses, study

curvo curved

CH

chabacano trashy, cheap

Chamorro, Violeta *president of Nicaragua (1990–　　)*

chapeado closed in with metal plates (**chapas**)

charco pool, puddle

charla chat, talk

charlar to chat

chaval *m* child, boy

chayote *m* vegetable pear (*tropical fruit*)

chiflado crazy, mentally disturbed, unbalanced

chinchulines *m pl* barbecued tripe (*Argentina*)

chiringuito *open-air restaurant on beach (Spain)*

chistulari *m* flute player

chivo kid, goat

chocar (qu) [1] to shock; to crash, collide

chorizo *type of Spanish pork sausage*

chorro stream (*squirting liquid or gas*)

chuleta chop (*cut of meat*)

chupadoras de sangre bloodsuckers

chupar to suck; to sip

churro fritter (*dough fried and sugared*)

D

dama lady; female

dañado *pp of* **dañar** to damage, hurt, harm

daño damage, harm

dar (*irr*) [27] to give; **—a conocer** to make known; **—contra** to strike, hit, run into; **—una vuelta** to take a drive, ride; **—vueltas** to circle, go around in circles; **—se cuenta (de)** to realize

dato fact, piece of data

de vez en cuando now and then, from time to time

debajo (de) underneath, below

deber must, should, ought; to owe; *mn* duty, obligation

debidamente duly, properly

debido a due to

débil weak

decano dean

decidirse a to decide to

decir (i; *irr*) [28, 48] to say, tell; **es—** that is to say

dedicarse (qu) a [1] to devote oneself to

defender (ie) [9] to defend

dejar to leave (*tr*); to let, allow; **—caer** to drop; **—de +** *inf* to stop + *pr p*

delante (de) in front (of)

delantero *n* forward (*soccer*); *adj* front

delco car battery

deletrear to spell

delfín *m* dolphin

demás rest, other, remaining; **por lo—** as for the rest

demasiado too much; **—s** too many

denigrante demeaning

dentadura denture

dentro (de) inside

denunciar to charge with an offense or a crime; to report, turn in (*to police*); to denounce, accuse

deportes *pl* sports

deportivo *adj* sports

depósito container; **—de gasolina** gas tank

deprimido depressed

derecha *n* right (*direction*); **a la—** to, on the right

derecho *n* law (*academic discipline*); *adj* right; *adv* straight; **todo—** straight ahead

desagüe *m* drain

desambular to wander

desarmar to disarm, defuse; to take apart

desarraigado *pp of* **desarraigar (gu)** [3] to uproot

desarrollo development

desayunar to have breakfast

desayuno breakfast

descansar to rest; to relax

descanso rest; relaxation

descaradamente boldly

descompuesto *pp* [48] *of* **descomponer (*irr*)** [36] to break, take apart

desconocer (*irr*; z) [24; 7] not to know, to be unaware of, to be unfamiliar with

desconocido stranger

descorazonado disheartened, discouraged

descubrimiento discovery

descubrir [48] to discover

descuento discount

desdeñable unimportant, negligible

desempeño carrying out, performance

desesperado *adj* desperate; *n* outlaw

desestimar to disregard

desfallecer (*irr*; z) [17; 7] to pass out, faint

desfile *m* parade

desgracia misfortune

deshacer (*irr*) [31, 48] to break, undo, take apart; **—se de** to get rid of

deslizar(se) (c) [5] to slip, glide

deslumbrar to dazzle

desmontar to disassemble, take apart; to take off, down

desnatado with the fat removed

despacio slow(ly)

despacho office

despedida goodbye, farewell

despedir (i, i) [11] to see off; to dismiss, fire; **—se (de)** to say goodbye (to)

despegar (ie; gu) [9; 3] to take off (*plane*)

desperdicios *pl* garbage; leftovers; **triturador** *m* **de—**

garbage disposal (*kitchen appliance*)

despertador *m* alarm clock

despertar (**ie**) [9] to wake up (*tr*); **—se** to wake up (*intr*)

desprendido released, set loose

después (de) after, later

desquitarse to get even, retaliate

destructor / a destructive

destruir (*irr*) [21] to destroy

detener (**ie**; *irr*) [43] to stop, detain; to arrest

detrás (de) in back (of), behind

deuda debt

devolución return, giving back

devolver (**ue**) [12, 48] to return (*tr*)

día *m* day; **—de Acción de Gracias** Thanksgiving Day; **— de fiesta** holiday; **—s fijos** specific days; **— laborable** weekday, working day; **al—** up-to-date

diagonales: en las— on the field (*football*)

diariamente *adv* daily

diario *adj* daily; *n* daily newspaper; **a—** *adv* daily

dibujar to draw

dibujo drawing; *pl* cartoons (*newspaper*); **—s animados** cartoons (*movies, television*)

dicho saying, proverb; *pp* [48] of **decir** (*irr*) [28] to say

diente *m* tooth

diezmado *pp* of **diezmar** to decimate

digno worthy

diluir (*irr*) [21] to dilute

dineral *m* large sum of money

dirección direction; address; **barra de—** steering column

director *m* editor-in-chief; director

dirigente *m, f* manager, director

dirigir (**j**) [2] to direct; **—se a** to address, go up to (talk to)

disco disk; record

discurso speech

discutir to discuss; to argue

diseñar to design

disfrazado disguised, wearing a mask

disfrutar (**de**) to enjoy

disgustar to displease, annoy; **—se** to be displeased, get angry

disparar to fire, shoot

disparo shot

disponer (*irr*) [36, 48] to dispose; **—se a** to get ready to

disponibilidad availability

disponible available

dispuesto *pp* [48] *of* **disponer** (*irr*) [36] ready, disposed

distinguir (**g**) [4] to distinguish

distintivo *n* sign, distinguishing mark

distinto distinct, different

distraer (*irr*) [44] to distract

distribuir (*irr*) [21] to distribute

diversión *f* amusement, entertainment, game

divertir (**ie, i**) [16] to amuse, entertain, **—se** to be amused, entertained; to have a good time

doblador *m* *in bullring a person with cape who attracts bull toward an exit gate*

doblar to double, fold; to turn (*corner*); to dub (*movie dialog*)

doblete *m* double (*baseball*)

documental *m* documentary

doler (**ue**) [12] to hurt, pain

dolorosamente painfully

domar to tame, domesticate; to train

domicilio dwelling; **a—** at home; to the house, home (*as in* **entrega a—** home delivery)

domingo Sunday

dominguero picnicker

dominicano Dominican (*from the Dominican Republic*)

dorado golden

dormir (**ue, u**) [13] to sleep; **—se** to go to sleep, fall asleep

dormitorio bedroom

dote *m* gift

ducha shower

duda doubt

dudar to doubt; to hesitate

dudoso doubtful

duelo duel

dueño owner

Duero *river of western Spain and Portugal*

dulce sweet

duradero lasting

durar to last

duro hard, harsh; **huevo—** hard-boiled egg; *n Spanish coin worth 5 pesetas*

E

ecuador *m* equator

echar to throw, cast, toss; to mail; to pour

edad age; **hijo de corta—** young son

EE.UU. *abbrev for* **Estados Unidos** United States

efectivamente really, actually, in truth, in effect

efectivo cash

eficaz effective, efficacious

ejecutivo executive

ejemplar *m* example, copy (*book*)

ejemplo example

elaborar to construct, make up

elección election; choice

electrodoméstico household appliance

elegir (**i, i; j**) [11; 2] to choose, elect

eludir to elude, avoid

embajador *m* ambassador

embargo: sin— however

emboscada ambush

embutido sausage

emisión *f* broadcast

emitir to emit, broadcast; to send

emocionante exciting, thrilling, moving

emocionarse to get excited; **—(con)** to be moved (by)

empanada filled pastry; meat pie, patty

emparrillado gridiron

empatado tied (*sports*)

empeñado (en) determined, bound (to)

empezar (**ie**; **c**) [9; 5] to begin, start

empleado employee

emplear to use, employ

empleo job, employment

empresa company, enterprise, business

empresario manager, business man

empujar to push

en:—cuanto as soon as; —**cuanto a** as for, with regard to; —**seguida** right away, at once, immediately

enagua (*often pl*) underskirt, petticoat

enamorado person in love; lover

enamorar to court, woo; —**se** (**de**) to fall in love (with)

enanismo smallness, shortness of stature

encantar to delight, be very pleasing to

encañonar to aim, point

encarcelado *pp of* **encarcelar** to jail, imprison

encargado (**de**) in charge (of)

encargar (**gu**) [3] to put in charge

encargo assignment, job

encarnar to embody

encebollado beef stew with onions

encender (**ie**) [9] to turn on, light; to set on fire

encendido turned on; lit, lighted

encierro confinement, shutting in; *running of the bulls to enclosed pens*

encima (**de**) over, on top (of); on one's person

encimera burners (*top of stove*)

encontrar (**ue**) [12] to find; to meet; —**se** to be, be found

endemoniado possessed by the devil

enero January

enfermarse to get sick

enfermera nurse

enfermería infirmary

enfermizo sickly

enfermo sick

enfrentarse (**a**) to face, meet (*an opponent*)

enfrente in front; opposite

enfriar (*irr*) [23] to cool, chill

enganche *m* down payment ("hooking up") (*Mexico*)

engañar to deceive, fool, cheat

engordar to gain weight

enjuague *m* rinse; —**bucal** mouthwash

enojado angry, annoyed

enojar to anger, annoy; —**se** to get angry, annoyed

ensalada salad

ensayo essay; effort, attempt

enseñar to teach; to show

ensuciarse to get dirty

entender (**ie**) [9] to understand

enterar to inform, tell, let know; —**se** (**de**) to find out (about), be informed (of, about)

entero entire; whole

entidad entity; business organization

entonces then, at that time

entrada entrance; ticket

entraña entrail, tripe; intestine

entrecot (*French*) *m* ribeye steak

entrega delivery

entregar (**gu**) [3] to deliver; to hand in, over

entremés *m* appetizer

entrenador *m* coach (sports)

entrenamiento training

entrenarse to practice, rehearse

entretener (**ie**; *irr*) [43] to amuse, entertain

entrevista interview

envase *m* container (*bottle, can, etc.*)

envenenamiento poisoning

enviar (*irr*) [23] to send

envidioso envious

envolver (**ue**) [12, 48] to wrap (up)

Epifanía Epiphany (*Jan. 6*); Twelfth Night (*of Christmas*); Feast of Magi

época time, season

equipaje *m* baggage

equipo team; equipment; appliance

equivocarse (**qu**) [1] to make a mistake

ermita abandoned chapel, hermitage

es decir that is to say

escala stop (*on a flight*); ladder

escalera stairs, stairway

escalope *m* scallop (*thin slice of meat*)

escándalo scandal; commotion, loud noise

escapada quick trip; getaway

escasear to be scarce

escoger (**j**) [2] to choose

escolar *m* student; *adj* academic, student

escolaridad preparatoria preparatory school education

escondite *m* hiding place

escopeta de cartuchos shotgun

escribir [48] to write

escuadra team

escuchar to listen (to)

escupir to spit

escurrir to drain

esfinge *f* sphinx

esforzado tough

esforzarse (**ue**; **c**)(**por** + *inf*) [12; 5] to make an effort (to + *v*)

eso: por— therefore

espalda back (*body*)

espantar to frighten, scare

español: a lo— Spanish-style

espárrago asparagus

especializado: centro— *school specializing in one course of study*

especializarse (**c**)**en** [5] to major in; to specialize in

espejo mirror

espeluznante terrifying, hairraising

espera wait

esperanza hope

esperar to wait (for)

espeso thick, dense (*food, liquids, underbrush, etc.*)

espía *m, f* spy

espina bone (*fish*), thorn

espíritu *m* **de superación** desire to advance, get ahead

esqueleto skeleton

esquina corner (*outside*)

estación season

estadio stadium

estado status; —**civil** marital status

estampilla postage stamp

estar (*irr*) [29] to be; **sala de—** living room

estatura height

esterilizada: gata— neutered female cat

estilo style; **por el—** of that kind, like that

estimado *n* estimate, proposed cost

Estocolmo Stockholm

Estrasburgo Strasbourg (*France*)

estrechez *f* narrowness

estrecho narrow

estrella star

estrellarse to crash, be smashed

estreno debut, first appearance, use, *or* performance

estupor *m* amazement

evitar to avoid

evocador / a evocative

examen de aprendizaje *m* examination for learner's permit

exigente demanding

exigir (j) [2] to require, demand

exitazo *augmentative of* **éxito** huge success, "smash hit"

éxito success

expiatorio for atonement

expirar to expire; to die

explicar (qu) [1] to explain

exponer (*irr*) [36, 48] to expose, leave unprotected

extranjero *adj* foreign; *n* foreigner

extrañar to miss (*emotional reaction*)

extraño strange

extremaunción last rites

extrovertido *n* extrovert; *adj* extroverted, gregarious

F

fábrica factory

fabricar (qu) [1] to manufacture

facilidad ease, facility

facturar to check through (*baggage*)

falta lack; mistake, error; **hacer** (*irr*) [31, 48] — to be needed; **sin—** without fail

faltar to be missing, lacking; **—a** to miss, fail to attend;

no faltaba más how absurd, this is ridiculous, the "last straw"

fallar to fail, break down

fallo malfunction, defect

familiar *m* family member; *adj* family; familiar

fandango *Spanish folk dance*

fantasma *m* ghost

farmacia drugstore, pharmacy

favor *m* kindness, favor; **—de presentarse** please appear, show up

fe *f* faith; **a—** truly

fecha date; **—de vencimiento** expiration date

feria market, fair

ferretería hardware store

festivo: días—s holidays; holy days

fideos *pl* noodles

fiduciario: departamento— trust department (*bank*)

fiebre *f* fever

fiel faithful

fiero wild, untamed

fiesta festive occasion, seasonal festivities; party; **—s patronales** *local festivities held annually in honor of town's patron saint or protector;* **día de —** holiday

fijarse (en) to notice

fijo fixed, set; **días—s** specific days

fila row

filtro filter

fin *m* end, ending; purpose, goal; **a—es de** at the end of; **en—** so, anyway, at any rate

financiación financing

financiamiento financing

finés / a Finnish (*also* **finlandés / a**)

fingir (j) [2] to pretend, feign

fino delicate, fine; exquisite; of high quality; refined; **yegua de paso—** show horse

firma signature

firmar to sign (*one's name*)

físico *adj* physical; *m* physicist

flan *m* custard

flor *f* flower

Florida: Pascua— Easter

fluoruro fluoride

foco center, focus

folleto pamphlet, brochure

fonda inn

fondo back, rear; bottom; **a—** thoroughly

footing *m* jogging

forastero stranger (*from another town or region*)

forcejear to struggle

forma: estar (*irr*) [29] **en—** to be in shape; **ponerse** (*irr*) **en—** to get in shape

formación training

formulario form, application blank

foro forum; stage

forro lining

fortaleza fortress

foto *f* photo

F.P. = Formación Profesional (*school curriculum in Spain*)

fracasar to fail

fracaso failure

fragua forge, machine shop

fraile *m* friar, monk, priest

fraude *m* fraud

fregadero kitchen sink

fregona mop

freír (i, i) [38, 48] to fry

frenazo jamming on of the brakes

freno brake

frente *m* front; *f* forehead; **de—** face-to-face

fresa strawberry

fresco *n* cool(-ness); *adj* cool; fresh

frigorífico refrigerator (*Spain*)

frío cold

frito *pp* [48] *of* **freír (i, i;** *irr*) [38] to fry

fuego fire; **—s artificiales** *pl* fireworks

fuera outside

fuerte strong

fuerza force, power, strength; **a la—** of necessity, forcibly

fumar to smoke

función function, duty, job

funcionario public employee

fustigar (gu) [3] to lash

fut *m* soccer, football (*slang*)

G

gabinete pedagógico teaching laboratory

gafas *pl* glasses (*eyeglasses*)

gaitero bagpipe player

gala gala; specialty; choicest part, favorite; "pride and joy"

galán *m* beau, boyfriend, suitor

galería gallery; corridor

gallego Galician (*from Galicia, section of northwestern Spain*)

gallina hen

ganadería cattle farming

ganadito *dim of* **ganado** cattle

ganancia profit, gain

ganar to win, beat; to earn, gain; **—se el pan** to earn a living

ganas *pl* desire, eagerness; **tener (ie;** *irr***) [43] —** to feel like (it)

garganta throat

gas: a todo— at top speed

gaseosa soft drink

gastar to spend; to waste

gasto expense

gato cat

gazpacho *cold vegetable soup*

gélido frigid, frozen, freezing (-cold)

general: por lo— in general

Génova Genoa (*Italy*)

gentil courteous

gerente *m* manager

gestión *f* management, negotiations; **—inmobiliaria** real estate transactions

gesto gesture

gigante *m* giant

gimnasia gymnastics, exercise

girar to spin, revolve; **—se** to spin, turn around

gitano Gypsy

globo globe; balloon

goleada scoring of many goals

golero goalkeeper

goloso sweet-toothed, greedy

golpe *m* blow

gordito *dim of* **gordo** fat

gota drop

gozar (c)(de) [5] to enjoy

grabar to record (*on tape or disk*)

gracia grace; humor; **Día de Acción de—s** Thanksgiving Day

gracioso amusing, funny; attractive, graceful

grado degree

graduarse (*irr*) [25] to graduate

gral. *abbrev. of* **general**

gramática grammar

grasa fat, grease

grasiento greasy

gratis *adv* free, without charge

griego Greek

grifo faucet

gripe *f* flu

gris gray

grito shout, cry

grueso thick, heavy

Guadalquivir *m river in southern Spain*

guagua bus (*Caribbean, eastern U.S., Canary Islands of Spain*)

Guantanamera *popular Cuban song*

guante *m* glove

guapete *dim of* **guapo** good-looking

guapo good-looking, handsome; pretty

guaraní *m* Guarani (*Indian language in Paraguay*)

guardameta *m, f* goalkeeper

guardián *m* watchman, guard

guarida lair, den

guía *m, f* guide; *f* guidebook, directory

guisante *m* pea

guiso cooked dish

guitarra guitar

gustar to be pleasing to, "to like"

gusto taste, pleasure

H

haber (*irr*) [30] to have (*aux*)

habilidad ability, skill

habitación room

habitante *m, f* resident, inhabitant

hacer (*irr*) [31, 48] to do, make; **—falta** to be needed; **—una pregunta** to ask a question; **—se** to become, get

hacia towards

hache *f letter* h

halcón *m* falcon

hallarse to be, be found

hambre *f* hunger; **pasar—** to be hungry; **tener (ie;** *irr***) [43]—** to be hungry

harina flour; meal

hasta until, up to; as far as; **—luego** see you later, bye; **—que** until

hebreo Hebrew

hecho fact, deed

helado *pp of* **helar** (**ie**) [9] to freeze; *n* ice cream

herida wound, injury

herir (ie, i) [10] to wound

hermanastra stepsister

hermoso beautiful

herramienta tool

herrería forge, machine shop

Hi-Fi: cadena— stereo system

hielo ice

hierro iron

hijo de corta edad young son

hindi *m* Hindi (*a language of India*)

hipermercado supermarket

hispanoparlante *m, f* Spanish speaker

hogar *m* home

hogar-escuela *m* boarding school, public day school

hombro shoulder

hondo deep

horario schedule

horno oven

hospitalario hospitable

hostelería hotels and tourism, hospitality industry

hoyo hole

hueco space, hole

huelga strike (*labor*)

huella track, footprint; trace

huésped / a guest

huevo egg; **—duro** hard-boiled egg

huir (*irr*) [21] to flee, run away

humareda cloud of smoke

humilde humble

humor *m* mood, humor

hundir (*tr*) to sink, submerge

I

ida y vuelta round-trip
idioma *m* language
iglesia church
ilusión *f* enthusiasm
imagen *f* picture, image
impar *adj* odd (*as opposed to "even"*)
impedir (**i, i**) [11] to prevent; to impede
implantación establishment, setting up
importar to matter, be important
imprescindible essential, indispensable
impresora printer (*machine*)
imprimir [48] to print
impuesto *n* tax; *pp* [48] *of* **imponer** (*irr*) [36] imposed
impulsar to push; to knock, bat in (*runs in baseball*)
Inca *a member of the ruling family in the Quechua Indian empire in Peru at the time of the arrival of the Spaniards*
incansable untiring
incendio fire
incierto uncertain
inclinarse to lean over, bend over, bow
incluir (*irr*) [21] to include
incogible *adj* unstoppable, uncatchable; *mn* hit (*baseball*)
incorporarse to sit up (*from a lying position*)
índole *f* kind, class, type
infalsificable impossible to counterfeit, forge
informática data processing
informe *m* report, account; information
infusión *f* tea (*after brewed*)
ingeniero / a engineer
ingerido *pp of* **ingerir** (**ie, i**) [10] to ingest, swallow
ingestión *f* ingestion, something swallowed
ingrato ungrateful
ingreso enrollment, entrance
inhalado *pp of* **inhalar** to inhale
inmobiliario: gestión —a real-estate transactions
inodoro toilet bowl

inolvidable unforgettable
inquieto restless, disturbing
inquilino / a tenant, renter
inscribirse [48] to register, enroll
inseguro unsafe, insecure; unsure
insistir (**en**) to insist (on)
insólito unusual
instancia petition
instante: al— at once
integrante *m* member
intercederse to intercede
internarse (**en**) to go into, penetrate
intrépido intrepid, fearless
introducir (*irr*) [22; 7] to introduce, put in(to)
inversión *f* investment
inverso *adj* reverse
invierno winter
invitado *n* guest
ir (*irr*) [32] to go; **—de compras** to go shopping; **—se** to leave, go away
I.V.A. = Impuesto de Valor Agregado sales tax (*"value added tax"*)
izquierda *n* left: **a la—** to, on the left

J

Jaén *city in southern Spain*
jamás never
jamón *m* ham
jardín *m* garden; outfield (*baseball*)
jardinero gardener; outfielder
jefe / a boss, manager; chief
jit *m* hit (*baseball*)
jonrón *m* homerun
jota *Spanish folk dance; letter* j
joven young
joya jewel
jubilado *pp of* **jubilarse** to retire
juerga partying, spree
jueves *m* Thursday
juez *m, f* judge
jugada play (*sports*); move (*games*); trick
jugador *m* player; gambler
jugar (**ue; gu**) [14; 3] to play (*games, sports*)

jugo juice
juguete *m* toy
junta council, governing board
juntar to join, unite; **—se** to come together, assemble
junto together, near; **—(a)** next (to), close (to), together (with)
jurado sworn, bound by an oath (*pp of* **jurar** to swear)
justicia justice; law; police

L

La Coruña *city in northwestern Spain*
labio lip
lácteo *adj* dairy; **—s** dairy products
lado side; **al—de** beside, next to
ladrón *m* thief
lambada *popular dance, originally Brazilian*
lana wool
langosta lobster
lanzador *m* pitcher (*baseball*)
lanzar (**c**) [5] to shoot, launch; to pitch
lápiz *m* pencil
largo long; **a lo—de** along
lasca thick slice
lástima pity, shame
lastimar to hurt, pain; **—se** to get hurt
lata can (*container*)
lavabo bathroom; basin
lavado washing, laundry (*clean*)
lavadora washing machine, washer
lavamanos *m sing* basin
lavavajillas *m sing* dishwasher
lavar to wash
laxante *m* laxative
lección lesson
lectura reading
leche *f* milk; **¡—!** Damn!
lechero *adj* milk; dairy
lechuga lettuce
leer (*irr*) [26] to read
legumbre *f* vegetable
lejano *adj* far (away)
lejos (**de**) far (from)
lengua language; tongue
lenguado sole (*fish*)

lenguaje *m* language (*manner of speech*)

lentejas *pl* lentils

lentes *m* or *f pl* eyeglasses

lento slow

lesionado injured

letrero sign, notice

levantar to raise, lift; **—se** to stand up, get up

ley *f* law

liana vine

liarse (*irr*) [23] to get tangled, mixed up

Líbano Lebanon

libertad liberty, freedom

libre free; open, vacant

librería bookstore

licenciado *person with a master's degree*; lawyer (*Mexico, Central America, Argentina*)

liderato first place; leadership

liga league

ligero light (*in weight, Spain*); slight; fast

Lima *capital of Peru*

limpia cleaning; clean sweep (*sports*)

limpiador *m* cleaner

limpiar to clean

limpio clean; fair (*sports*); **picadillo—** lean ground beef

lindo pretty; nice (*Sp Am*)

línea line

lío confusion, mix-up, mess; entanglement, "affair"

listo ready; smart, clever

lo: a—largo de along

local *m* place, site, premises

localización locating, localizing

locura madness, insanity

lograr to gain, win; to achieve, get, attain, succeed (in)

lomo loin; pork

lucha fight, struggle

luego then, later; **hasta—** see you later, bye

lugar *m* place

lugareño villager

lujo luxury; **de—** first-class

luna moon

lunes *m* Monday

lustro five-year period

luz *f* light

LL

llama *wooly ruminant animal of South America*

llamada call

llamamiento call, appeal

llamarse to be called, named

llanta tire (*car*)

llave *f* key; **—en mano** immediate occupancy; **ama de—s** housekeeper

llavero keycase; key ring

llegar (**gu**) [3] to arrive; **—a ser** to get to be; to become

llenar (**de**) to fill (with)

lleno full; **solicitud—a** application filled out

llevar to carry, take; to wear (*clothes*) **—a cabo** to carry out, complete; **—se a cabo** to be carried out, take place

llover (**ue**) [12] to rain

llovizna drizzle

lloviznar to drizzle, sprinkle

lluvia rain

lluvioso rainy

M

Machu Picchu *hidden fortress city of the Inca empire in Peru*

madrugada dawn, early morning

maduro ripe, mature

maestro master; teacher

maíz *m* corn; maize

mal *m* evil

mala: de—uva ill-tempered, in a bad mood

maleta suitcase

maletín *m* briefcase, hand luggage

maleza thick weeds

maltrato mistreatment, abuse

manchego of La Mancha (*region of central Spain*)

mandar to send; to order

mandato command

manejar to operate, handle; to manage; to drive (*Sp Am*)

manejo operation; driving; handling

manera: de todas —s at any rate, anyway

mango mango (*tropical fruit*)

manguera hose

manifestación demonstration in public, rally

mano *f* hand; **— de trabajo** workforce; **llave en—** immediate occupancy

manso gentle, mild; tame

manta blanket

mantequilla butter

manzana apple

mañana *f* morning; *m* tomorrow; **pasado—** day after tomorrow

manzanilla *type of olive; type of sherry;* camomile tea

maqueta model, likeness (*on reduced scale*)

maquinaria machinery

mar *m* sea

Maradona, Diego *professional soccer player from Argentina*

maraña thicket

maravilla wonder, marvel

maravillar to astonish

marca brand

marcar (**qu**) [1] to score; to dial (*telephone*); to mark

marchar to march; **—se** to leave, depart, go away

marginal *adj* fringe; **beneficios—es** fringe benefits

marido husband

marinero seaman, sailor; **salsa—a** marinera sauce (*based on tomato, garlic, herbs*)

mariposa butterfly

mariscal marshall; **—de campo** quarterback

mariscos *pl* shellfish

marrón brown

Marsella Marseilles (*city in southern France*)

martes *m* Tuesday

Martí, José *Cuban patriot and writer of the late 19th century*

marzo March

más more; most; plus; **a— tardar** at the latest; **cada vez—** more and more; **sin— ni—** without beating around the bush, without further ado

masa dough; **—agria** sourdough

masacrar to massacre
máscara mask
masculino masculine
matanza slaughter
matar to kill
matrícula car registration; tuition; registration (*college*)
matricularse to register (*college*)
mayonesa mayonnaise
mayor older; bigger, greater; **misa—** High Mass
mayoría majority
mazazo blow with a hammer, mallet
medalla medal
medianoche *f* midnight
mediante by means of, through
mediar to intervene, interfere
medias *pl* stockings
mediodía *m* noon
medir (**i**, **i**) [11] to measure; to be . . . tall
mejor better; best; **a lo—** maybe, most likely
mejorar to improve (*intr, tr*); **—se** (*intr*) to improve
mellizo twin
menestra stew; stir-fried food
Meninas (Las) painting by 17th-century Spanish artist Diego Velázquez, in Madrid's El Prado museum
menor smaller; younger; minor
menos less, least; **—mal** it's just as well that, it's a good thing that; **a—que** unless
mensaje *m* message
mente *f* mind
mentir (**ie**, **i**) [10] to lie (*tell a falsehood*)
menudo *n* well-seasoned dish of tripe, also called **mondongo** (*Mexico*); *adv* **a—** often
mercado market(place)
mercancía merchandise, goods
merecer (*irr*; **z**) [17; 7] to deserve
merengue *m* Dominican (*nickname for inhabitant of Dominican Republic*); *popular dance from the Dominican Republic*
merluza hake (*type of codfish*)
mesero waiter

meseta plateau
mesón *m* inn, tavern
meter to put (in); **—se** to meddle, interfere, butt into
metralleta submachine gun
metro meter (*3.28 ft.*); subway
mezclar to mix
microlentillas *pl* contact lenses
microonda microwave
miedo fear; **tener** (**ie**; *irr*) [43] **—** to be afraid
miel *f* honey
mientras while, as long as; **—tanto** meanwhile
miércoles *m* Wednesday
miga crumb; **pan de—** bread crumbs, soft part of bread
mil one thousand
milagroso miraculous
Milán Milan (*city in Italy*)
milanesa: **a la—** *food breaded and sauteed*
milenario millennium
minuta menu
mirar to look (at), watch
miras: **con—al futuro** looking to improve
Miró, Joan *20th-century Spanish painter*
misa Mass (*religious service*); **—mayor** High Mass
misiva letter (*communication*)
mitad half
mitigar (**gu**) [3] to mitigate, lessen
mito myth
moca mocha (*coffee*)
moda style, fashion; **estar de—** to be in style
modos: **de todos—** at any rate, anyway
mojar to soak, dunk
molestar to bother, annoy
molestia bother, annoyance
momento: **en algún—** at any time
momia mummy
monstruo monster
montaje *m* installing, setting up
montar to put up; to go up, get on
monte *m* woods; mountain; countryside

montón *m* pile, heap; lots, great number, "bunch"
morado purple
morder (**ue**) [12] to bite
moreno dark, brunette
morir (**ue**, **u**) [13, 48] to die
morro: **beber a—** to drink straight from the bottle
morrón: **pimiento—** sweet (bell) pepper
mostrador *m* counter
mostrar (**ue**) [12] to show; **—se** to appear, look
mote *m* boiled corn
motivo reason; **con—de** because of, on the occasion of
moto *f* motorbike
mover (**ue**) [12] to move (*tr*); **—se** to move (around) (*intr*)
moza girl
mozo boy
mudanza move, moving (*of house contents*)
muerto *adj* dead; *n* corpse
muestra sign, evidence, sample
mujer *f* woman
mula mule
multa fine (*penalty*)
mundial *adj* world(wide)
mundo world
municipio city, town; municipality
murciélago bat (*animal*)
musical: **compacto—** compact disk player
músico musician

N

nacer (*irr*; **z**) [33; 7] to be born
nacimiento birth
nada nothing; not anything; not at all; **de—** you're welcome
nadar to swim
nadie no one, nobody
nana nursemaid (*Sp Am*)
naranja orange
narcotraficante *m* drug trafficker, drug dealer
nariz *f* nose; nostril
natal *adj* native
naturaleza nature

nave *f* nave; aisle
Navidad Christmas; **—es** Christmas season
negar (**ie**; **gu**) [9; 3] to deny; **—se** (**a**) to refuse (to)
negocio business deal, transaction; *pl* business
negro black
nevada snowfall
neoyorquino *adj from New York*
ni siquiera not even
nido nest
ninguno none, not any; no one, nobody
nivel *m* level
Niza Nice (*city in France*)
Noche Vieja New Year's Eve
Nochebuena Christmas Eve
nombrar to name, appoint
nombre *m* name
noquear to knock out, KO
nota grade, mark (*school*); note
notable *m* B (*grade*)
noticias *pl* news
noticiero newscast
novecientos nine hundred
novia girlfriend; fiancée; bride
noviazgo betrothal, engagement
novio boyfriend; fiancé; groom
nube *f* cloud
nublado cloudy
nuevo new; **de—** again
nunca never

O

obedecer (*irr*; **z**) [17; 7] to obey
obra work
obrero worker
obtener (**ie**; *irr*) [43] to obtain
ocioso lazy, idle
ocupado busy
ocuparse de to be in charge of, provide (*services*)
ocurrírsele a uno to occur to one
odiar to hate
odisea odyssey
oeste *m* west
ofender to offend, insult; **—se** to be offended
oferta offer
oficio office, position, job

ofrecer (*irr*; **z**) [17; 7] to offer
oír (*irr*) [34] to hear
¡ojalá ! How I wish, If only . . .
ojo eye; **¡—!** Attention!, Note!, Be careful!, Look out!
ola wave; **correr—s** to surf
oler (**hue**) (**a**) [15] to smell (like); *also tr*
olor *m* smell, odor
olvidar to forget; **—se** (**de**) to forget (about)
O.N.C.E. = **Organización Nacional de Ciegos** (*blind*) **de España**
onda wave (*radio, sound*)
oponerse (*irr*) **a** [36, 48] to oppose
optativo optional
oración prayer
orden *m* order (*arrangement*); *f* order (*command, religious organization*)
orilla shore
oro gold
oscuro dark
oso bear (*animal*); **—de peluche** teddy bear
ovoide *adj* egg-shaped; *mn* football (*nickname*)

P

pabellón *m* pavillion; **—de fiestas** entertainment center
padrino godfather
paella *typical Spanish dish (from Valencia) based on rice and seafood*
página page
pago payment
país *m* country
paisaje *m* landscape
pajar *m* hayloft
pájaro bird
palabra word
palabrota swearword
palo stick; **De tal—, tal astilla** A chip off the old block
pan bread; **—de miga** bread crumbs, soft part of bread; **—de Muerto** *pastry eaten to celebrate All Saints' and All Souls' Days (Mexico)*; **ganarse el—** to earn a living

panadería bakery
pañal *m* diaper
pañuelo handkerchief
papa potato (*Sp Am*)
Papa *m* Pope
papel *m* paper; role; **—es** citizen's documents, identification
papelera trash container, wastebasket
paquete *m* package
par *mn* pair; *adj* even (*as opposed to "odd"*)
parada stop, stopping place
paraguas *m sing* umbrella
parar to stop, stay (*take lodging*); **—se** to stop; to stand up (*Sp Am*)
parecer (*irr*; **z**) [17; 7] to seem, appear; **—se a** to look like, resemble
parecido similar
pared wall (*interior*)
pareja couple, pair
párpado eyelid
parque *m* **de atracciones** amusement park
parrilla grill (*cooking*)
parrillada grilled food (*usually meat*)
párroco parish priest
parte: por mi— as for me; **todas—s** everywhere
partido game (*sports contest*)
partir to split; to depart
pasado *m* past; **—mañana** the day after tomorrow
pasar hambre to suffer hunger
pasaje *m* passage; fare, ticket
Pascua Easter; Passover; **—Florida** Easter
pasear(se) to stroll, walk; to take a walk
paseíto, *dim of* **paseo** walk, stroll
paseo boulevard, avenue; **yegua de—** walking horse
pasillo aisle, hall(way)
paso step; passage; **—a—** step by step; **ceder el—** to yield (*right of way*); **de—** in passing; **yegua de—fino** show horse
pastel *m* pastry; pie, cake
pastelería pastry shop
pastilla pill, tablet

pastorela *Nativity play given during Christmas season in Mexico*

pataleo stamping of feet

patrocinar to sponsor

patrona patron (*female saint*)

patronal *adj* patronal, patron; **fiestas—es** *local festivities held annually in honor of town's patron saint or protector*

patrullando *pr p of* **patrullar** to patrol

paz *f* peace

Paz, Octavio *contemporary Mexican novelist, winner of Nobel prize for literature in 1990*

pecado sin

pecar (**qu**) [1] to sin

pecho chest, breast

pedagógico pedagogical (*teaching*)

pedido order, request

pedir (**i, i**) [11] to order; to ask for; **—prestado** to borrow

pegar (**gu**) [3] to hit, strike; to stick; **—se** to stick, cling

pelar to peel, shell, skin

pelea fight, quarrel, argument, scuffle

película film, movie

peligrar to be in danger

peligroso dangerous

pelo hair

pelota ball; baseball

pelotari jai alai player

pelotazo hard-hit ball (*baseball*)

pelotero baseball player

peluche felt, plush; **oso de—** teddy bear

peluquero hairdresser

pena grief, sorrow; worry

pensar (**ie**) (**en**) [9] to think (about, of); **— +** *inf* to plan, intend to + *v*

pensión *f* pension, boarding house

pensionista *m, f person receiving room and board*

peña social group or club

peor worse

pequeño small

pera pear

perder (**ie**) [9] to lose; to miss (*usually a vehicle*); to waste; **—se** to miss (*an event of great importance or interest*)

pérdida loss

peregrinación pilgrimage

perezoso lazy

periferia outskirts

periódico periodical, newspaper

periodismo journalism

periodista *m, f* journalist

permanecer (*irr*; **z**) [17; 7] to stay, remain

permiso permission; permit; **—de conducir** driver's license

perplejo confused, perplexed

perrazo big dog

perro dog; **— -guía** seeing-eye dog

perseguir (**i, i**; **g**) [11; 4] to pursue, harass

personal *m* personnel

personaje *m* character (*in fiction*)

pertenecer (*irr*; **z**) [17; 7] to belong

pesado heavy

pesar to weigh

pescado fish (*after caught*)

pese a despite, in spite of

peseta *monetary unit of Spain*

pésimo terrible, very bad

peso weight; *monetary unit of many Hispanic countries*

petrolero *adj* oil

picadero "bachelor pad," "love nest"

picadillo ground beef; **— limpio** lean ground beef

picante hot, spicy

Picapiedra: los— the Flintstones

picar (**qu**) [1] to chop, pick; to sting, bite, itch, hurt

pico tiny bit

pie *m* foot

piedra stone

piel *f* skin; fur; leather

pierna leg (*human*)

pieza part, piece; **—de recambio** spare part

pimiento morrón large sweet (bell) pepper

pinchar to puncture, pierce; to have a flat tire

pintar to paint

pintoresco picturesque

pintura painting; paint

piña pineapple

piñata *decorated hanging container filled with sweets, fruits, etc.*

piscina swimming pool

piso floor; apartment, condominium (*Spain*)

pista runway, track

pizarra blackboard, slate

placer *m* pleasure

plancha iron (*home appliance*); **a la—** grilled

planear to plan, outline

planicie *m* plain, flat area, level ground

plano map (*city*)

planta plant; **—baja** ground floor; **trabajo de—** permanent work (*Mexico*)

plantilla regular staff (*employees*)

plasmar to shape, mold

plata silver

plátano plaintain (*type of banana cooked before eaten*)

playa beach

playeras *pl* beach sandals

plaza room, seat, place, opening; municipal square; bullring

plazo term, time period

plegar (**ie**; **gu**) [9; 3] to fold, bend

pleito lawsuit

pleno full; **en—a vía pública** in broad daylight

plomería plumbing

plomero plumber

población population; village, town

poder (**ue**; *irr*) [35] to be able, can; *mn* power

poderoso powerful

podrido rotten

polaco Polish

pollo chicken

pomelo grapefruit

ponchado strikeout (*baseball*)

ponchar to punch; to strike out (*baseball*)

poner (*irr*) [36, 48] to place, put, set; to put on (*clothing*); to lay (*eggs*); **—por caso** to take as an example; **—se** to become, get; **—se en forma** to get in shape; **—se a +** *inf* to begin, go about + *pr p*

por for; through; per; on behalf of; for the sake of; — **consiguiente** consequently; **—eso** therefore; **—lo demás** as for the rest; **—lo pronto** for the present, provisionally; **—lo tanto** therefore; **—lo visto** apparently; **—mi parte** as for me; **—si acaso** just in case; **—supuesto** of course

porrón *m* wine pitcher with side spout

portazo door slam

portero goalkeeper (*soccer*); janitor; doorman

postre *m* dessert

potro colt

pote *m* *soup of beans, ham, greens*; clay cookpot

práctica practice; exercise

precio price

precisar to require, need

preciso necessary

preferente preferable

preferir (**ie, i**) [10] to prefer

pregunta question; **hacer** (*irr*) [31, 48] **una—** to ask a question

preguntar to ask; **—por** to ask for, inquire about

premio prize

prensa press (*newspapers, radio, etc.*)

preocupado *pp of* **preocupar** to worry

presentarse to appear, show up

presionar to pressure

prestado *pp of* **prestar**: **pedir** (**i, i**) [11]— to borrow

préstamo loan

prestar to lend, loan; — **atención** to pay attention

prevalecer (*irr*; **z**) [17; 7] to prevail

prevenir (**ie**; *irr*) [46] to prevent, avoid

previo prior, previous

previsto foreseen; **tener** (**ie**; *irr*) [43]— to anticipate

primavera spring (*season*)

primerísimo first-rate, top, best

principiante *m,f* beginner, novice

prisa haste, hurry; **tener** (**ie**; *irr*) [43] — to be in a hurry

privilegiado favored, privileged

probar (**ue**) [12] to prove; to test, try (out)

proceso trial; process

producir (*irr*; **z**) [22; 7] to produce

programación programming

promedio *n* average

promesa promise

promoción promotion, advancement; class, year (*academic*)

promover (**ue**) [12] to promote, advance, further

pronto soon; **de—** suddenly; **por lo—** for the present, provisionally; **tan—como** as soon as

propiciatorio propitious, favorable; likely, probable

propietario owner

propina tip, gratuity

propio own, same; proper

proponer (*irr*) [36, 48] to propose

propósito purpose; **a—** by the way

propuesta proposal

protagonista *m, f* protagonist, main character

protagonizado: **programa—por** program starring

proteger (**j**) [2] to protect

provecho: **buen—** *Bon appétit!*, Enjoy your meal!

provisional temporary

proximidades *pl* outskirts

próximo next (*future*)

prueba test, trial; quiz, exam; proof; **campo de—s** proving ground

pta *abbrev for* **peseta** (*pl* **pts**)

pública: **en plena vía—** in broad daylight

Puebla *city in southeastern Mexico*

pueblo town, village; people (*ethnic or political group*)

puerto port

pues well (*sentence introducer*)

puesto job, position

pulga flea

pulgada inch

pulsar to push (*button, key, etc.*)

punta tip, point

puñetazo blow with the fist

puño fist

puro pure; "nothing but"; **la—a verdad** nothing but the truth

Q

¡qué va! My goodness!, What the devil!, What do you mean!, No way!

quebrar (**ie**) [9] to break

quechua Quechua (*name of large Indian group in Andes countries of South America and also their language*)

quedar(se) to remain, stay; to be; **—le a uno** to have left

quehacer *m* chore, duty, task

quejarse (**de**) to complain (about)

quemar to burn (*tr*)

querer (**ie**; *irr*) [37] to want; to love, like

querido dear

quesadilla cheese turnover

queso cheese

quieto motionless, still

Quijote, el *novel written in two parts (1605 and 1615) by Spanish author Miguel de Cervantes*

quinientos five hundred

quitar to remove, take away, take off (*clothing*)

quiteño *inhabitant of Quito, Ecuador*

quizá(s) perhaps, maybe

R

rabia rage, anger

rabo tail

racha string; series; "streak"

radiografía X-ray

ramo field (*line of work*), branch; bouquet (*flowers*)

rapidez *f* speed, rapidity

rapto kidnapping

raro strange

rato while, short time

rayo ray; bolt of lightning

raza race, lineage; breed (*animals*)

razón *f* reason; right; **tener** (**ie**; *irr*) [43]— to be right

real real, actual; royal; of the highest rank (*as in* **camino real**); **R—Madrid** *professional soccer team* (*Madrid*)

realizar (**c**) [5] to carry out, fulfill

recambio: pieza de— spare part

recepción check-in desk (*hotel*)

receta recipe

recibo receipt

recién recently, new; **— llegado / a** newcomer

recinto campus

recio strong, robust

recobrar to recover

recoger (**j**) [2] to pick up, gather

recolección harvest

reconocer (*irr*; **z**) [24; 7] to recognize

recordar (**ue**) [12] to remember; to remind

recorrer to cover, go over

recorrido trajectory, run; distance traveled

recto straight

recuperar to recover, get back

rechazar (**c**) [5] to reject, turn down

red net; network

redactor *m* editor

redondo round

referente referring

referirse (**ie**, **i**) **a** [10] to refer to

reflejo reflex

refresco cold drink (*normally "soft"*)

refrigerado refrigerated; air-conditioned

refugiarse to take refuge

regalar to give (*as a gift*)

regalo gift

régimen *m* status; plan

regla rule

reglamentado regulated

regresar to return

rehén *m, f* hostage

reino kingdom

reír (**i, i**; *irr*) [38] to laugh

relacionado con related to

relacionar to bring together

relatar to relate, tell, narrate

relato story, narrative

reloj *m* watch, clock

relleno stuffed; *n* stuffing, filling (*food*)

remate *m* final touch, crowning blow

remolcar (**qu**) [1] to tow; to drive in (*runs in baseball*)

RENFE = Red Nacional de los Ferrocarriles Españoles (*Spanish national railroad system*)

renglón *m* line (*written or printed*)

renta income, profit; rent, rental

rentabilidad profitability, capacity of producing income

reñido hard-fought

reparación repair

repartido *pp of* **repartir** to distribute, spread

reparto delivery

repente: de— suddenly

repetir (**i, i**) [11] to repeat

reponerse (*irr*) [36, 48] to get well, recover one's health

repuesto spare part

requerir (**ie**) [10] to require

réquiem *m* requiem (*prayer for the dead*)

requisito requirement

res *f* beef; head of cattle

rescate *m* ransom; save (*baseball*)

reserva reservation

residencia residence; dormitory

resolver (**ue**) [12, 48] to resolve, solve

respirar to breathe

responsable *m, f* person in charge, manager

respuesta answer, response

resultado result; score (*sports*)

resumen *m* resumé, summary; **en—** to sum it all up

retirada withdrawal, retreat

retirarse to withdraw, retreat, move back; to retire

reunir (*irr*) [39] to gather (*tr*); **—se** to gather, meet, get together

reventar (**ie**) [9] to burst

revisar to examine, check, review

revista magazine

rey *m* king

ribera bank (*river*)

rico rich; tasty, delicious

riesgo risk

rincón *m* corner (*interior*)

riñón *m* kidney

río river

rioplatense *from Buenos Aires, Argentina* (*from city's main river, the* **Río Plata**)

riqueza wealth

ristra string (*of garlic, onions, etc.*)

rizado wavy, curly

robar to rob; to steal

robo robbery, theft

rocoso rocky

rodar (**ue**) [12] to roll, tumble, fall tumbling

rogar (**ue**; **gu**) [12; 3] to request, beg, ask

rojo red; rare (*meat*)

romana: a la— deep-fried

romero pilgrim (*on religious retreat*)

romper [48] to break, tear (*tr*); **—se** to break, tear (*intr*)

roncar (**qu**) [1] to snore

ropa clothing; **—vieja** shredded beef (*Cuban dish*)

rosado pink

rotulación label

rubio blond

rueda wheel

ruedo circuit, turn; bullring

ruido noise

ruidoso noisy

ruiseñor *m* nightingale

ruso Russian

ruta route

S

S.A. = Sociedad Anónima corporation (*used in titles like "Inc." in English*)

sábado Saturday

saber (*irr*) [40] to know, find out; **—a** to taste like; *mn* knowledge, wisdom

sabor *m* flavor; **—es surtidos** assorted flavors

saborear to savor

sabroso delicious

sacar (**qu**) [1] to take out; to get (*grades*); **—se el carné** to get one's driver's license
sacudir to shake
sal *f* salt
sala room; hall; **—de estar** living room; **—de vídeo** video room (*for use of videotapes*)
salado witty, amusing, lively
salchicha sausage
salida departure, exit
Salieri, Antonio *Italian composer of late 18th and early 19th centuries*
salir (*irr*) [41] to go, come out; to leave; **—bien** to win, pass (*a test, course, etc.*); to come out OK
salsa marinera marinara sauce (*based on tomato, garlic, herbs*)
saltar jump
saltarín *m* acrobatic dancer
saltear to make jump, leap; to quick-fry
salud health
saludar to greet, say hello
saludo greeting
salvaje wild, savage
salvo except; safe
Salzburgo Salzburg (*city in Austria; birthplace of Mozart*)
San Juan St. John's Day (*June 24*)
sancocho *stew of meat or fish, cassava, banana, etc.* (*Sp Am*)
Sánchez, Hugo *professional soccer player from Mexico*
sandez *f* idiotic remark, action
sanfermines *m pl nine days of festivities in Pamplona, city in northern Spain, to celebrate San Fermín's day, July 7*
sangre *f* blood
sangría *beverage of red wine and fruit juice*
sanidad health
sanitario restroom
sano healthy, sound
Santiago *city on southeastern coast of Cuba*
santiguar (**ü**) [8] to make the sign of the cross; (*colloquial*) to slap, strike, beat, hit, punish
santo holy; saint
sábado Saturday

sea...o... whether...or...
secar (**qu**) [1] to dry
seco dry
secuestrar to kidnap, seize
secuestro kidnapping
secular secular, worldly, temporal
sed thirst; **tener** (**ie**; *irr*) [43] **—** to be thirsty
seda silk
sede *f* seat, headquarters
seducir (*irr*) [22] to seduce; to entice, attract, charm
seguida: en— right away, at once, immediately
seguido consecutive
seguir (**i, i; g**) [11; 4] to follow, continue, keep on; to take (*courses*)
según according to
seguridad safety
seguro safe; certain, sure; *m pl* insurance
selección national team, all-star team
selva jungle, forest
sello stamp
semana week
semanal weekly
semanario *n* weekly newspaper
sembrar (**ie**) [9] to sow, seed
semejante similar
semejanza similarity
semental: toro— bull for breeding
semilla seed
senda path
seno bosom
sensato sensible, prudent
sentar (**ie**) [9] to seat; **—se** to sit (down)
sentido sense, meaning
sentir (**ie, i**) [10] to feel; to regret; **—se** to feel
señal *f* sign, signal
señalar to show, point out, indicate
señalizado *pp of* **senalizar (c)** [5] to identify with a sign; to put up a sign
señuelo bait, decoy
separar to separate; to reserve, set aside
ser (*irr*) [42] to be; **llegar (gu)** [3] **a—** to get to be, become

serbocroata *m* Serbo-Croatian (*from region of Yugoslavia*)
serie *f* series; serial
servicios *pl* toilets, restrooms
servir (**i, i**) [11] to serve; to be of value, be of use, be any good, "do"
sesos *pl* brains
setecientos seven hundred
sevillana *Spanish folk dance*
sexto sixth
SIDA *m* AIDS
sidra cider
siempre always
siestecita *dim of* **siesta** short nap
siglo century
siguiente following, next (*past*)
silla chair
sillón *m* armchair
sin falta without fail
siquiera: ni— not even
sitio place, spot, site
sito *adj* located, situated
sobre over, on, on top of; about, concerning
sobrino nephew
socio member
sofrito *base for stews and sauces* (*onion, tomato, peppers, etc.*)
sol *m* sun
soledad solitude
solemnidad solemnity; solemn ceremony
solicitante *m, f* applicant, person applying
solicitar to request, solicit; to seek, look for
solicitud application; application blank, form
solito *dim of* **solo** all alone, all by oneself; lonely
solo alone
sólo only
solsticio solstice (*days when sun is farthest from equator— June 21 and Dec. 21*)
soltar (**ue**) [12] to let out, release
soltera unmarried woman; **apellido de—** maiden name
soltería group of unwed people
soltero bachelor
sometido *pp of* **someter** to submit

sonar (ue) [12] *tr, intr* to sound, ring

sonido sound

sonreír (i, i; *irr*) [38] to smile

sonrisa smile

soñar (ue) (con) [12] to dream (about, of)

sope *m* filled corn tortilla (*round rather than flat, Mexico*)

soplar to blow

soportar to endure, stand; to hold up, bear

sorbete *m* sherbet

sorbo sip, swallow

sordo deaf

sorprender to surprise; **—se (de)** to be surprised (at, by)

sorpresa surprise

soso insipid, dull, uninteresting

sospechar to suspect

sospechoso suspicious

sótano basement, cellar

sotobosque *m* underbrush

Sr. (*abbrev*) **Señor**

Sra. (*abbrev*) **Señora**

Srta. (*abbrev*) **Señorita**

suavidad: con— gently, softly

subasta auction

subir to take, bring up, raise; to go, come up(stairs); **—(se)** to go, come up; to get on, in (*a vehicle*)

súbito sudden

subrayar to underline

suceder to occur, happen

sucio dirty

suculento succulent, delicious; juicy

sucursal *f* branch (*office*)

sudar to sweat

Suecia Sweden

sueco Swedish

suegra mother-in-law

sueldo salary, wage

suelo ground; floor

suelta de vaquillas *releasing young heifers in a bullring to run about after the local youth*

sueño dream; sleep; **tener (ie;** *irr*) [43] **—** to be sleepy

suerte *f* luck, fate; **—tonta** dumb, blind luck

sufrir to suffer, undergo

sugerir (ie, i) [10] to suggest

Suiza Switzerland

sumamente very, extremely

sumidero sink, drain

superación: espíritu de— desire to advance, get ahead

superar to complete; to overtake, surpass; **—se** to advance, get ahead (*profesionally*)

superganga supersaver (*fare*)

supervivencia survival

suplidor *m* supplier

suponer (*irr*) [36, 48] to suppose

supuesto: por— of course

sur *m* south

surtido supply, stock; *adj* mixed, assorted

suspender to fail

susto fright, scare

sustracción subtraction

T

tabaquero *adj from* **tabaco** tobacco

tal: con—que provided (that); **—vez** maybe, perhaps

talón *m* ticket stub

taller *m* repair shop, workshop, garage (*commercial*)

tamal *m* tamale (*chili-sauced meat rolled in a tortilla*)

tamaño size; **—s surtidos** assorted sizes

tambor *m* drum

tam-tam *sound of drum*

tan pronto como as soon as

tanto point (*sports*); **mientras—** meanwhile; **no es para—** there's no reason to get upset, it's no big deal; **por lo—** therefore

tapa bite, snack; cover

tardar to delay, take (time); **a más—** at the latest

tarea homework assignment

tarifa fare

tarjeta card; **—de compras** department store credit card

tarta cake, tart, pie; **—borracha** whiskey cake

taza cup

tazón *m* cup, bowl

té *m* tea

tebeos *pl* comics (*Spain*)

técnico technician, repairman, service employee; expert (*in a given field*)

techo roof, ceiling; **bajo—** indoors

tela cloth, textile

tele *f* TV (*short for* **televisión**)

telefonía celular cellular phoning

Telefónica, la *n* telephone company

telenovela soap opera

teleoportunidades television ads (*for jobs, sales, etc.*)

televidente *m, f* television viewer

televisor *m* television set

tema *m* theme, topic, subject

temblar (ie) [9] to tremble, shake

temblor *m* tremor, trembling

temer(se) to be afraid

templo church, temple

temporada season (*sports, hunting, crops*)

temporal temporary

temprano early

tendido stretched, spread out

tenedor de libros bookkeeper

tener (ie; *irr*) [43] to have; **—calor** to be hot; **—éxito** to be successful, succeed; **—frío** to be cold; **—ganas** to feel like; **—hambre** to be hungry; **—previsto** to anticipate; **—que** to have to; **—sed** to be thirsty; **—sueño** to be sleepy

terminar de + *inf* to finish + *pr p*

ternera veal

terremoto earthquake

terrenal earthly

terreno lot, plot of ground; field

Teruel *city in eastern Spain*

tesoro treasure

testigo *m, f* witness

tiburón *m* shark

tico Costa Rican (*nickname*)

tiempo time; weather; half (*soccer game*); **a—** on, in time

tienda store, shop

tierra land; **—adentro** inland

Tierra del Fuego *extreme southern tip of South America, part of Argentina*

tijeras *pl* scissors

timo "rip-off," swindle, fraud

tina bathtub

tinto: **(vino)**— red wine

tío uncle

tipo type; guy, fellow

tira strip; stripe; —**s cómicas** comic strips

tirada press run

tirar to throw; to throw away; —**(de)** to pull (on)

tirita small piece, strip

tiro shot

titulación degree (*education*)

titular *mn* headline; *adj* regular, on the first team

título degree (*education*); certificate

toalla towel

tocadiscos *m sing* record player

tocado headwear, headdress

tocar (**qu**) [1] to touch; to play (*an instrument*); to ring; —**le a uno** to be one's turn

todavía still, yet; —**no** still not, not yet

todo all; —**derecho** straight ahead; —**as partes** everywhere; **de**—**as maneras** at any rate, anyway; **de**—**s modos** at any rate, anyway; **del**— completely; **en**—**caso** in any case

Todos (los) Santos All Saints' Day (*Nov. 1*)

tomar to take; to eat, drink, have; —**una copa** to have a drink

tómbola raffle, game of chance

tomo tome, volume

tonto foolish, silly, dumb; **suerte**—**a** dumb, blind luck

tope: **hasta el**— fed up

torero bullfighter

torneo tournament

torno: **en**—**a** around

toro bull; —**semental** bull for breeding

torpedero torpedo boat; shortstop

torta torte, round cake

tortilla thin cornmeal cake (*Sp Am*); omelet (*Spain*)

tortillería taco restaurant; tortilla kitchen

toser to cough

tostada *deep-fried tortilla topped with refried beans, meat, etc.*

tostado *pp* of **tostar** (**ue**) [12] to toast

trabajador / a worker; *adj* hardworking

traducción translation

traducir (*irr*; **z**) [22; 7] to translate

traductor / a translator; —**jurado** *translator who has officially been sworn in prior to employment*

traer (*irr*) [44] to bring

tragar (**gu**) [3] to swallow

traje *m* suit, costume; —**de novia** bridal gown

tramo flight of stairs; short distance

trampa trick, trap

transcurrir to pass, transpire, elapse

trapo rag, cloth

tras behind, after

trasero *adj* rear

trasladar to move, transfer

tratamiento treatment

tratar to treat; —**de** + *inf* to try to + *v*; to deal with, handle, treat; —**se de** to be a question of; —**de que** + ... *subjunctive* to try to have ... + *v*

trato deal, pact

través: **a**—**de** through, across

tren *m* train; —**de vida** life style

tripulante *m, f* crew member

triste sad

triturador *m* **de desperdicios** garbage disposal (*kitchen appliance*)

tronar (**ue**) [12] to thunder

tropezar(se) (**ie**; **c**) [9; 5] **con** to meet, encounter, run into

trozo piece, bit

trueno thunder

tubo pipe (*plumbing*)

tulipán *m* tulip

tumbar to knock down; —**se** to fall, drop, lie down

¡tun tun! *sound of banging on door*

turno turn, shift (*work*)

Tutankamón Tutankhamen (*Pharaoh of ancient Egypt*)

tuteo *use of second-person sing pronoun* **tú** *and corresponding verb forms*

U

ubicado located

últimamente recently, lately

una: **de**—**vez** once and for all

usuario user, owner, holder (*as of a credit card*)

utilizar (**c**) [5] to use

uva grape; **de mala**— illtempered, in a bad mood

va: **¡qué**—**!** My goodness!, What the devil!, What do you mean!, No way!

vacío *n* empty space, emptiness, vacuum; **caer** (*irr*) [20] **al**— to fall out (*of a window, for example*); *adj* empty

vacunado *pp* of **vacunar** to vaccinate

vainilla vanilla

vale OK, good enough, coming right up (*or any expression of agreement*) (*Spain*)

valenciano Valencian (*from Valencia, region on east coast of Spain*)

valer (*irr*) [45] to cost, be worth

valoración appraisal, evaluation

valla fence, wall, barrier

vallado fenced-in

vano: **en**— in vain

vaquero cowboy

vaquillas: **suelta de**— *releasing young heifers in a bullring to run about after local youth*

Vargas Llosa, Mario *contemporary Peruvian novelist and presidential candidate in 1990*

variable *adj* variable; *mn* income on commission

varón *m* man, male

vaso glass (*container*)

¡Vaya! Well, now, What a ...!

vecindario *adj* neighborhood

vecino neighbor, resident

velo veil

velocidad speed

veloz rapid, fast

vencer (**z**) [6] to defeat, overcome, conquer; to win; to expire

vencido overdue, expired

vencimiento expiration (*date*)

venda bandage

vendado *pp of* **vendar** to bandage

vendedor *m* salesman

vender to sell

vendimia grape harvest

veneno poison

venir (**ie**; *irr*) [46] to come

venta sale

ventaja advantage

ventana window

ventilador *m* fan

ver (*irr*) [47, 48] to see; **—se** to be, find oneself (*in a situation*)

veranear to vacation, spend the summer

veras: de— truly, really

verdadero true, real

verde green

verduras *pl* greens, green vegetables

vergüenza shame, embarrassment

verso back (*of document, sheet, etc.*)

vertiginoso dizzy

vestir (**i**, **i**) [11] to dress, wear

vez: cada—más more and more; **de—en cuando** now and then, from time to time; **de una—** once and for all; **tal—** maybe, perhaps

vía way, track; **en plena— pública** in broad daylight

viajar to travel

viaje *m* trip, journey; walk (*baseball*)

viajero traveler

vídeo VCR

viejo old; **ropa—a** shredded beef (*Cuban dish*)

viento wind

viernes *m* Friday

vigente in force, effective

vigilado *pp of* **vigilar** to watch, guard, protect

vinagreta *salad dressing made of oil, vinegar, and seasonings*

viña vineyard

violación rape; violation

virreyna *older spelling of* **virreina** wife of a viceroy

virtud virtue

vista sight; **con—s a** with a view to

visto: por lo— apparently

vistoso showy, flashy, "loud"

vivienda dwelling

vivo alive; lively, quick-witted, clever; **en—** live (*telecast*)

vizcaíno Basque, Biscayan; **a la—a** *food cooked in a* **sofrito** *of tomato, onion, garlic*

vocero spokesman

volante *m* steering wheel

volar (**ue**) [12] to fly

voltejear to cartwheel

voluntad will, willpower

volver (**ue**) [12, 48] to return, go, come back; **—se** to turn around; to turn back; to turn, become, get, go (*crazy, blind, deaf, etc.*) **—a** + *inf* to + *v* + again

vos you (*familiar, sing.*)

voseo *use of second-person sing. pronoun* **vos** *and corresponding verb forms, found in several Spanish American countries*

votante *m, f* voter

voto vow; vote

voz *f* voice; **en—alta** out loud

vuelo flight

vuelta turn; change (*money*); **de—** back; **ida y—** round-trip; **dar—s** to circle, go around in circles; **dar una—** to take a drive, ride

W

wáter *m* restroom, toilet (*from British "water closet"*); toilet bowl

Y

ya already, now; **—no** no longer, not anymore; **—que** since

yegua mare; **—de paseo** walking horse; **—de paso fino** show horse

yerno son-in-law

yuca cassava (*starchy vegetable used in Cuban cooking*)

Z

zapatilla slipper; running shoe

zapato shoe

zarzuela musical comedy; *seafood dish*

zumbido buzz(ing)

zurdo left-handed

English-Spanish

The bracketed numbers indicate the verb groups as listed in the preceding
Verb Tables.

A

abandon abandonar, dejar
able: to be—(to) poder (ue;
irr) [35]
about: to ask— preguntar por;
to think— pensar (ie) [9] en
ache doler (ue) [12]
achieve conseguir (i, i; g) [11;
4], lograr
acquainted: to be—with
conocer (irr; z) [24]
acquire adquirir (ie) [16]
across: to run— cruzarse (c)
[5] con
actually en realidad, realmente
ad(vertisement) anuncio
address dirección, señas pl
admit admitir, confesar (ie)
[9]
advantage ventaja; **to be to
one's—** convenirle (ie; irr)
[46] a uno; **to take—(of)**
aprovecharse (de)
advice consejos pl
advisable preferible, aconse-
jable, conveniente
advise aconsejar
affair asunto
afraid: to be— tener (ie; irr)
[43] miedo
after después (de), tras; **to
look—** atender (ie) [9]
afternoon tarde f; **all—long**
toda la tarde
again otra vez, de nuevo; **to
do + v + —** volver (ue) [12,
48] a + inf
against contra

ago: a year— hace un año
air aire m
alive vivo
all todo; **—afternoon long**
toda la tarde; **—day long**
todo el día
alone solo
already ya
also también; además
although aunque
always siempre
amuse entretener (ie; irr) [43]
analysis análisis m
anchovy boquerón m
ancient antiguo
angry enojado, bravo; **to get—**
enojarse
anise-flavored brandy anís m
another otro
answer contestar, responder
any adj, pro cualquier(a), alguno; **at—rate** de todos modos, de todas maneras
anymore: not— ya no
anyone alguien, alguno;
cualquiera
anything algo; **not—** nada
anyway de todos modos, de
todas maneras
apparently por lo visto
apparition aparición
appear aparecer (irr; z) [17, 7];
—+ adj mostrarse (ue) [12]
+ adj
appetizing: to find— apetecerle (irr; z) [17, 7] a uno
approach acercarse (qu) (a) [1]
appropriate: to be— convenirle (ie; irr) [46] a uno
April abril m

arm brazo
aroma aroma m
arrive llegar (gu) [3]; **upon —
ing** al llegar
as: —far— hasta; **— for me**
por mi parte; **—for the rest**
por lo demás; **— long —**
mientras, siempre que; **—
many —** tantos / as como;
— much — tanto como;
— soon — tan pronto
como, en cuanto; **the
same —** (just like)
igual a
ashamed: to be — avergonzarse (üe; c) [12; 5]
ask preguntar; **to — about**
preguntar por; **to — for**
pedir (i, i) [11], preguntar
por
asleep: to fall — dormirse (ue,
u) [13]
at: — first al principio; **—
last** por fin; **— least** por lo
menos; **— times** a veces,
algunas veces
athlete atleta m, f
atmosphere ambiente m
attend asistir (a)
attract atraer (irr) [44]
attractive atractivo, guapo
August agosto
author autor / a
avail oneself (of) aprovecharse
(de)
aware: to become—(of) enterarse (de)
away: far— lejos; **to go—** irse
(irr) [32], marcharse, partir;
to take — quitar

B

B notable (*grade*)
baby eels angulas
bachelor soltero
back:—ward para atrás, hacia atrás; to come— volver (ue) [12, 48], regresar; in—of tras, detrás de; to give— devolver (ue) [12, 48]; to go— volver (ue) [12, 48], regresar
baker panadero / a
ball bola, pelota (*small*), balón *m*(*large and inflatable*); crystal— bola de cristal *m*
bar (*tavern*) bar *m*
base *v* basar
baseball béisbol *m*
basin lavabo, lavamanos *m sing*
basket canasta
basketball baloncesto, básquet(bol)
bat murciélago
bath: to take a— bañarse
bathe bañar
bathing suit bañador, traje *m* de baño
bathroom baño
bathtub bañera, tina
battle batalla
battlefront frente *m*
be estar (*irr*) [29], ser (*irr*) [42]
beach playa; —sandals playeras
beautiful hermoso, bello, lindo
because of a causa de, debido a, por
become ponerse (*irr*) [36, 48], hacerse (*irr*) [31, 48], llegar (gu) [3] a ser; to—aware (of) enterarse (de); to—tired (of) cansarse (de)
bed cama; to go to— acostarse (ue) [12]
bedroom alcoba, dormitorio
beef carne *f*, carne de vaca, carne de res
before antes (de); (*conj*) antes de que
begin empezar (ie; c) [9, 5], comenzar (ie; c) [9, 5]; to— + *inf* ponerse (*irr*) [36, 48] a + *inf*

behind detrás de, tras
believe creer (*irr*) [26]
belong pertenecer (*irr*) [17, 7]
best mejor; to be— convenirle (ie; *irr*) [46] a uno
better mejor
between entre
bill cuenta
bird pájaro, ave *f*
bit: a little— un poco; quite a— bastante
bite morder (ue) [12]
bitter agrio, amargo
black negro
blanket manta
blue azul
body cadáver *m* (*corpse*)
bomb: neutron— bomba de neutrones
bone (*fish*) espina
bookstore librería
bore aburrir
boring aburrido
boss jefe / a
botanist botánico / a
both ambos, los / las dos
bother molestar
bottom fondo; from the—of my heart de todo corazón *m*
boyfriend novio
brandy: anise-flavored— anís *m*
break romper [48] (*tr*), romperse (*intr*); —down fallar
breakfast desayuno
breathe respirar
bring traer (*irr*) [44]; to—(take) down bajar
broken descompuesto, roto
brother hermano
build construir (*irr*) [21]
bus bus *m*, camión *m* (*Mexico*), autobús *m*, guagua (*Caribbean, eastern U.S., Canary Islands of Spain*), autocar *m*; city—driver conductor / a (de autobuses) del municipio
busy ocupado
but pero, sino
butter mantequilla
buy comprar

C

call llamar; to be—ed llamarse
calm calma, tranquilidad; to— down calmar (*tr*), calmarse (*intr*)
can *v* poder (ue; *irr*) [35]
Canary Islands Islas Canarias (*Spanish islands off the Northwest coast of Africa*)
cape capa
capital (*city*) capital *f*; (*money*) capital *m*
car carro, auto, coche *m*
card tarjeta; credit— tarjeta de crédito
care cuidado; to take—of atender (ie) [9]
caress acariciar
carpenter carpintero
Caribbean Caribe *m*
carry traer (*irr*) [44]; to—out cumplir (con)
cartoons dibujos (animados) (*television*)
case: in— en caso de que; just in— por si acaso
cashier cajero / a
Catholic católico
celebrate celebrar
centimeter centímetro
certain cierto
change *v* cambiar, convertir (ie, i) [10]; *n* (*money*) vuelta, cambio
chapter capítulo
character carácter *m*, personaje *m*, protagonista, *m, f*
charge: without— gratis *adv*
cheap barato
chicken pollo; —and rice arroz *m* con pollo
child niño / a, hijo / a
chilly fresco
choose escoger (j) [2], elegir (i, i; j) [11; 2]
chop (*cut of meat*) chuleta
circumstance circunstancia
city ciudad —bus driver conductor / a (de autobuses) del municipio; provincial— ciudad de provincias
class: first — de lujo
classroom aula

clean limpio
close: to get—(to) acercarse (qu) (a) [1]
close cerrar (ie) [9]
clothes ropa
cloud nube *f*
clove (*garlic*) diente *m*
coffee café *m*
cold frío; **to be—** tener (ie; *irr*) [43] frío
come venir (ie; *irr*) [46]; **to— back** volver (ue) [12], regresar; **to—downstairs** bajar; **to—in(to)** entrar (a); **to— up** subir; **to—upstairs** subir
comet cometa *m*
comfortable cómodo
comics tebeos *pl* (*Spain*)
coming right up! de acuerdo, vale
compete competir (i, i) [11]
complain quejarse
comply (with) cumplir (con)
compose componer (*irr*) [36, 48]
computer computadora, ordenadora
conclude concluir (*irr*) [21]
confess confesar (ie) [9]
confession: to make a— confesar (ie) [9] algo
confused confundido, perplejo
connection conexión *f*
consequently por consiguiente
consist of consistir en
contain contener (*ie; irr*) [43]
continue seguir (i, i; g) [11; 4], continuar (*irr*) [25]
contrary: on the— al contrario
contribute contribuir (*irr*) [21]
cook *n* cocinero / a; **pastry—** pastelero / a; *v* cocinar
copy machine máquina copiadora
corner rincón *m* (*interior*), esquina (*outside*); **—shot** (*soccer*) tiro de esquina
corpse cadáver *m*
correct corregir (i, i; j) [11; 2]
cost costar (ue) [12], valer (*irr*) [45]
cotton algodón *m*

count (*nobleman*) conde *m*; *v* contar (ue) [12]; **to— on** contar con
counter (*in store*) mostrador *m*
country país *m*; campo
course: of— por supuesto
cover cubrir [48]
cream: ice— helado
credit card tarjeta de crédito
crisis crisis *f*
critic crítico / a
cross cruzar (c) [5], atravesar (ie) [9]
crossword puzzle crucigrama *m*
crystal cristal *m*; **—ball** bola de cristal
cure cura
currently actualmente
cut cortar
cyclist ciclista *m*, *f*

D

daily cotidiano
dance bailar
dare atreverse (a)
dark oscuro
date fecha; cita (*appointment*)
dawn amanecer *m*; madrugada
day: every— todos los días, cada día; **all—long** todo el día; **the—after tomorrow** pasado mañana
deaf sordo
deal with tratar de
dear (beloved) querido / a, amado / a; **my—** amor *m* mío
December diciembre *m*
decide (to) decidirse (a)
decision decisión *f*
deep-fried a la romana
defend defender (ie) [9]
defender (*soccer*) defensa *m*
delicious delicioso, sabroso
deliver entregar (gu) [3]
Democrat demócrata *m*, *f*
dentist dentista *m*, *f*
deny negar (ie; gu) [9; 3]
departure salida
depend (on) depender (de)
deserve merecer (*irr*) [17; 7]
destroy destruir (*irr*) [21]

detain detener (ie; *irr*) [43]
detective detective *m*; **—story** cuento de detectives, cuento policial
determined: to be — to decidirse a
devote oneself to dedicarse (qu) a [1]
dictionary diccionario
die morir (ue, u) [13, 48]
difficult difícil
diligent diligente
dinner comida, cena; **to have—** comer, cenar
directly directamente
dirty sucio
disappear desaparecer (*irr*) [17; 7]
discuss discutir
dish plato
dismal triste
dismiss despedir (i, i) [11]
disposal: garbage— triturador *m* de desperdicios
dispose disponer (*irr*) [36, 48]
distract distraer (*irr*) [44]
distribute distribuir (*irr*) [21]
do hacer (*irr*) [31, 48]; **to— ... again** volver (ue) [12] a + *inf*
doctor médico / a, doctor / a
dormitory residencia
doubt dudar
doubtful dudoso
doughnut churro
down: to break— fallar; **to bring (take)—** bajar; **to calm—** calmar (*tr*), calmarse (*intr*); **to fall—** caerse (*irr*) [20]; **to kneel—** arrodillarse; **to knock—** tumbar; **to lie—** acostarse (ue) [12]
downstairs: to come— bajar
downtown centro
downward para abajo, hacia abajo
drag tirar (de), arrastrar
drain desagüe *m*, sumidero
dream (of) soñar (ue) (con) [12]
dress vestir (i, i) [11]
drink beber, tomar; **something to—** algo de beber
drive manejar, conducir (*irr*; z) [22; 7]

driver: **city bus**— conductor / a (de autobuses) del municipio; —**'s license** permiso de conducir, carné *m* (*Spain*), permiso de manejar (*Sp Am*)

drop dejar caer

drown ahogarse (gu) [3]

dub (*movie dialogue*) doblar

due to debido a

dunk mojar

E

each cada; *pro* cada uno / a

eagle águila

earlier antes

early temprano

easy fácil

eat comer

eels: **baby**— angulas

egotist egoísta *m*, *f*

elect elegir (i, i; j) [11; 2]

elegant elegante

embarrassed: **to be**— avergonzarse (üe; c) [12; 5]

embrace *n* abrazo; *v* abrazar (c) [5]

emphasis énfasis *m*

employee empleado

end *n* final *m*, fondo; *v* acabar, terminar

engine motor *m*; máquina

engineer ingeniero / a

enjoy disfrutar (de), gozar (c) [5] (de)

enough suficiente, bastante

entertain entretener (ie; *irr*) [43]

entire entero

entrance entrada

envious envidioso

environment ambiente *m*

especially sobre todo, especialmente

etc. etcétera

even siquiera, hasta, aun; —**though** aunque; **not**— ni siquiera

evening tarde *f*; noche *f*; **good**— buenas noches

ever alguna vez (*past*), algún día (*future*); **more (less) than**— más (menos) que nunca

every cada; —**day** todos los días, cada día

everyday *adj* cotidiano

everything todo; —**that** todo lo que

everywhere todas partes

exam examen *m*

exit salida

expensive caro

experience experiencia

explain explicar (qu) [1]

eye ojo

F

fact hecho

factory fábrica

fail + *inf* dejar de + *inf*

fall caer (*irr*) [20]; **to**—(*through space*) caer al vacío; **to**—**asleep** dormirse (ue, u) [13]; **to**—**down** caerse; **to**—**in love (with)** enamorarse (de); **to**—**to** tocarle (qu) [1] a uno

famous famoso

fan (*sports*) aficionado, fanático; (*machine*) ventilador *m*

far lejos; —**away** muy lejos; **as**—**as** hasta

farewell despedida

fascinate encantarle a uno

fast *adj* rápido, veloz; *adv* de prisa, rápidamente, velozmente

faucet grifo

February febrero

fed up: **to be**— estar hasta el tope

feed oneself mantenerse (ie; *irr*) [43]

feel sentir (ie, i) [10] (*tr*); **to**— + *adj* sentirse + adj; **to**—**like** tener (ie; *irr*) [43] ganas (de)

few pocos; **a**— unos, unos pocos, unos cuantos; **quite a**— bastantes

field campo, cancha (*sports*)

film película, film *m*

finally por fin

find encontrar (ue) [12], hallar; **to**—**appetizing** apetecerle (*irr*; z) [17; 7] a uno; **to**—

out (**about**) enterarse (de); (*preterit*) saber (*irr*) [40]

fine *n* multa

finish acabar, terminar; —+ **-ing** terminar de + *inf*

fire (*hurl*) lanzar (c) [5]; **to set on** — encender (ie) [9]

first:—**class** de lujo; **at**— al principio

fish (*before caught*) pez *m*; (*after caught*) pescado

fit *v* caber (*irr*) [19]

flee *v* huir (*irr*) [21]

floor piso, suelo

fly volar (ue) [12]; **to let**— lanzar (c) [5]

follow seguir (i, i; g) [11; 4]

food comida

foot pie *m*

for:—**heaven's sake** por Dios; —**that reason** por eso; **to look**— buscar (qu) [1]

forehead frente *f*

forget olvidarse (de)

former viejo, antiguo

forward (*soccer*) ala *m*

free gratis *adv*

French francés / a; —**fries** papas fritas (*Sp Am*), patatas fritas (*Spain*)

frequent frecuente; —**ly** con frecuencia, a menudo

Friday viernes *m*

friendly simpático, amable, amistoso

fries: **French**— papas fritas (*Sp Am*), patatas fritas (*Spain*)

front frente *m*; **in**—**of** enfrente de, delante de

frozen helado

fruit frutas *pl*

fulfill cumplir (con)

full lleno

furiously furiosamente

furthermore además

G

garbage basura; —**disposal** triturador *m* de desperdicios

garden jardín *m*

garlic ajo

gather reunir (*irr*) [39] (*tr*), reunirse (*intr*)

general: in— por lo general, generalmente
gentlemen caballeros, señores
get conseguir (i, i; g) [11; 4]; tener (ie; *irr*) [43] (*preterit*); (*grades*) sacar (qu) [1]; **to— +** *adj* ponerse (*irr*) [36, 48] + *adj*; **to—angry** enojarse; **to— close (to)** acercarse (qu) [1] (a); **to—hot** calentarse (ie) [9]; **to—mad** enojarse; **to— married (to)** casarse (con); **to—on** subir (a); **to—ready** prepararse; **to—sick** enfermarse; **to—tired** cansarse; **to—to be** llegar (gu) [3] a ser; **to—up** levantarse
ghost fantasma *m*
girlfriend novia
give dar (*irr*) [27]; **to—back** devolver (ue) [12]
glass cristal *m*
go ir (*irr*) [32]; **to—about + -ing** dedicarse (qu) [1] a + *inf*, ponerse (*irr*) [36, 48] a + *inf*; **to—away** irse, marcharse, partir; **to—back** volver (ue) [12], regresar; **to—in** entrar; **to—out** salir (*irr*) [41]; **to—to bed** acostarse (ue) [12]; **to—to sleep** dormirse (ue, u) [13]; **to—toward** dirigirse (j) [2] a; **to—up** subir; **to—upstairs** subir; **to—wrong** (*fail, break down*) fallar
goal gol *m*; **scoring of many—s** goleada
goalie golero, portero, arquero, guardameta *m*
godfather padrino
good bueno; bien; **—evening** buenas noches; **—heavens!** ¡Dios mío!; **— looking** guapo
goodbye: to say—(to) despedirse (i, i) [11] (de)
grab coger (j) [2]
grade (*mark*) nota
grandmother abuela
gray gris
grayish: sort of— tirando a gris
great gran(de)
greater / greatest mayor

green verde
grilled a la parrilla
guest invitado, huésped / a
guide (*person*) guía *m, f*; (*object*) guía *f*

H

hair pelo
half (*soccer game*) tiempo
hallway pasillo
hand in, out, over entregar (gu) [3]
hang (up) colgar (ue; gu) [12; 3]
happen pasar, suceder, ocurrir
harass perseguir (i, i; g) [11; 4]
hat sombrero
hate odiar
have haber (*irr*) [30] (*aux*), tener (ie; *irr*) [43]; (*eat, drink*) tomar; **to—dinner** comer, cenar; **to—left** quedarle a uno; **to—lunch** almorzar (ue; c) [12; 5]; **to—to** tener (ie; *irr*) [43] que
head (*boss*) jefe / a; (*body*) cabeza; *v* **to—for** dirigirse (j) [2] a; irse (*irr*) [32] para
heal curar (*tr*), curarse (*intr*)
hear oír (*irr*) [34]
heart corazón *m*; **from the bottom of my—** de todo corazón
heat calor *m*
heaven: for —'s sake por Dios; **Thank—!** ¡Gracias a Dios!; **good—s** ¡Dios mío!
hello hola, buenos días
help ayudar; *n* ayuda
here aquí; **right—** aquí mismo
hi hola
high alto
highway carretera
hope esperar
hopeless triste, desesperado
hospital hospital *m*
hot caliente; **to be—** hacer (*irr*) [31] calor (*weather*); tener (ie; *irr*) [43] calor (*person*); **to get—** calentarse (ie) [9]
house casa

how cómo; **—I wish!** ¡ojalá!
hug abrazar (c) [5]
huge enorme, tremendo, grande
hundred cien, ciento
hungry: to be— tener (ie; *irr*) [43] hambre *f*
hurry *v* apurarse, apresurarse; **to be in a—** tener (ie; *irr*) [43] prisa
hurt doler (ue) [12]; *tr* lastimar, lesionar
husband esposo, marido

I

ice cream helado
idea idea
important importante
impossible imposible
improve mejorar(se)
in:—case en caso de que; **to go—** entrar; **to hand—** entregar (gu) [3]
include incluir (*irr*) [21]
infirmary enfermería
injure lastimarse
inland tierra adentro
inside dentro, adentro
insist (on) insistir (en)
instead of en vez de, en lugar de
intelligent inteligente
intend + *inf* pensar (ie) [9], proponerse (*irr*) [36, 48] + *inf*
intense intenso
interest *v* interesarle a uno
interpreter intérprete *m, f*
into: to come — entrar a
introduce presentar, introducir (*irr*; z) [22; 7]
invite invitar
Italian italiano

J

jacket chaqueta, anorak *m*, saco
jail: in — encarcelado
January enero
job trabajo, puesto
journalist periodista *m, f*
judge juez *m, f*
July julio

jump saltar
June junio
just: — **in case** por si acaso; — **like** (**the same as**) igual a

K

keep on + *pr p* seguir (i, i; g) [11; 3], continuar (*irr*) [25] + *pr p*
key llave *f*
kiss besar
kite cometa *f*
kneel down arrodillarse
knock down tumbar
know (*be acquainted with*) conocer (*irr*; z) [24, 7]; (*know how, have knowledge of*) saber (*irr*) [40]; **to—what to say** saber qué decir

L

language idioma *m*, lengua; lenguaje *m* (*manner of speech*)
large grande
larger / largest mayor
last: último; final; *v* durar; — **night** anoche; —**week** la semana pasada; — **year** el año pasado; **at—** por fin
late tarde
later después, luego, más tarde
Latin latino; *n* (*language*) latín *m*
laugh reír(se) (i, i; *irr*) [38]; **to — at** reírse de
law ley *f*
lawyer abogado / a
lazy ocioso, perezoso
lead conducir (*irr*) [22; 7]
lean over inclinarse
least menos; **at —** por lo menos
leave (*intr*) irse (*irr*) [32], marcharse, partir, salir (*irr*) [41]; (*tr*) dejar, abandonar
left: **to have —** quedarle a uno
leg (*human*) pierna; (*animal, furniture*) pata
lentil lenteja
less menor; — (**more**) **than**

ever menos (más) que nunca
lesson lección
let dejar, permitir; **to —fly** lanzar (c)[5]
letter (*alphabet*) letra; (*communication*) carta
liberty libertad
library biblioteca
license: **driver's —** permiso de conducir, carné *m* (*Spain*), permiso de manejar (*Sp Am*)
lie (*tell a falsehood*) mentir (ie, i) [10]; **to — down** acostarse (ue) [12]
like *adv, prep* como; *v* gustarle a uno (*literally* **to be pleasing to**); **just —** (**the same as**) igual a; **to feel —** tener (ie; *irr*) [43] ganas de; **to look —** parecerse (*irr*; z) [17; 7] a
lining forro
Lisbon Lisboa
listen (**to**) escuchar
little poco; pequeño, chico; **a — bit** un poco
live vivir
long largo; **all afternoon —** toda la tarde; **all day —** todo el día **as — as** mientras, siempre que
longer: **no —** ya no
look (**at**) mirar; **to — +** *adj* mostrarse (ue) [12] + *adj*; **to — after** atender (ie) [9]; **to—for** buscar (qu) [1]; **to—like** parecerse (*irr*; z) [17; 7] a
lose perder (ie) [9]
lot: **a—of** (**—s of**) mucho; una gran cantidad de
loud *adj* ruidoso; fuerte; *adv* en voz alta, fuerte
love amor *m*, cariño; **to fall in — (with)** enamorarse (de); *v* amar, querer (ie; *irr*) [37]; **to — + inf** encantarle a uno + *inf*
low bajo; **in a — voice** en voz baja
lunch *n* almuerzo; **to have —** almorzar (ue; c) [12; 5]

M

machine: **copy —** máquina copiadora

mad: **to get —** enojarse; **to go —** volverse (ue) [12; 48] loco
madly locamente
madness locura
make hacer (*irr*) [31, 48]; **to — a confession** confesar (ie) [9] algo; **to — a mistake** equivocarse (qu) [1]
man hombre; **single —** soltero
many muchos; **as — as** tantos como; **so —** tantos; **too —** demasiados
March marzo
married: **to get —** (**to**) casarse (con)
matter: **to be a — of** tratarse de
May mayo
maybe a lo mejor, quizá (s), tal vez
me: **as for —** por mi parte
mean querer (ie; *irr*) [37] decir, significar (qu) [l]
meat carne *f*
medium rare un poco rojo
meet (*for the first time*) conocer (*irr*; z)[24; 7]; encontrar (ue) [12]
meeting reunión *f*
menu minuta, menú *m*
midnight medianoche *f*; **at —** a (la) medianoche
millennium milenario
minibikini minibiquini *m*
miraculously milagrosamente
mirror espejo
miss perder (ie) [9] (*lose*) ; extrañar, echar de menos (*long for*); faltar a (*not show up*)
missing: **to be —** faltar
mistake: **to make a —** equivocarse (qu) [1]
model modelo *m*, *f*
moderately moderadamente
mom mamá
Monday lunes *m*
money dinero
month mes *m*; **the whole —** todo el mes, el mes entero
moon luna
more más; — (**less**) **than ever** más (menos) que nunca
morning mañana; **tomorrow —** mañana por la mañana

mother madre, mamá
mountains montes *m pl*; montañas
move mover (ue) [12] (*tr*); moverse (*intr*)
moved: to be — (by) emocionarse (con)
movie película, film *m*; **—s** cine *m*
much mucho; **as—as** tanto como; **so—** tanto; **too—** demasiado; **very—** muchísmo
music música
must deber
my dear amor mío
mysterious misterioso

N

name nombre *m*
named: to be — llamarse
nap: short — siestecita
natural natural
near(by) cerca
necessary necesario
need necesitar, hacerle (*irr*) [31, 48] falta a uno; faltarle a uno; **to—to** necesitar, tener (ie; *irr*)[43] que
neither ni; ni . . . tampoco
net red
network red
neutron bomb bomba de neutrones
never nunca, jamás
new nuevo
newcomer recién llegado / a
newspaper periódico, diario
next próximo (*future only*), siguiente
night noche *f*; **last—** anoche
nightingale ruiseñor *m*
no: — longer ya no; **— one** nadie, ninguno; **— way** de ningún modo, de ninguna manera
nobody nadie, ninguno
normal normal
not: — anymore ya no; **— even** ni siquiera
nothing nada
novel novela
November noviembre *m*
now ahora, ya; **— then** ahora bien

nowhere ninguna parte
number: phone — número de teléfono
nurse enfermero / a

O

obey obedecer (*irr*; z) [17;7]
obtain obtener (*irr*) [43]
occur ocurrir, suceder (*happen*); ocurrírsele a uno (*come to mind*)
October octubre *m*
of course cómo no, por supuesto
off: to see — despedir (i, i) [11]; **to take —** quitarse; **to turn —** apagar (gu) [3]
offend ofender; **to be —ed** ofenderse
offer ofrecer (*irr*; z) [17; 7]
often con frecuencia, a menudo
oil aceite *m*; petróleo; **olive —** aceite *m* de oliva
OK bien, está bien; vale (*Spain*)
old viejo, antiguo, anciano
olive oil aceite *m* de oliva
on en, sobre, encima de; **— arriving** al llegar; **— patrol** de patrulla; **— the right** a la derecha; **— time** a tiempo; **— top of** sobre, encima de; **to count —** contar (ue) [12] con; **to keep —** + *pr p* seguir (i, i; g) [11; 4] continuar (*irr*) [25] + *pr p*; **to turn —** encender (ie) [9], poner (*irr*) [36; 48]
once una vez
only *adj* único; *adv* sólo, solamente
open abrir
oppose oponer (*irr*) [36, 48]
order *n* pedido (*request*); orden *m* (*arrangement*); orden *f* (*command, religious organization*); *v* pedir (i, i) [11], ordenar, mandar; **in — to** para, a fin de
other otro
ought deber
out fuera (de), afuera; **to find —** (about) enterarse (de), saber (*irr*) [46] (*preterit*); **to**

go — salir (*irr*) [41]; **to hand —** entregar (gu) [3]; **to put —** apagar (gu) [3]; **to spread —** extenderse (ie) [9]; **to stretch —** extenderse; **to take —** sacar (qu) [1]
outfielder jardinero
outrageous: to be— ser (*irr*) [42] un escándalo
outside (a)fuera; fuera de
over sobre, (por) encima de; **to be —** terminar, acabar; **to lean —** inclinarse
overcome vencer (z) [6]
own *adj* propio
owner dueño / a

P

page página, hoja
pajamas pijamas *m pl* (*Spain*), piyamas *m pl* (*Sp Am*)
pardon *v* perdonar
parish priest párroco
participate participar
particular particular
party fiesta
pass pasar
passion pasión *f*
pastry cook pastelero / a
patience paciencia
patrol: on — patrullando
pay pagar (gu) [3]
peace paz *f*
pension (*boarding house*) pensión *f*
people gente *f*, personas
per por
perhaps quizá (s), tal vez, acaso
permit permitir, dejar
person persona
pessimist pesimista *m, f*
phone number número de teléfono
picnicker dominguero
pipe tubo, caño
pitcher: wine — porrón *m*
pity lástima
pizza pizza
place *v* poner (*irr*) [36; 48]; **to take —** tener (ie; *irr*) [43] lugar
plan *n* plan *m*; proyecto; **to —** + *inf* pensar (ie) [9] + *inf*

plane avión *m*
planet planeta *m*
play (*games*) jugar (ue; gu) [14; 3]; (*music*) tocar (qu) [1]
please gustar, agradar
pleasing: to be —ing gustar
plenty (of) bastante
poem poema *m*
poet poeta *m, f* (*also* poetisa *f*)
point (*scoring*) tanto
police policía, agentes *m pl*; **—man** policía *m*, agente *m*
Pope Papa *m*
Portuguese portugués / a
possess tener (ie; *irr*) [43], poseer [26]
possible posible
potato papa (*Sp Am*), patata (*Spain*)
power poder *m*
prefer preferir (ie, i) [10]
preferable preferible, conveniente
prepare preparar
presently actualmente
president presidente *m, f*
pretend fingir (j) [2]
prevent impedir (i, i) [11]
price precio
priest cura *m*; **parish —** párroco
problem problema *m*
produce producir (*irr*; z) [22; 7]
professor profesor / a
program programa *m*
promise prometer
pronounce pronunciar
propose proponer (*irr*) [36; 48]; **to —** + *inf* proponerse + *inf*
protect proteger (j) [2]
prove probar (ue) [12]
provincial de provincias, provinciano; **— city** ciudad de provincias
pull tirar (de)
pursue perseguir (i, i; g) [11; 3]
pursuit persecución
put poner (*irr*) [36; 48]; **to — on** ponerse; **to — out** apagar (gu) [3]
puzzle: crossword crucigrama *m*

Q

Quechua quechua (*name of large Indian group in Andes countries of South America and also their language*)
question: to be a — of tratarse de
quite: bastante; **— a bit** bastante; **— a few** bastantes

R

rain llover (ue) [12]
raise (*lift*) levantar
rapidly rápidamente
rare: medium — un poco rojo
rate: at any — de todos modos, de todas maneras
rather algo
raw crudo
reach alcanzar (c) [5]; (*go as far as*) llegar (gu) [3] a
read leer [26]
ready listo, dispuesto; **to get —** prepararse, disponerse (*irr*) [36; 48]
realize darse (*irr*) [27] cuenta (de)
really de veras, en realidad, realmente
reason razón *f*; **the — why** la razón por la que; **for that —** por eso
receive recibir
recognize reconocer (*irr*; z) [24; 7]
recover recobrar
red rojo
refer to referirse (ie, e) [10] a
referee árbitro
refrigerator refrigerador *m*, nevera, frigorífico
refuse (to) negarse (ie; gu) [9; 3] (a)
register matricularse
regret sentir (ie, i) [10]
remain permanecer (*irr*; z) [17; 7], quedar(se)
remember recordar (ue), acordarse (ue) (de) [12]
repeat repetir (i, i) [11]
republic república
Republican republicano
respond contestar, responder

rest: as for the — por lo demás
restaurant restaurante *m*
restroom cuarto de caballeros / damas, servicio(s); wáter *m*
return volver (ue) [12, 48] (*intr*), devolver (ue) [12, 48] (*tr*)
revolution revolución
rice arroz *m*; **chicken and —** arroz con pollo
right *n* derecho; **— here** aquí mismo; **on, to the —** a la derecha; **to be —** tener (ie; *irr*) [43] razón, convenirle (ie; *irr*) [46] a uno
ripe maduro
road camino, carretera
rocky rocoso
room cuarto, habitación, sala
roommate compañero / a de cuarto
rotten podrido
run correr; **to — across** cruzarse (c) [5] con
running shoes zapatillas

S

sad triste
sake: for heaven's — por Dios
sale venta
same mismo, igual; **the — as** (**just like**) igual a; **at the — time** al mismo tiempo, a la vez
sandals: beach — playeras
Saturday sábado
say decir (i; *irr*) [28, 48]; **to — goodbye (to)** despedirse (i, i) [11] (de); **to know what to —** saber (*irr*) [40] qué decir
saying dicho
scarcely apenas
scare susto
scared: to be — asustarse
score marcar (qu) [1]
scoring of many goals goleada
scream *v* gritar
sea mar *m*
secretary secretario / a
see ver (*irr*) [47; 48]; **to — off** despedir (i, i) [11]
seem parecer (*irr*; z) [17; 7]
sell vender

send mandar, enviar (*irr*) [23]
September se(p)tiembre *m*
serious serio, grave
serve servir (i, i) [11]
set on fire encender (ie) [9]
several varios, unos, algunos, unos pocos, unos cuantos
shall I ...? *pr tense of verb, for example*: **Shall I open the window?** ¿Abro la ventana?
sharp astuto
shave afeitar
shoes zapatos; **running —** zapatillas
shoreline orilla
shot: **corner—** (*soccer*) tiro de esquina
shout gritar
show mostrar (ue) [12]
shower ducha
sick enfermo; malo; **to get —** enfermarse
sidewalk acera
silence silencio
sin *n* pecado; *v* pecar (qu) [1]
sing cantar
single man soltero
sink fregadero (*kitchen*); lavabo, lavamanos *m sing* (*bathroom*)
sit down sentarse (ie) [9]
sleep dormir (ue, u) [13]; **to go to —** dormirse
sleepy: **to be —** tener (ie; *irr*) [43] sueño
slowly despacio
smaller / smallest menor
smell *n* olor *m*; *v* oler (hue) [15] (*tr*, *intr*)
smile sonreír (i, i; *irr*) [38]
so:**—many** tantos; **—much** tanto; **—that** para que, de modo que, de manera que
soak mojar
some alguno, unos, algunos; algo de, un poco de
somebody alguien, alguno
someday algún día
somehow de algún modo, de alguna manera
someone alguien, alguno
something algo; alguna cosa; **— to drink** algo de beber
sometime alguna vez; **— s** a veces, algunas veces
somewhat algo

somewhere alguna parte
soon pronto; **as — as** tan pronto como, en cuanto
sorry: **to be —** sentir (ie, i) [10]
sort of grayish tirando a gris
Spaniard español / a
speak hablar
spend pasar (*time*); gastar (*money*)
spicy picante
sports *adj* deportivo
spread out extenderse (ie) [9]
square (*shape*) cuadrado; (*municipality*) plaza
star estrella
station estación
stay quedarse; parar (*take lodging*)
stepsister hermanastra
stereo estéreo
still aún, todavía
stone piedra
stop parar (*tr*, *intr*); parar(se) (*intr*); detener (ie; *irr*) [43] (*tr*); detenerse (*intr*); **— + -ing** dejar de + *inf*
store tienda, almacén
story cuento, historia; **detective —** cuento de detectives *m pl*, cuento policial
strange raro, extraño
stranger desconocido, forastero (*from another place*)
street calle *f*; **up the —** calle arriba
stretch out extenderse (ie) [9]
string (*garlic, onions, etc.*) ristra; **a whole —** toda una ristra, una ristra entera
stroll *n* paseíto; *v* pasear(se)
strong fuerte
student alumno / a, estudiante
study estudiar
subjunctive subjuntivo
substitute sustituir (*irr*) [21]
subway metro
succeed tener (ie; *irr*) [43] éxito; **to — in + -ing** lograr + *inf*
success éxito
successful: **to be —** tener (ie; *irr*) [43] éxito
such tal, semejante
suddenly de pronto, de súbito, de repente

suffer sufrir
suggest sugerir (ie, i) [10]
suit: **bathing —** bañador *m*, traje *m* de baño
suitable: **to be —** convenirle (ie; *irr*) a uno [46]
suitcase maleta
summer verano
Sunday domingo
sunglasses gafas de sol
sunny: **to be —** hacer (*irr*) [31, 48] sol
supermarket supermercado, hipermercado
support mantener (ie; *irr*) [43]
suppose suponer (*irr*) [36, 48]
sure seguro, cierto
surprise sorprender; **to be —d** sorprenderse
sweater suéter *m*
system sistema *m*

T

T-shirt camiseta
table mesa
take tomar, llevar; coger (j) [2]; **to — a bath** bañarse; **to — advantage (of)** aprovecharse (de); **to — away** quitar; **to — care of** atender (ie) [9]; **to — (bring) down** bajar; **to — off** quitarse; **to — out** sacar (qu) [1]; **to — place** tener (ie; *irr*) [43] lugar
tall alto
team equipo
tear *v* romper [48]
telegram telegrama *m*
television televisión *f*, tele *f* (*colloquial*)
tell decir (i; *irr*) [28, 48], contar (ue) [12]
temperature temperatura
terrible terrible
test probar (ue) [12]
thank agradecer (*irr*; z) [17; 7] dar (*irr*) [27] gracias a; **— goodness, — heaven!** ¡Gracias a Dios!
Thanksgiving Day Día de Acción de Gracias
theme tema *m*
then luego, entonces; **now —** ahora bien; **well —** pues, pues bien

there is, there are hay

therefore por eso, por lo tanto

think pensar (ie) [9], creer [26]; to — about pensar en

thirsty: to be — tener (ie; *irr*) [43] sed

though: even — aunque

thousand mil

throw echar, tirar, arrojar

Thursday jueves *m*

ticket boleto (*Sp Am*), billete *m* (*Spain*)

tie (*sports*) empatar *v*; empate *mn*

time tiempo; hora; vez; at the same — al mismo tiempo, a la vez; at —s a veces, algunas veces; on — a tiempo; this — esta vez

timid tímido

tired: to become — (of) cansarse (de)

title título

to: — the right a la derecha

today hoy; a week from — de hoy en ocho días

toilet baño (*room*); inodoro, wáter *m* (*bowl*)

tomorrow mañana; — morning mañana por la mañana the day after — pasado mañana

tonight esta noche *f*

too: — many demasiados; — much demasiado

tooth diente *m*

top: on — of sobre, encima de

torn roto (*pp* [48] *of* romper); rasgado

total total; —ly totalmente, completamente

totebag bolsa

touch tocar (qu) [1]

tourist turista *m*, *f*

toward hacia, para; to go — dirigirse (j) [2] a

towel toalla

toy juguete *m*

tranquility tranquilidad

translate traducir (*irr*; z) [22; 7]

translation traducción

translator traductor / a

travel viajar

tremble temblar (ie) [9]

trial proceso

trip viaje *m*

trouble: to be worth the — valer (*irr*) [45] la pena, merecer (irr; z) [17; 7] la pena

truck camión *m*

true verdad *fn*; verdadero, cierto *adj*; to be — ser verdad

truly de veras

trust fiar (*irr*) [23], fiarse (de), confiar (*irr*) [23]

truth verdad

try (out) probar (ue) [12]; to — to tratar de, intentar

Tuesday martes *m*

turn volver (ue) [12]; to — off apagar (gu) [3]; to — on encender (ie) [9], poner (*irr*) [36; 48]; to be one's — tocarle (qu) [1] a uno

type tipo

U

unable: to be — no poder (ue; *irr*) [35]

uncle tío

under bajo, debajo de

understand comprender, entender (ie) [9]

unfortunate pobre, desafortunado

unhappy infeliz, triste

unique único

until *prep* hasta; *conj* hasta que

up arriba; — the street calle arriba; — to hasta; to be — to tocarle (qu) [1] a uno; to come (go) — subir; to get —levantarse

upon en, encima de, sobre; — arriving al llegar

upstairs arriba; to go (come) — subir

upward (para, hacia) arriba

use usar, emplear

usually por lo común, generalmente

V

various varios

veal ternera

very muy; — much muchísimo

view panorama, vista

village pueblo, aldea, población

voice voz *f*; in a low — en voz baja

W

wait (*for*) esperar

waiter mesero, camarero

waitress mesera, camarera

wake up despertar (ie) [9] (*tr*), despertarse (*intr*)

walk andar (*irr*) [18], caminar

want querer (ie; *irr*) [37]; desear

war guerra

wash lavar

waste perder (ie) [9]

watch mirar

water agua

wave *n* ola; *v* blandir

way modo, manera; no — de ningún modo, de ninguna manera

wear llevar; vestir (i, i) [11]

weather tiempo, clima *m*

wedding boda

Wednesday miércoles *m*

week semana; last — la semana pasada; a — from today de hoy en ocho días

welcome *adj* bienvenido; *n* bienvenida

well bien; — (then) pues, pues bien

what ¿qué?, ¿cuál / es?; lo que

whenever cuando, cuandoquiera

which ¿cuál / es?, ¿qué?; que, el / la / los / las que, el / la cual, los / las cuales, lo cual, lo que

white blanco

whoever el que, quienquiera que, cualquiera que

whole todo, entero; a — string toda una ristra, una ristra entera; the — month todo el mes, el mes entero

whose ¿de quién / es?; *conj* cuyo

why ¿por qué?; the reason — la razón por la que

will *n* voluntad *f*

win ganar

wind viento; **to be —y** hacer (*irr*) [31, 48] viento

window ventana

wine vino; **—pitcher** porrón *m*

wing ala

winter invierno

wish: How I —! ¡ojalá!

without *prep* sin; *conj* sin que; **— charge** gratis *adv*

witness testigo *m, f*

woman mujer

wool lana

word palabra

work *n* trabajo; *v* trabajar

worry preocupar (*tr*), preocuparse (*intr*)

worse / worst peor

worth: to be — valer (*irr*) [45]; **to be — the trouble** valer la pena, merecer (*irr*; z) [17; 7] la pena

wrath ira

write escribir

wrong: to go — (*fail, break down*) fallar

Y

year año; **a — ago** hace un año; **last —** el año pasado

yell gritar

yesterday ayer

yet aún, todavía

younger / youngest menor

Photo Credits

Paso preliminar I
Page 8: D. Donne Bryant.

Unit 1
Pages 18 and 22: Peter Menzel / Stock, Boston.

Unit 6
Page 44: Mike Mazzaschi / Stock, Boston. Page 50: Dion Ogust / The Image Works.

Unit 7
Page 53: Hugh Rogers / Monkmeyer Press.

Unit 10
Page 62: Peter Menzel / Stock, Boston.

Unit 12
Page 69: Ulrike Welsch.

Unit 13
Page 75: Alan Carey / The Image Works.

Unit 14
Page 80: Ulrike Welsch.

Unit 17
Page 98: Stuart Cohen / Comstock.

Unit 25
Page 135: Paul Conklin.

Unit 31
Page 170: Peter Menzel / Stock, Boston. Page 175: Mike Mazzaschi / Stock, Boston.

Unit 32
Page 184: Copyright © Tom Hurst 1991.

Unit 35
Page 201: David Alan Harvey / Woodfin Camp and Associates.

Unit 37
Pages 218 and 220: Joe Viesti / Viesti Associates. Page 221: Owen Franken / Stock, Boston.

Unit 41
Page 238: Mark Antman / The Image Works.

Unit 42
Page 244: Stuart Cohen / Comstock.

Unit 43
Page 252: Mark Antman / The Image Works.

Unit 46
Page 268: Peter Menzel / Stock, Boston.

Unit 48
Page 277: Colombia Information Service. Page 280: Jeremy Barnard / The Picture Cube.

Index

Arabic numerals refer to regular grammar units. Other designations: **Paso** = **Paso preliminar**; **Diversión** = **Diversión y práctica**. (Note: The grammar unit immediately preceding the **Diversión** or the **Lectura** is indicated in parentheses.)